12-15

The Healing
Energies
of Music

DISCARD

The Healing
Energies
of Music

Hal A. Lingerman

A publication supported by
THE KERN FOUNDATION

Quest Books
Theosophical Publishing House

Wheaton, Illinois ◆ Chennai (Madras), India

MANCOS
PUBLIC LIBRARY

Copyright 1983, 1995 by
Hal A. Lingerman
First Quest Edition 1983. Second Edition 1995.
All rights reserved. No part of this book may be
reproduced in any manner without written permission
except for quotations embodied in critical articles
or reviews. For additional information write to:

The Theosophical Publishing House
P. O. Box 270
Wheaton, IL 60189-0270

A publication of the Theosophical Publishing House,
a department of the Theosophical Society in America.

*This publication made possible with
the assistance of the Kern Foundation*

Library of Congress Cataloging-in-Publication Data

Lingerman, Hal A., 1943–
    The healing energies of music / Hal A. Lingerman.
        p.   cm.
    "A Quest book."
    Includes bibliographical references and index.
    ISBN 0-8356-0722-4
    1. Music therapy.   I. Title
ML3920.L695   1995   94-36151
615.85154—dc20   CIP
                                                             MN
            9 8 7 6 5 4 3 2   *   98 99

This edition is printed on acid-free paper that meets the
American National Standards Institute Z39.48 Standard

Printed in the United States of America by Versa Press

Contents

Preface to the Revised Edition

Music opens us to the rapture of being alive; music suggests the Mystery that moves through all things.

I deeply value the transforming power of beautiful music! Although I am not a trained musician, I am a longtime lover of music who is deeply indebted to music for the many ways it has always enriched my life. For me music is far more than entertainment; it is a vital food, filled with energies and beauty that nourish me daily. I believe that great music, carefully selected and experienced, can be a unique agent for healing, for partnering joy and sorrow, for empowerment, attunement, and inspiration, and for expanding one's spiritual consciousness.

Professionally, I am a college teacher, counselor, and nonsectarian minister. In each of these areas, music helps and inspires me in ways that are both obvious and subtle. Whatever I have felt and learned about music through the years, I have enjoyed sharing with others. The results have been gratifying and mysterious. I have observed music improve people's physical health, emotional stability, mental focus, and spiritual sensitivity. In my own life, I have felt repeatedly how beautiful music contributes toward refocusing me and integrating parts of my personality, offering harmony and peace to my psyche and empowerment and gladness to my soul.

In this book I would like to share with you some of the impressions and discoveries that have come to me from experiencing beautiful and uplifting music. My approach is synthesis: Many pieces of music cut across different fields of study, such as politics, history and biography, psychology, philosophy, science, medicine, religion, metaphysics, and esoteric studies. I have been led by my own love of music to follow an intuitive and mystical path of investigation. During my years in teaching and the ministry, I have moved through various orthodox, metaphysical, and esoteric groups, finding truth in all places and in all religions and philosophies of the world. I believe strongly in the teaching of multiple lifetimes and in the progressive consciousness of all lives, in the existence of beings in nature who work through the inner dimensions of life, in the great reality of angels and higher powers in God that inspire us. I acknowledge gratefully the abiding love of the Divine Presence as the inspiration for humanity. Also, I acknowledge God's helpers, both visible and invisible, with whom we are linked in the great ladder of light (mentioned in the Old Testament story of Jacob's Ladder), as we serve the cause of the highest that we know.

Years of seeking spiritually, behind the literal or merely academic view of things, have only confirmed my conviction that truth is far deeper and more subtle than any one literal approach or interpretation. We are reminded, "By their fruits ye shall know them." One's life is always larger than one's belief systems; whatever path we follow, our lives will require increasing refinement—of mind, emotions, and body. Disharmony or imbalance on any level of consciousness produces fear and stress within the total temperament, and if these concerns are not dealt with, they can eventually lead to frustration, dis-ease, and even illness.

We live today in a critical and demanding time that is uncertain and full of sudden changes. In many places, we can observe a decline in excellence and a decreasing sensitivity to others' needs. In many areas of life, high quality and a sense of purpose seem to be lacking. However, at the same time, many persons are also feeling a new hunger for a life that is less self-seeking, less exploitive, more respectful, and more spiritually meaningful. Internal and external growing pains in humankind are demanding serious questioning of ideas that for many years have been accepted or taken on faith. Old systems and assumptions are breaking apart. Old solutions are no longer helpful. New energies and new seeds of possibility are now leading individuals to share in a new spirit of cooperation. Such persons are contributing their creative energies to helping our planet function more healthily as part of God's universe. People are now developing deeper intuition and insight that will lead us eventually into future times of increased well-being, caring, and loving good will.

Some persons among us today hold to pessimistic and fatalistic views of humankind's future. I prefer to see our times as a dynamic opportunity for individual and planetary transformation. Now is the time to dig in, get involved, and work for a cause greater than one's own pleasure or self-interest. Enough individuals, working together in networks of light and prayer-filled activity, can make a huge difference. They can help to create a brighter future in all places. Every life of service and every act of genuine good will can help to bring about a new cleansing and healing.

I believe music can be one such catalyst for good. Music, as the empowering sound of divinity, is an extremely important carrier of the Creator's holy Presence. When sound is used wisely and effectively, it can attune people to higher sources of love, union, and power, thus strengthening their character and increasing their receptivity and attunement.

I wrote *The Healing Energies of Music* in 1980–81. Since its publication in 1983, the book has gone through five printings and has been translated into German, Swedish, and Portuguese. During the past eleven years, I have been privileged to receive letters from around the world, written by readers who have shared with me in many ways their love of beautiful music. I deeply appreciate these enthusiastic responses. This new and updated book offers music lovers everywhere many more selections and possibilities.

In 1980 the compact disk was little more than a rumor. Now, with the amazing turnaround in technology and the music industry, the LP, although still loved and collected by many, has largely become a dinosaur. Cassette sales are also dwindling, and the compact disk reigns supreme. During the past ten years, many beautiful recordings have appeared on compact disk. Many obsolete 78 and LP records and out-of-print cassette recordings have been remastered and rereleased on compact disk. These restored recordings are almost "like new," with distortions, pops, clicks, and hisses largely removed, and sound quality is improving continuously.

However, at the same time that so many "old friends" and new recordings are rapidly appearing, music lovers are facing new challenges:

1. How do we find out about the new recordings that are becoming available so rapidly?
2. How can we sample and listen to these new recordings in order to choose the ones that we want to buy and add to our listening library?
3. How can we access the new recordings we want to buy?
4. How can we locate and buy new recordings before they go out of print? (The average life span of a new CD is often one to two years, sometimes shorter, and sometimes only one to two thousand CDs are made at a single pressing.)

These challenges point to why so few persons are even aware of the music that is currently available. In what follows, I will suggest several strategies for discovering, sampling, and locating beautiful music. It is my hope as well that this book itself will be a resource for dealing with these problems.

It is clear that music offers tremendous opportunities for enjoyment, healing, inspiration, and transformation. From my classes and workshops, however, I find that many listeners are just beginning to make contact with the music that can touch their deepest feelings and open their hearts and souls. Surveys indicate that in the midst of a supposedly booming CD industry, only five to seven percent of the population is buying the kind of immortal music that for more than five hundred years has stirred people's consciousness, inspired them, and helped heal their psyches.

During the years since I wrote *The Healing Energies of Music*, I have continued to seek out the compositions and recordings which have proved to be enjoyable, inspiring, therapeutically uplifting, and spiritually dynamic. Some of what I have discovered suggests new and promising possibilities. For instance, a new World Music is evolving rapidly today, which like other aspects of the growing multimedia culture, expresses an expanding synthesis of styles, forms, ideas, feelings, timbres, and harmonies. In these days of accelerated change and rapid transformation, powerful music from all nations and cultures is now offering us all its unique healing power: a more global music is emerging.

As a practical resource, this new edition includes a thorough listing of many new recordings (CD and cassette), including conductor, orchestra (or group), artists, and the label and distributor. I have also provided as many addresses as possible for ordering the recordings I mention and list. I have tried to provide some description of the listed recordings, without telling the reader-listener how or what to hear. When many recordings of the same musical work exist, it is difficult to know which interpretation to choose. My suggestions for particular interpretations are the results of personal taste and more than twenty years of careful research. Compare different recordings of the same musical work to find the energies, shadings, and interpretations that benefit you the most.

The *Schwann Opus Catalogue*, available almost anywhere, is also a valuable resource for finding the composer, label, order number, and distributor for a musical selection you are seeking, such as a piece of music heard on the radio that you would like to purchase. Refer also to the *Music Masters Catalogue*, c/o Musical Heritage, 1710 Highway 35, Ocean, NJ 07712 (908-531-3375). For New Age musical recordings, please refer to White Swan Music, Inc., 1705 Fourteenth Street, Box 143, Boulder, CO 80302. For special imported classical recordings, I have found the following sources most helpful:

1. Records International, P.O. Box 1140, Goleta, CA 93116-1140 (1-805-687-0327).
2. Allegro Imports, 12630 NE Marx Street, Portland, OR 97230-1059 (1-800-288-2007).
3. Qualiton Imports, 24-02 Fortieth Avenue, Long Island City, NY 11101 (1-718-937-8515).

I have also listed additional sources that can help you to keep updated and informed about existing and new recordings. As a reliable music store, I recommend Tower Records, which has proven to be helpful and cooperative whenever I have needed to find a recording. I suggest that you talk to record store employees about the music you want to hear, get on mailing lists from various record companies, who will usually send you free announcements of new recordings, and keep a listening journal of pieces of music that uplift and feed you.

I have also included in this new book a chapter on women composers and their music. Amazingly, when I originally wrote *The Healing Energies of Music*, many fewer recordings by women composers/artists existed. Now, happily, more and more women's music is appearing. Even more hopeful, as I write today, is the number of recordings appearing in which men and women are collaborating and performing music together—as friends and companions who mutually love to make music.

I look forward to hearing from you and learning from you about the beautiful music that you love and cherish in your daily life. I hope this book will help to lead you into many new experiences in your lifelong enjoyment of beautiful music.

I wish to thank the many friends who have helped me and inspired me to write this new edition: in particular, my mother (an organist and teacher) and my father (accountant, college teacher, attorney, spiritual seeker, animal lover, and entrepreneur), who often encouraged my love of music, Ruth Stockton and Gwen Hulbert for their valuable editorial suggestions, Paul M. and Paul G. Traudl, Marge and Elden, Stan, Tom, Elsie, Lynn, Dr. Dika Newlin, Jerrie, Ken, Trudy, Helen, Walter, Lucy, Joy, Clare, Robert and Jeri Hannah, Tony A., Kent, Joe, Norman, Dr. David Amos, and Dr. Benjamin Kimpel. I'm especially grateful to Rosemary, my patient, wonderful wife, whose kindness and loving friendship enrich my life each day, and also to Aria, my creative and magical daughter, whose love and joy always bring me new gifts and surprises. I deeply thank the Reverend Flower A. Newhouse, spiritual teacher and Christian mystic, founder of Questhaven Retreat in Escondido, California, whose sensitivity to music and nature has provided me with many valuable insights, some of which appear in this book. Thanks also to Dr. John Diamond, whose book *Your Body Doesn't Lie* has confirmed through kinesiology so many of my own findings. I also wish to thank Dr. Karl Haas, who has inspired me greatly with his illuminating radio series on music of the great composers, *Adventures in Good Music*. I also am deeply grateful to the many composers, conductors, and performing artists, past and present, whose sensitivity and talents have enhanced my life and the lives of millions of listeners throughout the Earth. I also want to acknowledge the encouragement and expertise of Dr. Helen Bonny, one of the pioneers in the field of musical therapy and her work in integrating psychology, music, and spirituality.

The powers that can be communicated to earth by means of music are as yet scarcely suspected by the average individual.

But the time is fast approaching when man will select his music with the same intelligent care and knowledge he now uses to select his food. When that time comes, music will become a principal source of healing for many individual and social ills, and human evolution will be tremendously accelerated.

ESOTERIC MUSIC, CORINNE HELINE

That music always round me,
Unceasing, unbeginning—
yet long untaught I did not hear;
But now the chorus I hear
and am elated; . . .
I hear not the volumes of sound
merely—I am
moved by the exquisite meanings,
I listen to the different voices
winding in and out,
. . . now I think I begin to know them.

LEAVES OF GRASS, WALT WHITMAN

Introduction

Just as much information is given by a great symphony as is imparted by a remarkable book. It is just as important that a person become evolved and enlightened in music as it is that someone become improved by thought.

FLOWER A. NEWHOUSE

Music is the universal language.

RICHARD WAGNER

Sound, color, and number influence every area of life. How we respond to these great universal forces will condition a large part of our health and happiness. It is, therefore, essential to learn how to use sound, color, and number more wisely, so that their energies can flow into us and our environment, filling our life with joy, vitality, and clarity.

We live in *music*. The universe is a tonal harmony composed of many moving sounds—many lives interacting and vibrating together as they resonate in music coming through the silence of the Infinite. Each individual human life either contributes to this creative harmony or produces discord. We make either music or noise.

Music is the positive pole of sound; its rhythms and life-enhancing melodies echo the eternal harmonies sounding through the heavens. In this way music is a mirror of holy resonance; it opens transparencies in us, enlarging our horizons and helping us to feel what is beautiful and inspiring. Great music nourishes us. It is always strengthening, because it attunes us to powerful waves of life energy and to the unfathomable Source of all good.

Noise is the opposite of music. It is "sound gone crazy," for its insanity is really its disconnectedness—its failure to find any unity or harmony with the universe in which it is moving. Great music resolves chaos dynamically, bringing peace, beauty, synthesis, and transformation; noise emphasizes separation, ugliness, and distortion.

Stories come down to us about how sensitive and skilled the ancients were in using music as a healing art. For them music was not just a form of entertainment; it was also a source of health, containing chords of rhythm and melody that would harmonize and rebalance the human organism, draining away its impurities. From Manly Hall, a prolific writer on esoteric traditions, we learn that in ancient Greece an angry man charged an enemy, sword drawn, ready to kill. Suddenly "a wise Pythagorean," sensing the situation, struck one chord on his lyre. Instantly, all anger and hatred were drawn out of the would-be attacker, and he became gentle as a lamb.

Pythagoras of Samos, a very wise teacher of ancient Greece, knew how to work with sound. In his mystery schools in Delphi and Crotona, he taught his students how certain musical chords and melodies could produce responses within the human organism. He demonstrated that the right sequence of sounds, played musically on an instrument, can change behavior patterns and accelerate the healing process.

In the Old Testament we also read about the power and therapeutic value of beautiful music. Saul, an ancient king, was troubled "by an evil spirit." He was advised as follows:

> . . . seek out a man, who is a wise player on a harp: and it shall come to pass . . . that he shall play with his hand and thou shalt be well.
>
> 1 SAM. 16:16

Saul sent for David, whom he "found favorable in his sight," and when David played his lyre for the king, these were the results:

> David took a harp, and played with his hand: and Saul was refreshed, and was well, and the evil spirit departed from him.
>
> 1 SAM. 16:23

From these examples and others, it is clear that the ancients sensed the power and value of beautiful music and knew how to use it to promote harmony and well-being in their lives. They knew in their consciousness the difference between uplifting and degrading music. Likewise, today we can rediscover the therapeutic and spiritual potencies of healing music.

In my work I have been able to observe many situations in which music has been a powerful factor for change and improvement, both for individuals and for groups. Certain pieces of music, played with appropriate timing and good taste, have helped to alter behavior and awareness. Musical selections have helped to calm the heartbeat and nervous system, have promoted greater relaxation, have deepened constructive attitudes and brought a willingness to listen and to be receptive to new directions. I have also observed how specific musical selections can contribute to changing the mood of an environment or a relationship. I remember, for example, several patients in nursing homes who sat inert and unresponsive in their seats until a certain piece of music was played to them. Then, suddenly, they began to move, clapping their hands, smiling, humming, singing, talking with each other, and keeping time with their feet. When a certain woman, who was almost catatonic, heard the waltzes of Chopin, she suddenly began singing and yelling happily. A single piece of music, carefully played, can transform the entire atmosphere and conduct in a place. Dr. John Diamond, a well-known medical doctor and researcher into the powerful factor of music in our lives, demonstrated this fact in his book *Your Body Doesn't Lie:*

> One factory in particular, a manufacturing and repair plant for sophisticated electronic equipment, where concentration and clearheadedness are essential, was playing a great deal of rock on its continual music broadcast system. It was recommended that this be eliminated. The management changed to different music and found to their delight an immediate increase in productivity and an equally pleasing decrease in errors, even though the employees were quite vocal about their dissatisfaction at having had their favorite music removed.

These experiences and others like them offer immense value for our lives. They speak to our times of increasing stress and challenge and point the way to a rediscovery of the healing energies of great music. They tell how we can use music to increase harmony and clarity in our working environment, our homes, and our relationships. Music, wisely chosen, can refresh us in our leisure hours, at our jobs, or wherever we may be. I use the word *healing* to suggest whatever contributes to the increasing balance and integration of all the ingredients of the personality. Music, properly used, can help to bring clearing and purification to the body, emotions, and thinking patterns. Music can also open listeners to deeper dimensions of soul and of spiritual strength within and around them.

I believe that great music is always inspired. In its own way it is immortal; its unique essence overrides personal tastes and preferences, so that it pours through listeners like a life fluid, gaining access and opening doors where all else has failed. Often great music influences persons therapeutically, despite previous conditioning, opinions, or experiences. Finally, music that is truly immortal is greater than its particular style or the historical period in which it was composed, and it transmits an abiding essence which speaks to every generation.

I remember playing certain musical selections for a friend in New Jersey several years ago. When he heard this music for the first, and even the tenth time, he ridiculed it. He said he found it "weird, far out, and too different." Subliminally, however, he must have found it intriguing, as it triggered strong emotional responses in him. He soon returned and asked for more of "that strange stuff." I obliged. Gradually, he became fascinated by the sounds of the symphony orchestra, with so many melodies interweaving. He was captivated by the colors and sonorities of different instruments blending together. He responded particularly to the strings and powerful crescendos of the brass and timpani. I noticed that he was concentrating and really giving himself to the music for the first time. Whereas previously he had paced up and down in the room, talking nervously, he now chose to sit down. His breathing changed, and he became more introspective—even meditative.

By the end of that year he had bought more than two hundred new recordings, most of them containing "that weird stuff." Later, he wrote to me, telling me how some pieces of music had inspired him to write a book of poetry. He mentioned to me how different he felt: " . . . more connected and centered—more interested in things." I noticed how he had become more purposeful in his job, and how much more carefully he chose his working environment. The nourishing power of the music he found overrode all previous experiences and tastes. It awakened a deeper layer in him and affected his responses to daily ups and downs. It increased attunement to his own life path. Today great music still nourishes him.

Our life's highest purpose is to live completely in conscious union with God. The more we cultivate great music in our lives, the greater will be our attunement to unlimited sources of the Creator's power and direction. Such music will strengthen us to define and accomplish our earthly goals.

Develop a deeper friendship with great music and you will see many areas of your life begin to open. Beautiful music can:

Increase physical vitality, relieve fatigue and inertia.
Pierce through moods, calm anxiety and tensions, uplift feelings.
Focus thinking, clarify goals, release courage and follow-through.
Deepen relationships, enrich friendships.
Stimulate creativity and sensitivity.
Strengthen character and constructive behavior.
Expand consciousness of God and horizons of spiritual attunement.

We were all created equal, but we are born into each lifetime with different temperaments, personalities, and inclinations, which we learn to harmonize. Choosing our path with discernment and sharing with each other, we move toward fuller expression of the Divine Presence. Often, we may feel the light at the center of us and beyond us, which fills our blind spots and clarifies our motivations. Particular pieces of great music, pouring their healing energies through us, help to emphasize the light of Divinity; they remind us to focus on the best in ourselves, which is of God, while we attend to those distorted areas that need correction.

Seek out music that increases your well-being and transforms ugliness and chaos. Such music can lead you into activities and horizons of consciousness that are as beautiful as your greatest dreams and life goals.

CHAPTER 1

Music and You—A Closer Relationship

Each time we listen to beautiful music, we select an impression to weave into the harmony of our unfoldment.

FLOWER A. NEWHOUSE

It seems to me that, above all, music must stir the heart.

C. P. E. BACH

How deeply do you feel music? How much of yourself do you give? The more you can give of yourself to the music you are experiencing, the more vibrations of power will sound through you. If you come to great music with an open heart, a willing mind, and a relaxed body, it will enter you and renew you. Great music brings healing streams and electrical chargings, but these cannot enter and revitalize you as deeply if you are distracted, tense and resistant, critical, impatient, ungrateful, or poorly prepared.

If our attunement is faulty and we are scattered, we sometimes miss the finest things in life. A poet has written, "The Angels come to visit us, and we know them only after they are gone." If you take time to prepare yourself beforehand for your music, it will play *through you*, not just around you. You will receive the full power and beauty of great music by learning better how to relax and link with the melodies you are hearing.

Take a comfortable position, either sitting in your favorite chair or lying on the floor. If you are outside, lie down on the grass or relax against a favorite tree. Use these ten keys for a more meaningful musical experience.

BEFORE BEGINNING THE MUSIC

1. Come to quiet for a minute. Speak to your body; tell any tense areas to relax. Speak to your feelings; tell them to be calm. Speak to your mind; let go of racing thoughts. Realize the Divine Presence in whom you are listening. You might want to use an affirmation or

verse to center yourself, such as "Be still and know that I am God." Keep this exercise short, simple, and enjoyable.

2. Be grateful for the music you are about to experience. Say, "Thank you." Be expectant!

3. Surrender to the music. Try to open yourself to the music you hear.

WHILE THE MUSIC IS PLAYING

4. Release all tensions into the music. Feel the music pulling you out of all negativity and tension. Wherever there is a block in yourself, visualize an opening. Breathe deeply, taking in the music. Let go completely.

5. Feel the music embracing and filling you. Release all need to dominate or control the situation. Open to the healing, revitalizing currents of melody that are entering you. Go inside the sound.

6. Give yourself to the music. Enjoy the music wherever it takes you. Let surprises happen.

7. Be filled with joy and praise. Move into mystery!

8. Do not play music for too long at one time.

WHEN THE MUSIC IS OVER

9. Take time to absorb the music. Sit quietly for a few minutes after it has finished.

10. When appropriate, combine experiencing music with other activity, such as keeping a diary, sketching, dancing or moving, or doing chores such as housework, cooking, or working in the shop. Even before you hear the first note, it matters greatly *where* you hear the music. Is the setting beautiful?

Take the time to cultivate the most advantageous surroundings for your musical experiences. Here are four suggestions to help you:

— Experience music in a beautiful place. Avoid clutter, heaviness, ugliness, and darkness. Clear the atmosphere, heighten colors, and seek light.

— Play your music in a quiet place. Minimize outer noise and distractions. Turn off the TV, avoid loud hums of electrical appliances. Let your music emerge out of quiet, or listen to music in nature. Be sensitive to the sounds of nature—bird calls, rain, woods, streams, wind, ocean—as these combine with musical melodies to uplift you and link you with the Eternal. Find the particular volume that is best for you. Avoid overkill.

— Buy good equipment. Find a stereo or sound system with speakers that play music with a clear tone and minimal distortion. Choose your equipment carefully and patiently, after hearing some of your favorite recordings played on it. Trust your own ear. Explore many different speaker systems before deciding. Do not buy, necessarily, according to brand name or advertising.

— Take good care of your system, CDs, tapes, and recordings. Avoid excess heat. Touch your CDs only around the edges, never on the top or bottom surfaces. Before original tapes stretch or tear, copy them for your own use on quality blanks. Clean your records when they are dusty. Do not stack your records. Play one record at a time. Clean the tape heads regularly and remove dust from needles, carefully.

For increased therapeutic value, try not to be too critical of the music you are experiencing. If you are too fussy a listener, you will not soar. The quality of performances and pressings varies. Find recordings you can live with and love them unconditionally for all they have to offer. Emphasize the treasures of the music, not the defects. Listen behind the notes for the overtones, the larger melodies, and the archetypes that the composer may have "heard" and partially brought through. Move into the silences between the notes. Such an attitude of openness and gratitude will expand the range and depth of the musical experiences that come to you. In an atmosphere of joyful acceptance, the healing vibrations of great music can more easily find entrance into you and will bring you the greatest possible enjoyment and upliftment.

Discover the great golden moments in music and arrange them into healing and beneficial sequences that will meet your various needs. Arrange your favorite selections into a healing continuum that sustains you and lifts your consciousness. Use the lists through this book and the further suggestions in the Appendixes to help you find just the right music for you.

From thorough scientific research, Dr. John Diamond and others have found that many early digital recordings are not as "warm" or as therapeutic as the original recordings. I have no proof of this myself, but I still often prefer older recordings, which now in many cases have been beautifully remastered on CD. I believe that each recording is unique. You may feel some recordings are more powerful than others, yet in certain cases, even though the sound may be less clear, warm, or immediate, this particular version "speaks to you." Keep listening, remain receptive to new impressions, and try to hear all the music that you can discover. Every musical masterpiece remains vast and potentially ever new.

CHAPTER 2

Music for Better Health and Well-Being

The only correct music is that which is beautiful and noble.

RALPH VAUGHAN WILLIAMS

I will sing with the spirit, and I will sing with the understanding also.

1 COR. 14:15

While the greatest pieces of music will energize and inspire all levels of your being, there are musical works that may appeal more specifically to certain parts of your make-up. Some music affects primarily your physical body. Such compositions activate you and make you feel stronger and more powerful in your movements; other pieces might make you want to move more rapidly, perhaps through dancing, house cleaning, painting, or even typing (I remember learning to type as a teenager to *The Blue Danube Waltz,* which the teacher played frequently). Music with strong, regular rhythms tends to activate the body, while also coordinating and focusing the mind.

Other selections will affect your feelings-emotions more. Perhaps a certain tune or song will make you cry, while another will bring out greater devotion, joy, sadness, or even anger. The music of such Romantics as Chopin, Tchaikovsky, and Rachmaninov is often very moving emotionally.

Another selection of music will appeal mostly to your mind, inspiring you with new ideas, seed thoughts for new possibilities, and creativity. The music of the Baroque is structured and seems to be especially effective for a listener who wishes to study, organize ideas, or focus on goals.

Finally, there are those pieces of music that penetrate through all your outer layers. This kind of music speaks directly to your heart and soul, reminding you of your wholeness, divine connection and highest selfhood in God. The early celestial music of Palestrina, Tallis, Taverner, Victoria,

J. S. Bach's *Goldberg Variations,* especially as played by Rosalyn Tureck, and Vaughan Williams's *Fantasia on a Theme of Thomas Tallis* can open deeper soul contact and deepen aspirations toward divinity.

Different instruments also affect particular parts of your make-up. Melodic music, played by certain solo instruments and chamber ensembles, may be quieting. Music such as Mendelssohn's *Songs without Words,* a Mozart sonata, or a Schubert quartet, especially when heard late at night, is more soothing than a great symphony, replete with the potencies of full orchestral sound. Play symphonies, concertos, cantatas, and similar larger works when you want a stronger, more demanding and invigorating blast of musical sound. Cultivate lovely chamber music and small-scaled, "cameo" selections of string music for intimate, quiet times, when you desire a more calming influence. Here are some general guidelines to follow in choosing instruments to best suit your goals:

1. Physical Body—brass, percussion (drums), heavy bass notes; electronic music and amplified sounds.
2. Emotional Body—woodwinds and strings.
3. Mental Body—strings.
4. Soul Body—high strings, harp, bells, and organ (very powerful and stimulating to all the bodies); wind chimes; high strings.

Seek out the kind of music you need to balance and awaken all of you. Discover the times and sequences in which musical selections are most appropriate.

Keep a journal of musical experiences and specific pieces and how they inspire you or make you feel. List any imagery or empowerments that might come through to you from hearing pieces of music.

MUSIC FOR THE PHYSICAL BODY

The physical body is the earthly temple for the soul. It is important to love and care for your physical body in every possible way. As you would seek to feed, clothe, clean, exercise, and rest your body wisely, so can you wisely select and use music to bathe, purify, and energize your physical vehicle. Observe what kinds of sounds irritate or frighten you; feel what music is either good for you (life-enhancing) or harmful (depleting).

Use musical selections to pierce through physical inertia and lumpiness. (I find that Beethoven's music, especially the *Emperor Concerto,* often motivates people, gives them courage, and strengthens the willpower.) Use other musical favorites to sound through hyperactivity and tension, thus relaxing your nerves and muscles.

If your physical body needs energizing, play music with stronger rhythms and more powerful contrasts, such as marches and peppy tunes. Instrumentally, choose music for piano, or feel the stronger sounds of brass and percussion (listen especially to the beautiful Venetian brass and choral music of Gabrieli or to the stirring sonatas of the Slavic composer, Vejvanovsky). Pieces for trumpets, horns, tubas, saxhorns, trombones, timpani, cymbals, and gongs are very powerful. They will ground you very quickly, if you feel you are too lethargic or spaced out. F. J. Haydn's Trumpet Concerto in E-flat, as interpreted by Håkan Hardenberger (Philips 420203-2) and Mozart's horn concertos are outstanding examples of stirring music.

However, be careful *not to play this kind of music too much, too long, or too loudly*. If you overexpose yourself to the powerful sounds of bass or percussion, even if such sounds are melodious, you may shock and exhaust yourself very quickly.

Big moments in music always build up from quietness; mighty crescendos emerge out of silence. The great artist and composer Pablo Casals said that all musical masterpieces are created from the resolution between tension and release. Although we may seek peace and tranquility, such states must be earned. Music that achieves harmony from a dynamic reconciliation of opposites will make you feel strong and victorious. Your body will feel better each time you experience music that harmonizes the emotional conflicts and dissonances of life with a new musical solution.

Avoid continuous blasts of noise and chaos without melody. A horrendous, life-denying deluge of junk sounds will dehumanize you and eventually leave you with a hole in your soul. In the same way, avoid merely pleasant, linear music that leaves you feeling stale, dull, and equally unsatisfied. Choose life-enhancing, melodic music that expands your dreams and creative horizons and makes you feel that you are welcomed and included meaningfully in the cosmic dance of life. Beautiful music is that which makes you feel more caring and affirmative, more glad to be alive, more connected to the totality.

Marches. Many marches and their rhythms are composed for orchestra or brass band. They provide a healthy stimulus to your physical body. Marches pierce through inertia and lethargy. They call you to attention and focus you, stirring and directing you to clarify your goals and take decisive action. In a larger way, some marches promote greater cooperation and fellow-feeling; they inspire and motivate. Marches can awaken loyalty and often serve as a powerful medicine for combating an enemy, either external or within oneself. I also think here of the empowering qualities of many Native American dances and pow-wow music, now available. Here are some suggestions for marches that will inspire and activate your physical body. See the appendix for label numbers and more suggestions.

Pomp and Circumstance no. 1 by Sir Edward Elgar (Philips 6502001): This great, ennobling piece of music (and the other marches in this series) is vivid and very powerful. It lifts you in every area of your being, not just the physical body. It will stir you with energy and desire for group mobilization to achieve common purposes and goals. If played at a memorial service, it will scatter sorrow and depression, making those present feel the value of time and earthly opportunity still available to them.

Powerful chords of melody, like beacons of white light, sound through this music, charging and filling your body with renewed energy. It is a thrilling experience to see and feel the power of unity that occurs each year in London at the last night of the Proms, when many thousands of people sing this tune together to the words of *Land of Hope and Glory*. Helene Nagel, a poet and mystic, has written a hymn to the angels to be sung to Elgar's melody:

Angels of Glory

Angels of Glory, Angels of Prayer,
Angels of Worship, may we be aware
Of octaves of beauty, of forms of light,
Of streams of color, beyond earthly sight,
As chanting His praises, we do honor the Christ.

Angels of cleansing, Angels of Fire,
Watching over the altar, hear our holy desire;
In rivers of spirit, washed clean and pure,
We bring our whole being; may that only endure
Which in adoration kneels to honor the Christ.

Angels of Music, Angels of Song,
In joyous procession our spirits do long
To echo thy chorus, our glad voices raise
To the gateway of glory, great anthems of praise,
As chanting His splendor, we do honor the Christ.

Angels of Healing, Angels of Love,
The streams of God's mercy pour down from above,
Touching deeply each soul who sends forth a prayer,
For lifting of burdens, for healing of cares,
As chanting His goodness, we do honor the Christ.

Angels of Power, Warriors of Light,
Who vanquish the darkness and strengthen the right,
Gird us with the armor of the Holy Word;
With the shield of spirit, let our voices be heard,
As chanting His power we do honor the Christ.

When you listen to *Pomp and Circumstance*, envision the purity of white light filling you with galvanizing power to build and work for the good. One listener, who tuned into this melody in her own way, felt it to be like the chant of angel ordination, emanating from the heavens and empowering whoever hums or sings it.

Several years ago, as I played this marchlike music of Elgar in a nursing home, where I was offering a music therapy class, I noticed several patients in wheelchairs. They had been sitting with heads bowed and bodies inert, almost catatonic. Suddenly they stirred in their seats. They looked up with eyes opening wide. As the climax of energy came through the music, I saw that many persons in the room were smiling, humming along, and keeping time with their hands and feet. The entire atmosphere was changed. The nurses smiled at each other, the spirits of the patients were uplifted, and for some time afterwards their conversations became more animated. Their faces looked less aimless and more focused. One woman said to me, "Boy, that piece really made me feel powerful again."

Triumphal March (from *Aida*) by Giuseppe Verdi (Solti – London 430226): This dramatic march with its accompanying, exultant chorus brings in great strength and power. It lifts the emotions as well as the body. Its festivity rises to disperse all heaviness. Notice the strong melody throughout and the blaze of trumpets that lifts you. Strong rhythms are often repeated in the melody. These accents kindle stronger purpose and constancy in the listener. It reminds us that by facing a challenge bravely, it becomes possible to overcome it. As it is written to celebrate the victory of a returning army, so will it stir feelings of triumph in you.

I remember hearing this piece played once in a local record store. Persons browsing through the bins stopped, stood at attention, and raised their heads upward with dignity and joy. One man, smiling broadly, began to conduct the march with arms raised. After the chorus mounted toward the final crescendo and finished singing, everyone applauded. Three persons bought the recording. Many of the choruses from the operas of Verdi, Puccini, Mozart, and others bring in vibrations of great power when they are played.

Marche Slave by Peter Ilyich Tchaikovsky (Järvi – DGG 429984-2): Varied rhythms and strong, melodic flavors characterize this festive, explosive music. While some of Tchaikovsky's music is manic and contains many shadings of joys and deep melancholy, this piece is far more dynamic and sweeps the listener along. You can sing this music, and you can march to it. The strong rhythms and powerful brass choirs send trumpeting energies through your body. I defy you to sit still while you listen to this piece. Enjoy it! The music is very powerful. (Also try Tchaikovsky's *Capriccio Italien*).

It is interesting to note that the great maestro, Leopold Stokowski, who has now passed on, conducted this showpiece as the concluding selection at a concert in Royal Festival Hall in London to celebrate the sixtieth anniversary of his first appearance with the London Symphony Orchestra. That recording captures the power and fireworks of the music, and at the conclusion you will hear a great roar from the audience. For readers who appreciate this great maestro's exceptionally dramatic and uniquely vivid recordings, please contact and join The Leopold Stokowski Society of America, 106 E. Curtis Street, Mount Vernon, OH 43050.

Other Music to Energize the Physical Body:

Berlioz – *Hungarian March* (Rákóczy)
Sousa – *Stars and Stripes Forever*
Sibelius – *Alla Marcia* (from *Karelia Suite*)
Schubert – *Marche Militaire*
Beethoven – *Turkish March* (from *Ruins of Athens*)
Clarke – *Trumpet Voluntary*
Johann Strauss, Sr. – *Radetzky March*
Arthur Fiedler (cond.) – *Pops Roundup* (cowboy songs)
Prokofiev – *March* (from *The Love for Three Oranges*)
Lumbye – *Marches and Galops*
L. Anderson – *Bugler's Holiday*
Alwyn – *Elizabethan Dances*
Grieg – *Homage March* (from *Sigurd Jorsalfar*)
Mozart – Marches

Walton – *Orb and Sceptre*
Khachaturian – *Sabre Dance* (from *Gayaneh*)
Respighi – *Tarantella* and *Cancan* (from *La Boutique fantasque*)
Offenbach – *Cancan* (from *Gaîté Parisienne*)
Kabalevsky – *Comedians' Galop*
Ponchielli – *Galop* (from *Dance of the Hours*)
Gould – *American Salute; Declaration Suite*
Grainger – *Molly on the Shore* and *Gum-Suckers' March*
Tom Varner – *Long Night Big Day* (New World)

Overtures. Overtures in general contain parts that are peppy and dynamic. Happy and energetic sections are especially good for activating the physical body. For best results, play the overtures and let yourself move freely as the music inspires you.

Wagner – *Die Meistersinger* (ends in triumph)
Dvořák – *Carnival* (explodes with energy)
Weber – *Euryanthe; Oberon* (mystery leads to powerful release)
Johann Strauss, Jr. – *Die Fledermaus* (fast middle section)
Mozart – *Abduction from the Seraglio; Don Giovanni; Magic Flute* (mysterious and also enlivening)
Rossini – *William Tell* (note especially the rousing finale, used as theme for *The Lone Ranger*); *Silken Ladder* and *The Thieving Magpie*
Mendelssohn – *A Midsummer Night's Dream*
Sibelius – *Karelia Overture and Suite*
W. Schuman – *American Festival Overture*
Copland – *Outdoor Overture*
John Williams – *The Cowboys Overture*
Berlioz – *Roman Carnival*
M. Arnold – *Beckus the Dandiprat*
Barber – *School for Scandal*
Mason – *Chanticleer*
Brahms – *Academic Festival Overture*
Walton – *Portsmouth Point*
Schreker – *Fantastic Overture*
Suppé – *Poet and Peasant; Light Cavalry*
Nielsen – *Helios*
Moeran – *Overture for a Masque*
Holst – *A Fugal Overture*
Douglas Lilburn – *Aotearoa Overture*

These pieces of music are very powerful. Use them wisely and let their activating power fill you.

Fanfares, lively songs, epic soundtracks, and dances are also types of music that will vitalize you with their strong frequencies. Explore the pieces to find those that do the most for you. Most of these selections are very strong, so play just a few at a time, then absorb the power before playing more of this kind of music.

Fanfares. Many of these pieces were composed for royal festivals and celebrations. The strong brass sounds will stimulate your physical body and your emotions. The majestic trumpets and crashing cymbals will vitalize you, especially when you are feeling lethargic or sorry for yourself. If these pieces prove to be too strong and make you feel withdrawn or angry, then play lighter music.

Mouret – Fanfares (used on *Masterpiece Theatre*)
De La Lande – *Symphonies for the King's Suppers*
Twenty Fanfares for the Common Man (Mester-Koch)
Bliss – *Investiture Antiphonal Fanfare* (Cala 1010)
Copland – *Fanfare for the Common Man*
Dukas – *La Péri*
Josephs – Fanfare
Stravinsky – *Fanfare* (from *Rake's Progress*)
Joan Tower – *Fanfare for an Uncommon Woman*
Helen Stanley – Fanfare (Koch)

Lively Songs. A class that I worked with discussed the kind of music that made them feel recharged and physically renewed. They preferred lively, popular pieces. They also pointed out that they liked music with perky rhythms. Here are some of the pieces and performers they liked the most:

Mitch Leigh – *Man of La Mancha* (MCA 31065)
Huayucaltia (Brotherhood) – *Caminos* and *Horizontes* (lovely and lively Mesoamerican songs)
Victoria de los Angeles – sings Spanish zarzuelas (EMI)
Anastasia (Broadway musical)
Stephen Foster – *Favorite Songs* (Gregg Smith and Raymond Beegle; conductors – Vox Allegretto ACD 8167)
A Cockeyed Optimist – South Pacific
Oh, What a Beautiful Morning – Oklahoma!
Germaine Montero – *Folk Songs of Spain* (Vanguard 8081)

Yentl: Songs (Barbra Streisand)
Fiddler on the Roof
Songs of Stephen Sondheim
Songs of Andrew Lloyd Webber (specifically, *I Don't Know How to Love Him* from *Jesus Christ Superstar*, *Memory* from *Cats*, *Music of the Night* from *Phantom of the Opera*, *Don't Cry for Me, Argentina* from *Evita*, and *Love Changes Everything* from *Aspects of Love*)
Wayland Jennings – country songs
Johnny Cash – *Wabash Cannonball*
Kenny Rogers
Tanya Tucker
Garth Brooks
Nat King Cole
Ruth Crawford Seeger – *American Folksongs for Children* (Wireless Audio, Minnesota Public Radio, P.O. Box 64454, St. Paul, MN 55165-0454)
Pete Seeger – *The Bitter and the Sweet* (folk songs)

I remember an evening with a dear friend, when we listened together to the beautiful, enlivening melodies of *Brigadoon*. At the end of the performance, my friend said, "I always feel so good after seeing a musical like this; it makes me feel so lively."

I find particularly beautiful the haunting folk songs and ballads of Gordon Bok. Don't miss the deep and timeless feelings of Bok's *Peter Kagan and the Wind*, *Bay of Fundy*, and *Turning Toward the Morning*. I especially like *Return to the Land* (Folk-Legacy Recordings CD-118, Sharon, CT 06069).

In a similar way, I notice with interest how one contemporary church group uses as its opening hymn the tune to *Oh, What a Beautiful Morning* from *Oklahoma*. Although they have changed the words to fit their religious philosophy, they have picked up on the tune's highly charged energies. The music lifts and stimulates people with feelings of expectancy that last for the entire service.

Heroic and Epic Soundtracks. Have you noticed how certain musical soundtracks add so much to the plot and the physical and emotional action going on in the scenes? Some of the strong soundtracks from the great motion picture epics will provide physical renewal and will increase vitality. You will find that, even if you cannot remember the exact scene during which the music was played, the memories of certain musical themes can galvanize your body. Sometimes, it is not even necessary to see the movie;

just hearing the recording of the music itself is enough to charge you. My wife Rosemary and I often share the following humorous dialogue: "Great movie, Hal. Do you remember that scene where . . . ?" "No, Rosie, I never saw it, but I have the soundtrack—beautiful music!" Here are some of the soundtracks, which happen to be personal favorites of mine. The best place to find and order soundtracks is from Craig Spaulding, Screen Archives Entertainment, P.O. Box 34792, Washington DC 20043 (1-202-328-1434).

Ben Hur – Miklos Rózsa
King of Kings – Rózsa
Quo Vadis – Rózsa
El Cid – Rózsa
Lust for Life – Rózsa
Time after Time – Rózsa
Dead Men Don't Wear Plaid – Rózsa
Julius Caesar – Rózsa
Far and Away – John Williams
Superman – Williams
Star Wars – Williams
The Empire Strikes Back – Williams
E.T. – Williams
Odd Man Out – William Alwyn
Born Free – John Barry
Out of Africa – Barry
Gandhi – Maurice Jarre
Jesus of Nazareth – Jarre
Lawrence of Arabia – Jarre
The Message – Jarre
Lion of the Desert – Jarre
Gone with the Wind – Max Steiner
Day of the Dolphin – Georges Delerue
A Little Romance – Delerue
Forest of the Amazon – Heitor Villa-Lobos
Caravans – Mike Batt
The Man from Snowy River – Bruce Rowland
The Good, the Bad and the Ugly – Ennio Morricone
Once Upon a Time in the West – Morricone
The Mission – Morricone
Casualties of War – Morricone
Chariots of Fire – Vangelis
How the West Was Won – Alfred Newman

The Robe – Newman
Nevada Smith – Newman
Son of the Morning Star – Craig Safan
Silverado – Bruce Broughton
O Pioneers – Broughton
North by Northwest – Bernard Herrmann
The Ghost and Mrs. Muir – Herrmann
Mysterious Island – Herrmann
The Kentuckian – Herrmann
Obsession – Herrmann
The Seahawk – Erich Korngold
Old Gringo – Lee Holdridge
Lonesome Dove – Basil Poledouris (Cabin Fever Music)
Blue Lagoon – Poledouris
Quigley Down Under – Poledouris
Moby Dick – Philip Sainton
The Best Years of Our Life – Hugo Friedhofer
One-Eyed Jacks – Friedhofer
The Agony and the Ecstasy – Jerry Goldsmith
100 Rifles – Goldsmith
The Sand Pebbles – Goldsmith
Lilies of the Field – Goldsmith
Stagecoach – Goldsmith
Bad Girls – Goldsmith
The Big Country – Jerome Moross
The Wild Bunch – Jerry Fielding
The Magnificent Seven – Elmer Bernstein
The Hallelujah Trail – Bernstein
Hawaii – Bernstein
Geronimo – Ry Cooder
Alfred the Great – Raymond Leppard
Heaven and Earth – Kitaro
Dream Rider – Randy Miller
How the West Was Lost – Peter Kater and R. Carlos Nakai
Lost Horizon – Dimitri Tiomkin
Giant – Tiomkin
Ran – Toru Takemitsu
The Bridge on the River Kwai – Malcolm Arnold
The Roots of Heaven – Arnold
Scott of the Antarctic (Symphony no. 7) – Ralph Vaughan Williams
Hoffa – James Newton Howard

Wyatt Earp – Howard
Rebecca – Franz Waxman
The Nun's Story – Waxman
The Spirit of St. Louis – Waxman
The Music of the Lone Ranger – Alberto Colombo, Karl Hajos, William
  Lava, and Cy Feuer

As a boy I thrilled to the adventures of the Lone Ranger and his companion, Tonto—heroic champions and true fighters for justice, who may seem
tame by today's Hollywood eruptive, "max-out electronic glitz" standards,
or who may seem dull in the face of the dehumanizing cult of violence,
exploitation, and antiheroic trends of our time. I especially loved the dramatic and pictorial musical accompaniments to the various episodes. These
selections, almost always classical, revealed a genius of imagination and
integration.

Most persons know about Rossini's *William Tell Overture* (finale), which
is the basic theme song for the program. Other classical selections, from
Wagner, Mendelssohn, Liszt, and Tchaikovsky further enhanced the scenes.
I never could locate a few pieces of music that I especially enjoyed. The
mystery for me was solved a few years ago by Reginald M. Jones, Jr., who
writes about this "extra" music for "The Lone Ranger" in his outstanding
book *The Mystery of the Masked Man's Music* (The Scarecrow Press, Inc.,
Metuchen, New Jersey, 1987). Today, the additional background music to
"The Lone Ranger" is available on a wonderfully nostalgic CD recording,
The Music of the Lone Ranger, (Intersound, 11810 Wills Road, P.O. Box
1724, Roswell, GA 30077). It is a real find for anyone who loves the West,
the genre of the Western movie and soundtrack, and the heroic in music.

When you play these soundtracks, notice the particular tracks on each
CD that appeal to you the most. Program your favorite cues in the order
that you prefer. With soundtrack recordings, there is usually a wide range
of musical moods and content. In general, you will find that the main theme
(usually the first and last tracks of the CD) is the strongest, sometimes is
repeated most often, and in many cases is the most memorable.

Dances and Folk songs. Certain music makes you want to dance. The best
music of this kind frees and restores your physical body. It does not jar you,
deplete your energies, or make you feel scattered and frenzied. Folk dances
and other pieces of beautiful dance music are different from disco and hard
rock, in which wiggling hips and navels are often the main attraction, and
the energy focuses more in the genitals than in the heart.

Zorba the Greek (in the terrific novel by Nikos Kazantzakis) points out that life itself is a dance; so too melodic dance music puts you in touch with your energy and helps you to feel genuine intimacy in close physical contact and rhythmical movement with another person. I think especially of many beautiful tango compositions by Astor Piazzolla. Dancing gracefully with vitality to a song or melody is a way to share deeply with one you feel close to, and such an experience enables you to touch and embrace the other physically and soulfully in an affectionate, wholesome way. Also, such dancelike music provides you with an uplifting form of exercise. It clears out staleness in your emotions, limbs, and muscles, and helps you to breathe in new energy through your lungs and bloodstream.

Here are some musical selections of beautiful and lively music that may make you feel like dancing:

Music that Makes You Feel Like Dancing

Tumbalalaika (Yiddish folk songs without words) (Vanguard)
Tony Elman – *Shakin' Down the Acorns* (White Swan Distributors)
Brewer, Rumbel, and Tingstad – *Emerald*
Piazzolla – *Symphonic Tango* (Stratta – Teldec 1 76997)
Praetorius – *Dances from Terpsichore*
Dvořák – *Slavonic Dances*
Brahms – *Hungarian Dances*
Enesco – *Romanian Rhapsodies*
Borodin – *Polovtsian Dances* (from *Prince Igor*)
Respighi – *Ancient Dances and Airs*
Ippolitov-Ivanov – *Caucasian Sketches*
Paul Fetler – *Contrasts for Orchestra*
Bartók – *Dance Suite*
Turina – *Fantastic Dances*
Granados – *Ten Spanish Dances*
Sarasate – *Spanish Dances*
Bernstein – *Dances* (from *West Side Story*)
Copland – *Cuban Dance*
Virgil Thomson – *Acadian Songs and Dances*
Debussy – *Dance; Sacred and Profane Dances*
Chopin – Waltzes
Theodorakis – *Dances* from *Zorba the Greek*
Weber – *Invitation to the Dance*
Tchaikovsky – *Dances* from *Swan Lake* and *Sleeping Beauty*
Shostakovich – *Polka* (from *Age of Gold*); *Tea for Two*

Delibes – *Coppélia* and *Sylvia*
Minkus – *La Bayadere; Don Quixote; Paquita*
Messager – *The Two Pigeons*
Copland – *Rodeo*
The Chieftains (especially their album *Celtic Harp*)

MUSIC FOR FEELINGS AND MOODS

The most challenging area in our make-up is the emotions. Just as the physical body releases energy through movement and activity, the emotions give out energy through the expression of feelings. One of the most important aspects of a balanced and creative life is to nurture and maintain a healthy, happy, and constructive emotional nature.

We usually feel before thinking, even if it is very quickly. Observe your emotional responses. If something happens that makes you feel happy, how do you express this feeling? Do you sing, do you cry out in joy, do you speak out, do you show happiness by moving your body—running, hopping, smiling, hugging—or some other way? Pay close attention to your responses to feelings of joy, anger, fear, sadness, tenseness, confusion, guilt, and so forth. How do you release your emotions? Music can help you.

The key to a healthy emotional nature is beautiful expression, not repression, of your feelings. Creative expression and balancing your emotions take time and careful attention, especially if you have repressed your feelings for many years. The important thing is to learn how to release your feelings constructively.

A while ago, a friend was told, "You are so angry! Why are you so filled with anger?" My friend answered that he was not angry *at anyone* he could remember. "No," he was reminded, "you are just filled with anger itself—the stored-up feelings of old angers that were never expressed. You are a carrier of rage."

My friend went home alone and considered carefully what he had been told. During the next year he discovered many memories of childhood and earlier times when he had felt very angry. Behind many of the angry feelings was extreme grief and memories of pain and loss. Out of propriety, good manners, or fear, he had mostly swallowed and "stuffed" his anger, thus building a tightness in his head and solar plexus that increased with the years and with each new instance of turning his angry feelings inside. It took my friend a long time to begin to work through the anger and frustration he had stored up. During this process, often involving talking and journaling, he discovered deep memories of painful scenes, when he had wanted to respond emotionally, but instead had choked back his feelings and repressed the situation. I remember that when he finally got in touch with his deep emotions, he said, "If I had gone on like this, some day I might have killed somebody."

If you deny or repress your feelings, you may remain numbed and unresponsive, feel melancholic and full of sadness, or become violent and destructive. The creative release of positive and negative emotions brings catharsis and clearing, leaving you feeling stronger and more vital. The therapeutic progression often consists of moving through anger to grief and then to release. Laughter and the energizing which comes from creative activity can help this process.

In terms of health, repressed anger may also lead to migraines, ulcers, strokes, or tumors; prolonged fears may make you tense and may bring eczema, shingles, psoriasis, or arthritis. It is essential, therefore, to find healthy outlets and creative ways through which to channel your emotions. Your daily diet—of food, mental attitudes, spiritual devotion, and study— must be supplemented by emotionally rewarding and satisfying interests.

Great music is one aid to healthy emotional release. In general the creative arts offer you wonderful opportunities to transmute negative, suppressed emotional energies. Use artistic outlets like singing, painting, dancing, moving with music, working with clay, writing poetry, or keeping a journal to channel the energies and pockets of feeling that are alive in you. And, let music come into you, music that stirs you and at the same time acts as a clearing agent that will take and absorb the feelings you release into it.

You can often clear out emotional blockages with music. I have found generally that music for woodwinds will often help to clear out some emotional tensions and blockage. The transparent sounds of the flute, piccolo, oboe, English horn (really an alto oboe), clarinet, and sometimes the bassoon, playing beautiful, melodic music, are wonderful healing agents for strained emotions. *La Mer* (The Sea), a strong, melodic piece by the French composer Debussy, is especially effective in breaking up tensions in the emotions.

During a serious business meeting, I remember playing a recording of Jean-Pierre Rampal's performance for flute of J. S. Bach's *Badinerie* to a group of rather angry and tense listeners. Soon, their looks changed. The music was pulling the strain out of them. As the piece bathed them with fountains of effervescent melody, they began to relax. The fighting mood of the group changed, and smiles appeared on some faces. One listener offered the woman next to him a cigarette, which she gratefully accepted. After the music session had ended, the meeting proceeded more smoothly, and an attitude of cooperation prevailed.

Sometimes woodwinds are combined with strings to provide a different kind of healing musical experience. A striking example of a piece of this type is the Adagio, third movement of Rachmaninov's Second Symphony. In this marvelously rhapsodic and therapeutic musical movement, the clarinet leads and carries the melody. The tune is quiet but gradually rises and eventually soars with the full orchestra, carrying a listener into great heights. To hear this music is to feel all emotional negativity and tension drained away. This music not only absorbs the energies you release into it, but also carries you into a higher, devotional, and spiritually elevated state of consciousness. It is one of the greatest works that Rachmaninov was ever inspired to compose. The movement comes full circle to recede and close in quietness.

Releasing Anger. Music can also be used to release anger. *Anger* is the word we use to describe one kind of emotional displeasure. Depending on what kind of temperament you have, you will need to find the most appropriate ways to defuse and discharge your anger. Perhaps you can go outside and chop wood; or you might begin to beat the rugs, hit pillows, jog, scrub floors, sing loudly, ride your motorcycle, play racquetball, or some equally vigorous activity. Sounding tones (such as "HO, HO!") is an especially effective way to release energy through the voice. Obviously, you would want to find some constructive way to release this energy, for it never helps to react destructively (for example, yelling and screaming), thus adding decibels to the trouble and confusion already disturbing the atmosphere.

Certain music provides a reservoir or "tank," which can receive and store a discharge of strong, angry feelings and energies. At the same time, in the alchemy of exchange, such music often refills and empowers you with its own cleansing currents and healing essences. Release and receive! Many wonderful examples of such "deep release" music come from the Slavic and Celtic-Irish cultures. For example, Mussorgsky's *Great Gate of Kiev*, the final section from *Pictures at an Exhibition* (especially the phenomenal version that includes an apocalyptic pipe organ, Eduardo Diaz-munoz conducting, OMCD80107DDD), Rimsky-Korsakov's *Russian Easter Overture* (preferably by Leopold Stokowski on RCA Silver Seal 60487-2 or by Charles Gerhardt on Menuet 160002-2), Shostakovich's Symphony no. 5, and *Song of the Forests* (by Vladimir Ashkenazy on London 436 762-2), Shaun Davey's *Relief of Derry Symphony* (Tara CD3024), and songs by composer and singer Enya and the group Clannad offer listeners opportunities for deep release.

I also deeply love the powerful, yet lyrical and melodic works of American composers Roy Harris, Howard Hanson, David Diamond, Walter

Piston, William Schuman, Otto Luening, Norman Dello Joio (especially his
Antiphonal Fantasy for Organ and Orchestra, Summit DCD 145, Albany
Distributors), Samuel Barber. and Alan Hovhaness. Such outstanding con-
ductors as maestros David Amos, Gerard Schwarz, Kenneth Klein, Dennis
Russell Davies, Leonard Slatkin, and James Sedares are currently cham-
pioning these wonderful American composers in their recordings, as did
Bernstein, Ormandy, and others in the past.

Interestingly, I have found that people react very differently in times
of anger. Some will go to any extreme to avoid controversy and conflict.
Others, needing a strong adrenalin discharge, attack viciously and look for
ways to blow off steam in assertive, fiery, explosive outbursts. Musical taste
and temperament often go together. My books *Living Your Destiny* and
Taking Account of Your Life (Samuel Weiser, York Beach, Maine) contain
useful information on temperaments, as do Dr. Helen Bonny's *Music and
Your Mind* and Jean Shinoda Bolen's *Gods in Every Man* and *Goddesses
in Every Woman*. Our differing temperaments and energy responses to
life situations and relationships make our musical choices quite varied and
subjective. I list below many types and selections of music, each of which
can help to release strong feelings through rhythms, melodies, and timbres.

Strong Music to Air Out Anger

Holst – *The Planets* (especially *Mars*)
Dello Joio – *Antiphonal Fantasy on a Theme of Vincenzo Albrici for
Organ and Orchestra*
Beethoven – *Egmont Overture;* Symphonies nos. 3, 5, and 9
Tchaikovsky – Symphony no. 5 (last movement); Symphony no. 6
(good for getting down into grief and depression); Piano Concerto no.
1 (Finales to first and third movements)
Saint-Saëns – Symphony no. 3 *(Organ)* (last movement is especially
grand and heroic, rising to great heights and glory)
Rheinberger – Organ concertos and Suite for Organ and Orchestra
Mahler – Symphony no. 1 *(Titan)*
Nielsen – Symphony no. 5 and Finale of Symphony no. 4
Villa-Lobos – *Genesis*
Rachmaninov – Piano Concerto no. 3
Janáček – *Sinfonietta* (powerful brass and strings); *Glagolitic Mass*
(passionate choral sections and organ/orchestral parts)
Borodin – Symphony no. 2 (powerful brass and strong rhythms in outer
movements)
Creston – *Toccata* (Schwarz – Delos 3127)

Wagner – *Ride of the Valkyries; Entrance of the Gods into Valhalla* (powerful release)

Poulenc – Concerto for Organ, Timpani and Strings (highly energizing, with some very introspective sections)

Copland – Symphonies nos. 1 and 3

Britten – *Four Sea Interludes* (from *Peter Grimes*)

Jongen – *Symphonie Concertante for Organ and Orchestra* (supercharged, with very mystical, quiet third movement)

Verdi – *Dies Irae* (from *Requiem*)

Boito – Prologue to *Mefistofele* (very strong)

Ginastera – *Estancia* (activating rhythms); Symphony no. 3 *(Pampeana)*

Theodorakis – Symphony no. 3

de Falla – *El Amor Brujo, Nights in the Gardens of Spain,* and *El Sombrero de Tres Picos*

Brahms – Piano Concerto no. 1 (strong sections of struggle, combining with sections of peace and yearning)

The more *yang,* or strong, musical selections just mentioned are good for receiving and absorbing angry feelings. These pieces are large enough to contain your release.

Another approach, however, is to use calmer, more *yin* music to diffuse and transmute strong emotions. Very often this kind of music will help you to relax at all levels and release anger through interior processes. These pieces will either rebalance you, making you wonder how you could have become so agitated with temper, or they will make you move toward positive outer expression of the anger by lifting it into a more constructive creative activity.

Quiet Music to Calm Anger

Alfredo Ortiz – *Harp for Quiet Moments* (I, II)

J. S. Bach – Two Concertos for Two Pianos

Boccherini – *Guitar quintets* (Naxos)

Echoes of Nature – *Morning Songbirds* (Laserlight); *Loons of Mirror Lake*

Robert Tree Cody – *Dreams from the Grandfather*

Mozart – *Sonatas for Violin and Piano; Cassations*

Rostropovich and Tachezi – *Cello and Organ* (Teldec)

Michael Conway Baker – *Washington Square* (haunting and beautiful) (Summit DCD 165)

Handel – *Harp Concerto* (Boston Skyline)

Lyrical Melodies of Japan (flute-harp) (Denon)

Mike Rowland – *The Fairy Ring* (gets beneath anger down into grief and deep release; good with massage; even more effective when combined with ocean sounds)

Music for Quiet Listening (Hanson – Mercury 434 347-2)

Patrick Ball – *Secret Isles* and *From a Distant Time* (for Celtic harp)

Daniel Kobialka – *Going Home* (Willow Music, P.O. Box 151439, San Rafael, CA 94915) (very compassionate music, good for releasing pain and grief)

Rod McKuen – *Balloon Concerto*

Michael Jones – *Magical Child*

Hilary Stagg – *Feather Light* (harp) (Real Music, 85 Libertyship Way, Sausalito, CA 94965)

Schubert – Prelude to *Rosamunde*

John Williams – *Schindler's List* (soundtrack)

Silvius Leopold Weiss – Sonatas for Lute

Christoph Gluck – *Dance of the Blessed Spirits*

Ron Dexter – *Golden Voyage I*

Jacob van Eyck – *Music for the Recorder*

Andy Williams – miscellaneous songs

Perry Como – miscellaneous songs

Roger Whittaker – miscellaneous songs

Jacques Burtin – *The Inner Song* (music for African kora) (Studio SM – Paris 12 22.91)

Relieving Tension. Sometimes the schedule of a busy day makes you tense. You may feel wound up, physically and emotionally. To unwind and slow down, you may need to play music that is quiet, melodically pleasing, and slow in rhythm and pacing. Here are some suggestions:

Music to Relieve Hyperactivity

J. S. Bach – *Air on a G String*

Rod McKuen – *Concerto for Balloon and Orchestra* (Stanyan label)

Grieg – *Holberg Suite*

Beethoven – Symphony no. 6 (first and second movements)

Pachelbel – *Canon in D*

Alan Hovhaness – *Mysterious Mountain* (RCA)

Marvin Hamlisch – *Sophie's Choice* (soundtrack)

David Michael and Randy Mead – *Petals in the Stream* (Fortuna label)

Mozart – Concerto for Flute and Harp; Concertos for Flute and Orchestra (1, 2)

Vivaldi – Flute concertos; *Four Seasons*

Mario Giulani – Guitar concertos

Rodrigo – *Aranjuez Concerto* (guitar and orchestra)

Mantovani – *Songs of Love; Italian Suite*

Depression and Fear. If you are feeling dejected, tired, and negative about life, sleep is often the best therapy. Before getting the rest you need, play a quiet piece of music, such as the ones mentioned above. If sleep is not possible, or you are not tired but just low and feeling the "blues," music can help lift you out of gloom. Try to find music that ends on an up note, with a rhythm that keeps moving you forward—neither too hurried nor too lethargic. I suggest these musical selections to pierce through melancholy, fears, doubts, and apprehensions:

Music to Relieve Depression, Fear, and Grief

Alturas – *From the Heights* (music from the Andes)

J. S. Bach – Keyboard concertos; *Thou Art with Me* (Ormandy – CBS 38915)

Haydn – Flute quartets

Mendelssohn – *Capriccio brillante;* Piano concertos

Bizet – Symphony in C

Sousa – Marches

Tchaikovsky – Piano Concerto no. 1 (finale)

Rachmaninov – Piano Concerto no. 2 (finale) (composed by Rachmaninov to help himself conquer his own manic-depressive tendencies)

Viennese Operetta Arias (sung by Lucia Popp) (EMI)

Saint-Saëns – Symphony no. 3 (*Organ*) (power finale lifts the listener into radiance and triumph)

Mark Isham – *A River Runs Through It* (soundtrack)

National Parks and Sanctuaries (*Solitudes*/Dan Gibson Environmental Sound Experiences)

Debussy – *La Mer (The Sea)*

Delibes – *Coppélia* (beautiful dance melodies)

Beethoven – Piano Concerto no. 5 *(Emperor)*

Dvořák – Symphony no. 8; *Slavonic Dances*

Mozart – Symphonies nos. 35 *(Haffner);* 41 *(Jupiter)*

Handel – *Water Music; Music for the Royal Fireworks*

Classical Loon (NorthWord Press, P.O. Box 1360, Minocqua, WI 54548) (very relaxing)

Grofé – *Grand Canyon Suite; Mississippi Suite*

Mendelssohn – Symphony no. 4 *(Italian)*

Parry – *Jerusalem* (used in *Chariots of Fire)*

Rick Erlien – *Music of Yosemite* (Real Music, Sausalito, CA)

Boredom. Sometimes boredom is caused by a lack of variety in our schedules or by an unimaginative, grudge-filled, and ungrateful attitude toward the gift of our lifetime. When we feel that we are in a rut, we need to change either our attitude or our approach to the assignment. Find the best proportion for each day, in which you combine regularity and spontaneity. There will also be certain spaces in your life, called Open Key periods, in which you are "between assignments." These can be times of great opportunity, if you approach them creatively and with receptivity. Music can be a stimulus to help in these areas.

However, if you use free time to worry, or waste in idleness, you may lose a great gift and may look back later, seeing how you could have used this time more wisely. Ultimately, your own creativity and your spiritual connections are the best ways out of depression and anxiety. Go down into your grief and pain, and you may find there deeper wellsprings of inspiration and new joy. There is always so much to learn, so many areas in which you can grow; it is extremely wasteful, especially in our times, to feel excessive self-pity and boredom. The following musical selections tend to awaken new enthusiasm, vision, and vitality:

Music to Relieve Boredom

Gottschalk – *Grande Tarantelle* (piano and orchestra) (Vanguard)

Liszt – *Hungarian Rhapsodies* (Dorati – Mercury)

Respighi – *Ancient Dances and Airs; Pines of Rome* (Dorati – Mercury)

F. J. Haydn – Trumpet Concerto

Rodrigo – *Fantasy for a Courtier*

Rimsky-Korsakov – *Scheherazade* (Beecham – EMI or Stokowski – RCA)

Prokofiev – *Lt. Kijé Suite*

Babbling Brook (the beautiful combination of Bach and a brook) (Distributions Madacy, Box 1445, St. Laurent, Quebec, Canada H4L 4Z1)

Kevin Locke – *Dream Catcher* (Native American flute and environmental sounds) (White Swan Distributors)

Vincent d'Indy – *Symphony on a French Mountain Air* (Naxos or London)

Bizet – *Carmen* (selections) (Beecham – EMI)

Stevan Pasero – *Seasons* (guitar, strings, panflutes)

Amy Beach – Piano Concerto (Vox)

Authentic Greek Folksongs and Dances (Legacy 318)

Richard Diciedue – *Violin Concerto in D* (Lefkowitz/Amos – Cambria 1064)

Strength and Courage. At the times in your life when you need greater courage—either to make a decision or to stand firm in the path you have chosen—music can help to focus you and strengthen you in your determination and constructive willpower.

A friend of mine, who has long struggled with a compulsion to overeat went through many self-help programs, including weight-watching programs, nutrition classes, and the like. But her main problem was lack of self-discipline—simply not being able to use willpower to push herself away from the table. She found that certain musical pieces served as chargings to help her to stand up to her demanding appetite. By listening to specific musical selections, she was able to conquer excess and to eat more intelligently. She used Kabalevsky's *Comedians* and selections from Rózsa *Ben Hur.*

Another friend uses music to help him meet difficulties in business relationships. Just before going out to deal with a difficult person, he plays certain powerful musical pieces that gear him for the challenge. Being by nature rather retiring and peace loving, he finds that these musical choices galvanize him sufficiently to negotiate effectively and stand up for his position. He no longer allows himself to be bullied, and the music gives him courage, without making him overly aggressive or tyrannical.

Here are some suggestions for music that can awaken deeper courage in you. This music is also a stimulant to the physical body. It often causes increases of blood flow, speed of circulation, and muscular energy and metabolism.

Music for Strength and Courage

Robert Russell Bennett – *Stephen Foster Commemoration Symphony* (Steinberg – Legacy 332)

Elgar – *Pomp and Circumstance March no. 1*

Beethoven – Piano Concerto no. 5 *(Emperor)*; Choral Fantasy for Piano and Orchestra; Symphony no. 3 *(Eroica)*; *Egmont Overture*

Brahms – Symphony no. 2 (final movement)

Julia Ward Howe and William Steffe – *Battle Hymn of the Republic*

La Marseillaise (arranged by Hector Berlioz)

Copland – *Fanfare for the Common Man; A Lincoln Portrait; Suite of Old American Songs* (Try also Copland's beautiful *Tender Land Suite.* This beautiful music, especially the finale *The Promise of Living,* based on the revivalist song *Zion's Walls,* brings through a power and beauty that are very special. Look up the version conducted by James Sedares on Koch 3-7092-2 or the wonderful rendition conducted by Copland himself – RCA 6802 or 09026.)

Richard Strauss – *Sunrise* (from *Thus Spake Zarathustra* – used in the movie *2001: A Space Odyssey*)

Hendrick Andriessen – Symphony no. 4 (Olympia)

Respighi – Suite for Organ and Orchestra

Rachmaninov – *Concerto élégiaque* (orchestrated by Alan Kogosowski, conducted by Neeme Järvi – Chandos 9261)

Star-Spangled Banner and other national anthems (Legacy)

Wolf – *Beyond Words* (especially the Native American tone poem *Sooh Ichilay,* or *Many Thundering Horses,* composed for thundering horses, kettledrums, and environmental thunderstorm)

Relaxation and Reverie. After a long day at work, there will be times when you may wish just to put your feet up and relax. As some persons prefer to use this time to mellow out with a friend or brood creatively with a newspaper, you may wish to use music to help you unwind. Certain music allows you to release stressful feelings as you recall certain lovely past experiences, memories, and places of beauty that you can now revisit in consciousness, if not in actual travel.

Music for Relaxation, Reverie, and Imagery

Bearns and Dexter – *The Golden Voyage* (vol. 1)

Chris Valentino – *The Musical Sea of Tranquility* (a beautiful, relaxing guided imagery with harp and ocean) (Jonella, Box 522, Englewood, NJ 07631)

Nancy Enslin – *Mystic Shores* (harp and ocean)

Rachel Portman – *The Joy Luck Club* (soundtrack)

John Williams – *Presumed Innocent* (soundtrack)

Daniel Kobialka – *Fragrances of a Dream; Afternoon of a Fawn*

James Galway – *Nocturne* (flute); *Song of the Seashore* (RCA)

Frederic Delius – *Brigg Fair; Appalachia*

Toumani Diabate – *Kaira* (*Peace*) (African music for kora – beautiful and meditative) (Hannibal 1338)

Opera without Words (RCA or Sony) (Kostelanetz – CBS)

Bizet – *Carmen without Words* (Kostelanetz – CBS)

Chopin – Nocturne in E-flat Major

Salvador Bacarisse – Concertino for Guitar and Orchestra

Wagner – *Evening Star* (from *Tannhäuser* conducted by Mantovani)

Gheorghe Zamfir – *Romantic Flute of Pan* (especially Zamfir's own composition, *To Thee O God)*

Annie Locke – *Memories*

Debussy – *Clair de lune; Reverie; Arabesque no. 1* (also *Debussy by the Sea* – Special Music Company)

Ravel – *Pavane for a Dead Princess; Introduction and Allegro* (Harp, Flute, Clarinet, and String Quartet)

Timo Korhonen – *Sevilla* (beautiful Spanish solo guitar music of Tárrega, Torroba, and Albéniz)

Somei Satoh – *Toward the Night*

Andrés Segovia – Miscellaneous guitar music

Torroba – Sonatina for Guitar and Orchestra

Cry of the Loon – Environmental sounds

Terry Oldfield – *Out of the Depths; Reverence* (flute, ocean, and whale songs)

Serenity (Tranquil Moods: L.D.M.I., Box 1445, St. Laurent, Quebec, H4L 4Z1, Canada)

Alan Stivell – *Renaissance of the Celtic Harp* (Rounder Records or CD 3067)

Enya – *Exile* and *Evening Falls* (from *Watermark)*

Michael Gettel – *San Juan Island Suite*

Bach by the Sea (Special Music Company, Englewood Cliffs, NJ)

Bruch – *Scottish Fantasy*

Kreisler – *Humoresque*

Copland – *Quiet City; Appalachian Spring; Our Town*

Vivaldi – Oboe concertos

Love and Devotion. Erich Fromm in *The Art of Loving* has written that love is a decision, not just an emotion. In the midst of all temporary ups and downs in your life, you have, innately within you, an enormous God-given power, the power to express unconditional love. Such love is constant caring and devotion, coupled with understanding and discernment.

Certain pieces of music, with their melodies and sonorities, can especially help to awaken the power of love within you. These pieces appeal more directly to your heart center, and they will bathe you in love-energy.

As a general rule such music emphasizes the high strings of the orchestra, the harp, and the organ. Some of these pieces have been composed for the whole orchestra, which will bombard your atmosphere more powerfully than would just a few instruments or a piece of chamber music. Such pieces are like great beams of light (to some they often appear as rose and blue) that penetrate you and your environment, filling every space around you with the devotional energies of love.

Music for Love and Devotion

Franck – *Panis angelicus*
John Denver-Placido Domingo – *Perhaps Love*
Rachmaninov – *Love Theme* (Eighteenth Variation from *Rhapsody on a Theme of Paganini*)
Nino Rota – *Symphony on a Love Song*
Mozart – *I Shall Love Her* (Aria from *Il re pastore*)
Orff – *In trutina* (from *Carmina Burana*)
Saint-Saëns – *Softly Awaken My Heart* (from *Samson and Delilah*)
Bruch – *Romance for Viola and Orchestra*
Vaughan Williams – *Serenade to Music*
Frank Bridge – *Rosemary*
Elgar – *Rosemary*
Linda Ronstadt – *Canciones de mi Padre*
Smetana – Largo (from *Má Vlast*)
Grieg – *I Love Thee (Ich Liebe Dich)*
Delibes – *Bell Song* (from *Lakmé*) (sung by Lily Pons – CBS Portrait 45694)
Wagner – *Liebestod* (from *Tristan und Isolde*); Prelude to Act 1 *(Parsifal)*
Marian Anderson – *Spirituals*
Jessye Norman – *Sacred Songs*
Luciano Pavarotti – *O Sole Mio* and *Turn to Sorrento*
Placido Domingo – *Be My Love*
Liszt – Schubert Song Transcriptions; Consolation no. 3
Chopin – Piano Concerto no. 1 (slow movement) (Gilels on Sony SMK 46336)
Beethoven – *For Elise*
Korngold – *Garden Scene* (from *Much Ado About Nothing*)
Judy Loman and Daniel Domb – *Meditations* (beautiful music for harp/cello)
Emile Pandolfi – *Once Upon a Romance*
Goldmark – *In the Garden* (from *Rustic Wedding Symphony*)

J. S. Bach – *Jesu, Joy of Man's Desiring* (conducted by Stokowski or sung by Kirsten Flagstad)

Fauré – *Cantique de Jean Racine*

Handel – Largo (from *Xerxes*)

Mahalia Jackson – Miscellaneous hymns

Victor Herbert – *Ah, Sweet Mystery of Life* (sung by Beverly Sills)

John Barry – *Somewhere in Time* (soundtrack); *Moviola*

Mendelssohn – Violin Concerto

Parkening Plays Bach (guitar solo)

World's Greatest Love Songs (orchestral) (Intersound CDM 8006) (includes *The Look of Love, Misty, Stardust, Lover, And I Love Her, Michelle, We've Only Just Begun,* and many others)

Once, in a television interview, Seiji Ozawa, conductor of the Boston Symphony Orchestra, said that the way great music has helped him the most is to make him feel a particular emotion such as happiness or sadness in hundreds of different ways. The various instrumental colors, melodies, and harmonies of music stimulate many overtones and subtleties of feeling. Music helps us to get in touch with our larger interior palette of nuances of feeling, and it calls us to externalize those feelings in our relationships, in conversation, in worship, or in the expression of common goals worked out together. We can use the profound content of music to awaken the feeling, caring parts of ourselves.

Explore the wide range of musical choices that have been suggested. Find those pieces that help you the most to contact, release, and refine your larger spectrum of emotional response.

CLEAR THINKING, MENTAL POWER

Just as certain selections of music can nourish your physical and emotional layers, so other musical works can bring greater health to your mind. Music can help you find greater mental clarity and focus.

Your attitudes affect what happens to you. As experience, itself, is neutral, it is your attitude, your thoughts and feelings, that determine largely what you will make of your challenges and opportunities. It is the sign of a healthy mind in each of us when we see but do not condemn or judge, hold no limiting, rigid opinions based on the past, and remain alive to new impressions and new possibilities. Such a mind is an alert, observant, and well-directed instrument for the soul. As your mind can remain flexible, expectant, and clearly attuned, not rigid, so will your life bring you many new opportunities.

Generally, music most pleasing to the mind will be simple and clear melodically and rhythmically. Music of the Baroque period (early to mid–1700s) is wonderful for focus and mental clarity. It is ordered, melodic, and contains few surprises. It tends to flow along pleasingly, like vibrant currents of a river. Such music helps the mind to focus, plan, and execute the thoughts and desires you are seeking to fulfill. The music of the Baroque period also contains regular rhythms that correspond to a normal, healthy heartbeat. Look up the melodic and buoyant concertos of Vivaldi, Marcello, Corelli, Torelli, Albinoni, Quantz, Tartini, Manfredini, Stamitz, and others. These works will relieve your stressful feelings and, within their reliable frame of order and beauty, will always prove satisfying.

Much music of the twentieth century is also intellectual. However, less music of our time is melodic, so although the structure is well thought out, it tends to grate on the listener (at least this listener) and is often hard logic without deep feeling or inspiration. Cultivate music that inspires you; avoid computerized, mental sounds, composed out of mere curiosity or cleverness. Certain selections will help you move into your day with planning and directed energy. Here are some musical pieces for a more healthy, attuned mind:

Music for Clear Thinking

J. S. Bach – *Brandenburg Concertos; The Four Suites*
Haydn – Piano trios
Boccherini – Symphonies; Quartets
Telemann – Concerto for Three Violins and Orchestra
Frederick the Great – Flute concertos
Handel – *Water Music*
Kuhlau – Flute quintets
Alessandro Scarlatti – Sinfonias
Domenico Scarlatti – 555 Harpsichord sonatas (various labels)
Fernando Sor – *Fantasies and Etudes* (Timo Korhonen, guitar – Ondine);
  Trio Sonata Encore (Boston Skyline)
François de Fossa – *Guitar trios* (Naxos)
Mozart – Church sonatas
Baroque string music of Telemann, Vivaldi, Albinoni, Manfredini,
  Corelli, Torelli, and others.

MUSIC AND MEDITATION

The greatest, most inspiring music speaks to your heart and soul. Certain wonderful, timeless melodies and harmonies emerge and return to the heavens, linking you with the Eternal. As you can let yourself move inside these masterpieces, you will feel more expanded, light-filled, attuned and in communion with the Source of all life. Such music will always send you back into the world with renewed hope, vigor, and dynamic, joyful serenity. You may feel that you are accompanied by innumerable Hosts who call you to let go of heaviness and negativity so that you can receive and absorb greater frequencies of energy. Such music brings God's infinite worlds nearer. Your deepest experience of music becomes a spiritual sacrament. No longer are you interested only in bettering earthly conditions or in getting somewhere else beyond earth. Heaven and earth are connected.

There will be many times of meditation and prayer when you will want to keep totally silent. However, a very special piece of music can prepare you for your devotions. Such music will still your body, emotions, and mind, so that your soul center can speak through you, grounding whatever light is available. You will come away enriched and empowered to meet whatever life gives you.

Here are some guidelines to prepare for a more effective meditation preceded by music:

1. Begin by treating this musical meditation as a holy time. Listen in an attitude of reverence and praise. You may want to speak an affirmation or Bible verse. For example; "I will pray with the Spirit and with understanding also" (1 Cor. 14:15), or "The music of the Heavens fills me with the Love of God."

2. Be open to the spiritualizing energies of the music. Something will happen to you spiritually as you are listening. Feel the music moving through all parts of you.

3. Keep a notebook handy, so that you can jot down any impressions or imagery you may receive.

4. Describe any impressions that the melodies might awaken in you. (These may come in the form of places, colors, presences, shapes, archetypes, ideas, and so forth.)

5. Ask yourself, "What feelings does the music awaken in me?" (These may be joy, peace, power, warmth, or some other feeling.) Do you feel better or worse?

6. In what part of your body do you feel the music the most? (For example, in the groin, stomach, solar plexus, heart, throat, forehead, crown of head, muscles, joints.) It is important to realize consciously *where* you feel the music. This is a signal that either more energy is needed in this area, or that dispersing the energy is what is called for.

In this sense, the music serves as a balancing device or tuning fork and will help to harmonize your body, emotions, mind, and soul.

7. When the music has finished, lift up your heart in thankfulness for the enrichments that the music has brought you. A grateful heart keeps the doors open for continuous blessings to enter your life.

Gradually, you will find those special pieces of music that best lead you into the greater mysteries of the Divine. Keep a list of the selections that attune and enrich you the most. Play them often and know that you can depend on them to help you deepen your sensitivity to the Source.

These are some of the musical selections I have found to be most helpful in times of meditation, prayer, and heightened devotion:

Music for Meditation and Prayer

Sergei Rachmaninov – *Vocalise* (Moffo/Stokowski – RCA)

Vaughan Williams – *Fantasia on a Theme of Thomas Tallis* (Ormandy – RCA 09026-61724); *Symphony no. 5* (Barbirolli – EMI 7243 565110)

Arnold Rosner – *Responses, Hosanna and Fugue* (Amos – Harmonia Mundi 906012)

Hovhaness – *Mysterious Mountain* (conducted by Reiner – RCA 5733)

Palestrina – *Pope Marcellus Mass* (Tallis Scholars – Gimell CDGIM 339)

Beethoven – Adagio (from Symphony no. 9)

Schubert – *The Last Quintet op. 163* (arranged for string orchestra by Dalia Atlas ITM 950005)

Tchaikovsky – *Adagio cantabile* (from *Souvenir de Florence*) (Rachlevsky – Claves CD 50-9317)

Kurt Atterberg – *Suite no. 3 for Violin, Viola and Orchestra* (Lysy – Claves CD 50-8507))

Humperdinck – *Children's Prayer* (from *Hansel and Gretel*) (conducted by Ormandy on CBS MLK 45736)

Handel – Largo (from *Xerxes*)

Dvořák – *Largo* (from *Symphony no. 9*) (conducted by Bernstein on Sony SMK 47547)

Elgar – *Nimrod* (from *Enigma Variations*) (conducted by Sir Adrian Boult on EMI CDM 64748)

J. S. Bach – *Come Sweet Death; Toccata and Fugue in D* (orchestral version, conducted by Leopold Stokowski on RCA 09026-61267-4)

Bruckner – *Symphony no. 8* (third movement) (conducted by Horenstein on Vox Box 2-CDX 5504)

Mahler – *Symphony no. 3* (final movement, conducted by Leonard Bernstein on Sony SM2K 47 576); *Symphony no. 4* (Wit – Naxos 8.550527)

Evening Bells – Russian folk melody (Nekrasov – Mobile Fidelity MFCD 859)

O Sanctissima – Music for Prayer (flute and harp)

Wagner – Prelude to Act 1 (from *Lohengrin*); *Prelude* and *Good Friday Music* (from *Parsifal*) (conducted by Bruno Walter on CBS MK 42050 or Stokowski on Pearl PEA 9448)

Bloch – *Prayer for Cello and Strings* (Lysy – Claves CD 50-8507)

Lekeu – *Adagio* (Claves)

Saint-Saëns – *Symphony no. 3* (second movement: *Poco Adagio*) (conducted by Munch on RCA Red Seal 09026-61500-2)

Fauré – *In Paradise* (from *Requiem*) (conducted by Rutter on Collegium COLCD 109)

Chris Valentino – *Musical Sea of Tranquility* (quiet harp and ocean) (Jonella Recording Company, P.O. Box 522, Englewood, NJ 07631)

Rod McKuen – *Concerto for Balloon and Orchestra* (Stanyan STZ 103-2)

Coyote Oldman – *Tear of the Moon* (Indian pan pipes and Native American flute) (Coyote Oldman Music, 434 Chautauqua Avenue, Norman, OK 73069)

Mozart – *Vesperae Solennes de Confessore (Sanctus); Ave Verum Corpus* (conducted by Sir Colin Davis on Philips)

Robert Tree Cody – *Dreams from the Grandfather* (White Swan)

MUSIC IN LIVE PERFORMANCE

It is important to experience your music privately—in the intimacy of your own home—and at times it is also beneficial to go to live concerts. Music in the home can flow into you with little interference or "static" from other persons and vibrations. On the other hand, a powerful live concert that is a happening gathers a whole audience and lifts it into a higher group consciousness, either through group clearance or even a spiritual experience. Buy live recordings whenever possible.

Certain performing artists serve as highly charged vehicles for emotional communication among an audience; their artistry is a therapeutic agent to help others to transmute negative feelings into positive emotional outpouring, through the medium of music. I have experienced this response while listening to a live performance by Arthur Rubinstein, and another, in a different way, by Vladimir Horowitz. Rubinstein's joy and delight with life always sparkle through the music that he plays and will fill the people who hear his recordings. His feelings are infectious, and they help to raise many low spirits. Horowitz channels great power and delivers sparks of electricity through his playing. Listeners are often stimulated by the high-voltage energy of his masterful technique, which combines with inner power and vitality. From the most quiet, delicate pianissimos to the mightiest crescendos, Horowitz spans the keyboard and the chords of human emotions. The music that he performs releases coils of directed energy that charge the audience with new strength and remove various blockages of repressed feelings and memories. In an interview, Horowitz stated that one of his greatest aims in making music was to have the piano sound like an orchestra, and thus his recordings today offer a full spectrum of sound that bathes the listener throughout his or her whole being—physical, emotional, mental, and soulful.

Johnny Cash. In a different way, the country singer Johnny Cash, with his renditions of ballads, gospel songs, and personally interpreted folk music, elicits sustained emotional catharsis from his audience. Cash, whose craggy, Old Testament-prophet look, mixed with a tough "coolness," continues to come across like a folk hero to many of his fans. He has passed through many personal challenges and tragedies, but always struggling toward the open road, he emerges before his audience, singing and pushing ahead with the courageous spirit of one who overcomes. I have always felt a strong appeal for Johnny Cash, as singer and person. In his own unique way, he is a survivor. He continues to generate strong charisma, while also creating genuine emotional rapport with those who hear him. True to the title of his 1975 autobiography, *Man in Black*, published by Zondervan, he dresses in black. His voice is not as smooth any longer, but it contains a rough-hewn honesty and a strong, gutsy quality which empathizes with the human condition and one's personal suffering. His songs combine strength and compassion, the masculine and feminine poles of feeling, which finally neither condone nor condemn. Cash's definition of spirituality is "to use one's ability, through God, to rise above yourself and to feel power that is not your own. . . . Spirituality is . . . ego-less." (*Pulse Magazine,* June 1994, p. 100.)

Johnny Cash's songs proclaim a yearning for freedom on the open road, the desire in the human heart to overcome pain, limitations, and confinements to find love and union with another person and the Infinite beyond—a dream that is often seemingly thwarted by the "fates" and frailties of earthly existence. Listen to the tremendous outpouring of feeling which

Cash generated when he visited San Quentin and Folsom Prison to do live concerts for the inmates (Columbia CDs). These powerful recordings, made in the late 1960s, are still a testimony to the basic longings of humankind, no matter how seemingly distorted, for some ineffable union in the Spirit. In their own countryish way, Cash and his songs are analogous to the heart-rending synthesis of joy and sorrow which Horowitz achieves in his live performance CD of Rachmaninov's Piano Concerto no. 3. Behind many of Cash's songs (such as in the album *Ride This Train*)—as performed with the guitar, harmonica, and the human voice, most recently in his voice-acoustical guitar album for American Recordings-Warner Brothers—a listener can still hear the continuous, driving rhythm of a fiery locomotive, steaming along its tracks, gaining momentum and breaking into freedom and total release. I've always delighted in the sight and sounds of trains and locomotives, thanks largely to Dan McFadden, a New Jersey friend from college years. The sounds of a powerful steam train or an express train, such as those heard in *The Power and the Glory*, I and II on Mobile Fidelity CD, evoke in me feelings of the struggle and the yearning of the human soul to break free of its earthly prisons and confinements. The soul in struggle, like Prometheus trying to break free of his chains and weight, resembles a locomotive that roars in joy with smoke and whistle, as it chugs and steams along the tracks leading onward toward vast open spaces.

In these ways Johnny Cash generates raw energy and a powerful emotional bond in his audience. I definitely feel that his music is stimulating, for it does contain strong waves of feeling which arouse the listener in very grounded, earthy ways. Cash takes us away with him, but he brings us back—now more savvy and compassionate—to help and to share what he has learned through life's sufferings.

Play Johnny Cash's songs when you are feeling strongly about facing challenges in the physical world and when you wish to release your emotions, perhaps getting in touch with nostalgic memories. (Note: Johnny Cash's album, *Cash*, on American Recordings 9-45520.)

Some of the many other country singers who have maintained their popularity through the years include Dolly Parton, Willie Nelson, Marty Robbins, Waylon Jennings, Roy Orbison, and Kris Kristofferson.

CHAPTER 3

Finding Your Music

Music rebukes us, for it is wider and richer than any of us knows.

CLAUDIO ARRAU

My purpose is to create music for all people, music which is beautiful and healing, to attempt what old Chinese painters called "spirit resonance" in melody and sound.

ALAN HOVHANESS

Many factors influence our musical needs and choices. Among these are the following:

1. Soul experience; prior experiences/tendencies
2. Temperament and personality
3. Childhood memories and our earliest exposure to music, even while in the womb
4. Stimuli from home and work environment; how we respond to others' musical tastes
5. Our continuous self-education and learning
6. Our deeper desires and aspirations; the ideals we follow most in this lifetime
7. Our desire to love and be loved

Each of us was born into this lifetime with a specific temperament, through which we master and express our dreams and purpose. Each person's temperament is unique and will never again be repeated with exactly the same tones. The Creator's light and our own responses and choices come through our temperaments in varied shadings of energy, sometimes said to correspond to the four elements: Fire, Earth, Air, and Water. The Chinese add a fifth element: Wood. Spiritual teachings through the ages have recognized these modes as a way of describing our life expression. The ancient Greeks considered the four elements to be psychological forces, alive and interacting in different proportions in everyone. They correspond in the person to the will (Fire), the body and action (Earth), the mind and thinking (Air), and the emotions (Water).

In astrological teachings, Fire refers to the sun signs—Aries, Leo, and Sagittarius; Earth refers to the energies of Taurus, Virgo, and Capricorn; Air describes the energies of Gemini, Libra, and Aquarius; and Water suggests the energies of Cancer, Scorpio, and Pisces. Each of us expresses the divine purpose and our own life desires through the particular blending of these four elements in our temperaments.

Find yourself in the four elements as they are described below. Such understanding can help you begin to release more light through your personality and to develop your strengths and work on your weaknesses and blind spots. Use music, too, to cultivate and activate your expression of energies as they emerge through the four temperaments.

FIRE

This area of the temperament is very intense and high-voltage. It acts instantly and gives off sparks. On the negative side, it can be too impulsive, often speaking out or acting before thinking. The fiery element can be tense, hyperactive, domineering, and judgmental, at times taking issue or criticizing before considering others' intentions. The fiery side likes to win, eagerly accepting challenge and competition. Usually, it is fearless, and sometimes it is foolhardy. At other times, the fiery side considers itself too highly and becomes inflated with pride and ego. When being expressed negatively, the fire side often goes off on a power trip, willing to do anything to be the star of the show. Its flames then cause constant turmoil.

When the fiery side acts constructively, the person can be a dynamic leader, a confronting, courageous pioneer, and a fearless worker who makes necessary decisions quickly and moves forward. Positive fire energy is decisive yet teachable, explosive but not destructive, fast yet patient with those who are slower or hold differing opinions. Even with its strong direction, constructive fire energy expresses appreciation and consideration for others. It emanates self-worth without seeming superior and pompous.

In developing the Fire in us, we need to love and purify, listen more patiently, and avoid impulsiveness, aggressiveness, and insensitivity.

Musically, our fiery nature likes power, surging sound, strong rhythms, and romantic yet dynamic melodies—music of strength. I have observed that the fiery element often responds well to music of victory:

Music of Fire

J. S. Bach – *Toccata and Fugue* (orchestral version, conducted by Leopold Stokowski – London or Chandos – conducted by Matthias Bamert)

Wagner – Overture and Prelude to *Die Meistersinger; Ride of the Valkyries; Dawn and Siegfried's Rhine Journey* (from *Die Götterdämmerung*)

Beethoven – *Choral Fantasy for Piano and Chorus and Orchestra;* Symphony no. 9; Symphony no. 5

Verdi – *Grand March* (from *Aida*)

Rachmaninov – Piano Concertos nos. 2 and 3; *Rhapsody on a Theme of Paganini*

d'Indy – *Symphony on a French Mountain Air*

Sibelius – *Finlandia; Autre Fois; Tapiola*

Suppé – *Poet and Peasant Overture; Light Cavalry Overture; Boccaccio Overture*

Berlioz – *Roman Carnival Overture; Rob Roy Overture*

F. J. Haydn – *The Creation; The Seasons;* masses; piano trios

David Fanshawe – *African Sanctus* (Silva Classics)

Missa Luba (African setting of the Mass) (Philips)

Ramirez – *Missa Criolla* (Philips)

Peña – *Misa Flamenca* (Nimbus)

Vangelis – *Chariots of Fire*

EARTH

The earth side of the temperament tends to be more cautious, concrete, and old-fashioned. It emphasizes details, practicality, maintenance activities, structure, set routine, and stability. It needs security to feel at ease. This side of our temperament is dependable, gradual, follows orders well, and aims for usefulness. Rarely does it welcome sudden changes, daring imagination, new opinions, ideas, or ventures into the unknown. It is modest, loyal, and moves to keep things clear. It keeps closely to plans and budgets; it measures, and it is grounding.

When the Earth side acts constructively, it is constant without being rigid, and it is restful without being lethargic. Likewise, it is definite and more traditional without being judgmental or provincial. The Earth side deeply feels and appreciates the beauty of the good Earth and nature. It thrives on activities that beautify the home and earthly places, such as gardening, painting, and interior decorating. It is happy doing manual work and achieving practical results.

In developing Earth we will be steadfast and practical but must avoid rigidity, inertia, and provincial, judgmental attitudes by expanding horizons and interests.

Musically, the Earth side seeks melodies that are warm, homey, settled, traditional, and evocative of friendship and earthly comforts. Music of nature appeals to this temperament, especially that which is nostalgic and suggestive of repose. Since this side likes practicality, it often favors music with definite lyrics and meaningful poetry. It prefers literal statement to spatial suggestiveness or more aleatoric styles. Simple themes and rhythms, often repeated, appeal to it, especially beautiful, restful tunes.

The warm, poignant melodies of Stephen Foster celebrate the home and domestic happiness, both of which delight the Earth side. The more predictable rhythms and colorations of Baroque music are often comforting to this side of us. Other pieces that will be in tune with Earth include the following selections, which are warm, melodically pleasing and definite in form:

Music of Earth

Dvořák – Cello Concerto; *Overture to Nature, Life and Love; Silent Woods; Humoresque; My Home Overture; Cypresses* (Koch 3-1628-2)

Brahms – *Lullaby;* Symphony no. 3

Bruch – *Scottish Fantasy;* Violin Concerto no. 1

Massenet – *Meditation* (from *Thais*)

Debussy – *Clair de lune*

Fauré – *Requiem*

Goldmark – *Rustic Wedding Symphony*

Emile Pandolfi – *By Request; Remember Me* (piano)

Yas-Kaz – *Jungle Book*

Music of Irving Berlin and Jerome Kern

Songs of Perry Como, Bing Crosby, Barbara Mandrell, John Denver, Gordon Bok, Johnny Mathis, Captain and Tennille, Mamas and the Papas, Johnny Cash, Barry Manilow, Pete Seeger, Cat Stevens

Music of Giacomo Puccini

Music of Mantovani

AIR

The Air element in our temperament is more mercurial; like a chameleon, it is constantly changing, according to the present company, the thoughts, and the impressions being absorbed from the environment. Air begins with the more mental and conceptual, moving from the abstract into concrete and tactile situations. It enjoys the perpetual motion of ideas and theories, and it seeks endless variety. It is rarely contemplative but often avoids hard, physical work. The Air side likes to fantasize, and then may disown its dreams when they become too demanding. It is very independent and resents restrictions. The airy part of the nature thinks before it feels and tends to analyze situations and persons. Sometimes it sees only its own point of view and may be insensitive to others' feelings or perspectives. It can be shallow and selfish.

At its best, the Air side considers with clarity and thinks through difficulties to find the best solution. It probes and penetrates, making sudden connections and penetrating obstacles with energies that cleanse and direct. Most constructively, the Air side often synthesizes, seeing the best in every person and challenge and combining forces to promote greater well-being and creativity. It is versatile and varied, like the many facets of a diamond, and can draw upon talents and powers to meet every need. Usually it is objective and wastes little time showing sentiment.

To develop the Air in us, we need to explore ideas and possibilities. We need to learn to follow through and avoid scatteredness and superficiality. It is important to communicate clearly with focus.

What helps us to balance our Air side is to find focus, follow through, and finalize our intentions. Grounding and anchoring our dreams is very important.

Musically, the Air side needs rhythmical variety, interesting pictures and suggestive imagery in sound, and clear melodies. It likes more experimental music that moves ahead in a certain direction, yet encompasses a wide spectrum of variety and color. It often responds to experimental music, such as the twelve-tone scale, sound clusters, minimalist techniques, and various aleatoric works. Extroverted music often appeals to Air, especially current songs and promotional hit tunes, though too much emotion in music may seem puzzling. Contemporary sounds and textures fascinate the Air temperament for a short period until it becomes bored.

Here are some musical selections with strong rhythms and movement and many colors that the Air side might find enjoyable:

Music of Air

Robert Whitesides-Woo – *Miracles*
Kim Robertson – *Water Spirit*
John Rainer – *Songs of the Indian Flute I, II*

Iasos – *Angels of Comfort*
R. Carlos Nakai – *Canyon Trilogy*
Kevin Locke – *The Flash of the Mirror*
Ray Lynch – *The Sky of Mind*
Ravi Shankar – Indian ragas
Lee Holdridge – *Other Side of the Mountain, Part 2*
John Barry – *Born Free* (soundtrack)
Mozart – Horn concertos; Clarinet Concerto
George Gershwin – *Rhapsody in Blue*; Piano Concerto in F;
 – *Kiri Te Kanawa Sings Gershwin*
Richard Rodgers – *Slaughter on Tenth Avenue*
Wolff and Hennings – *Tibetan Bells I, II, III*
Elgar – *Enigma Variations*
Scott Joplin – Rags
Poulenc – *Rustic Concerto for Harpsichord and Orchestra*
Songs of Bob Dylan, Mason Williams, Judy Collins, Gordon Lightfoot,
 Dan Fogelburg, and James Taylor
Richard Strauss – *Don Juan; A Hero's Life*

WATER

The fourth aspect of the human temperament is expressed through the element of Water. This part is more introspective, emotional, at times brooding and melancholic, even to the point of self-indulgence. It often needs to be alone but not for too long, lest it become morbid. We must guard against the watery side's emphasizing the negative and exaggerating a situation or condition. It is wise to avoid its self-pity, self-deprecation, and martyrdom. Still, our watery side, or our deep feelings, needs to come forward out of hiding to find true expression.

When it can get out of itself—usually by talking oneself out or by feeling others' needs to be more important than its own—this side is very caring, generous, and compassionate. At its best, the watery side is loyal beyond its emotional ups and downs. Often, it can feel with a great intuitive perspective, sensing and "knowing" in ways that are not logically explainable.

The watery element grows through experiences of great joy and suffering. When working at its best, the watery side will lift up all tragedy into the light, overcoming tendencies toward moodiness, pessimism, and self-pity. It will find itself best by losing itself in loving service with others and one-pointed devotion to God or some high ideal. Often, its energies will be expressed through dedication to a cause.

We could well advise our watery side to "get out of yourself, forgive and forget, give yourself to something larger than yourself, avoid depleting moods, and fight out of heaviness no matter what the cost. Remember your joy."

Musically, the watery element seeks pieces with deep feeling and contrasting polarities of emotion which bring a total response from the heart. This temperament feels before it thinks. If you tend toward the dramatic, musical evocations of melancholy and tragedy will appeal to you. Even more, you enjoy hearing the melodies and power of triumph and victory, as they drive away tears and suffering. Great love themes, deep passions, and human striving arouse the watery side with their many moods. Remember the deep feelings contained especially in Slavic, Celtic, Irish, Hebrew, and Italian music.

Here are several melodic and dramatic musical selections that will stimulate your Water side:

Music of Water

Handel – *Water Music*
Luciano Pavarotti – *Verismo Arias; Neapolitan Songs; Passione*
Vito Paternoster – *Inzaffirio (Adornments)* (available from Records International, Goleta, CA)
Chopin – Nocturnes
de Falla – *Nights in the Gardens of Spain*
Johann Strauss, Jr. – *Blue Danube Waltz*
Tchaikovsky – *None But the Lonely Heart;* Symphony no. 6 *(Pathetique); Romeo and Juliet Overture*
Mahler – Symphonies nos. 4 and 6
Wagner – Prelude and *Liebestod* (from *Tristan und Isolde*)
Rimsky-Korsakov – *Scheherazade*
Alan Stivell – *Renaissance of the Celtic Harp*
Richard Addinsell – *Warsaw Concerto; Goodbye Mr. Chips* (Marco Polo)
Maurice Jarre – *Lara's Theme* (from *Dr. Zhivago*)
Ernest Gold – *Love Theme* (from *Exodus*)
Music of Mantovani (especially *Italian Suite*)
Nat King Cole – *Stardust; When the World was Young*
Danny Boy (traditional Irish melody) (conducted by Slatkin on Telarc)
Debussy by the Sea (Special Music Company, 560 Sylvan Avenue, Englewood Cliffs, NJ 07632)
Bach by the Sea (Special Music Company)

Chopin by the Sea (Special Music Company)
J. S. Bach – *Come Sweet Death*
Hubert Bath – *Cornish Rhapsody*
Emil Reznicek – *Donna Diana Overture*
Ernest Bloch – *Schelomo*
Joan Baez – Miscellaneous folk songs
Water Music of the Impressionists (Rosenberger – Delos 3006)

YOUR TEMPERAMENT

We cannot change our basic temperament, but we can expand it. Relationships of various kinds can help. Seek relationships that call forth your best, but also cultivate friendships and contacts that open new channels for your life's expression. Take every opportunity to fill in your blind spots.

Through music you can learn to utilize each element and shading of your temperament more dynamically and beautifully. From the lists you have just read and from other suggestions listed in the appendixes, you can explore the music that will enhance what you already are and will awaken unexpressed areas. If, for example, you find that you may be overemphasizing Fire and Air elements with music that is always loud, heavy, and fast, bring out new elements in your life by listening to music that is more quiet, reflective, and lyrical. You will find that such music will expand your temperament, bring your life into better balance and tone, and enable you to approach your relationships as a more well-rounded person who can be adaptable in every situation. As you choose your music wisely and appropriately, all of your sensory organs will be quickened and, in some cases, your whole being will be rebalanced and harmonized.

Share your music with friends, but care about them enough to uplift them with music that best fits their true temperament and their needs as well. Use music as a tonic for your life. Enlarge your musical horizons continuously, so that you grow in your capacity to express sound.

Visualizing. The visual sense responds to colors, shadings, designs, and formations. Great music stimulates the imagination and helps you to picture scenes, persons, places, and dimensions of life that become more real to you. The conductor Charles Munch mentions this aspect of music in his autobiography, *I Am a Conductor*:

> Music is an art that expresses the inexpressible. It rises far above what words can mean or the intelligence define. Its domain is the imponderable and the impalpable land of the unconscious. . . . Music always suggests something to me: just a color or a landscape or perhaps a sensation that can be felt and expressed only in sound.

The musical compositions of Claude Debussy, at times emanating vibrations of green (see chapter 10 for a discussion of music and color vibrations), often awaken in a listener scenes and pictures of water, kingdoms of the sea, and nature beings inhabiting woods and forests. Sounds of a Hawaiian love song conjure up scenes of the islands and beckoning sunsets. A Nat King Cole lyric can recall nostalgic memories and relationships from the past. *Ebb Tide*, with its actual sounds of gulls and ocean waves will remind listeners of beaches, surf, the seashore, and endless horizons of life. In another way, Wagner's Prelude to *Lohengrin* (Act I) evokes the archetypal pattern-shape of a chalice, which expresses the theme of the Holy Grail descending and humankind's quest for spiritual light.

Much well-known program music contains definite stories and themes, which the composer describes through melodies and tone colors. Such music will enhance your visual sensitivity and stimulate your powers of visualization. Unlike television, music will not "do it for you," but instead will cause you to activate your own imagination. No two persons will "see" or feel a piece of music in the same way, and there is no single way to respond or just one meaning to look for.

Play musical offerings with a relaxed and expectant attitude. Let the melodies and colors of the music stream through you, evoking whatever scenes or impressions may come. Avoid outer distractions. Be open to the music, accepting whatever it might bring up in you. The real wonder and magic of music become clear as you let it "stir up the gift of God within you" (2 Tim. 1:6). You may be taken to other places and dimensions of consciousness, or you may see loved ones and familiar landscapes rising out of deep memories. You may see yourself in new roles, with a different appearance, or you may travel in consciousness to other times and landscapes that are evoked by the music.

Here are a few choice selections of evocative, pictorial music:

Music that Paints Pictures

Beethoven – Symphony no. 6 *(Pastorale)*
Grieg – *Morning* (from *Peer Gynt*)
Debussy – *The Sea*; Nocturnes; *The Engulfed Cathedral*
Mendelssohn – Symphony no. 3 *(Scotch); Hebrides Overture; Calm Sea, Prosperous Voyage Overture*
Holst – *The Planets*
Stravinsky – *The Firebird; Petrouchka*
Mussorgsky – *Pictures at an Exhibition*
Wagner – *Evening Star* (from *Tannhäuser*)

Berlioz – *Fantastic Symphony*
Vaughan Williams – *Lark Ascending; Antarctic Symphony*
Johann Strauss, Jr. – *Blue Danube Waltz*
Tchaikovsky – *The Storm*
Respighi – *Pines of Rome; Roman Festivals*
Schumann – Symphony no. 1 *(Spring)*
Glazunov – *The Forest; The Sea*
Kim Robertson – *Angels in Disguise*
Delius – *Appalachia; Brigg Fair*
Miklós Rózsa – *Ivanhoe* (soundtrack) (Intrada 7055)

Through the years I have been impressed by the fine work that Dr. Helen Bonny and her associates have done in the fields of creative music listening and music therapy. Though I offer my suggestions as a music lover, not as a musician, Dr. Bonny and I share many tastes and impressions. I especially recommend her book relating psychology and music, *Music and Your Mind,* and her three monographs *Guided Imagery and Music 1, 2,* and *3.* In these booklets, she explains the importance of building a sound continuum which helps the listener to focus and move through various processes of imagination, release, balance, and clearance. Along the same lines, I also recommend the annotated guide to the Institute for Consciousness and Music taped music programs, called *Conscious Listening,* by Linda H. Keiser. It is available from the Institute for Consciousness and Music, Box 173, Port Townsend, WA 98368. Dr. Bonny can be contacted at 418 Charles, Salina, KS 67401.

Entering into the sound of music. You will never lose your identity. Rather, you go into the inviting continuum of sounds and melodies to link with the timeless, moving eternities of life itself. Music, like an induction, offers you a world of its own, created by the movement and interaction of energies that vibrate through you. Unlike words or physical objects, music is always becoming, always noticeably moving beyond itself. The ephemeral quality of music is beautifully expressed by Anais Nin:

> Music holds the movements of life, the chained incidents which compose it, the eternal melting of one note before another to create song. The notes must melt before one another; they must be lost after they have given their soul, for the sake of the whole. It may be a beautiful note, but it cannot strike alone forever. It must pass, as all things must pass, to make up the immense composition that is life.

Musical sounds, especially melodious ones, lift you out of stress, heaviness, and limitations. They help you to break through rigidity and dull repetition. Listen to the expansive tones of a flute, and you will begin to fly with wings or soar like hawks in the wind. Enter the lilt and glissando of harps, and you can feel free and weightless, able to rise into lighter atmospheres and expanded feelings. The sound of a cello is deeper and very soulful, and it often awakens the feelings of focused reflection and longing. (Note especially the Suites for Solo Cello, by J. S. Bach and the hauntingly beautiful work for cello, strings, and soprano, by Vito Paternoster, called *Inzaffirio* [Adornments], available from Records International, P.O. Box 1140, Goleta, CA 93116.)

Listen, also, to the sounds of nature, flowing streams, waterfalls, the wind playing through trees, bird songs, or the surging waves of the ocean. Such living, environmental music can help to attune you to celestial, cosmic forces that will inspire and help you. Beautiful nature music is like a magic carpet that lifts you into God's grandeur and connects you with the resonances and harmonies of the spheres. I especially like *Loons on Mirror Lake* (Nature Recordings Reference Series), used in the soundtrack *On Golden Pond*.

Here are a few selected pieces of music that will expand your auditory faculties, lifting your consciousness:

Music to Expand Hearing

Lawrence Ashmore – *Four Seasons* (RCA 60437)
Paul Horn – *Inside the Taj Mahal*
Wendy Carlos – *Sonic Seasonings* (especially *Fall*)
Environments (miscellaneous recordings)
Bearns and Dexter – *Golden Voyage I, III*
Nakai – *Sundance Season*
Palestrina – *Pope Marcellus Mass* (celestial)
Humperdinck – *Children's Prayer* (from *Hansel and Gretel*)
Hovhaness – *Mysterious Mountain*
Benedictine Nuns – *Ave Maria* (White Swan)
Kay Gardner – *Emerging; Ouroboros* (Ladyslipper Distributors)
Inkuyo – *Land of the Incas*
Georgia Kelly – *Seapeace*
Paganini – *The Convent of Mount Saint Bernard* (Dynamic Recordings)
Nóirín Ní Riain – *Soundings: Spiritual Songs from Many Traditions*
Dean Evenson – *Ocean Dreams; Peaceful Pond*
Terry Riley – *June Buddhas*
Ida Gotkovsky – *Song of the Forest* (Qualiton Imports)

A certain musical selection may cause you to feel more happy, coura-geous, and loving, while another piece may arouse in you feelings of agitation, anger, or confusion. Find music that helps you. Realize that music is far more than background noise. Its vibrations are continuously producing their effects on you. Avoid sounds that deplete and scatter you. Be selective with your music. Fill your life with beautiful sounds, not just background noise. Cultivate upliftment from your music.

Keep an active listening journal to track the music that is most helpful and inspirational to you. Notice where your music affects you. Does it expand your heart center, making you feel more loving and filled with good will? Does it stimulate your mind and allow your brain to function with greater clarity? Does a certain selection help you to grieve or to recover past memories? What effects does your music produce in your physical body? Do you feel stronger, more fluid and graceful? Do you feel like dancing in movements that are freeing, or does your music cause you to twitch irritably and shake with agitation and nervous headaches? By becoming aware of areas in you affected by music, you can use music to direct energy to places that need it or to disperse energy in you that is congested.

The power of great music can also help you to discover and change certain habits and behavior patterns that you may be holding from childhood. From childhood influences and from even deeper soul memories, we have absorbed experiences and impressions that remain in us today, like deep fingerprints in the conscious and subconscious mind. Dr. Alexander Lowen (author of *Bioenergetics*) and Moshe Feldenkrais (movement therapist and author of *Awareness through Movement*) are pioneers in showing how the body stores memories in muscles and joints. They have demonstrated in their studies of body response that even our muscles and whole physical organisms often retain the memories and reflex patterns of the past. Some-times just one unpleasant childhood memory sticks in us like glue, either locking up our joints and muscles, or cramping our emotions and thought patterns. Exercises of the body can release memories in the mind. Music can facilitate this process and help release many of the blocks and crisscrosses in the system, even those we may have never consciously realized. Great music can cause increased flow of energy to circulate through the physical body, the emotions, and the mind. Great music awakens us to our soul.

From my workshops in musical therapy, conducted privately and in schools and nursing homes, I have seen the healing power of music unlock frozen joints and stiff muscles. I have seen a woman who was catatonic begin to move freely in her wheelchair to the sounds of Bizet's *Carmen (Toreador's Dance)*; later she smiled and released even more fear and tension as she listened to Chopin's waltzes. Another patient—a man who was often quarrelsome and difficult to manage—became more helpful after hearing Bach's *Brandenburg Concerto no. 4* and a Haydn symphony.

The great composer Sergei Rachmaninov found deep healing through composing his own Piano Concerto no. 2. His main challenge was to overcome depression, largely caused by childhood scenes and the feelings of separation and homesickness he felt for his native Russia. With the help of Dr. Dahl, a Russian doctor and hypnotherapist, he made headway in this challenge through the practice of visualization and mental suggestion, and through the vibrations of music itself.

One amazing experience that I remember happened at Unity Village, Lee's Summit, Missouri, many years ago during a summer class in creative writing which I was teaching. Students ranged in age from nine to eighty-two. During one sequence I played the mysterious Adagio from Bartók's *Music for Strings, Percussion and Celesta*. Imagine my amazement when, after the piece ended, a man came running forward, saying, "What was that music? It gave me the ending to a story that I've been working on for years." Even more amazing was what he told me next. He had begun the story in a small boardinghouse, located in Asheville, North Carolina. It turned out to be the same building in which at an earlier time, Thomas Wolfe, the American novelist, had written *Look Homeward, Angel*. After Wolfe came the great Hungarian composer Béla Bartók, who was dying of leukemia; he had received a commission from Serge Koussevitsky, conductor of the Boston Symphony Orchestra, to write a new work for orchestra. Bartók went to Asheville, North Carolina, and composed the Concerto for Orchestra in the same room in which Wolfe had written his book. And now, in a marvelous, serendipitous "golden thread" of continuity, the gentleman in my class told me that he had stayed in the very same room as Wolfe and Bartók, and a piece of Bartók's music was the completing link for the man's own short story. I've always enjoyed telling this experience.

You too can find those musical pieces that will pierce through a mood, a repressed memory, or a blocked area in yourself. Here are some directives to help your progress:

Recall and release the past. Choose three pieces of music (instrumental pieces or songs) that you love deeply because they make you feel good. Arrange these or other pieces in a pleasing continuum of sounds (either record them on a cassette or program them in a certain order on a CD player). Begin to listen to these pieces, keeping a notebook next to you. Be aware of how and where you are feeling the music. Then, allow yourself to go back into your childhood. Be open to scenes and memories stored deep inside you. Allow these to surface and write them down.

In an attitude of gratefulness and acceptance, ask the Eternal Presence to reveal to you, through music, what you need to know in order to remove the block or hindrance you might be feeling. It may be an early scene with parents or brothers and sisters. It may be the memory of a pet, a painful sight or sound, a personal disappointment. Or there may be something in your life that is still unfinished—something you feel you must complete.

Closure, or dealing with unfinished business, at least to some extent, is often necessary before we can go forward. If death or separation makes this closure physically impossible, you can still talk, feel, and act out constructively now, to release whatever you have held inside for so long. If necessary, imagine the person you wish to speak to. See the person sitting in an empty chair or in a particular scene; speak to that individual as you would if he/she were sitting in front of you. As you speak out loud, in the present tense and in the first person, let the music drain out of you whatever deep feelings you wish to release. Feel yourself letting go of long-held emotions that have cramped and stifled you. Complete *now,* in a loving and constructive way, whatever has frustrated you and remained incomplete inside you. Avoid deliberately hurtful and destructive responses, for these will only prolong discord and deplete your energies. At the same time, do not be insincere nor overly polite. Through music, you can speak firmly, honestly, and lovingly to another; you can allow yourself to forgive and be forgiven; and you can find the best ways to complete unfinished, unresolved, unexpressed experiences. In addition to this technique, you may also write your feelings in a letter or a journal or say them into a cassette. Read what you have written out loud; then throw it away, releasing it all into the music.

Great music of any style or genre can bring many kinds of solutions. It can help you to repair broken relationships and inspire you to build new ones. Beautiful music also stimulates you to overcome your own inertia, negativity, and procrastination. The dynamic chargings of great music will not allow you to remain in attitudes of anger, self-pity, frustration, regret, or sadness (which is often anger turned inward). Rather, the most healing music will always call you forward and upward, helping you to find ways to release the past and awakening in you joy and creativity. It opens your heart center to feel the energy of unconditional love.

Remember beautiful experiences that have included music. Keep a journal and scrapbook of favorite musical memories, any favorite experiences in connection with music. Did anyone sing to you as a child? Recall a song or melody you may have learned as a child and try to sing it now; remember your first contact with a musical instrument, either bought or homemade. What concerts do you remember, and what feelings can you recall from experiencing them? Do you have memories of singing in a choir? Did music ever bring you together with new friends? What favorite trips or places do you associate with certain musical pieces? When did you buy your first recording, and what were your feelings as you listened to it playing? How do you use music now, with your children or with family and friends? Write down in your notebook the treasured memories that great music has brought into your life.

How has music expanded your sensitivity and perspective? How has music enabled you to appreciate more the colors, sounds, customs, and essences of other nationalities, cultures, religious traditions, and historical periods? How are you using music now to grow, interpersonally, socially, and spiritually?

Recently, I sat down and spent an hour recalling the many ways in which music has enriched my life. Partly as a means of sharing with my readers and partly to suggest a possible approach to keeping a musical notebook, I include some of my most intimate memories which music has provided:

Born in New York City, on Broadway in Manhattan, I experienced music early and in great ethnic variety. Even now as I write, I can hear the beautiful Welsh songs and hymns my mother sang throughout the household. I can still hear her sing the Welsh lullaby, *The Ash Grove,* which her mother taught her. Later, as I played stickball on the sidewalks of our neighborhood, I can recall the mixture of international sounds, pouring together out of apartment windows, alleys, and storefronts. From Blumental's Laundry up the block, and from Miller's living room on the first floor, I remember soulful Hebrew, cantorial chanting, and Israeli folk songs. From across the street came the strains of the Blues and strong, colorful Puerto Rican and Latino rhythms, rhumbas, and festive party music that lasted into the early morning hours. From our courtyard came sounds of an Oriental koto and flute. Behind our apartment building was a small convent with a garden where I heard the songs of birds accompanying the nuns' singing of Gregorian chants and other such devotional music, offered up each morning. Getting off our elevator on the eleventh floor, I often heard coming from the Druckers' apartment various nostalgic violin melodies, composed or played by Fritz Kreisler, lively polkas, and Strauss waltzes from Vienna.

Down on the seventh floor in the apartment of my Russian friend Nicholas, I first heard the Russian melodies of Anton Rubinstein, Tchaikovsky, Glinka, and Glazunov, the basso voice of Chaliapin, and the sounds of balalaikas in the night. I remember especially the beautiful, haunting melody of *Evening Bells*. On Thursday nights I always listened to the Lone Ranger and Tonto subduing bank robbers and other outlaws with a straight one-two punch, as the bad guys often hit the ground with a thud on the final note of the crescendo from Wagner's *Flying Dutchman Overture*. Then, to the thrilling finale of Rossini's *William Tell Overture*, the masked man and Tonto rode off into the hills and sunset. Away from home and neighborhood, in school I sang the devotional hymns and liturgical music of the Episcopalian and Lutheran churches, which we learned in chapel each morning. My first real introduction to opera came when my mother took me to hear Mario Lanza playing the role of Caruso.

My greatest thrill still remains the first time I heard the magic of a live symphony orchestra, with more than one hundred musicians making music together. This experience came in the early fifties in Lewisohn Stadium in New York City, when a young, crew-cut Japanese visitor to America named Seiji Ozawa led the Stadium Symphony Orchestra at sunset in a dynamic performance of Tchaikovsky's Fourth Symphony. I have always felt close to Ozawa and have even dreamed of talking with him. Perhaps this is because of those clear memories of his arrival in America, or because I also happened to be working near Boston when he began his tenure as Music Director and Conductor of the magnificent Boston Symphony Orchestra. Through these past twenty years, I have admired the good work Ozawa and his associates are carrying on, for example, through their friendship with China and their mutual sharing and playing of great music, East and West, especially the music of outstanding composers, such as Toru Takemitsu, R. Murray Schafer (whose book *Tuning the World* is a unique reading experience), and John Harbison (most recently, Harbison's Cello Concerto). I have also deeply enjoyed seeing Ozawa leading a new orchestra, the Saito Kinen Orchestra, as the players performed the Brahms Symphonies. And before Ozawa, I treasure my memories of hearing conductors William Steinberg, Erich Leinsdorf, and Charles Munch, in their passionate, ecstatic performances with the Boston Symphony Orchestra.

I remember, also, as a young boy, the feeling of joy and grandeur of being swept up into power one morning, in Riverside Church, after a sermon by the guest speaker Dr. Martin Luther King, Jr. More than three thousand people rose and sang together the *Battle Hymn of the Republic,* and the organist Virgil Fox, as I remember, played the mighty pipe organ with such full potency that I could feel a deep vibration and expansion through my heart center and solar plexus. That morning, the giant sanctuary was filled with cascades of melody. A deep religious fervor in the large congregation reached upward and seemed to join with the singing of heavenly choirs, descending to inspire us. It seemed to me that many of those present were lifted out of themselves for a few minutes to spiral upward, above Grant's Tomb, across the street, and then even higher than the huge cathedral tower, reaching toward the sky. I will always carry many deep and wonderful memories of my years at Riverside Church and, later, as a student, of my six semesters at Union Theological Seminary, across the street from Riverside Church.

Since the day of my twelfth birthday, when I bought my first records in an old bookstore near the Bronx Zoo—two musty 78s containing Mozart's Fortieth Symphony and Beethoven's *Egmont Overture*—music has been with me like a holy companion. Although I am not a performing artist this lifetime, I have found music to be an intimate and faithful friend that has continuously enriched my life and helped me in many ways.

In an even deeper way, music for me has often been a gateway into God's presence. At various times, the magnetic currents of great, transcendental music have made me feel both humble and invincible. Through music I have experienced a joy and ecstasy beyond words and genuine glimpses into the all-embracing light of the Creator's presence, which for me can only be called mystical and profoundly spiritual.

I remember reading a statement by the composer Hector Berlioz, that music and love are "the two wings of the soul," and I agree with these inspired words from the great composer Frederick Delius:

Music is a cry of the soul. It is a revelation, a thing to be reverenced. Performances of a great musical work are for us what the rites and festivals of religion were to the ancients—an initiation into the mysteries of God and the human soul.

Music can change our moods, energize us, and lift us to spiritual heights. Everyday sounds affect us, too. Consider for a few minutes to what degree sounds around you influence your life. What kinds of sounds surround your home and working environments? How many of these sounds are pleasing to you? Which give you energy upliftment, and which sounds that you hear each day are confusing, noisy, chaotic, or depleting? The psychiatrist James E. Johnson in his book *Freedom from Depression* advocates wholesome music but cautions against the adverse effects of contemporary beats and the cacophony of much rock-and-roll, which he feels is sound masquerading as music. He has found that certain beats in this kind of music contribute dangerously to depression and hypertension. This observation has been surfacing repeatedly from many disciplines, but a decrease in the popularity of rock is unlikely since it gathers billions of profit dollars. Most recently, Martha Bayles, in her excellent book *Hole in Our Soul: The Loss of Beauty and Meaning in American Popular Music*, warns:

People used to tap their feet and smile when they listened to American popular music. Now they sit open-mouthed and stare: at heavy metal virtuosos who treat music as a form of warfare; at "pop" singers who reduce love to soft-core pornography; at "grunge" rockers who squall cheap despair while smashing expensive guitars; at "gangsta" rappers who sell more records when under indictment for assault, rape, and murder than when they are merely posing as violent criminals. Conjuring nothing but aggression, anxiety, lust and rage (and malignant moods), such fare could not be more different from the best blues, jazz, gospel and country, in which such negative feelings are balanced with tenderness, grace and wit. Indeed, the great vigor of our music has always been its ability to blend opposites. What has happened to this vigor?

Dr. John Diamond, in his excellent and informative book, *Your Body Doesn't Lie*, talks about how sound and music play a very large role in our lives. Dr. Diamond is a well-known therapist in the field of behavioral kinesiology, or the study of bodily movement and response based upon energies within the system and in the environment. He writes:

> Surrounded by the right sounds, we all can be invigorated, energized, and balanced. It has been demonstrated clinically that music adds to our general health and well-being. Music, then, can be an important part of our program of primary prevention—the prevention of illness at the prephysical, energy-imbalance level.

Given the importance of music in our lives, the next question is "Which music is the best?" In the later pages of his book, Dr. Diamond shares the findings of careful research—findings which correlate with other researchers'—into the effects of music on plants and the human organism. He measured muscle response after listening to music and reports:

> Using hundreds of subjects, I found that listening to (certain) rock music frequently causes all the muscles in the body to go weak. The normal pressure required to overpower a strong deltoid muscle in an adult male is about 40 to 45 pounds. When rock music is played, only 10 to 15 pounds is needed.
> . . . every major muscle of the body relates to an organ. This means that all the organs of our body are being affected by a large proportion of the popular music to which we are exposed each day. If we add up the hours of radio play throughout the world, we can see how enormous a problem this is.

Dr. Diamond discovered that some rock music, such as that of the Beatles, does not have this effect, but the rhythm itself tends to be harmful:

The abnormal rhythm of the rock beat (anapestic – da-da-DA) and the volume of noise level (combine) to induce weakness in us. Noise may be defined as sound which, when it reaches a certain level of intensity, decreases body energy. Detrimental music reduces energy at any volume. Good music and nearly all natural sounds strengthen at any level. But even if you play good music so loudly over a sound system that distortion occurs, a level will be reached at which the sound weakens a person's energy.

Studies have shown that certain music, if listened to repeatedly, has the effect of depleting one's energy systems and causes confusion in thinking, disorientation of feeling, and a reversal of value systems. It has been reported that listening to too many discordant sounds produces a numbness in the body and a confusion between the two sides of the brain, which seems to cause responses and perceptions "to switch" from one side of the brain to the other. This process often seems to impair the person's sensitivity in ways that accentuate irritability, increase one's intolerance for stress and fears, and may often lead to antisocial, addictive behaviors. The heavy beat and bass vibrations also cause the energy in a person to focus on and overload the sexual chakras or energy centers. Such overload may stimulate physical violence, rage, and/or sexual addiction as well as other physical excesses and disorders, such as drug or alcohol abuse.

Albert Roustit, in his book *Prophecy in Music*, describes this effect:

The distinction between music and noise seems to be blurring: melody and words are being replaced by shrieks for which the only accompaniment is a frenetic rhythm, and the result, as we have all many times observed, is a sort of collective hysteria similar to that of primitive people.

To put oneself into a trance under the effect of certain rhythmic excitation is to leave momentarily the civilized state to fall into a savage one, at which point, from the depths of human nature, the individual's bestiality can make its appearance too strongly for a weakened spirituality to correct.

Unfortunately, this state has become more the norm today, so that persons usually under the influence of the anapestic hard rock beat and other addictive influences often need their own "detoxification" process, or some new exposure in healthy conditions in order to realize that there is an antidote to destructive noise. Unfortunately, such an alternative often becomes possible only in a time of extreme sickness or when choice is no longer an option. This is why future healing environments must be sensibly controlled, especially in regard to the music that is played inside them.

After a point, even the anticipation of certain unheard music can de-humanize unsuspecting listeners. As the Greek writer Nikos Kazantzakis, author of *Zorba the Greek*, points out, "We all carry our primitive ancestors with us." Some sounds can lower us to what we were in consciousness a long time ago, while other melodies and music will carry us forward, ennobling and lifting our entire being toward increasing harmonies and expressions of refinement, beauty, creativity, and evolution out of addiction, degeneracy, cruelty, and even criminal activity. To a large degree, "We are what we hear."

Today we stand at a crossroads. More than ever, humankind is resisting human-UNkind, both within ourselves and in the outer environment. Light and destructive forces are becoming increasingly polarized. Unlike ancient societies, which carefully monitored the music they permitted to be played, our times currently have an "anything goes" attitude. Thus, the only hope in the midst of our free choice is for us to educate ourselves to deepen our sensitivity and discernment so that we can learn how to feel what is truly healthy for the greater well-being of ourselves and our society. Real tastes develop out of consciousness, not hype.

To move ahead into clarity, health, and a new awakening in caring, we are faced with many important decisions and choices, even in the music we buy and listen to. One group of young people some years ago gathered all their recordings of destructive, chaotic music and burned them in public. The burning pyre of records was a statement against what they considered to be ugly, degrading musical influences in their lives. They decided to go in a different direction while they still had the sensitivity to choose.

Destructive music causes damage, not only to your physical body, but to your emotions and mental processes. Such sounds affect your entire aura, often making you feel psychically torn apart, fragmented, hostile, fright-ened, combative, isolated, hypervigilant, defensive, tense, and disconnected. Such stressful, ugly sounds can also scatter your plans and concentration, and they can fog and frustrate your goals. Most tragically, discordant music can alienate you from your inner center of guidance, cutting you off from conscious union with the celestial worlds and the Creator, leaving you feeling abandoned and exposing you to the invasions and controlling energies of negative vibrations and "users." And, as Dorothy Retallack and others have proven, certain ugly music will even kill plants.

How much more joyous and effective life can become as we bring beautiful melodies into our daily environment. The outstanding Finnish composer Jean Sibelius was right when he said that melody is the soul of great, healing music. In the following chapters and in the appendixes, you can discover more of those musical selections drawn from different genres which have helped others and can nourish you with their renewing melodies, rhythms, and harmonies. Others will hear the music you are playing and, if they are receptive to such music, it will grow on them until they will actually come to expect it, because such music will always feed them.

What are your deepest aspirations this lifetime? Are they centered mainly in worldly fame and achievement? Are they to be found mostly in the areas of peer acceptance and relationships formed to achieve popularity and status? Are they focused mainly in the areas of home and family intimacy, or in artistic expression, or scientific pursuit? Or are they largely invisible, inward desires to know and love the Creator more through increased attunement and service?

Whatever the desire, you can use music to help these dreams come true. Suggestions in this book can help you to find those musical selections that speak to you most deeply and empower you toward your greatest desires and life purpose.

As you take time to become more sensitized and educated to great music, I believe that your exposure to it can expand each day of your life. Music can awaken in you a stronger sense of purpose, greater power and creativity, and it can help you to contact and feel your feelings in all their complexities. Music can strengthen your follow-through and can reveal to you a clearer vision of your highest goals and ideals for this lifetime.

The joy of music, ultimately, seems connected to sadness. The sadness is that of existence. The more you are filled with the pure happiness of music-making (or music-listening), the deeper the sadness is.

TORU TAKEMITSU

CHAPTER 4

Music for Daily Life

When I had a family of my own, I wanted music to be a part of all our lives, so I did the same thing my mother did—I had it playing all the time. . . . It wasn't just for the kids, of course. I was playing music for my own pleasure, and even now that all three are grown and no longer live with me, I still have music on almost constantly.

JOAN KENNEDY, THE JOY OF CLASSICAL MUSIC

If we could devise an arrangement for providing everybody with music in their homes, perfect in quality, unlimited in quantity, suited to every mood, and beginning and ceasing at will, we should consider the limit of human felicity (to be) already attained.

EDWARD BELLAMY

Your day is now! Every day of your life is important and contains many new opportunities to grow. The more creatively and receptively you can see your lifetime, the less possible it is for you ever to feel bored or defeated.

In order to be ready for as many opportunities as possible, you can plan and simplify your day. Find the amount of routine necessary for you to feel secure and discover how much variety and spontaneity you can handle. Music, appropriately selected, can help you to increase stability, variety, and the creative opportunities that you need. Beautiful melodies and harmonies, carefully chosen for your daily schedule, will help you to focus and meet stress with strength. Beautiful pieces of music can also bring into each day a new vitality and upliftment that can enrich your life, causing it to flow more smoothly, even in the midst of stress and challenges.

WAKING UP

It is very unnerving and stressful to wake up to a loud alarm clock. It is much more healthy to wake up naturally, with the sun, the sounds of nature, or the melodies of beautiful music. As you may dream and sometimes may travel far in your sleep, so must you return gradually and smoothly into your body.

During sleep you can reach into light—like a great stream of energy emanating from your physical body—to visit, to heal and serve in other places, or to work through a challenge in your own subconscious or un-conscious mind. While sleeping, you may have experienced inwardly going to another place, perhaps to learn or observe something valuable that can be used later when you are physically awake. The Bible mentions such astral projection or soul travel through your "silver cord" (Eccles. 12:6). Today, many persons have experienced such extended travel, especially during near-death experiences. When you return to your physical body, you do not want to come back in wrong or enter with a jolt. Therefore, choose wisely the way in which you wake up. Avoid as many shocks to your psyche as possible. Before going to sleep, send out the prayer and invocation that you will wake up at the necessary time each morning. Trust the helpful promptings of God's watchers and guardian angels and your own deeper awareness to help you in this need.

If this approach does not work at first, then set a clock-radio on a music station that plays beautiful, quiet pieces with melodies that bring you back slowly into the new day. You may also use a cassette or CD of quiet music. Melodic music for strings or flute is especially good. Gregorian chants or nature sounds may also be helpful. If you are prone to going back to sleep, try music that is a bit more peppy, but without heavy bass sounds. The tune *Whistle While You Work* is the kind of energetic upper that will not shock you, yet may stir you enough to get out of bed. Also, Vivaldi's flute, guitar, or violin concertos, Mozart's flute quartets, and Telemann's string compositions are helpful. They are bright and airy, inviting you joyfully into your new day. In general, play Baroque music in the morning as a means for focusing. Other suggestions include Prologue to *Sound of Music* and *Morning* from *Peer Gynt*, by Grieg. Baroque composers whose music is tuneful, focusing, and directive include Vivaldi, Torelli, Corelli, Kuhlau, Manfredini, Albinoni, Carulli, Quantz, Handel, Telemann, Tartini, and Stamitz.

DAILY GOALS

Each morning scan your day. Perhaps you will find better focus and will accomplish more by making a list of five or six things you want to get done. As you are planning your day, play some music in the background that will clear your mind and direct you toward your desired goals. Play music that will help you to envision all tasks, meetings, and projects as going well, in the best order you can conceive.

Here are some musical selections for early morning planning:

Giulani – Guitar concertos
Vivaldi – Flute concertos; violin and guitar concertos; piccolo concertos
J. S. Bach – Harpsichord concertos; Brandenburg Concertos
C. P. E. Bach – Miscellaneous concertos
Stamitz – Flute concertos
Mozart – Flute quartets; Clarinet Concerto; Concerto for Flute and Harp
Corelli – Concerti Grossi
Boccherini – *Guitar quintets* (Naxos)
Manfredini – Trumpet concerti
Whistle While You Work
When You Wish Upon a Star
Oh, What a Beautiful Morning

Cultivate music in the morning that is joyous and transparent, not heavy or thickly orchestrated; avoid dissonances and crossed harmonies, which can easily jangle your nerves. Keep the music clear, just as you want your own thoughts and energies to be clear and well-focused. Notice as you drive to work how much a beautiful Baroque concerto will help you to focus and plan your day.

MEALS AND GOOD DIGESTION

In his very informative book *The Doctor Prescribes Music,* Dr. Edward Podolsky talks about the value of music with our meals. According to him, beautiful music played while we eat aids digestion, actually stimulating the digestive processes and helping them to function better. He mentions a fascinating scientific discovery that the principal nerve of the tympanum (middle ear) ends in the center of the tongue and connects with the brain, reacting alike to sensations of taste and sound. This is scientific support that good food and good music go together. Music that is pleasing to the ear heightens the taste buds; both processes, hearing beautiful music and eating food, work together to promote good digestion. It is no accident that in ancient cultures court musicians played while the nobility ate. Even today, beautiful music such as violin, guitar, or harp melodies—played in restaurants—relaxes us, makes us feel good, and helps our bodily functions to run more smoothly, reacting favorably on glands and nerves.

Dr. Podolsky goes on to describe the opposite effects on our system:

Unpleasant emotions bring about certain changes, which give rise to distress. When the stomach is upset, the pylorus (a muscular structure at the base of the stomach) closes. The contents are backed up in the stomach, the organ remains awash and sensations of heaviness, distension and acid risings result. If unpleasant emotions continue to plague the stomach, matters become worse. The person is thus upset and shows drowsiness, mental inefficiency and a tendency to abstraction and day-dreaming. His temper begins to wear thin. He becomes irritable. . . .

Music is the best antidote for unpleasantness at the dinner table. When there is beautiful music to be heard, there is an outpouring of gastric juice. This acts as a flushing device. The food is digested properly, it passes from the stomach into the duodenum through a wide-open pylorus.

When choosing music for meals, avoid brass, bass, and timpani. Avoid heavy beats. Select music that is not heavy or loud; avoid loud contrasts, for counter-rhythms may interfere with smooth digestion. Choose happy music that is light and airy (especially violin, flute, and harp), without deep emotional or intellectual content. Keep your music simple at all meals.

Here are a few suggestions for better eating and digestion:

Telemann – *Table Music*
Vivaldi – Lute concertos; oboe concertos
Handel – Harp Concerto; flute sonatas
Marcello – Sonatas for Recorder
Mozart – Flute quartets; flute concertos; Concerto for Flute and Harp
Mendelssohn – *Songs Without Words;* string trios
Grieg – *The Last Spring; Heart Wounds;* Piano Concerto (second
  movement); *Holberg Suite*
van Eyck – Music for Recorder
Albéniz – *Iberia* (solo guitar music)
Chopin – Piano Concerto no. 1 (second movement)
Domenico Scarlatti – Miscellaneous sonatas
Clementi – Miscellaneous sonatas

Also note the CBS *Dinner Classics Series,* designed to combine good eating with good listening. The Intersound *Music and Menus* series consists of two CDs of regional and classical music to accompany meals, including music from Mexico, China, Switzerland, Israel, France, Hawaii, Germany, Greece, Spain, and Italy (Intersound International, P.O. Box 1724, Roswell, GA 30077).

INSOMNIA

Insomnia is a challenge for many. You can take sedatives or sleeping pills that may dull your senses, or you can move into sleep creatively. Cultivate quiet, dreamy music for bedtime. Avoid late television shows that are either violent or too mentally stimulating. Try not to eat just before retiring.

As you prepare to go to sleep, first give thanks to God and review your day with a joyful heart. Release all cares into the Creator's keeping, and visualize the quiet night of sleep that you need. Prepare yourself even further by selecting a quiet piece of music for harp or strings. You might find the following recordings helpful: Chris Valentino's *The Musical Sea of Tranquility* – harp and ocean waves; John Barry's *Somewhere in Time* – strings; and Mike Rowland's *Fairy Ring* – strings. I also like Philip Elcano's *Rain Dance* and Robert Tree Cody's *Dreams from the Grandfather*. A Haydn string quartet may also prove soothing. Daniel Kobialka's *Going Home* is especially restful. These sounds can enfold you with soft melodies, which can induce fast and restful sleep. Play just one or two of them before going to sleep. Turn your lights out as you listen. Keep the volume low.

Here is a more comprehensive list of musical selections that will help you to go to sleep quickly and soundly:

Aeoliah – *Majesty; Love in the Wind*
Chris Valentino – *The Musical Sea of Tranquility*
Daniel Kobialka – *Going Home; When You Wish Upon a Star; Rainbows*
David Naegele – *Temple in the Forest*
Nancy Enslin – *Mystic Shores* (harp and ocean)
Mike Rowland – *Fairy Ring*
Daniel Domb and Judy Loman – *Meditations* (cello/harp)
Emile Pandolfi – *An Affair to Remember*
F. J. Haydn – Adagios (from his string quartets)
Vivaldi – Adagios (from his many concertos for varied instruments, especially works for strings)
James Galway – *Song of the Seashore*
Schubert – *Ave Maria* (preferably nonvocal); Quintet for Strings (op. 163)
Massenet – *Meditation* (from *Thais*)
Brahms – *Lullaby*
Schumann – *Träumerei* (Dreams)
Debussy – *Clair de lune; Arabesque no. 1; Reverie*
J. S. Bach – *Air on a G String; Arioso; Come Sweet Death; Thou Art with Me*

Palestrina – *Pope Marcellus Mass*
Pachelbel – *Canon in D* (conducted by Paillard)
Vaughan Williams – *Fantasia on a Theme of Thomas Tallis*
Barber – Adagio for Strings
Humperdinck – *Children's Prayer* (from *Hansel and Gretel*) (conducted by Ormandy on CBS)
Gregorian chants (miscellaneous, nuns singing)

Let these pieces of quiet, melodic music fill you; let them bring you peace, calm, and release you safely into the night or daytime of your sleep.

CHAPTER 5

Music for Home and Family

I believe that music can be an inspirational force in all our lives – that its eloquence and the depth of its meaning are all-important, and that all personal considerations concerning musicians and public are relatively unimportant – that music comes from the heart and returns to the heart – that music is spontaneous, impulsive expression – that its range is without limit – that music is forever growing – that music can be one element to help us build a new conception of life in which the madness and cruelty of wars will be replaced by a simple understanding of the brotherhood of man [and woman].

LEOPOLD STOKOWSKI

Music touches our innermost being and in that way produces new life, a life that gives exaltation to the whole being, raising it to that perfection in which lies the fulfillment of man's life.

HAZRAT INAYAT KHAN

Children, especially very young ones, have entered into this incarnation with memory threads of the kingdoms of light that they left in order to come to earth. They should not be hurried. Likewise, every soul, awaiting entrance into a new lifetime, absorbs impressions in the womb of the mother. This important process is vividly described in Dr. Thomas Verny's wonderful book *The Secret Life of the Unborn Child*, which I believe should be required reading for every expectant mother and father. Dr. Verny vividly describes his own musical memories from the womb, and he outlines the research into what music is most appealing to a growing fetus. He mentions how beneficial the melodies of Mozart and Vivaldi are and how happily the baby responds to this music when it is played in the environment.

With beautiful music wisely selected and a harmonious atmosphere alive in the home, you can help your child to enter into this lifetime peacefully, with less anxiety and trauma. And as a result of the warmer, more loving environment you provide for your children, they will remain more consciously linked with the Eternal Presence that surrounds them. Infants are sensitive to sounds that first enter their psyches. It is wise to avoid as many shocks as possible in today's stress-filled world, both in your own life and in your children's. Just as the warm voice of a caring parent or friend will encourage them, so beautiful music instills hope, nurturing, and confidence to meet challenges. Beautiful music deepens trust and a sense of well-being. It makes anyone feel more at home on earth.

Following are suggestions for different kinds of music that will appeal to different sides of your child's make-up.

QUIET YOUR HOME

Every person and every home needs to balance times of great activity with periods of rest and reflection. This practice helps us find poise and renewal in a busy world. Whenever you feel tension building in yourself or your home, you can use music to help regain the sense of peace and attunement. Cultivate stability and joy by playing some of these musical selections:

Daniel Kobialka – *Rainbows* (lovely children's songs) (White Swan Distributors); *When You Wish Upon a Star* (very calming) (White Swan Distributors); *Velvet Dreams; Afternoon of a Fawn* (very restful)

Vivaldi – Miscellaneous concertos, such as the flute concertos; *The Four Seasons; L'estro armonico*, etc.

J. S. Bach – Brandenburg Concerto no. 4

Pachelbel – *Canon in D* (conducted by Paillard on RCA)

Grainger – *Blithe Bells; Country Gardens*

Grieg – *Morning* (from *Peer Gynt*); *Lyric Suite; Holberg Suite*

Mozart – Flute quartets; *Haffner Serenade; Posthorn Serenade;* flute concertos; Concerto for Flute and Harp

Telemann – Flute concertos; Concerto for Three Violins and Orchestra

James Galway (soloist) – *The Magic Flute; Annie's Song; Song of the Seashore*

Gluck – *Dance of the Blessed Spirits*

Rodrigo – *Fantasy for a Courtier*

Debussy – *Clair de lune*

Susann McDonald – Miscellaneous harp music, especially Zabel: *The Source*

Mendelssohn – *Songs without Words;* quartets; Octet

Chopin – Waltzes; preludes; etudes (I recommend Lipatti as pianist for the waltzes)

Tchaikovsky – Waltzes from *Sleeping Beauty; Swan Lake; Nutcracker*
Kreisler-Dvořák – *Humoresque*

These pieces are especially good as accompaniment to coming down after
the day's work when loved ones come back together. They are valuable for
treating stress, worry, and high-strung, emotional states.

It is very therapeutic and lovingly intimate to sing to your children,
especially at bedtime. Keep beautiful tunes and songs alive in the environment. This is a way to tell them through music how much they mean to
you. You may also wish to play them a pleasant recorded story as they
drift off to sleep.

CONSTRUCTIVE ACTIVITY

By now, it should be clear that music falls into three categories:

1. Music that helps you and gives you strength and joy.
2. Music that is emotionally neutral ("blah" music).
3. Music that hurts and weakens you.

How can you tell the difference among these kinds of music? First, you
can observe your feelings and responses to the music you are experiencing.
Do you feel stronger, happier, more at peace and in tune with life, with
persons, with your work, and with your interests? Is the music helping to
release endorphins and peptides in you that give you more vitality and joy?
Does the music bore you? Does the music make you feel tense, agitated,
restless, annoyed, angry, or violent? Observe how you feel as you listen to
a piece of music.

Dr. John Diamond, in *Your Body Doesn't Lie*, mentions his investigations
into the music children listen to. He says this about the music many
children play and parents allow in the home:

> With the rock beat . . . the entire body is thrown into a state of alarm. The
> perceptual changes that occur may well manifest themselves in children as
> decreased performance in school, hyperactivity and restlessness; in adults,
> as decreased work output, increased errors, general inefficiency, reduced
> decision-making capacity on the job, and a nagging feeling that things
> just aren't right—in short the loss of energy for no apparent reason.
> This has been observed clinically hundreds of times. In my practice I
> have found that the academic records of many schoolchildren improve
> considerably after they stop listening to rock music while studying.

The anapestic hard rock beat (˘˘/) seriously hampers energy flow, dis-
torts brain response, and fragments the senses, mental abilities, and spiritual

attunement. I recall tutoring a boy who was having severe nervous problems, both in school and at home. He listened constantly to music with an anapestic beat. Although at first he found the new music "strange," he soon responded very strongly and positively to the soothing melodies of Dvořák's Largo from his Symphony no. 9 and was able to do his homework much more easily and creatively. He also said that this piece calmed him down, while a trumpet concerto by Haydn enabled him "to think straighter." (Incidentally, this former lover of anapestic hard rock really enjoyed Haydn.)

This incident proved to me again that good work is enhanced by the sounds of beautiful, harmonious music. Interestingly, in almost all the music appreciation classes I teach at the university, a clear pattern is evident. In the beginning the students, many of whom have been adversely affected by listening repeatedly to the anapestic hard rock beat, complain about the "crummy, awful music" they are now hearing (often for the first time). Then as the class continues, their brains realign themselves, and they love the music they formerly hated. They wind up introducing the "new" music (especially Vivaldi and Bach) to others.

Stimulating the imagination. Many examples of great music are dramatic in a particularly descriptive way. Sometimes this music has been called program music, for it is often inspired by mythology, a story, or by nature, or it paints a story or a scene with sound. Such music can stimulate you and your child to paint pictures inwardly with your powers of imagination and visualization. You may find fantasies and dreams coming alive, thus awakening greater creative outlet and expression. Such music energizes and inspires you in your work, your relationships, and your recreation.

These selections are good antidotes for anyone with a passive, dulled, and overly "TV-ed" consciousness; they are especially helpful for children and adults who might tend to be slaves of television and other electronic/video machines. Much of this music has been used in films and shows, since it is colorful and stimulating to the imagination. You might want to listen to these pieces with your eyes closed or with a notebook by your side, to jot down impressions and pictures that come to mind. Where possible, avoid words and lyrics.

Mozart – Piano Concerto no. 21 (slow movement); Symphony no. 40; horn concertos
Beethoven – Symphony no. 6 *(Pastorale)*
Smetana – *The High Castle; Moldau*
The Cry of the Loon – Gentle Persuasion (Special Music-Essex Entertainment, 87 Hackensack Street, Hackensack, NJ 07601)

Liszt – Hungarian rhapsodies

Yas-Kaz – *Jungle Book* (from *Darkness in Dreams*) (Kuckuck 11092 – Celestial Harmonies, P.O. Box 30122, Tucson, AZ 85751) (marvelous music to take children into an imaginary tropical jungle)

Rod McKuen – *Balloon Concerto* (Stanford – Stanyan STZ103–2) (DCC Compact Classics, 8300 Tampa Avenue, Suite G, Northridge, CA 91324)

Dvořák – Slavonic dances

Brahms – Hungarian dances

David and Steve Gordon – *Sanctuary* (recorded at Sequoia National Forest) (White Swan Distributors)

Hovhaness – *And God Created Great Whales* (conducted by David Amos – Crystal CD–810); *Mysterious Mountain* (Reiner on RCA 5733)

Rodrigo – *Aranjuez Concerto*

Robert Bearns and Ron Dexter – *Golden Voyage I* (a galactic exploration through celestial harmonics) (White Swan Distributors)

Britten – *Four Sea Interludes* (from *Peter Grimes*)

Delius – *Florida Suite*

Chick Corea – *Children's Songs* (Naxos 8.550341)

Quilter – *Children's Overture* (EMI CDM 64131)

Rimsky-Korsakov – *Russian Easter Festival Overture; Sadko; The Tale of the Tsar Saltan; Golden Cockerel* (EMI 568098)

Copland – *Lincoln Portrait; Quiet City; Appalachian Spring; The Tender Land*

Bloch – Concerto Grosso no. 1

Berlioz – *Roman Carnival Overture; Rob Roy Overture; Harold in Italy*

Ravel – *Fairy Garden* (from *Mother Goose*)

Ketélbey – *Bells Across the Meadow; In a Monastery Garden*

Handel – *Messiah* (choruses)

Johann Strauss, Jr. – *Blue Danube Waltz; Tales from the Vienna Woods; Emperor Waltz*

Juventino Rosas – *Over the Waves* (played at the circus)

Ivanovici – *Danube Waves*

Martinu – Double Concerto (highly dramatic)

Weber – *Invitation to the Dance*

RELEASE YOUR CHILD'S ENERGY

Your children deserve to be bathed in beautiful, melodic music—the best that you can find for them. Particularly when they are very young, it is best to avoid playing stressful, clashing sounds and chaotic or depressing songs. Children (and many adults) are very open at subconscious levels to any sounds or suggestions that come to them from the environment. Also, in a constructive sense, as they get older, you will find that music with more defined rhythms and pleasing melodies can help to direct and motivate their energies.

Certain beautiful and very rhythmical music, like a Haydn symphony or even the melodious love song from *Beauty and the Beast*, will often help them to concentrate on their homework, while other stressful and chaotic sounds will make them lose concentration and feel jumpy, even when they do not have work to do.

Here is some music that will stimulate your children of three years and older without attacking them or causing them to feel fragmented and confused:

Mozart – Sonatas for violin and piano
Villa-Lobos – *Little Train of the Caipira* (from *Bachianas Brasileiras no. 2*) (strong but visually exciting)
Anderson – *Sleigh Ride; The Typewriter; Syncopated Clock*
Stephen Foster – Songs (such as *My Old Kentucky Home; Beautiful Dreamer; Camptown Races*) (Vox Allegretto)
Delibes – *Coppélia; Sylvia; The Source*
Tchaikovsky – *Nutcracker* (with Christopher Plummer narrating on Caedmon or Kevin Kline on Rabbit Ears)
Saint-Saëns – *Carnival of the Animals*
Grainger – *Lincolnshire Posy; Country Gardens*
Mendelssohn – *A Midsummer Night's Dream*
Ponchielli – *Dance of the Hours*
Dukas – *The Sorcerer's Apprentice*
Hovhaness – *Sinbad the Sailor; And God Created Great Whales*
Copland – *Old American Songs*
Corigliano – *Pied Piper Fantasy*
Bizet – *Children's Games*
Jean Cras – *Children's Loves* (Cybelia) (Qualiton Imports)
Dan Welcher – *How Maui Snared the Sun* (with Richard Chamberlain as narrator on Marco Polo)
Dohnányi – *Variations on a Nursery Song*
Poulenc – *Story of Babar the Elephant; The Model Animals*
Raffi – *Songs for Children*
Gottschalk – *Grande Tarantelle*
Children's Stories of Great Composers (A & M Records, 939 Warden Avenue, Scarborough, Ontario, M1L 4C5, Canada):
　– Vivaldi – *Ring of Mystery*

   – *Beethoven Lives Upstairs*
   – *Mr. Bach Comes to Call*
   – Mozart – *Magic Fantasy* (story of *The Magic Flute*)
   – *Tchaikovsky's Life in Music*
Holdridge and Diamond – *Jonathan Livingston Seagull*
Soundtracks: *The Sound of Music; Mary Poppins; Aladdin; Snow White and the Seven Dwarfs; Fantasia; Winnie the Pooh; Sleeping Beauty; Cinderella; Beauty and the Beast; Black Beauty*
Haydn – *Toy Symphony*
Beethoven, Mozart – German dances
Prokofiev – *Peter and the Wolf*
Harsanyi – *Story of the Little Tailor*
Ravel – *Mother Goose; L'Enfant et les sortileges*
Rimsky-Korsakov – *Scheherazade; Golden Cockerel*
Kleinsinger – *Tubby the Tuba* (Caedmon CPN 1623)
Pete Seeger – *Songs for Children* (Vanguard)
Copland – *Billy the Kid; Rodeo; Danzon Cubano*
Britten – *Young Person's Guide to the Orchestra*
Offenbach – *Gaîté Parisienne*
Paul Winter – *Common Ground; Canyon; Whales Alive*
Judy Collins – *Whales and Nightingales* (especially *Farewell to Tarwathie* and *Amazing Grace*) (Elektra)
Andrew Lloyd Webber – *Joseph's Technicolor Dream Coat; Phantom of the Opera; Cats*
Shostakovich – *Polka* (from *Age of Gold*)
Hopkins – *John and the Magic Music Man*
Kim Robertson – *Tender Shepherd; Love Song to a Planet*

OTHER LANDS AND THE PAST

In spite of stress, increasing polarities, and the prophets of doom, many people today sense a new breakthrough in consciousness already appearing on the horizon. This is the coming New Age, or Age of Aquarius, which, according to higher teachings, will promote a fuller expression of empathy and the brotherhood of humankind. Times ahead will also emphasize greater interdependence of people freely sharing their good with others to produce win-win outcomes, a cooperative group effort toward peace and jointly constructive goals, scientific advances, creative synthesis in the arts, and greater international harmony, communication, and compassion.

Above all, our times are revealing to us how precious and valuable each life is, since we are all interconnected. In some way each of us can contribute to the greater totality and wholeness. By working together, we come to feel a greater reverence for life, and, by helping others, we open new pathways of service, recognizing more clearly our place as a receptor and channel in God's unfolding universe.

In the midst of this expanding consciousness and global communication, it is important to awaken in your child a growing awareness and appreciation for *all* cultures, nations, and traditions so as to develop a more universal perspective.

All of us are persons of color, the colors of God's Light, and we are sharing increasingly in the emerging multicultural richness that is becoming ever more present on our planet. Music of the world can help you to move into the larger consciousness of becoming a global citizen. As various media can now take viewers on instant trips to many lands, and many colleges and schools are providing armchair travel courses, so music can help to awaken deeper appreciation and feelings, past, present, and future, of the many places and races on this planet.

While appreciating your own particular national heritage and background, you can use the following musical pieces to help your child to become a more sensitive planetary citizen. As you share such music with your children, try to show accompanying pictures of lands and peoples, perhaps from *Highlights Magazine, National Geographic Magazine, Smithsonian,* and other travel periodicals and history books. These pieces of music may need some introduction because the language and the instruments may seem new and different. Blend such music into your home environment appropriately, for example, on certain festival days and special holiday celebrations. (See Catherine Milinaire's lovely book *Celebrations,* which celebrates many world rituals and festivals, and David Maybury-Lewis's classic work *Millennium,* a celebration of tribal wisdom in the modern world, also available on video.)

The *Nonesuch Explorer* series of recordings, the anthologies *Global Celebration* and *Global Meditation,* and many other newer recordings are an excellent way to travel around the world musically. Now, in many music stores, you will find a special section called World Music. Music is a wonderful way to expand your consciousness of other countries and cultures.

The World Music recordings below are listed in most cases by distributor. Many of these recordings are available through White Swan Music, Inc., 1705 Fourteenth Street, Box 143, Boulder, CO 80302; Allegro Imports, 12630 NE Marx Street, Portland, OR 97230-1059; and Qualiton Imports Limited, 24-02 Fortieth Avenue, Long Island City, NY 11101. Also, contact Records International, P.O. Box 1140, Goleta, CA 93116-1140, a source that I have always found to be most helpful. Records International specializes in unusual, often striking recordings from other countries. Since labels of recording companies often remain the same but individual label numbers change frequently, it is sometimes better to order directly through the distributors (or through the sources I have just mentioned) rather than through stores.

ANTHOLOGIES OF WORLD MUSIC

Around the World for a Song (Ryko RCD 00217)
A Musical World Tour (Arion ARN 64080) (Allegro Imports)
Voices of Forgotten Worlds (Ellipsis Arts CD 3252) (plus booklet)
World Music (Nimbus NI 7008)
Dances of Universal Peace (Sufi Islamia/Prophecy Publications, 114
  Forest Avenue, Fairfax, CA 94110)
Global Meditation and *Global Celebration* (4 CDs each) (Ellipsis Arts:
  Relaxation Company, 20 Lumber Road, Roslyn, NY 11576)
Worlds of Music (MacMillan, 866 Third Avenue, New York, NY 10022)
  (plus booklet)

Celtic, Hebridean, and Welsh

Currie and Gibson – *Songs of Scotland* (ASV 2087)
Alan Stivell – *Renaissance of the Celtic Harp* and *Harps of the New
  Age; Celtic Symphony* (Rounder CD) (Cambridge, MA)
Lynette Johnson – *Twilight Airs: Songs for Celtic Harp* (Sierra Classical,
  P.O. Box 5853, Pasadena, CA 91117)
Patrick Ball – *Celtic Harp* (Fortuna) (Celestial Harmonies)
Kim Robertson – *Moonrise* (Invincible, P.O. Box 13054, Phoenix, AZ
  85002 or White Swan)
Jan Carter – *Where Angels Fly* (Larrikin) (Allegro Imports)
*The Enchanted Isles: Harp music of Ireland, Scotland, England and
  Wales* (Carol Thompson – harp) (Dorian) (Allegro Imports)
Joemy Wilson – *Celtic Dreams* (Dargason Music – Backroads)
Charles Tomlinson Griffes – *The Kairn of Koridwen* (De Cou – Koch
  7216)
Bantock – *Hebridean Symphony* (Hyperion)
  – *Celtic Symphony* (Hyperion)
  – *Pagan Symphony* (Hyperion)
Voice of Wales (Chandos 6540)
The Airs of Wales (Cheryl Ann Fulton – harp) (Koch)
Scott MacMillan – *Celtic Mass for the Sea* (Atlantica) (Allegro Imports)

Mexico, Central and South America

Sérgio and Odair Assad – *Alma Brasileira* (guitars) (Elektra Nonesuch)

Alturas – *From the Heights* (Terra Nova Records, P.O. Box 455, Sunland, CA 91041-0455); *The Enchanted Land* (Terra Nova)

Los Folkloristas – *Mexico: Horizonte Musical* (Discos Pueblo – Fonarte Latino)

Linda Ronstadt – *Canciones de mi Padre* (Elektra/Asylum Records)

Carlos Mabarak – *Balada de los Rios de Tabasco; Symphony* (Lozano – Forlane UCD 16712)

Miguel Jimenez – *Tres Cartas de Mexico; El Chueco* (ballet); *Angelus; Noche en Morelia* (Lozano – Forlane UCD 16712) (Records International)

Villafontana – *Magical Strings; Mexican Symphony* (Discos Mexicanos, Juarez, Mexico)

Daniel Catan – *Rappaccini's Daughter* (Private)

Guatemala: Its Celebrated Marimbas (Arion) (Allegro)

Sergio Cuevas – *Indian Harp of Paraguay* (Allegro Imports)

Traditional Music of Mexico (Mariachis) (Legacy)

Los Calchakis – *Latin American Harp, Marimbas and Guitars* (Arion) (Allegro Imports)

– *Flutes of the Incan Lands* (Allegro)

– *Under the Flight of the Condor* (Allegro)

Alfredo Ortiz – *Paraguayan Harp for Quiet Moments I, II* (P.O. Box 911, Corona, CA 91718)

Soleil Inca – *Peru, Bolivia, Ecuador, Chile and Colombia* (Playa Sound) (Allegro); *Flute, Guitar and Harp of the Andes* (Legacy International Box 6999, Beverly Hills, CA 90212)

Lee Holdridge – *El Pueblo del Sol* (Bay Cities)

Yma Sumac – *Voices of the Xatabay* (Capitol)

El Condor Pasa – *Indian Harps and Flutes* (Laserlight – Delta Music, Los Angeles, CA)

inti-Illimani – *Fragments of a Dream* and *Leyenda* (with John Williams) (Sony)

– *Imagination (El Mercado)* (Redwood Records, 6400 Hollis Street, Suite B, Emeryville, CA 94608)

Esteban Ramon – *Harp Magic from Latin America* (P.O. Box 722242, San Diego, CA 92172-2242)

Jaime Torres – *Charango* (Rounder)

Bernardo Rubaja – *Hill of the Seven Colors; Celebration in the Village* and *Song of the Americas* (from *Alma del Sur*) (Narada)

Bandolas de Venezuela (Dorian Discovery) (Allegro)

Savia Andina Classics – Bolivia (Sukay Records, Suite 523, 3315 Sacramento Street, San Francisco, CA 94118)

Huayucaltia – *Caminos; Horizontes* (ROM, Treasure Trove, P.O. Box 491212, Los Angeles, CA 90049)

Villa-Lobos – *The Discovery of Brazil; Genesis; Dawn in a Tropical Forest; Forest of the Amazon; Amazonas* (Marco Polo)
– *Bachianas Brasileiras* (Bátiz – EMI)
– *Magdalena* (CBS)

Juan Jose Castro – *The Cry of the Sierras* (Philips 510658-2- PolyGram)

Alberto Ginastera – *Ollantay* (Qualiton); *Symphony no. 3 (Pampas)* (Dorian) (Allegro); *Panambi* (especially the beautiful section, *Amanecer*, or *The Dawn*) (Largo 5122) (Qualiton Imports)

Astor Piazzolla – *Tangazo* (London Argo)

Antonio Estevez – *La Cantata Criolla* (Dorian) (Allegro)

Julian Orbon – *Three Symphonic Versions* (Dorian)

Agustin Lara – *Twenty Hits* (RCA 3307-2-RL)

Carlos Chávez – *The Six Symphonies* (Vox)

Augustin Barrios Mangore – *Guitar Works* (John Williams – guitar) (Sony)

Fiesta Mexicana (Francisco Araiza) (DGG – PolyGram)

Lalo Shifrin – *Cantos Aztecas* (Pro Arte)

Candelario Huizar (the Mexican Sibelius) – *Symphonies* (RCA)

Silvestre Revueltas – *The Night of the Mayans* (IMP – Allegro)

José Pablo Moncayo – *Huapango* (Unicorn-Kanchana); *Zapata* (Forlane 16688/9)

Missa Criolla and Missa Flamenca (Philips – PolyGram)

(For easy access to these recordings contact Ocean Song, c/o Apolonia-Virginia Igonda, 1438 Camino Del Mar, Del Mar, CA 92014; 1-619-755-7664. For beautiful music of the Andes, contact Tumi, 8-9 New Bond Street Place, Bath, Avon BA1 1BH, England.)

England and Ireland

Delius – *Appalachia* (London or EMI)

Chieftains – *The Celtic Harp* (RCA or BMG)

Hamilton Harty – *The Children of Lir* (Chandos)

Music of Vaughan Williams (especially *Oxford Elegy* and *To a Lark Ascending*) (EMI)

Bax – *Seven Symphonies* and *Tone Poems* (Chandos)

Britten – Miscellaneous works (London)

Rubbra – Symphonies and orchestral works (Lyrita); *Viola Concerto* (Conifer)

Walton – *Symphonies nos. 1, 2* (RCA)

Elgar – *Enigma Variations* and other miscellaneous works (EMI)

Danny Boy (sung by Robert White) (RCA)

Music of the Chieftains and Boys of the Lough (RCA)

Mary O'Hara – *Recital* (C5 Records, P.O. Box 328, Maidenhead, Berkshire, SL6 2NE, England)

Sean O'Riada – *I Am Ireland* (Shanachie)

Nóirín Ní Riain – *Spiritual Songs from Many Traditions; Songs from the Irish Traditions; Religious Songs from the Irish Tradition; Irish Religious Traditional Songs* (Caoineadh na Maighdine); *Vox de Nube* (beautiful sacred songs sung hauntingly by Nóirín and the monks of Glenstal Abbey: available only through Sounds True, 735 Walnut Street, Dept. FC6, Boulder, CO 80302)

Enya – *Shepherd Moons; Watermark* (Reprise – Warner) (many deeply haunting songs)

Anne Auffret – *Sacred Music from Brittany* (Keltia Musique)

Shaun Davey – *Relief of Derry Symphony* (Tara Records, 8 Anne's, Dublin 2, Ireland) (Koch Distributors)

Irish String Quartets (Chandos 9295)

Scotland

Bagpipe music and songs of Calum Kennedy (London)

Maxwell Davies – *Orkney Wedding with Sunrise* (Unicorn or Philips)

Valerie Dunbar – *I'll Say Farewell* (Klub Records – PRT, Inc.)

Tommy Scott – *Pipes and Strings of Scotland* (Scotdisc) (Qualiton Imports)

Scottish Songs of the Hebrides (Hyperion Records International)

France

Nana Mouskouri – *Cote Sud-Cote Coeur* (French and Greek) (Philips – PolyGram)

Offenbach – *Gaîté Parisienne* (RCA)

Michel Legrand Plays Legrand (Polydor)

Milhaud – *Suite Provençale* (Munch/RCA)

  – *Sacred Service* (Adda) (Qualiton)

India

Readers are referred to a special source for Indian music: Raga Records, P.O. Box 635, Village Station, NY 10014. Also, note the series of wonderful Indian music on the Nimbus label. Catalogue available from Nimbus Records, P.O. Box 7746, Charlottesville, VA 22906-7746.

Ali Akbar Khan – *Journey; Garden of Dreams* (Triloka – BMG)

Haridas – *Chants of Paramahansa Yogananda* (Living Joy Productions, 14618 Tyler Foote Road, Nevada City, CA 95959)

Shivkumar Sharma – *Ragas* (santoor and tabla) (Nimbus)

L. Subramaniam – *Sarasvati* (Water Lily Acoustics, P.O. Box 91448, Santa Barbara, CA 93190)

Call of the Valley – Indian classical instrumental music (EMI CD-PSLP 5002)

Lakshmi Shankar – *Evening Concert* (Ravi Shankar Music Circle, P.O. Box 46026, Los Angeles, CA 90046)

– *Songs of Devotion* (Ethnic – Auvidis)

Balachander – *Veena Virtuoso* (Seven Seas)

Ravi Shankar – *Concerto for Sitar and Orchestra; Morning Love* (EMI); *Sounds of India* (CBS); *Passages* (with Philip Glass) (Private Music, 9014 Melrose Avenue, Los Angeles, CA 90049)

Shivkumar Sharma (plays the strings of the santoor) (Chanda Dhara, Stuttgart, Germany)

These Still Waters – Lisa Moskow (sarod) and Genji Ito (shakuhachi and hischiriki) play a blend of Indian-Japanese reflective music (Casting Spells 4754 – 2126 Fifth Avenue, San Rafael, CA 94901)

Celestial Songs of Upanishad (Oriental Records, P.O. Box 387, Williston Park, NY 11596)

Imrat Khan (sitar and surbahar) – *Raga Marwa* (Nimbus)

Russia (See special appendix on Russian Sacred Choral Music)

Osipov Balalaika Russian Folk Orchestra (Melodiya)

Feenist Balalaika (Art and Electronics)

Rachmaninov – *Vespers, Liturgy of St. John Chrysostom*

Evening Bells (traditional) (Mobile Fidelity)

Red Army Chorus (EMI)

Serge Jaroff – *Midnight in Moscow* (Don Cossack Chorus) (Musikfest – DGG)

Russian Winter (Art and Electronics)
Balalaika Favorites (Balalaika Orchestra) (Mercury)

Japan

Art of the Japanese Bamboo Flute (Legacy)
The World of the Koto (Denon) (Allegro Imports)
Japanese Melodies (Denon 35C37-7330) (Allegro Imports)
Lyrical Melodies of Japan (Denon DC-8114) (Allegro Imports)
Hiraoki Ogawa – *Temples of Japan* (Arion) (Allegro Imports)
Evening Snow (koto and shakuhachi flute) (Backroads Distributors –
   1-800-825-4848)
Sound of Silk Strings (Tomoko Sunazaki – koto solo) (Fortuna)
Moon at Dawn (Tomoko Sunazaki – koto and Masayuki Koga –
   shakuhachi) (Fortuna) (listed on CD as Tegoto-Fortuna label)
Akira Ifukube – *Symphonic Eclogue for Koto and Strings* (Fontec)
   (Records International); *Gautama the Buddha: Symphonic Ode*
   (Futureland) (Records International)
Kohsaku Yamada – *The Dark Gate* (RCA Japan) (Records International)
Yasushi Akutagawa – *Symphonies* (Toshiba) (Records International)
Toru Takemitsu – *Ran* (Milan)
   – *Far Calls, Coming Far* (ABC – Albany)
Sakura (Rampal/Laskine) (CBS)
Japanese Melodies (vol. 3) (Rampal) (CBS)
Ikuma Dan – *Six Symphonies* (London FOOL-20466/9 – Japan) (Records
   International)
Koto Music of Japan (Laserlight 12184; 1-800-648-4844)
Kimio Eto Plays the Koto (Elektra)
Galway – *Song of the Seashore* (RCA 3534)
Tony Scott – *Music for Zen Meditation* (Elektra) (White Swan
   Distributors)
Ayako Lister – *The Japanese Koto* (ARC Music Int., P.O. Box 111, East
   Grinstead, West Sussex RH19 2YF, Great Britain)
Bunya Koh (Taiwan composer) – *Confucian Temple Rites* (Sunrise)
Minoru Miki – Requiem (koto and strings) (Records International)
Teruyuki Noda – *Adriatic Rhapsody for Guitar and Orchestra* (Camerata
   32CM 344)
Moonlit Castle (shakuhachi flute and harp) (Empty Bell Music, 609
   Jackson Street, #1, Albany, CA 94706)
Kitaro – *Silk Road Suite* (PolyGram)

Hovhaness – *Fantasy on Japanese Woodprints* (Etcetera KTC 1085)
(Qualiton Imports)
Japan (traditional instruments) (Arion) (Allegro Imports)
Music for Koto and Flute (Kudo and Asawa – Crystal CD–316)

China

Xian Xianghai – *Yellow River Concerto* (Nuova Era or Hong Kong)
Chi Gong Melody – good for healing (Sounds True)
Music for the Chinese Classical Orchestra (Legacy)
Eleven Centuries of Traditional Music of China (Legacy)
Phases of the Moon (Traditional Chinese Music) (CBS 36705)
Popular Cantonese Melodies (HK – One World)
Chinese Evergreens (HK – One World – BMG)
Twelve Heroines of Imperial China (HK – BMG)
Shu-Feng – *Chinese Pipa* (White Swan Distributors)
Chinese Bamboo Flute Music (Laserlight)
Chan Wing-Wah – *Celebration Overture* (HK – One World)
Zhang Yan (plays the double zheng) (HK – One World)
Wu Hai-lin – *Violin Concerto* (HK – One World)
Chen Gang – *Bells from the Temple* (HK – One World)
The Imperial Bells of China (Fortuna, P.O. Box 32016, Tucson, AZ
85751)

Germany and Austria/Bavaria

The Charm of Old Vienna (vols. 1, 2) (conductor Willi Boskovsky)
(Vanguard Classics)
Creampuffs from Vienna (conductor Willi Boskovsky) (Vanguard
Classics)
Schumann – Symphony no. 1 *(Spring)*
The Sound of Austria (Dorian – Allegro)
Joseph Lanner – *Waltzes* (Sony)
Johann Strauss, Jr. – *Waltzes* (Marco Polo)
Lucia Popp – *Vienna Operetta Arias*
Beverly Sills – *Vienna Album*

Roumania

Georges Enesco – *Roumanian Rhapsodies* (Mercury)
Gypsy Melodies (Zamfir on panflute) (Philips – PolyGram)

Old Roumanian Folksongs (Yumika: panflute) (Electrecord) (Allegro Imports)

Porumbescu – *Roumanian Rhapsody* (Olympia) (Allegro)

Constantinescu – *Violin Concerto* (Olympia 417) (Allegro)

Gypsy Music in Roumania (cimbalom and panflute) (Olympia) (Allegro)

Flute of Pan and Organ (Marcel Cellier and Gheorghe Zamfir) (Pierre Verany PVY 750001) (Allegro)

The Heart of Roumania (panflute and organ) (Pierre Verany PVY 750002) (Allegro)

Roumanian Gems (panflute, cimbalom, and pipe organ) (Pierre Verany PVY 750004) (Allegro)

Italy

Gioacchino Rossini – *Overtures* (London Weekend or RCA)

Luciano Pavarotti – *Arias and Neapolitan Songs* (London)

Mantovani – *Italian Suite* (London)

Renzo Arbore – *Due Punti e a Capo* (Blue 61676 Elektra Entertainment)

Ottorino Respighi – Miscellaneous works

Spain

Manolo Sanlucar – *Aljibe* (Andalucia Symphony) (a knockout!) (Records International)

Joaquin Rodrigo – *Concierto de Aranjuez; Concerto for a Fiesta* (Philips)

Roberto Gerhard – *Pandora Suite; Alegrias* (ballet); *Cancionera de Pedrell* (Pons – Harmonia Mundi HMC 901500) (Records International)

Timo Korhonen – *Sevilla* (solo guitar – beautiful!) (Ondine ODE 752-2) (Records International)

Pablo Casals – *Sacred Choral Music* (Koch Schwann)

Frederico Moreno Torroba – *Sonatina for Guitar and Orchestra and Two Interludes* (Analekta) (Allegro Imports); *Concerto from Castille* (Thorofon) (Qualiton Imports); *Concerto from Malaga, Flamenco Concerto* and *Iberian Concerto* (Philips – PolyGram)

Mario Castelnuovo-Tedesco – *Serenade; Guitar Concertos 1, 2* (RCA – BMG)

Anton Abril – *Concierto Mudejar; Concierto Aguadiano; Homenaje a Sor* (Analekta) (Allegro)

Salvador Bacarisse – *Concertino for Guitar and Orchestra* (DGG PolyGram)

Manuel Ponce – *Concierto del Sur* (MCA)
Zarzuelas (Hispavox and EMI) (Records International)
Cante Gitano (Nimbus) (Allegro)
Cante Flamenco (Nimbus) (Allegro)
Leo Brouwer – *Retrats Catalans* (London)
Antonio Ruiz-Pipo – *Tablas for Guitar and Orchestra* (DGG – PolyGram)
The Gypsy Kings (Polydor)
Victoria de los Angeles – *Zarzuela Aria*s (EMI Studio); *Traditional Catalan Songs* (Collins) (Allegro)
John Williams (guitar) – *Echoes of Spain* (music of Isaac Albéniz) (CBS MK36679)
Pasodobles (Asensio – Ensayo 3451)

Scandinavia

Kirsten Flagstad: Sings Grieg Songs (AS) (Allegro Imports); *Norwegian Songs* (EMI); see also London 5 CD Commemoration to Flagstad
Music of Edvard Grieg, especially *Olav Trygvason* and *Landsighting* (Unicorn-Kanchana)
Music of Jean Sibelius, especially *The Bard* and *Symphonies nos. 4, 7* (BIS) (Qualiton)
Music of Christian Sinding, especially *Piano Concerto* and *Symphony no. 1* (NCC) (Qualiton)
Hans Erik Philip – *Fiskerne* (soundtrack: beautiful and moving music for viola and orchestra) (Danica) (Albany Imports)
Robert Kajanus – *Aino* (symphonic poem) (Records International)

Hawaii

Jerre Tanner – *Boy with Goldfish* (Troy) (Albany Distributors)
Dan Welcher – *Haleakala: How Maui Snared the Sun* (Marco Polo)
Songs sung by Alfred Alpaka (MCA)

Israel

David Amos (conductor) – *Horn of Plenty: Lovely Songs of Israel* (anything conducted by David Amos is excellent!)
Richard Tucker – *A Passover Seder Festival; Kol Nidrei* (Sony)
Fifteen Jewish Songs for Cello and Piano (Adda) (Qualiton Imports)
Hebrew Melodies (Fidelio) (Qualiton)

Music of the Bible (White Label) (Qualiton)

Our Hope (male choir sings cantorial Jewish choral music) (MK) (Allegro Imports)

Jewish Folk Songs (Multisonic) (Allegro)

Unburden Your Heart: Jewish Folk Songs (Multisonic) (Allegro)

Israeli Melodies (Centaur 2140-Koch)

Hebraic and Russian Melodies (Mischa Elman, violin) (Vanguard OVC 8030)

Hatikvah; Kol Nidrei (Pro Arte)

Ernest Bloch – *Sacred Service* (Chandos or Sony); *Schelomo* (Solomon) (EMI); *Israel Symphony* (Vanguard); *Baal Shem* (CBS or ASV); *Violin Concerto* (Vanguard); *Voice in the Wilderness* (EBS) (Qualiton Imports); *Three Jewish Poems* (Vanguard)

Karmon Israeli – *Songs of the Sabras* (Vanguard)

Kletzmer music (miscellaneous)

Gordon Jenkins – *Soul of a People* (Bainbridge) (Allegro)

John Duffy – *Heritage* (Mehta – CBS)

Ami Maayani – *Symphony no. 4 on Popular Hebraic Themes* (Rodan – Music in Israel MII-CD-9) (available from Records International)

Castelnuovo-Tedesco – *Violin Concerto no. 2 (Prophets)* (Perlman/Mehta – EMI CDC 54296)

Ben-Haim – *Violin Concerto* (Perlman/Mehta – EMI)

Itzhak Perlman – *Tradition: Popular Jewish Melodies* (EMI)

Joseph Achron – *Hebrew Melody* (Intersound International – CCD 2222)

Hebraic Legacies (Aaron Rosand, violinist) (Audiofon CD 72033 – Albany Music)

Abraham Kaplan – *Glorious* (lovely settings of the Psalms of David – a real classic!) (North American Liturgy Resources, Phoenix, AZ 85029) – *K'Dusha Symphony (Holy, Holy, Holy)* (Music Department, Congregation B'Nai Amoona, 324 S. Mason Road, Saint Louis, MO 63141)

Jan Peerce – *The Art of the Cantor* (Vanguard)

Mordechai Seter – *Midnight Vigil* (Capriccio 10 368)

Noam Sheriff – *Revival of the Dead* (IMP) (Allegro)

Ben Steinberg – *Shomeir Yisrael* (Friday evening musical service) (Arkay Records) (Allegro Imports)

Tumbalalaika (Yiddish folk songs without words) (Vanguard)

Netania Davrath sings Yiddish folk songs (Vanguard)

Greece

Theodorakis – *Symphony no. 3* (Minos – Greek Video, 394 McGuinness Boulevard, Brooklyn, NY 11222); *Canto Olympico* (Intuition Records) (Records International); *Best of Mikis Theodorakis* (instrumental) (Koch-Schwann); *Zorba the Greek* (ballet) (Records International)

Christodoulos Halaris – *Music of the Aegean Sea* (vols. 1, 2) (Orata) (Allegro Imports)

Greek Party (The Helenes) (P.P.I., 88 St. Francis Street, Newark, NJ 07105)

Authentic Greek Songs and Dances (Legacy)

Music of Ancient Greece (Harmonia Mundi)

Agnes Baltsa – *Songs My Country Taught Me* (DGG – PolyGram)

Yanni – *In My Time* (Polydor)

Skalkottos – *Greek Dances* (Lyra)

Manolis Kalomiris – *Symphony no. 2* (Lyra) (Records International)

Africa

David Fanshawe – *African Sanctus* (Philips or Silva Classics 6003) (also a very fine documentary video on this extraordinary musical journey); *Salaams* (Philips – Polydor)

Spirit of African Sanctus (Saydisc) (Qualiton Imports)

Heartbeats of Africa (available through David Fanshawe) (You can contact David Fanshawe at this address: Fanshawe One World Music, P.O. Box 574, Marlborough, Wilts, SN8, 2SP, UK; Tel.: 44-01672-520211)

Al-Haji Papa Bunka Susso – *A Gathering of Elders* (Water Lily Acoustics)

Mass of the Keur Moussa (Senegal) (Sounds True)

Masses of Cameroun (Sounds True)

Koko du Burkina Faso: Balafons and African Drums (Playa Sound – Auvidis)

Les Ballets Africains (African Ballet of the Republic of Guinea) (DunDumB Records)

Paul Simon – *Graceland* (Polydor)

Miriam Makeeba Sings African Songs (Polydor)

Spirituals in Concert (Kathleen Battle and Jessye Norman) (DGG – PolyGram)

Singing in an Open Space: Zulu Rhythm and Harmony (Rounder)

Kronos Quartet: Pieces of Africa (Elektra-Nonesuch) (WEA – Warner)
David Hewitt – *An African Tapestry* (White Swan)
Ali Farka Toure and Ry Cooder – *Talking Timbuktu* (Rykodisc 1381)

Native American

All of the following musical selections are available through Four
Winds Trading Company, c/o Richard T. and Catherine Carey, 685
South Broadway, Suite A, Boulder, CO 80303, 1-800-456-5444. They
are very helpful also in answering your questions about individual
recordings.

Kaibah – Navaho songs
Wolf – *Beyond Words; Rides the Wind* (Anisnabe)
R. Carlos Nakai – *Canyon Trilogy; Cycles; Sundance Season; Earth
    Spirit; Desert Dance; Emergence; Changes; Journeys* (Navajo) (Canyon
    Records: see below)
James DeMars – *Spirit Horses; Two World Concerto; Two World
    Symphony* (very creative, dramatic music, especially *Spirit Horses*
    and *Lake That Speaks;* highly recommended, wonderful composer
    and person) (Canyon CDs, 4143 North Sixteenth Street, Phoenix, AZ
    85016)
Medicine Wheel (On Wings of Song and Robert Gass) (Spring Hill
    Music)
Kevin Locke – *Dream Catcher; The Flash of the Mirror; Keepers of the
    Dream* (Lakota)
Coyote Oldman – *Night Forest; Landscape; Tear of the Moon;
    Compassion; Thunder Chord*
Philip Elcano – *Rain Dance*
Fernando Cellicion – *Kokopeli Dreams; Buffalo Spirit*
John Rainer, Jr. – *Songs of the Indian Flute I, II*
Ralph Kotay – *Kiowa Hymns*
Jackalene Crow Hiendlmayr – *Legends of the North American Indians*
Louis Ballard – *Music for the Earth and the Sky*
Carl T. Fischer – *Reflections of an Indian Boy*
Chief Dan George – *Proud Earth*
Robert Tree Cody – *Dreams from the Grandfather* (Dakota/Maricopa)
J. Reuben Silverbird – *The World in Our Eyes: A Native American
    Vision of Creation* (Dine/Apache)
Chuna McIntyre – *Across the Tundra* (Eskimo)
Alice Gomez – *Flute Dreams* (Mestizo)

Robert Mirabal – *Something in the Fog* (Taos Pueblo)
Black Elk – *The Sacred Pipe; Black Elk Speaks*
Brian Akipa – *The Flute Player* (Sisseton Wahpeton Sioux)
William Gutierrez – *Calling the Eagle* (Ute/Dine)
Perry Silverbird – *The Blessing Way; Spirit of the Fire* (Dine/Apache)
James Bilagody – *Canyon Speak*
Anakwad – *The Spirit Sings* (Northstyle, P.O. Box 1360, Minocqua, WI 54548)
Eric Casillas – *Drumming in the Botanica Magia*
Native Flute Ensemble – *Gathering of Shamen*
John Huling – *Desert Plateaus; Canyon Spirit*
Jessita Reyes – *Deer Dancer; Seasons of the Eagle*
Douglas Spotted Eagle – *Sacred Feelings*
Paula Horne – *Heart Songs of Black Hills Woman* (Dakota Sioux)
Elizabeth Wilson – *Nez Perce Stories*
Lean "Sonny" Nevaquaya – *Spirit of the Flute*
Georgia Wettlin-Larsen (Whirling Cloud Woman) – *Songs for the People*
Joanne Shenandoah – *Loving Ways* (Dakota Sioux)
Steve Wall/Harvey Arden – *Wisdomkeepers: Meetings with Native American Spiritual Elders*
Dik Darnell – *Following the Circle; Winter Solstice Ceremony; Voice of the Four Winds* (Etherean Music, 9200 West Cross Drive #510, Littleton, CO 80123)

Australia and New Zealand

Douglas Lilburn – Symphonies nos. 1, 2, and 3; *Aotearoa Overture* (Kiwi CD SLD-90; Continuum 1069) (Records International)
St. Joseph Choir – *Maori Songs* (Kiwi)
Peter Sculthorpe – *Kakadu* (ABC Australia) (Albany Music); *Nourlangie* (Sony)
Barry Conyngham – *Vast* (Albany Music); *Southern Cross Concerto* (Cala)
Carl Vine – *Symphonies* (Albany Music); *Battlers* (Tall Poppies)
Don Kay – *Tasmania Symphony* (Albany Music)
Ross Edwards – *Maninyas-Concerto for Violin and Orchestra*; Piano Concerto
Larry Pruden – *Taranaki* (Kiwi)
Ashley Heenan – *Maori Suite* (Kiwi)
Ron Goodwin – *New Zealand Suite*

MISCELLANEOUS WORLD MUSIC RECORDINGS

Flemish: Lodewijk de Vocht – *Mass in Honor of the Angels; Annual Cycle of Spiritual Songs* (Rene Gailly) (Qualiton)

Cyprus: *Music of the Island of Saint Hilarion* (New Albion Records, 584 Castro #515, San Francisco, CA 94114)

Tibet: David Parsons – *Himalaya* (Fortuna)

Gyuto Monks – *Tibetan Buddhism* (Elektra-Nonesuch); *Freedom Chants from the Roof of the World* (Rykodisc, Pickering Wharf, Building C–3G, Salem, MA 01970)

One Hand Clapping (Tibetan Bells and environmental sounds) (Randall "Rain" Gray, 934 Fifteenth Street, Santa Monica, CA 90403)

Sacred Music, Sacred Dance (Tibetan Buddhist Monks from the Drepung Loseling Monastery) (Music & Arts 736)

Vietnam: *Dreams and Reality* (Playa Sound) (Allegro)

Thai Classical Music: *The Sleeping Angel* (Nimbus)

Bali: *Bali* (Elektra-Nonesuch)

O Bali (Colin McPhee) (CBC, P.O. Box 500, Station A, Toronto, Ontario, M5W 1E6, Canada)

Music of Lou Harrison and Gamelan Orchestra (MusicMasters, 1710 Highway 35, Ocean, NJ 07712); *La Koro Sutro* (New Albion Records, 584 Castro Street, #515, San Francisco, CA 94114)

Gamelan Semarpegulingan (JVC VICG–5024)

Arabian: *Anthology du Malouf* (Auvidis) (Qualiton Imports)

Al Gromer Khan – *Mahogany Nights* (Hearts of Space, P.O. Box 31321, San Francisco, CA 94131)

Turkey: *Sufi Music of Turkey* (CMP Records) (White Swan)

Music of the Whirling Dervishes (Finnadar/Atlantic Recording Corporation)

South Seas: David Fanshawe – *Musical Mariner: Pacific Journey* (Mercury); *Spirit of Polynesia* (Saydisc Records, Chipping Manor, The Chipping, Wotton-U-Edge, Glos, GL12 7Ad, England)

Tahiti: *Festival of Life* (ARC Music US, P.O. Box 11288, Oakland, CA 94611)

Tahitian Choir – *Rapa Iti* (Triloka 7192)

Pacifica: *Tales from the South Seas* (Larrikin) (Allegro Imports)

Cuba: *Homage to Ernesto Lecuona* (Seeco Tropical)

Malta: *Discover Malta* (Camilleri, Pulverenti, and Galea-Laus – Discover 920163)

MAGIC OF THE ORCHESTRA

What is more beautiful than a lovely moment in nature, a deep friendship, or the sounds of a hundred-piece orchestra making music! One of the greatest gifts you can give your children is to acquaint them with the subtle flavors, tones, and essences of the different instruments of the orchestra. As you take time to play for them, either live or recordings, observe what sounds, rhythms, melodies, and harmonies move them the most. You can recognize their needs more clearly, as you learn to sense their particular musical tastes.

Here are some basic selections to help you go through the whole orchestra with your child:

Britten – *Young Person's Guide to the Orchestra* (with narrator) (miscellaneous labels)
Saint-Saëns – *Carnival of the Animals* (Philips – Previn)
The Instruments of the Orchestra (narrated by Sir Adrian Boult) (EMI)
The Instruments of the Orchestra, by David Randolph (PolyGram)
Invitation to Music (narrated by Elie Siegmeister)
John and the Magic Music Man – Child's Guide to the Orchestra, by A. Hopkins

Brass: The brass instruments stimulate the physical body. They are very powerful and arouse feelings of nobility, potency, majesty, and at times can bring thunder and a sense of terror. Too much brass music at once may prove disturbing, especially to a very sensitive child.

Trumpets: Maurice Andre – *Art of Maurice Andre* (EMI and Erato)
Bruckner – Symphony no. 9
Wagner – Overture to *Die Meistersinger*
Torelli – *Complete Works for Trumpet(s) and Orchestra* (Bongiovanni 5523/24/25) (Qualiton)
Australian Trumpet Concertos (Lovelock, Mills) (ABC) (Albany Imports)
Canadian Trumpet Concertos (by Hetu, Forsyth, and Nimmons) (CBC SMCD 5130) (Allegro Imports)
Horns: Jean-Jacques Justafre: French Horn (Pierre Verany PVY 793091)
Mozart – Horn concertos
Britten – Serenade for Tenor, Horn, and Strings
Trombone: Christian Lindberg (various recordings on BIS)

Walker – *Trombone Concerto* (BIS) (Records International)
Mozart – *Requiem (Tuba Mirum)*
Tuba: Mussorgsky – *Bydlo (Ox Wagon)* from *Pictures at an Exhibition*
Berlioz – *Tuba Mirum* (from *Requiem)*
Vaughan Williams – *Tuba Concerto* (RCA)
Sibelius – Symphony no. 2 (finale)
Cornets: Debussy – *La Mer* (Bernstein – Sony)
Saxhorn: Mahler – *Symphony no. 7* (opening) (Haitink – Philips or
Bernstein – Sony)

Percussion: The percussion instruments also stimulate the physical body. These instruments are struck; they add rhythm, color, and sound-power to the orchestral texture. Like the brass, these instruments must be added into the work with good taste and proportion. Note especially the performances of the marvelous Scotland-born female composer and percussionist Evelyn Glennie, specifically *Light in Darkness* (RCA 60557-2-RC), *Rebounds* (RCA 09026-61277-4), and *Rhythm Song* (RCA 60242-2-RC). Note also Brian Slawson's wonderful recording *Bach on Wood* (CBS MK 39704).

Kettledrums: Handel oratorios and Bach cantatas; Gould – Spirituals
   Beethoven – Symphony no. 9
Snare drum: Shostakovich – Symphony no. 5
Tambourine: Tchaikovsky – *Arab Dance* (from *Nutcracker)*
Triangle: Respighi – *Pines of Rome*
Cymbals: Tchaikovsky – Symphony no. 4 (finale)
Gong: Respighi – *Pines of Rome* (Catacombs movement)
   Tchaikovsky – Symphony no. 6 (finale)
   Richard Strauss – *Also Sprach Zarathustra*
   Mussorgsky-Ravel – *Pictures at an Exhibition*
   Rachmaninov – *Symphonic Dances* (finale) (get the Slatkin version on
   Vox 3002 for full effect)
Castanets: Debussy – *Iberia*
Glockenspiel: Vaughan Williams – Symphony no. 8
Xylophone: Saint-Saëns – *Danse Macabre*
Vibraphone: Britten – *Spring Symphony* (opening section); Gould –
   Harvest
Bells: Karl Haas: Story of the Bells (WCLV/Seaway Productions, 26501
   Emery Industrial Parkway, Cleveland, OH 44128)
   Rachmaninov – *The Bells*
   Boiko – *Peter's Chimes* (or *Bells of Peter the Great*) (Svetlanov –
   Russian Disc 11045)

Mahler – Symphony no. 3 (fifth movement); Symphony no. 6 (cowbells); and Symphony no. 2 (finale) (bells, organ, choir, full orchestra)

Bells in Russia (Christophorus) (Qualiton Imports)

Good Friday Troparion (Cascavelle VEL 1023)

Ketélbey – *Bells Across the Meadow*

Pärt – *Cantus* (BIS)

Paganini – *The Convent of Mount Saint Bernard* (Dynamic CDS 27)

Morton Gould – *Declaration Suite*

William Schuman – *Credendum*

Evening Bells (traditional Russian folk song)

Hovhaness – *The Holy City; Island of Mysterious Bells;* Symphony no. 11

Vaughan Williams – *Shepherds of the Delectable Mountains*

Ginastera – *Ollantay* (last movement)

de Falla – *Bells of Dawn* (from *El Amor Brujo*)

Ravel – *Fairy Garden* (from *Mother Goose*)

Debussy – *Engulfed Cathedral* (Cala)

Khachaturian – Symphony no. 2 *(The Bell)*

Leopold Mozart – *Sleigh Bells*

Celestial Bells (Questhaven, 20560 Questhaven Road, Escondido, CA 92029)

Theodorakis – *Canto Olympico*

Westminster Concert Bell Choir (Gothic G–49042) (Koch)

Tubular Bells: Tchaikovsky – *1812 Overture*

Sibelius – Symphony no. 4 (final movement)

Celesta: Bartók – Music for Strings, Percussion, and Celesta

Anvil: Verdi – *Anvil Chorus* (from *Il Trovatore*)

Marimba: Creston – Concertino for Marimba and Orchestra

Hovhaness – *Fantasy on Japanese Woodprints*

Wind machine: Vaughan Williams – Symphony no. 7 *(Antarctica)*

Richard Strauss – *Alpine Symphony*

Woodwinds: The woodwinds maintain the melodic line and bring out the more airy, transparent quality of orchestral sound. Woodwinds will often affect the emotions and feelings, making you feel lighter and clearer.

Flute: Bach – Suite in B Minor

Vivaldi – Flute concertos

Mozart – Concerto for Flute and Harp

Piccolo: Vivaldi – Piccolo concertos

Oboe: Mozart – Concerto for Oboe
  Richard Strauss – Concerto for Oboe
  Randall Thompson – Suite for Oboe, Clarinet, and Viola
  Robert Bloom – *Requiem*
  Alec Wilder – Concerto for Oboe, Strings, and Percussion
English Horn: Sibelius – *Swan of Tuonela*
  Copland – *Quiet City*
Clarinet: Rachmaninov – Symphony no. 2 (slow movement)
  Weber – Clarinet Concerto
  Mozart – Clarinet Concerto
  Finzi – Clarinet Concerto
  Tavener – *The Repentant Thief*
Bass clarinet: Stravinsky – *Petrouchka*
Bassoon: Dukas – *Sorcerer's Apprentice*
  Mozart – Bassoon Concerto
  Vivaldi – Bassoon Concerto
Double bassoon: Ravel – *Piano Concerto for Left Hand* (opening)
Saxophone: Glazunov – Concerto for Saxophone
  Robert Ward – *Saxophone Concerto* (Albany)
  Paul Winter – *Canyon; Callings* (New Music)

Strings: Strings can soothe you, calm your fears, and bring a feeling of harmony and peace. They appeal more to your mind and to your soul, reminding you of continuity and the eternal music of the spheres.

Violin: Beethoven – Violin Concerto
  Mendelssohn – Violin Concerto
  Sibelius – Violin Concerto
  Brahms – Violin Concerto
  Philip Glass – Violin Concerto
  Samuel Barber – Violin Concerto
  Christopher Headington – Violin Concerto
  Howard Blake – Violin Concerto *(The Leeds)*
Cello: Dvořák – Cello Concerto; *Silent Woods*
  Tavener – *The Protecting Veil* (Virgin 59052)
  Nystroem – *Sinfonia concertante* (BIS 682)
  Taneyev – *Suite de Concert* (Koch 3-1135-2)
  Villa-Lobos – *Fantasia Concertante*
  Anton Rubinstein – Cello concertos
  Elgar – Cello Concerto

Dutilleux – *Tout un monde lointain*
Hersant – *Cello Concerto* (Harmonia Mundi France 905216)
Viola: Berlioz – *Harold in Italy*
   Walton – Viola Concerto
   Ahmet Saygun – Viola Concerto
   Bartók – Viola Concerto
Double bass: Mahler – Symphony no. 1 (funeral march)
Harp: Sibelius – *The Bard*
   Bruckner – Symphony no. 8 (third movement)
   William Mathias – Harp Concerto
   Hanson – Concerto for Organ, Strings, and Harp
   Handel – Harp Concerto in F
Guitar: Rodrigo – *Concierto de Aranjuez; Fantasy for a Courtier*
Mandolin: Mahler – Symphony no. 7
   Vivaldi – Mandolin concertos

Organ: Called the king of instruments, the organ brings in great power and, often, a connection with the celestial music of the spheres. Some organ pieces are especially uplifting to the soul; especially majestic are melodic works for organ and orchestra.

J. S. Bach – *Come Sweet Death* (as played by Virgil Fox)
Saint-Saëns – *Symphony no. 3 (Organ)* (Zamkochian/Munch – RCA)
Flor Peters – *Concerto for Organ and Orchestra* (Mottete 40161)
Jongen – *Symphonie Concertante for Organ and Orchestra* (Fox/Prétre
   – EMI)
Fétis – *Fantasy for Organ and Orchestra* (Koch-Schwann)
Poulenc – *Concerto for Organ, Timpani and Strings* (Chandos)
Rheinberger – *Suite for Organ, Violin, Cello and Strings* (Capriccio 10
   337) (available from Allegro)
Marco Enrico Bossi – *Concerto for Organ and Orchestra* (Bongiovanni)
   (available from Qualiton)
Paul Halley – *Nightwatch* (PolyGram) (a beautiful New Age organ
   improvisational composition; melodic and strong)
Tchaikovsky – *Manfred Symphony* (last movement)
Alexandre Guilmant – *Organ Concerto* (Chandos or ABC)
Havergal Brian – *In Memoriam* (organ, 2 harps, and orchestra) (Smith
   – Campion RR2CD 1331/2)

WEDDINGS

Weddings are beautiful, intimate occasions. They are often attended by great Presences and spiritual power. Good friends emanate love and warm wishes for a harmonious and productive marriage. As the ceremony begins, power builds. Beautiful music attunes the participants and sets the tone for the whole service.

Perhaps during the ceremony the couple will want a favorite piece of spiritual music sung or played. Later, a stirring recessional melody fills everyone with a sense of finality and a promise of friendship and unity in the future. The postlude allows all who are attending to come down again into the present, bringing new joy and dedication into their own relationships.

Very often we feel the power of angelic presences who seal the couple in auric union during their vows. It is, therefore, a good idea to play angelic music whenever possible (see Chapter 7). Given the spiritual significance of marriage, it is important for the couple to choose wedding music wisely. Harsh vibrations and all raucous music should be avoided. Pleasing, flowing melodies, especially if played on an organ or by strings or harp, bring majesty and reverence into the ceremony. A harp fills the atmosphere with a lifting transparency of sound, thus often opening doors to higher Presences attending. Strings provide purification and clarity for the feelings and thoughts of the participants.

Here are some suggestions for music at weddings:

Preludes:

Grieg – *Morning* (from *Peer Gynt*); *The Last Spring; I Love Thee*
Rachmaninov – *Love Theme* (Eighteenth Variation – from *Rhapsody on a Theme of Paganini*)
Elgar – *Nimrod Variation* (from *Enigma Variations*)
Mascagni – Intermezzo (from *Cavalleria Rusticana*)
Mozart – *Haffner Serenade*
Massenet – *Meditation* (from *Thais*)
Schubert – *Ave Maria*
Bach-Gounod – *Ave Maria*
Liszt – *Liebestraum*
Wagner – Prelude and *Liebestod* (from *Tristan und Isolde*)
Debussy – *Clair de lune*
Bach – *Sheep May Safely Graze*
Herbert – *Ah, Sweet Mystery of Life*

The Art of Virgil Fox (EMI 5 65426)
Streisand – *Evergreen*

Processionals:

Wagner – *Wedding March* (from *Lohengrin*)
Rodgers and Hammerstein – *Alleluia* (from *The Sound of Music*); *Climb
    Every Mountain* (from *Sound of Music*)
Rheinberger – *Organ Concertos* (E. Power Biggs) (Sony)
Schmidt – *Notre Dame* (Intermezzo)

Miscellaneous Wedding Music:

D'Hardelot – *Because*
Bond – *I Love You Truly*
DeKoven – *O Promise Me*
Cooke – *Love Sends a Little Gift of Roses*
Friml – *L'Amour, Toujours L'Amour*
Lehár – *Yours Is My Heart Alone*
Goss – *Praise My Soul*
Youmans-Heyman – *Through the Years*
Parry – *Bridal March*
Captain and Tennille – *There Is Love*

Specific Recordings:

There Is Love – The Wedding Songs (Scotti Brothers 72392 7562–2)
    (includes Wagner: *Lohengrin (Wedding March)*; Pachelbel: *Canon*;
    Schubert: *Ave Maria*; Debby Boone: *You Light Up My Life*; Buddy
    Holly: *True Love Ways*, etc.)
Bride's Book (Pro Arte CDS 564) (includes Williams: *Evergreen*; Herley-
    Silbar: *Wind Beneath My Wings*; Bernstein: *One Hand, One Heart*;
    Buffy Sainte Marie: *Wedding Song*; Richie: *Endless Love*, etc.)
Wedding Day (Pro Arte 569)
Music for Weddings (Angel CD2 762524–2)
The Wedding Album (RCA 6207 2-RC)
Today's Bride (Pro Arte CD 478)
Wedding Favorites (London Weekend Classics 421–638–2)
I Love You Truly (arranged by Richard Hayman) (contains Grieg's *I
    Love Thee*; *Wedding Day at Troldhaugen*; *Hawaiian Wedding Song*;
    and other selections) (Naxos 8.990019)

Music for Weddings (violin and organ) (Arion ARN 68048) (Allegro)
Everybody's Favorite Wedding Music (Essex Entertainment ESD 7050)

BIRTH

We come from light, and we return into light. The great opposites of life are birth and death, not life and death. Within the last ten years, much research has demonstrated that the veil between this life and the next dimension is very thin. Dr. Raymond Moody, Betty Eadie, Dr. Melvin Morse, Dannion Brinkley, Dr. Elisabeth Kübler-Ross, and many others have talked with thousands of people who clearly have seen across to the other side. Almost every one of these persons reports that many compassionate Presences of Love and Light surround us, prepare us for each new lifetime, and sustain us throughout this earthly existence and into the greater mansions of God's eternity, when our time of passing arrives.

As a mother conceives and begins to grow a fetus inside herself as a home for the soul attracted into incarnation through her, it is very important for her and others to cultivate a beautiful atmosphere for the incoming life. Dr. Thomas Verny, the Canadian physician, in his excellent book *The Secret Life of the Unborn Child,* mentions how impressionable every soul is who waits for his/her new body to form inside the mother. It is crucially important for parents and family to create a beautiful, constructive atmosphere of friendliness, harmony, and welcome. A home environment that is free of conflict and worry, alcohol, drugs, and violence, and is instead clean and lovely, filled with bright colors and paintings (as well as bright thoughts and feelings) will allow light to permeate the household and the consciousness of the householders.

Again, lovely music can help prepare the way for the incoming child, as it heightens the vibrations in the home. The awaiting soul hears, feels, and responds to whatever is played in the environment. Well I remember a man whom I once talked to, who complained that his wife could not sleep because the baby she was carrying was "kicking continuously." I asked the man if he played music in the house. He said, "Oh, sure; all the time." When I asked for a sample of such music, he played the most ghastly, chaotic, bass-filled, hard-drive noise that anyone could imagine: no beauty, no melody, and no harmony—only aggressive and assaultive blasts of ugly noise. I gave him a lovely tape recording of a harp concerto by Handel, and he grunted and left. But a few days later he returned, saying that his wife was enjoying a good night's sleep for the first time in her life, and "the kid wasn't kicking!"

Here are some calming, joyful, welcoming pieces that will help the infant to enter earth's density in joy and warm welcome:

Vivaldi – *The Four Seasons* and miscellaneous concertos (Vivaldi composed more than five hundred concertos) Dr. Verny reports that from his studies, most children respond the most joyfully to Vivaldi's and Mozart's music.

Baroque Trio sonatas (such as those by Telemann, Fasch, Handel, or other Baroque composers)

Saint-Saëns – *The Swan* (from *Carnival of the Animals*)

Humperdinck – *Children's Prayer* (from *Hansel and Gretel*) (attracts the Guardian Angel to her charge)

Massenet – *Meditation* (from *Thais*)

Fauré – *Requiem (In Paradiso)*

Debussy – *Clair de lune*

J. S. Bach – *Brandenburg Concertos; Jesu, Joy of Man's Desiring*

Handel – Largo (from *Xerxes*)

Kuhlau – Flute quintets

Braga – *Angels' Serenade*

Mozart – Piano Concerto no. 21 (second movement); flute concertos; flute quartets

Wagner – *Evening Star* (from *Tannhäuser*)

Gluck – *Dance of the Blessed Spirits*

Grieg – *Holberg Suite*

Dr. Hajime Murooka – *Lullaby from the Womb* (This recording, which many persons have found to be helpful, contains the rhythm of a healthy heartbeat, which plays under the music.)

TRANSITION

That which ages in us is only the abode;
the tenant does not age at all.

CHARLES GOUNOD

The best way we can prepare for our transition out of this life is to settle whatever negative emotions we may feel toward others and to forgive them totally, especially in those situations in which we may have felt anger and resentments. Try to practice instant forgiveness, avoid blaming (self or others), and work toward the greater well-being of the totality. Leonard Bernstein, the composer and conductor, put this idea of the importance of forgiveness into the finale of his noble and powerful musical composition,

The Chichester Psalms: "Behold, how good and how pleasant it is for brethren to dwell together in unity"(Ps. 133:1).

When our time comes, we take leave of our bodies to return into God's greater mansions of light. There is individual continuity: just our cloak (the physical body) is left behind. J. Krishnamurti said that "death is the beginning of something new." Alan Hovhaness is the composer of more than sixty symphonies and such beautiful, spiritually elevating musical masterpieces as *Mysterious Mountain, Avak the Healer, Prayer of Saint Gregory, The Celestial Gate,* and *Magnificat.* Now more than eighty years old, he was asked recently for his thoughts on dying. He answered simply, "I'm still composing, and my health isn't bad. But mainly I don't fear dying because I have so many friends waiting for me on the other side"(*Gramophone,* July, 1994). Very kindly, Hovhaness wrote a letter to me several years ago, sharing these inspiring words: "Handel to me is the greatest of all composers—Sibelius the most sublime of this century . . . I find that you speak the truth about angelic intelligences and divine guidance. I owe my life work to these spirit guides whom I try to follow as a spiritually blind man must be led through life. I am never satisfied with my music."

As we make our transition, we want the kind of musical accompaniment that resonates with the Eternal and clears our entrance into celestial light. Dr. Raymond Moody, a psychiatrist, and many others have thoroughly researched the accounts of thousands of persons who have seen over to the other side, especially those who have experienced NDEs (near-death experiences) and OBEs (out-of-body experiences). From these and other experiences, many persons in our time have lost their fears of death, annihilation, and eternal punishment or damnation.

At a memorial service, it is essential to play music that will sound the vibrations of joyful release, providing a smooth journey over to the other side, where angels, welcoming loved ones, and other messengers of light await us. Let joyful music ring out toward the beautiful, unlimited horizons of God's luminous habitations lovingly prepared for us.

Whatever music you choose for a person's passing, you are wise to select melodies that inspire, lift, and lighten the atmosphere. Your loved one's passing should be a time of great joy, as he/she finds release into larger, more beautiful dimensions of life. Play music that celebrates the loved one's transition as a true graduation and victory. Avoid music that is sorrowful, heavy-laden, or artificially sentimental: the veil between this world and the next is very thin.

At any passing and memorial service, choose music that supports these thoughts written by spiritual teacher Reverend Flower A. Newhouse in her book *Speak The Word:*

Life is endless, deathless, inexhaustible, and eternal. It becomes ever more purposeful, refined, and majestic as our grades are approached and completed. Eventually, the Earth will have nothing more to teach us, so there shall be no necessity for our return.

Realizing all this, we . . . release [name of person] not into death, but into the sublime consciousness of a freer, fuller, and happier life. Our thoughts and prayers shall follow [name of person] wherever he/she journeys, for in God there is no division of existence, and we dwell not in other worlds as much as upon other levels of awareness.

Here are some suggestions of beautiful, uplifting music to play at one's time of earthly transition and at the memorial service:

Dvořák – *Largo* (from *Symphony no. 9*) (conducted by Bernstein on Sony 47547)

Schubert – *Ave Maria* (string version)

R. Strauss – *Death and Transfiguration* (the closing section closely approximates the actual music that the departing soul can hear, sounding its transcendent and welcoming vibrations as this person is leaving the body and crossing over into the Light)
 – *At Parting* (from *Four Last Songs*)
 – Finale from *A Hero's Life*

Humperdinck – *Children's Prayer* (from *Hansel and Gretel*)

Wagner – *Pilgrim's Chorus*

C. Bohm – *Calm As the Night* (organ)

J. S. Bach – *Thou Art with Me; Air on a G String; Jesu, Joy of Man's Desiring*

J. S. Bach-Virgil Fox – *Come Sweet Death* (organ or strings)

Fauré – *Requiem (In Paradise)* (very celestial)

Victor Herbert – *Ah, Sweet Mystery of Life*

Elgar – *Pomp and Circumstance* (very strong)

Schmidt – Intermezzo (from *Notre Dame*)

Rodgers-Hammerstein – *Climb Every Mountain* (from *The Sound of Music*)

Mendelssohn – Selections from *Elijah*

Brahms – *How Lovely Is Thy Dwelling Place* (from *German Requiem*)

Gounod – *Sanctus* (from *Saint Cecilia Mass*)

Grieg – Piano Concerto (second movement)

Barber – Adagio for Strings (played at the memorial services of John F. Kennedy and Princess Grace)

Deep River (a spiritual)

Casals – *Song of the Birds*

Vaughan Williams – *Fantasia on a Theme of Thomas Tallis* (conducted by Ormandy – RCA)

Hanson – Andante tranquilo (from Symphony no. 3); Symphony no. 4

Kobialka – *Going Home* (White Swan Distributors)

Friesen – *Cathedral Pines*

Sibelius – *The Bard;* Symphony no. 7 (a beautiful, cosmic piece of music, used to great effect by Jacob Bronowski in his book and series of videos *The Ascent of Man*)

Mozart – *Ave Verum Corpus (Behold the True Body)*

Handel – Largo (from *Xerxes*)

Tchaikovsky – *Pas de deux (Nutcracker)*

As I write, I remember vividly a very good friend in the hospital, peacefully making his transition as he held his wife's hand and lifted out of his body with a smile of wonder in his eyes as he listened to *How Lovely Is Thy Dwelling Place*, from Brahms's *Requiem*. Like a magic carpet, a particular piece of music can bring us joy, relaxation, and total release, carrying us across into the greater light and love that embraces us from eternity.

> *O you my God, your mercy has left prayer to us as a connection, a blessed connection with you: as a blessing which gives us more than all fulfillment.*
>
> ARNOLD SCHOENBERG

HUMOR IN MUSIC

Sometimes music is simply good for a laugh, allowing a happy, fun-filled opportunity for release. Norman Cousins, in his helpful book *The Anatomy of an Illness*, points out the therapeutic value of genuine laughter, which unties knots in the emotions, the mind, and the body, and opens the whole system to the renewing energies of the universe.

Here is a short list of musical pieces that are filled with good humor and pleasing spirits:

P. D. Q. *Bach (P. D. Q. Bach) – Oedipus Tex; Bestiary; 1712 Overture; Prelude to Einstein on the Fritz; Preachers of Crimetheus; My Bonnie Lass, She Smelleth; Birthday Ode to Big Daddy Bach*

Garrison Keillor – *Lake Wobegon Loyalty Days* (Brunelle – Virgin VC 7 91109-2) (note especially *The Young Lutheran's Guide to the Orchestra*)

Praetorius – *Dances from Terpsichore*
Respighi – *Ancient Dances and Airs; The Birds*
Saint-Saëns – *Carnival of the Animals*
Tony Elman – *Shakin' Down the Acorns* (fiddle tunes on dulcimer)
  (White Swan)
Irish Night at the Pops – (Irish jigs) (Fiedler and Boston Pops – RCA
  60746-2)
D'Anna Fortunato – *Hurrah for Our National Game* (Newport Classics)
Tchaikovsky – *Dance of the Sugar Plum Fairy* (from the *Nutcracker
  Suite*)
Dvořák – *Carnival Overture*
Victor Borge – *Comedy in Music*
Anna Russell – Musical parodies (CBS)
Haydn – *Toy Symphony*
Mozart – *A Musical Joke; Posthorn Serenade*
Arnold – English, Cornish, Scottish, and Irish dances
Richard Strauss – *Till Eulenspiegel's Merry Pranks*
Grainger – *Handel in the Strand and Others*
Gilbert and Sullivan operettas (EMI)
Hoffnung Concerts (EMI)
Pete Seeger – Folk songs
I'm Gonna Wash That Man Right Out of My Hair (from *South Pacific*)
Walt Disney recordings for children, especially *Bambi, Dumbo, Mary
  Poppins, Winnie the Pooh*
Daniel Kobialka – *When You Wish Upon a Star; Rainbows*
Von Stade and Keillor – *Songs of the Cat* (RCA 09026-61161-2)
Britten – *Young Person's Guide to the Orchestra* (Britten – London)
Jackson Berkey – *Arvo the MagnifiCAT* (Soli Deo Gloria)

Learn to laugh more in life and see the good humor and fun in situations, persons, and opportunities. More important, learn to laugh at yourself, for it will bring you freedom and repeated possibilities for defusing negativity that will not only be enjoyable but can prove essential to your health.

> *We all return; it is this certainty that gives meaning to life, and
> it does not make the slightest difference whether or not in a
> later incarnation we remember the former life. What counts is
> not the individual and his/her comfort, but the great aspiration
> to the perfect and the pure which goes on each lifetime.*
>
> GUSTAV MAHLER

CHAPTER 6

The Music of Nature

And this our life, exempt from public haunt,
Finds tongues in trees, books in running brooks,
Sermons in stones, and good in everything.

WILLIAM SHAKESPEARE

I have learned my songs from the music of many birds, from
the music of many waters.

THE KALEVALA

Music and nature are two outstanding pathways leading you into God's expanding light. As you become more reverent and sensitive toward the many wonders of creation, you will feel new openings, moving you more deeply into the Divine Presence. The more you show care and kindness toward animals, trees, the environments of nature, and all living beings, the more you will feel how closely you are attended and nourished by the many higher Presences who look after nature as well as your own well-being. Such is the Gaia awareness.

Increase your attunement to nature by refining these areas:

1. Feel more love and appreciation for all lives surrounding you.
2. Increase study and acquaintance with nature. For example, read articles from *National Geographic*, the works of Edwin Way Teale, Hal Borland, John Muir, Henry Thoreau, Henry Beston, and Joseph Wood Krutch; the nature poetry of Li Po, Tu Fu, Rabindranath Tagore, William Wordsworth, Robert Frost, Robinson Jeffers, and many more. Take leisurely walks into nature; sit quietly in the woods or by streams, reflecting.
3. Listen continuously to great music of nature.
4. Reflect and meditate creatively on the mysteries and presences in nature. Keep a personal journal of your findings.
5. Take the time to get out into nature more; use all your senses and perception to experience its majesty.

Nature offers each of us so many simple joys and pleasures: the fragrances of pine trees; the colors and combined shadings of flowers growing side by side; the songs and cries of birds; the cool, damp vitality of soil held in the hands; the shapes and energy of stones; the rippling rhythms of a stream or lake; the pleasing sounds of an open meadow; eternity in the song of an ocean; the blazing majesty of a sunset. Notice these simple gifts of God; appreciate them more each day in your life. Take full advantage of the joys and gifts of nature, for these will continuously help balance and harmonize you in all the layers of your consciousness.

Certain composers have been especially sensitive to the colorful harmonies sounding through the kingdoms of nature. Often these great tone painters have heard the calls of fire, mountain, sea, and forest presences, and they have been able to describe their impressions in sound. Such composers can often translate these calls into musical themes and melodies.

It is interesting to see how various composers have tried in their own ways to describe the sounds and melodies of the nature kingdoms. For example, listen to Beethoven's *Pastorale* (Symphony no. 6) or Respighi's *Fountains of Rome*. Other composers, such as Sibelius, Grieg, and Hovhaness, in different ways, have tried to bring through angel songs in music and the sympathetic resonance of nature's soundings. Sometimes a great piece of nature music will sound either more elfin or more humanized to our ears (Grieg's Nocturne vs. Vivaldi's *Four Seasons*), while other nature music will sound more awesome and untamed, like roaring thunder in a primeval forest or savage and relentless ocean powers (Sibelius's *Tapiola, The Tempest, Oceanides,* or Symphony no. 4). The music of nature is unending in its variety and contrasts.

Following is a list of nature music and a few suggestive comments about what you might look for as you listen to them. Each area of the world has its own composers who describe musically nature's distinctive nuances. The world of nature is alive and excitingly different everywhere on earth. Remember also the earth's many "chakra points," which empower the planet. Often, such places can be found near great mountains, such as Mount Everest, the Himalayas, Mount Fuji, Mount Cook in New Zealand, the Sierras, Mount Rainier, or Mount McKinley, Alaska.

Use the following selections to tune into nature more deeply.

NORTH AMERICA

The greatest American nature music is fresh and alive, containing a vitality and spirit unlike any other. Beethoven said, "One must go to North America to give free vent to one's ideas." It is this sense of freedom and the vision of a new frontier—in nature and in consciousness—which make much American music unique. The following composers and their musical compositions are suggestive of nature's many moods and wonders:

Edward MacDowell
  Woodland Sketches; Sea Pieces; Fireside Tales; New England Idylls
    (Keene – Protone 2NRPR 2202/3)
  Suite no. 1, Suite no. 2 (Indian) (Hanson – Mercury 75026)
  To a Wild Rose (Ormandy – Columbia M30066)
  Two Piano Concertos (Amato/Freeman – Olympia OLY 353 or Cliburn/
    Hendl – RCA Gold Seal 60420–2)

MacDowell's music is refined, melodic, and impressionistic, suggesting to me various pastoral scenes and the gentle movements of the four elements.

Frederick Delius
  *Florida Suite; On Hearing the First Cuckoo in Spring; Summer
    Evening; Over the Hills and Far Away; Summer Night on the River;
    A Song Before Sunrise* (Beecham – EMI Angel CDCB 47509 or
    Boughton – Nimbus NI 5208 or Barbirolli – EMI ZDMB 565119)
  Appalachia (Barbirolli – Angel S-36756 or Hopkins – Marco Polo
    8.220452)
  Song of the High Hills; On the Heights (Beecham – Angel CDM
    64054)
  In a Summer Garden (Handley – Classics for Pleasure CDCFP 4568)

Delius, although born in England, lived in America and synthesized five major streams of influence: German, Scandinavian, French, English, and American. The *Florida Suite* (1887) suggests early American scenes in Florida at night among the intoxicating fragrance of orange groves, where Delius stayed for a time tending his father's property. I really like the atmospheric combination of the sounds of nature at night and orchestral strains of spirituals, moving on the waters.

Appalachia (1896) also suggests movements in nature, combining with the longings and feelings of a trek with sorrows. Again here, the choral sounds of old spirituals move across the distant horizon. Try to hear Sir John Barbirolli's rendition on EMI (CMS 565119).

Roy Harris
  Symphony no. 3 (Bernstein – DGG 419780)
  Symphony no. 4 (Folksong Symphony) (Golschmann – Vanguard
    Classics OVC 4076)

Symphony no. 5 (Whitney – Albany AR 012-2)
Symphony no. 6 (Gettysburg) (Clark – Albany Troy 064)
Symphonies nos. 1, 7 (Koussevitsky and Ormandy – Columbia MS-5095 or Mester – Albany AR 012-2)

To me the music of Roy Harris suggests the fields, prairies, and the relentless sun, storms, and open beauty of the Midwestern plains. I feel so often in this music the essential American spirit of freedom, the glory of harvest and labor, the sinewy, muscular quality in people, the call of the frontier and pioneers (much like the voice and writings of the legendary American poet, novelist, and historian Carl Sandburg) sounding through the reaping of stalks of corn and amber waves of grain.

Harris uses the brass in his works to great advantage, suggesting the blazing rays of bright sun starkly shining on soil and the sounds of cavalry bugles and horns reaching across the open plains. I find Harris's music unique for its spirit, its activating rhythms, and its strength in movement. It is powerful and therapeutic, startling, and boldly activating.

Howard Hanson
Symphonies nos. 1 (Nordic), 2 (Romantic), 3, 4 (Requiem), 5 (Sacred Symphony), 6, and 7 (A Sea Symphony) (Schwarz – Delos 4-DE-3150)
Symphony no. 2 (Romantic) (Hanson – Mercury 432008)
The Mystic Trumpeter (Schwarz – Delos DE 3160)

Maestro Gerard Schwarz and the Seattle Symphony have championed the beautiful, melodic works of Howard Hanson. Their series of Hanson recordings (Delos 4-De 3150) is a must for music lovers. Hanson's music is melodic and powerful, suggesting both the ancient bards and forests of Scandinavia and the woodlands of North America. Note the very beautiful slow movement of Symphony no. 2, which takes us deep into forests and woods, only to emerge into the clearing, revealing a panoramic view, perhaps, of ocean and mountain peaks.

Charles Ives
The Pond (Schuller – Columbia MS-7318)
Symphony no. 2 (especially slow movement) (Bernstein – Sony SMK 47568)
Symphony no. 3 (Hanson – Mercury 432755-2)
Symphony no. 4 (Stokowski – Sony Portrait MPK 46726) (coupled with *Robert Browning Overture*)
Three Places in New England (Thomas – DGG 423243)

The Unanswered Question (Bernstein – Sony SMK 46701)
From Steeples and Mountains (Hyperion CDA 66517)
The Universe Symphony (Samuel – Centaur 2205)

Ives's music is a fascinating combination of rugged good humor, criss-crossing tunes, complex rhythms, and a defiant Yankee temperament that is everything from feisty and brittle to warm and romantic. The pieces suggested above bring out Ives's sensitivity to nature during his long life in New England. His music is many-faceted, not always pleasant, but compelling. It suggests the shifting, winsome ambience of New England nature scenes.

The genius of Ives's works, I believe, is his ability to picture musically the great polarities of life and the human condition—the cold and warm, the heat and snow—mingled together in such scenes as the festive celebrations of villagers; old-time bands approaching, passing by, and leaving the silent desolation surrounding the fallen gravestones in forgotten cemeteries; and the waiting, watching eyes of hidden ponds, echoing with loons in the night. Enter into Ives's music with openness, imagination, and the ability to grieve and laugh at everything, even yourself. His music may not be pleasingly therapeutic or calming at all times, but deep feelings come through Ives's music.

Samuel Barber
Symphony no. 1 (Zinman – Argo 436288-2)
Music for a Scene from Shelley; Essay no. 2 for Orchestra; Serenade for String Orchestra (Golschmann – Vanguard OVC 4016)
Adagio for Strings (Munch – RCA Gold Seal 09026-61424 or Bernstein – DGG 431048-2)
Violin Concerto (Salerno-Sonnenberg/Shostakovich – EMI CDC 54314-2)
Fadograph of a Yestern Scene (Schenck – Koch 3-7010-2)

For me, much of Barber's music has freshly lyrical, powerful qualities, often evoking varied moods of wild, beautiful, peace-filled or windswept landscapes. Many of his compelling works are inspired by poetry and other literature of nature and the human condition.

Alan Hovhaness
Mysterious Mountain (Reiner – RCA 5733-2)
Mountains and Rivers without End (Hovhaness – Crystal CD 804)
Symphony no. 46 (To the Green Mountains) (Jordania – Koch 3-7208-2H1)
And God Created Great Whales (Amos – Crystal CD 810)

Avak the Healer (Nixon/Stevens – Crystal CD 806)
Mount St. Helens (Symphony no. 50); Angel of Light (from *Symphony no. 22*) (Schwarz – Delos DE 3137)
Return and Rebuild the Desolate Places (Clark – Koch 3-7221)

The music of Hovhaness is a uniquely beautiful synthesis of East and West. I love the strong Oriental quality in much of his work, as well as the strong flavor of Armenian liturgical music and his uniquely American hymn-filled lyricism and spirituality. In their own descriptive ways, Hovhaness's musical compositions reveal private worlds of spiritual mysticism, often describing nature's crystalline grottos, moonlit gardens, and spacious heights. The vision of universal brotherhood also permeates many of his works, especially *Symphony no. 11 (All Men Are Brothers)* (Crystal CD 801) and *Symphony no. 6 (The Celestial Gate)* (Crystal CD 807).

Lou Harrison
Seven Pastorales (Davies – MusicMasters 01612-67089-2)   .
Elegiac Symphony (Davies – MusicMasters 7021-2-C)
May Rain (harp) (Tanenbaum – New Albion NAO 55CD)
Double Concerto for Violin & Cello with Javanese Gamelan (Music & Arts CD 635)

Lou Harrison is a San Francisco-based composer who writes beautiful, accessible music. Like Hovhaness, Harrison offers a unique, melodic synthesis of East and West. Some of his music incorporates the exotic sounds of the gamelan orchestra into more Western-sounding instrumental ensembles. I especially like Harrison's spiritual philosophy that emphasizes cherishing, nurturing (conserving), and consideration (respect), all of which lead to increased creativity.

Rodgers and Hammerstein
The Sound of Music (RCA PCD1-2005)

The *Prologue, Climb Every Mountain,* and *Edelweiss* sections of this soundtrack contain very beautiful and powerful nature music. In these uplifting melodies the composer has captured the sounds of mountain devas and nature presences calling to each other. Each peak echoes its own tones, sending strong beams of light and healing energies into the receptive consciousness of the listener.

Ferde Grofé
The Grand Canyon Suite (Bernstein – Sony SMK 47544 or Kunzel – Telarc CD 80086 or Maazel – Sony SK 52491)

Charles T. Griffes
Poem for Flute and Orchestra; The White Peacock (Schwarz – Delos DE 3099)
George Chadwick
Symphony no. 3 (Järvi – Chandos 9253)
Walter Piston
Three New England Sketches (Schwarz – Delos DE 3106)

Maestro Schwarz and the Seattle Symphony have done some beautiful Piston recordings, as also have Maestro Leonard Slatkin and the Saint Louis Symphony.

Otto Luening
Wisconsin Suite (not yet recorded)
Kentucky Rondo (Smith – Louisville LCD 006)
Richard Adler
Wilderness Suite (Ketcham – RCA RCD1-5805)
Elie Siegmeister
Prairie Morning (from *Western Suite*) (Foss – Vox Allegretto ACD 8155)
John Alden Carpenter
Sea Drift (Hegyi – New World 321-2)
Wayne Barlow
The Winter's Past (Lucarelli/Barrett – Koch 37187)
John Knowles Paine
Symphony no. 2 (Im Frühling) (Mehta – New World NW 350-2)
David Diamond
Symphonies nos. 2, 4 (Schwarz – Delos 3093)
Virgil Thomson
The River; Plow that Broke the Plains (Stokowski – Vanguard OVC 8013)
Sea Piece with Birds (Ormandy – CR1-398)
Autumn (Marriner – Angel CDM 64306)
Randall Thompson
Symphony no. 2 (Schenck – Koch 3-7074-2 or Bernstein on Sony) (note the exquisite slow movement)
Aaron Copland
Appalachian Spring; The Tender Land (Copland – RCA Gold Seal 6802-2)
An Outdoor Overture (Abravanel – Vanguard OVC4037)
Tobias Picker
Old and Lost Rivers (Eschenbach – Virgin 59007)

John Duffy
  Symphony no. 1 (Utah) (Macal – Koss KC-1022)
John LaMontaine
  Wilderness Journal (based upon journals of Henry David Thoreau)
    (Dorati – Fredonia Discs, 3947 Fredonia Drive, Hollywood, CA 90063)
  Birds of Paradise (Fredonia)
Richard Nanes
  Nocturnes of the Celestial Seas (Delfon, 305 Third Avenue West,
    Newark, NJ 07107)
Edward MacDowell
  Suite for Large Orchestra (Hanson – Mercury 434-337)
Victor Herbert
  Sunset (Bernardi – CBC SMCD5050-2)
  Ah! Sweet Mystery of Life and *Moonbeams* (Sills/Kostelanetz – Angel
    CDC-7 47197-2)
  Hero and Leander (Maazel – Sony SK 52491)
Philip Glass
  Itaipu (Shaw – Sony SK 46352)
Paul Lloyd Warner
  Waterfalls (MPI – Music Poetry Images 104)
Eugene Friesen
  Cathedral Pines (for cello and pipe organ) (from the album *New
    Friend*) (Halley/Friesen – Living Music LD-0007)
Paul Winter
  Missa Gaia (contains the beautiful hymn by Kim Oler, *Blue Green
    Hills of Earth*); *Whales Alive* (Living Music/Windham Hill)
Thomas Canning
  Fantasy on Hymn of Justin Morgan (Stokowski-Everest 9004)
R. Carlos Nakai
  Canyon Trilogy (Canyon CR-610).

Nakai's *Canyon Trilogy* contains beautiful songs for flute that help to attune the listener to the nature kingdoms. Tony Shearer, part Lakota, writes these words in his wonderful book *The Praying Flute: Song of the Earth Mother:*

> Your flute is a gift from the Great One. It is ancient and sacred. Its voice is very wonderful, its spirit is very pure. . . . Your flute is not a playing flute—it is a praying flute. . . . When you pray with your flute, you're calling the Earth Mother's guardians. . . . In other words, you are talking to the trees and rivers, the flowers and the seeds of the unborn. . . . Flowers and trees do not speak, but they have hearts and spirits just like you and just like me. They can feel your love, hear your heart's message.

J. Reuben Silverbird
The World in Our Eyes (Celestial Harmonies 14040-2)

This powerful creation epic is expressed with Native American poetry, music, and nature sounds.

Wolf
Many Thundering Horses (from Beyond Words) (Kokopelli Flutes, Box 20125, Jackson, WY)

This a remarkably evocative piece of music, a miniature tone poem, which incorporates into the score flute, thunderstorm, kettledrums, and horses' hooves.

Tokeya Inajin (Kevin Locke)
Dream Catcher and *Keepers of the Dream*

These authentic flute music and chants of the Lakota (Sioux) are accompanied by winds, water, thunder, wolf calls, birds, and other sounds.

R. Murray Schafer (Canada)
The Darkly Splendid Earth (Israelievitch/Herbig – CBC SMCD 5114)
Dream Rainbow, Dream Thunder (Pauk – CBC SMCD 5101)
Jean Coulthard (Canada)
The Bird of Dawning Singeth All Night Long (Bernardi – CBC SMCD 5050-2)
Classical Loon (lovely classical music with haunting loon calls in the background) (NorthWord Press, P.O. Box 1360, Minocqua, WI 54548)
Dean Evenson
Peaceful Pond (Soundings of the Planet – SP-7122)
Ocean Dreams (7140); *Desert Moon Song* (7144)
Imant Raminsh (Canada-Latvian)
The Great Sea (Washburn – CBC SMCD 5116)
Carlos Chávez (Mexico)
Symphony no. 2 (Sinfonia India) (Mata – Vox Box 2-CDX 5061)

ENGLAND, SCOTLAND, AND WALES

Music, being identical with heaven, isn't a thing of momentary thrills, or even hourly ones. It's a condition of eternity.

GUSTAV HOLST

There is nothing quite so enchanting and appealing as an English pastoral scene—so serene, clear, and alive with guardian beings. Many English composers were particularly attuned to nature and were able to bring through musically the whisperings of woodland presences and the powerful energies moving among fields, trees, mountains, and sea. Many of the actual landscapes that inspired these composers are described visually and poetically in the wonderful book, *Musical Landscapes,* by John Burke (Webb & Bower, Exeter, England). Here are just a few musical selections that are filled with the presences of nature in the British Isles:

Ralph Vaughan Williams
   Lark Ascending (Bean/Boult – Angel CDM 64022)
   Norfolk Rhapsody no. 1 (Boult – Angel CDM 64022)
   In the Fen Country (Pople – ASV DCA 779)
   Symphony no. 1 (A Sea Symphony) (Lott/Summers/Haitink – Angel CDC 49911)
   Symphony no. 3 (Pastoral) (Harper/Previn – RCA Gold Seal 60583-2 or Price/Boult – Angel CDM 64018)
   Symphony no. 5 (Barbirolli – EMI CDM 5 65110 or Boult – Angel CDM 64018)
   Symphony no. 7 (Sinfonia Antarctica) (Boult – Angel CDM 64020) (Note: an interesting contrast to this theme in music comes with the Australian composer Nigel Westlake's stirring soundtrack *Antarctica,* on the Tall Poppies label, available through Albany Records.)
   Flos campi (Flower of the Field) (Riddle/Del Mar – Chandos 6545)

The music of Ralph Vaughan Williams always represents a strong emotional-spiritual experience, processed and polished through the mind into a refined and complete art form. I love nearly everything this great genius composed. I feel in this composer's music a natural affinity with nature that has been integrated and synthesized by a wise, urbane consciousness, bringing, as the result, a shining, though seemingly effortless, art form. I have always felt stirred and uplifted by Vaughan Williams' music, especially the nature pieces. His Libran balance produces a charging power and a transcendence in his music. There is a vision and grandeur to his compositions, which sweep the listener along and portray nobility through faith's upward reach of the heart.

George Butterworth
   Two English Idylls, The Banks of Green Willow, A Shropshire Lad (Boughton – Nimbus NI 5068 or Llewellyn – Argo 4364012)

Butterworth (1885–1916) is a poet of nature who composed just a few pieces of music before his death. He was killed in World War I at a tragically young age. His nature scenes for me are beautiful and at times sad, suggesting a yearning toward immortality in the midst of earthly feelings of solitude amid trees, streams, and woods. The listener is alone in nature, but always accompanied by haunting, invisible presences that breathe all around him or her. An idyllic, faerie-filled atmosphere pervades Butterworth's music.

Gerald Finzi
  A Severn Rhapsody; Nocturne; The Fall of the Leaf (Boult – Lyrita)
  Cello Concerto (Wallfisch/Handley – Chandos CHAN 8471)
  Clarinet Concerto (Stolzman/Guildhall – RCA 60437)

Finzi's music is removed and solitary but also paints beautiful, more austere nature scenes. It suggests the yearning for transition and the future joy of immortality, mixing with the sorrows of earthly transience.

Sir Arnold Bax
  The Garden of Fand; The Tale the Pine Trees Knew; The Happy Forest; In the Faery Hills; Into the Twilight; November Woods; Summer Music; Roscatha; Tintagel (Thomson – Chandos 8367; 6538; 8307)
  Spring Fire (Handley – Chandos 8464)
  Winter Legends (Fingerhut/Thomson – Chandos 8484)
  The Seven Symphonies (Thomson – Chandos)

The music of Sir Arnold Bax will take you into the untamed reaches of nature. Scenes of craggy coasts, storms in the forests, and wild cries of nature beings will open up to you. Listen to Bax at night, and you may well wish to have someone in the room with you, for his tone poems are often awesome. Bax's music can reveal the dark side of nature, with its storms, eruptions, and chaos.

Sir Granville Bantock
  Hebridean Symphony (Leaper – Marco Polo 8.223274)
  A Pagan Symphony (Handley – Hyperion CDA 66630)
  Celtic Symphony; The Sea Reivers (Handley – Hyperion CDA 66450) (mysterious and beautiful music)
Ernest Moeran
  Symphony (Dilkes – EMI/HMV-CSD 3705 or Handley – Chandos 8577)
  Lonely Waters (Handley – Chandos 8807)
  In the Mountain Country (Handley – Chandos 8639)

Benjamin Britten
  Four Sea Interludes (from *Peter Grimes*) (Giulini – Angel S-36215 or
    Boughton – Nimbus NI 5295)
John Ireland (an epic miniaturist)
  Concertino Pastorale (Hurst – Chandos 8375)
  Legend for Piano and Orchestra; Mai-Dun (Parkin/Thomson –
    Chandos 8461)
  The Forgotten Rite (Hickox – Chandos 8994)
Sir Edward Elgar
  Sea Pictures (Baker/Barbirolli – EMI CDC47329)
  Soliloquy for Oboe and Orchestra (Del Mar – Chandos Collect Chan
    6544)
Kenneth Leighton
  Veris gratia (Wallfisch/Handley – Chandos 8471); Concertino (BBC)
Augusta Holmes (English-Irish female composer)
  Irlande (Ireland); Night and Love (Friedmann and Davin – Marco Polo
    8.223449)
Thea Musgrave (Scotland)
  Song of the Enchanter (Comissiona – Ondine ODE 767-2)
Grace Williams (Wales)
  The Dancers (choral suite) (Hickox – Chandos CHAN ABR 1116)
Percy Grainger
  Hill-Songs; Beautiful Fresh Flower (Simon – Koch 3-7003-2)
Sir Hamilton Harty
  With the Wild Geese (Thomson – Chandos 8321)
  The Children of Lir (Harper/Thomson – Chandos 8387)
Frank Bridge
  The Sea (Handley – Chandos 8473)
  Norse Legend (Williams – Pearl PEA 9600)
  Enter Spring (Pearl 9601)
Philip Sainton
  The Island (Bamert – Chandos 9181)
  Moby Dick (soundtrack) (RCA – out of print)
Alan Bush
  Variations, Nocturne and Finale on an Old English Sea-Song (Snashall
    – PRT 8372)
Herbert Howells
  Elegy; Serenade for Strings (Hickox – Chandos 9161)
Sir Michael Tippett
  Fantasia on a Theme of Corelli (Andante) (Tippett – EMI 2-ZDMB-
    63522)

Sir Arthur Bliss
  Miracle in the Gorbals (Groves – EMI ASD 3342)
  Pastoral (Hickox – Chandos 8886)
  The World Is Charged with the Grandeur of God (Bliss – Lyrita SRCD
    225)
  Meditations on a Theme of John Blow (Wordsworth – Argo 443-170)
Gustav Holst
  A Somerset Rhapsody; Egdon Heath (Boult – London 425152-2)
  A Song of the Night; A Winter Idyll (Atherton – Lyrita SRCD 209)
William Alwyn
  Lyra Angelica (Angel Songs); Autumn Legend; Pastoral Fantasia
    (Hickox – Chandos CHAN 9065)
  Naiades (Nimbus or Chandos 9152)
Patrick Hadley
  The Trees So High (Bamert – Chandos 9181)
  The Hills (EMI – Odeon SAN393)
Edmund Rubbra
  Soliloquy for Cello and Orchestra (Handley – Lyrita SRCD 234)
  Viola Concerto (Little/Golani/Handley – Conifer 225)
Hamish Maccunn
  Land of the Mountain and the Flood (Gibson – Chandos 8379)
Sir John McEwen
  Border Ballads (Mitchell – Chandos CHN 9241)
Howard Blake
  Violin Concerto (The Leeds) (Edinger/Daniel – ASV 905)
William Mathias
  Symphony no. 2 (Summer Music) (Mathias – Nimbus NI 5260)
  The Enchanted Isles (Carol Thompson, harp – Dorian 90120)

FRANCE

French nature music is marked by two chief qualities—light, transparent
textures and drama. As a general rule, French music is not as thickly
orchestrated as English. Sometimes it is filled with spicy, playful sounds.
  Here are some of the more outstanding pieces of French music of nature:

Achille-Claude Debussy
  La Mer (Ansermet – London 421171-2 or Munch – RCA Red Seal
    09026)
  *Nocturnes; Prelude to the Afternoon of a Faun; Sacred and Profane
    Dances; Images* (Boulez – Odyssey 2-MB2K 45620)

*The Engulfed Cathedral; Clair de lune; Two Arabesques; The Island of
Joy* (Simon – Cala CACD 1001-2)
En bateau (Galway/Measham – RCA RCD1-4810)
Reverie (Ormandy – CBS MFK 45543)
Debussy by the Sea (Special Music Company 4961)

Debussy's music is green and aquamarine, mysteriously echoing another
world of nymphs and naiads, water devas, and sirens of the deep. Haunting
sounds of worlds underwater, such as the lost kingdom of Atlantis, are
strongly present in *The Engulfed Cathedral* (orchestrated beautifully by
Leopold Stokowski), which rises from the deep, only to disappear into total
submersion.

César Franck
Panis angelicus (Stokowski – Biddulph WHL 011)
The Aeolids (Breezes) (Van Otterloo – IMP X 9037)

Franck's music is filled with the presences of nature beings and angels.
According to Cyril Scott in his book *Music: Its Secret Influence Through
the Ages*, Franck's music forms a bridge between humans and devas and
angels.

Vincent d'Indy
Symphony on a French Mountain Air (Casadesus/Ormandy – Sony
Portrait or Collard/Janowski – Erato 2292 or Dutoit – London 430
278-2)
The Enchanted Forest (Dervaux – EMI CDM 7 63953)
Summer Morning on the Mountain (Dervaux – EMI CDM 7 64364)
Poem of the Shores; Mediterranean Diptych (Prétre – EMI CDM 7
63954)
Symphony no. 2 (Plasson – EMI CDM 7 63952)
Joseph Canteloube
Songs of the Auvergne (Davrath – Vanguard 8001-2 or Te Kanawa –
London 410004)
Shepherd Song (Bailero) (for cello and orchestra) (Julian Lloyd
Webber/Gerhardt – RCA Gold Seal 60695)
Hector Berlioz
Fantastic Symphony, third movement: *Scenes in the Country*
(Bernstein – EMI CDM 64630)
Francis Poulenc
Rustic Concerto (Concerto champetre) for Harpsichord and Orchestra

(Houbart/Soustrot – Pierre Verany PV 791001 or Va de Wiele/Prétre
– EMI CZS 7 62690-2)

Charles Koechlin
  Ballad for Piano and Orchestra (Rigutto/Myrat – EMI CDM 64369)
  The Jungle Book (Segerstam – Marco Polo 8.223484)
  The Persian Hours (Segerstam – Marco Polo 8.223504)

Maurice Ravel
  Daphnis and Chloe (Munch – RCA Gold Seal 60469)
  A Ship on the Ocean (Skrowaczewski – Vox Box 2CDX 5032)
  The Fairy Garden (from *Mother Goose*) (Martinon – Angel Studio
  CDM 69567)

Paul Gilson
  The Sea (inspired Debussy's *La Mer*) (Rickenbacher – Discover 920126)

Darius Milhaud
  Suite Provençale (Munch – RCA Gold Seal 09026-60685)

Ernest Chausson
  Poem of Love and the Sea (de los Angeles/Jacquillat – EMI 07777
  64365)
  Symphony in B-flat (Munch – RCA Gold Seal 09026-60683)

Emmanuel Chabrier
  Pastoral Suite (Ansermet – London 433720 or Tortelier – Chandos
  CHAN 8852)
  La Sulamite (Hendricks/Plasson – EMI 7 54004)

Albert Roussel
  Poem of the Forest (Symphony no. 1); A Flemish Rhapsody (Segerstam
  – Cybelia CY 801)

Charles Tournemire
  Symphonies (Bartholomee – Adda 581302-3 and Almeida – Marco
  Polo 8.223476 and 8.223478)

Olivier Messiaen
  From the Canyons to the Stars; Exotic Birds (Salonen – CBS 2-M2K
  44762)
  Turangalila Symphony (Chung – DGG 431781)

Lili Boulanger
  Nocturne (Galway/Measham – RCA RCD1-4810)
  Nocturne (from *Three Pieces for Violin/Piano*) (EMI CDM 764281-2)

Felicien David
  The Desert (Guida – Capriccio 10 379)

Henri Rabaud
  Eclogue (Dervaux – EMI CDM 7 63951-2 and Segerstam – Marco Polo
  223503)

CENTRAL AND SOUTH AMERICA AND SPAIN

Among the many South American composers and their striking compositions, I find that the following can take the listener into nature's realms:

Heitor Villa-Lobos (Brazil)
  Forest of the Amazon (United Artists UAS 8007) (record only)
  Bachianas Brasileiras 1–9 (Villa-Lobos – Angel 6CDZF 67229)
  Choros no. 6 (Villa-Lobos – Varèse Sarabande VCD 47257)
  Choros no. 8, 9 (Schernerhorn – Marco Polo 8.220322)
  Choros no. 10 (Mata – Dorian DIS 80101)
  Choros no. 12 (Bartholomee – Ricercar 007010)
  The Discovery of Brazil (Duarte – Marco Polo 8.223551)
  Genesis; Amazonas; Dawn in a Tropical Forest; Origin of the Amazon River (Duarte – Marco Polo 8.223357)
  Symphonic Dances; Rudepoema; African Dances (Duarte – Marco Polo 8.223552)
  The Piano Concertos (Ortiz/Gomez-Martinez – London 430 628-2)
  Fantasia for Cello and Orchestra; Choros no. 8; Uirapuru (Starker/de Carvalho – Delos DE 1017)

The powerful, exotic, and haunting music of this erratic genius is experiencing a strong revival. Villa-Lobos's music is unlike any other—folkish, yet serious, at times intensely dramatic, always melodic, spontaneous, highly rhythmical, and compelling. His nature music recalls lost waterfalls within the wild, exotic jungles of South America and contains haunting melodies of love and battle. The music is always exciting, often strange, sometimes profound.

Manuel de Falla (Spain)
  Nights in the Gardens of Spain (Rubinstein/Jorda – RCA Gold Seal 60046-2)
Ricardo Castillo
  Xibalbá (Almeida – Marco Polo 8.223710)
Alberto Ginastera (Argentina)
  Symphony no. 3 (Pampeana: Pastoral Symphony) (Whitney – Spanish Philips 510 658-2)
  The Dawn (from *Panambi*) (Borejko – Largo 5122)
Joaquin Rodrigo (Spain)
  Aranjuez Concerto; Pastoral Concerto; Music for a Garden; Summer Concerto; For the Flower of the Blue Lily; Distant Sarabande (Bátiz – EMI(4) 7 67435-2)

E. Salvador Bacarisse (Spain)
  Guitar Concerto, slow movement (Yepez/Fruhbeck de Burgos – DGG
  435845-2)

GERMANY AND AUSTRIA

Many composers have left us beautiful music that was inspired by Rhineland scenes of nature. The German-Austrian tradition usually offers music that is thickly orchestrated, often memorably melodic. The following composers have brought through music which strongly suggests nature's harmonies:

Ludwig van Beethoven
  Symphony no. 6 (Pastorale) (Klemperer – EMI CDM 63358-2 or
  Giulini – Sony SK53974)
Felix Mendelssohn
  A Midsummer Night's Dream (Flor – RCA 7764-2-RC)
  Symphony no. 3 (Scotch) (Munch – RCA Silver Seal 60483-2)
  Hebrides Overture; Calm Sea, Prosperous Voyage Overture (A.
  Springer – Vox Allegretto ACD 8145)
Robert Schumann
  Symphony no. 1 (Spring) (Munch – RCA Silver Seal 60488-2)
Johannes Brahms
  Symphony nos. 2, 3 (Karajan – DGG 429153)
Joachim Raff
  Symphony no. 3 (Im Walde) (D'Avalos – ASV CD DCA 793)
  Symphony no. 9 (In Summer) (Schneider – Marco Polo 8.223362)
  Symphony no. 11 (The Winter) (Venzago – Tudor 787)
Gustav Mahler
  Symphony nos. 3, 4, 6, 7 (miscellaneous labels)
Anton Bruckner
  Symphony no. 4 (Romantic) (Ormandy – Sony SBK 47653)
Richard Strauss
  An Alpine Symphony (Previn – Telarc CD 80211 or Karajan – DGG
  439017)
  From Italy (Aus italien) (Kempe – EMI3-CDZC 64350)
Richard Wagner
  Forest Murmurs (Stokowski – London 421020)
  Dawn; Siegfried's Rhine Journey; The Ride of the Valkyries (Stokowski
  – London 421020 or Ormandy – Odyssey MBK 38914)

SCANDINAVIA

Equally compelling in its own way is the pictorial music of nature by Scandinavian composers. Much of their music recalls the ancient bards and mythology. We are often taken back into solitary, primeval forests to hear the roar of Pan and the cries of nature spirits; melodies descend from mountain peaks and echo from icy streams and rivers.

Among the most striking examples of nature music from Scandinavia are these pieces:

Jean Sibelius (Finland)
The Bard; Once Upon a Time (listen to the beautiful vocalise, reminding the listener of deva music) (Järvi – BIS CD384)
Oceanides (Gibson – Chandos Collect 6538)
En Saga (Beecham – Koch Legacy 3-7061-2)
Swan of Tuonela (Ormandy – Odyssey MBK 39785)
Karelia Overture (Järvi – BIS CD222)
Tapiola (Karajan – EMI CDM 64331)
The Seven Symphonies (miscellaneous labels) (deva music of power; listen especially to Symphonies nos. 1, 4, and 6)
Edvard Grieg (Norway)
Olav Trygvason and Landsighting (Dreier – Unicorn-Kanchana UKCD 2056) (Grieg's strongest nature music)
Lyric Suite (Dreier – Unicorn UKCD 2005)
Piano Concerto (Andsnes/Kitaenko – Virgin 59613 or Bishop-Kovacevich/Davis – Philips 412923)
Peer Gynt (Beecham – EMI CDM 64751)
Holberg Suite (Karajan – DGG 419474)
Miscellaneous songs and piano music. (If possible, try to get recordings of Kirsten Flagstad singing this music. Her whole voice and being come from nature.)

Grieg gives us very beautiful, nurturing music of the nature beings. Grieg never composed an ugly note. It is music that is less powerful and often more melodic than Sibelius's compositions.

Ole Bull
The Herd Girl's Sunday; Visit to a Summer Farm; In Lonely Hours (Anderson – NCC – Norwegian Cultural Council – 50008-2)
Hugo Alfvén (Sweden)
A Legend of the Skerries (magnificent!) and *Symphony no. 4, From The Outermost Skerries*) (Järvi – BIS CD 505)

Kurt Atterberg (Sweden)
  Pastoral Suite no. 8 (Swedish Society SCD 1021)
  Symphony no. 6 (Hirokami – BIS CD 553)
  Suite no. 3 (Lysy – Claves CD 8507)
  Symphony no. 3 (*West Coast Pictures*) (Ehrling – Caprice 21364)
Tor Aulin (Sweden)
  Violin Concerto no. 3 (Bergqvist/Kamu – Musica Sveciae MSCD 622)
  Stormy Day (Klas – Musica Sveciae – MSCD 618)
Carl Nielsen (Denmark)
  *The Dream of Gunnar; Saga Drom; Pan and Syrinx; Rhapsodie
    Overture* (Rozhdestvensky – Chandos 9287)
  The Six Symphonies (various labels), especially no. 3 (*Expansiva*,
    conducted by Bernstein – Sony 47598 or Chung – BIS CD 321) and
    no. 4 (*Inextinguishable*, conducted by Blomstedt – London 421524)
Rued Langgaard (Denmark)
  Symphonies nos. 4, 5, 6 (Järvi – Chandos CHAN 9064)
  Symphony no. 15 (Sea Storm) (Stupel – Danacord 409)
Lars-Erik Larsson (Sweden)
  Pastoral Suite (Westerberg – Swedish Society SCD 1020)
  Symphonies nos. 1, 2 (Frank – BIS CD 426)
Christian Sinding (Norway)
  Piano Concerto and Symphony no. 1 (Knardahl/Fjeldstad – NCC
    50016-2)
Gösta Nystroem (Sweden)
  Arctic Ocean (Eros – Caprice CAP 21332 or Järvi – BIS 682)
  Symphony of the Sea (Soderstrom/Westerberg – Swedish Society SCD
    1015)
Oskar Lindberg (Sweden)
  Symphony in F Major; Three Impressions of Travel (Westerberg –
    Sterling 1015)
Wilhelm Stenhammar (Sweden)
  The Song (Blomstedt – Caprice CAP 21358)
  Late Summer Nights (Waldeland – Swedish Society SCD 1032)
  Mid-Winter (Järvi – BIS CD 438)
  Symphony no. 1 (Järvi – BIS CD 219)
  Symphony no. 2 (Järvi – BIS CD 251)
Hans Erik Philip (Denmark)
  Fiskerne (soundtrack) (Walter/Mikkelborg – Danica DCD 8127) (very
    beautiful suite for viola and orchestra)
Arne Nordheim (Norway)
  The Tempest (Darden – Aurora NCD-B 4932)

Anne-Marie Orbeck (Norway)
  Symphony (Dreier – Aurora ACD 4925)
  Gunnar de Frumerie (Sweden)
  Pastoral Suite (Nilson – Bluebell ABCD 019)
Dag Wirén (Sweden)
  Serenade for String Orchestra (Nilson – Bluebell ABCD 019)
Aarre Merikanto (Finland)
  Pan; Nocturne; Mysterious Largo (Segerstam – Finlandia FACD 349)
Einojuhani Rautavaara (Finland)
  Cantus Arcticus (Lahti – BIS CD 575)
Vaino Raitio (Finland)
  The Swans (Saraste – Ondine ODE 790-2)
  Icelandic Orchestral Music (Sakari – Chandos 9180)
Wilhelm Peterson-Berger (Sweden)
  Symphonie no. 3 (Same-Atnam) (Kohler – Musica Sveciae MSCD
  630) (Allegro Imports)

The Peterson-Berger Symphonie no. 3 is a uniquely beautiful pristine composition. It honors the clear, unspoiled wilderness of Lapland, and it especially describes the presences in mountain scenery. The sense of great wilderness and of nature before humans pervades the symphony. A distant beauty, alternating light and dark shadings, makes this work of music remote yet very appealing and powerful.

RUSSIAN AND SLAVIC

Much of the magnificent Slavic nature music pictures ancient legends and fairy tales, some colorful and enchanting (Tchaikovsky and Rimsky-Korsakov), while other music is often beautiful, unearthly, and remote, belonging to another world.

Antonín Dvořák (Czechoslovakia)
  In Nature's Realm (Ančerl – Supraphon 11 1242-2)
  The Silent Woods (Helmerson/Järvi – BIS CD245)
  Symphony no. 8 (Barbirolli – Angel CDM 64193)
  Symphony no. 9 (from the *New World*) (Bernstein – Sony SMK
  47547)
  Cello Concerto (Fournier/Szell – DGG 429155)

Dvořák was essentially a lyricist, combining Slavic moods and nature songs, especially lovely bird songs, played on different instruments (Cello Concerto and Symphony no. 8).

Bohuslav Martinu (Bohemia)
  Rhapsody-Concerto for Viola and Orchestra (Golani/Maag – Conifer CDCF 146 or Imai/DePriest – BIS CD 501) (a beautiful, flowing piece of nature music, often recalling old Moravian folk songs)
Anton Rubinstein (Russia)
  Symphony no. 2 (Ocean) (Gunzenhauser – Marco Polo 8.220449)
Boris Lyatoshinsky
  On the Banks of the Vistula (Gluschenko – Russian Disc 11 062)
Alexander Glazunov (Russia)
  Spring (Järvi – Chandos CHAN 8611)
  The Sea; The Forest (Svetlanov – Melodiya SUCD 10-00156)
  Idyll for Horn and Strings (Hammer/Starek – Koch Treasure 3-1611-2)
Peter Tchaikovsky (Russia)
  Swan Lake and *Sleeping Beauty* (various labels)
  Symphony no. 1 (Winter Dreams) (Markevitch – Philips 4-426848)
  The Storm (Rozhdestvensky – IMP Classics PCD 878)
Alexander Scriabin (Russia)
  Symphony no. 5 (Prometheus, the Poem of Fire) (Svetlanov – Russian Disc RC CD 11 058)
  Piano Concerto (Ashkenazy/Maazel – London 417252-2) (listen especially to the slow movement)
Anatol Liadov (Russia)
  The Enchanted Lake; Baba-Yaga (Svetlanov – Melodiya SUCD 10-00140)
Bedřich Smetana (Czechoslovakia)
  The Moldau River; The High Castle; From Bohemia's Woods and Meadows (from *My Country*) (Kubelik – DGG 429183-2 or Talich – Supraphon SUP 111896)
Nikolai Rimsky-Korsakov (Russia)
  Sadko (includes the famous *Song of India*) (Svetlanov – Melodiya SUCD 10-00180)
  May Night; Snow Maiden Suite (Järvi – 3 Chandos CHAN 8327/9)
Eduard Tubin (Estonia)
  Symphony no. 4 (Järvi – BIS CD227)
Nazib Zhiganov (Tatar)
  Symphonic Songs (Temirkanov – Russian Disc 11 046)

MISCELLANEOUS NATURE MUSIC

Douglas Lilburn (New Zealand)
  Symphonies nos. 1, 2 (Hopkins – Continuum 1069) (available from Records International, Box 1140, Goleta, CA 93116-1140)

Aotearoa Overture (Kiwi)
Landfall on an Unknown Shore (Hillary-Koch)

Having visited beautiful New Zealand, I was overjoyed to find this out-standing composer and his music. Lilburn studied with Vaughan Williams, and his music carries in itself a deep attunement with nature. To hear Symphony no. 2 and *Aotearoa Overture* is like being again near Queenstown, Te Anau, Wanaka, Tasman Glacier, Mount Sefton, Mount Aspiring, and Mount Cook, where I remember seeing the face of the Mountain Lord emerging from the peak. I can still remember feeling the power of Taklaw, the Lord of the Mountain, raying forth powerful currents of energy from the top of the mountain as it looks down on Hooker Valley and the fields of exquisitely colored lupines filling the surrounding landscape. My trips this lifetime to South Island, in New Zealand, come the closest to my dreams of paradise on earth. The writer Flower A. Newhouse talks about the great nature beings that are active in New Zealand, and she mentions the inner aspects of nature that are present at Mount Cook. She says that Taklaw, the Mountain Lord, clearly and telepathically shared his ideas with her:

> I am Taklaw, Guardian of the Future. My gift to you will be the support-ing of all your best desires for the future. Think of what you most need now, and I will help you. . . . Walk into the future with a brave, clean and resolved heart.

In like manner Geoffrey Hodson, who lived in New Zealand, shares his deep wisdom of the Deva and Angel kingdoms active there on North Island and South Island, in his marvelous book *Clairvoyant Investigations*.

Gideon Fagan
  Karoo Symphony (nature scenes from South Africa) (Marchbank – Marco Polo 8.223709)
Ron Goodwin (New Zealand)
  New Zealand Suite (Goodwin – EMI EJ 26 0172 4)

Goodwin's music, although not as deeply related to the inner worlds of the nature kingdom as Lilburn's, offers a beautiful, pictorial quality.

Peter Sculthorpe (Australia)
  Earth Cry; Kakadu; Irkauda IV (Challender ABC 426481) (Albany Imports) (ritualistic, desolate, often compelling.)
Richard Mills (Australia)
  Seaside Dances (Mills – ABC 432 251)

JAPAN

Toru Takemitsu
  Rain Coming; Waterways; Tree Line; River Run (Knussen – Virgin
    CDC 59020)
  Requiem for Strings (Wakasugi – CBC SMCD 5080)
  Dream Window (Harp Concerto) (Denon 78944)
  A Flock Descends into the Pentagonal Garden (Ozawa – DGG 423
    253-2)
  Dreamtime; Nostalghia (Iwaki – ABC Australia 426 998-2)
  November Steps (Ozawa – Philips 432176-2)
  To the Edge of Dream (Williams/Salonen – Sony SK 46720)
  Visions; Far Calls; Coming Far (Wakasugi – Denon 8723)
  Fantasma-Cantos; Waves (Otaka – RCA 09026-62537)

I especially enjoy Takemitsu's strange and mysterious nature pictures in
music. In his pieces, sensual, at times almost tactile sounds, mix with more
ominous, otherworldly feelings and presences.

SOUNDS OF NATURE: ENVIRONMENTAL RECORDINGS

Tim Crawford/Paul Stavenjord – *Mystic Visions; Guardian Spirits* (from
  Alaska, Native American flute with loons and acoustic guitar) (White
  Swan Distributors)
Sounds of Nature (nature sounds with musical background) – *Singing
  Birds; Golden Pond; Bayou* (Silver Bells Music, Nashville, TN 37203)
The Art of Relaxation: Nature Meditations (with music and sounds of
  nature) (Relaxation Company, 20 Lumber Road, Roslyn, NY 11576)
Soundings Tapestry (nature sounds and instrumental music) (Soundings
  of the Planet, P.O. Box 43512, Tucson, AZ 85733)
In Harmony with Nature (classical music selections with natural sounds)
  – *Waterfall Suite; Sounds of the Forest; Babbling Brook* (with Bach's
  Brandenburg Concertos) (Distributions Madacy, P.O. Box 1445, St.
  Laurent, Quebec, Canada H4L 4Z1)
Brazilian Soundscapes (Eloisa Matheu) – from *World's Soundscapes*
  (Sittelle 26106)
Soundings of the Planet – Dean Evenson (original New Age, flowing
  compositions, often for flute, cello, handharp, guitar, and some
  synthesizer sounds, accompanied by sounds of nature) (I especially
  like *Peaceful Pond, Desert Moon Song, Ocean Dreams, Gong with
  the Wind, Lifestreams, High Joy*) (Soundings of the Planet, P.O. Box
  43512, Tucson, AZ 85733)

Nature Recordings Reference Series: Bamboo Waterfall (waterfalls, songbirds, gentle streams, soft ocean waves, bamboo chimes, etc.) (Nature Recordings, P.O. Box 2749, Friday Harbor, WA 98250)

North Sound (nature or nature with classical/New Age musical backgrounds) (These are exceptionally lovely, often haunting, and in many cases good for attunement with nature. I especially like *Classical Loon I, II, Songbird Symphony, Classical Nature I, II, Loon Talk, Nature's Noel, Wolf Talk, Wilderness Thunderstorm,* and *Echoes of Yellowstone.*) (NorthWord Press, Inc., P.O. Box 1360, Minocqua, WI 54548)

Echoes of Nature (natural sounds of the wilderness with or without synthesizer music; I prefer just the natural sounds) (Laserlight-Delta Music, Santa Monica, CA 90404-3061) Series includes the following: *American Wilds; Ocean Waves; Wilderness River; Bayou; Frog Chorus; Rainforest; Thunderstorm,* etc. I especially like the *Sampler* (12 255), which offers a wide variety of nature sounds, and *Whales of the Pacific* (12-263), a very haunting, beautiful blending of whale sounds, ocean, and instrumental.

Terry Oldfield – *Reverence* (flute, whale songs, and ocean waves—lovely, haunting experience) (New World Company, Paradise Farm, Westhall, Halesworth, Suffolk IP19 8RH, England)

Chris Valentino – *Musical Sea of Tranquility* (beautiful and relaxing sounds of harp and ocean; a real help for restful, relaxed sleep) (Jonella Record Company, P.O. Box 522, Englewood, NJ 07631)

Mystic Shores (harp and ocean – wonderful, with a bit more mood variety than *Musical Sea of Tranquility*) (Intersound, Inc., 11810 Wills Road, P.O. Box 1724, Roswell, GA 30077)

David Naegele – *Eternal Sanctuary* and *Temple in the Forest* (synthesizers, stream, and piano) (very meditative and calming) (Valley of the Sun, Box 38, Malibu, CA 90265)

Paul Sullivan – *Sketches of Maine* (piano with some natural sounds) (River Music, Blue Hill Farms, ME 04615)

Bernie Krause – *Gentle Ocean* (just ocean and gulls) (The Nature Company, P.O. Box 2310, Berkeley, CA 94702)

Bearns and Dexter – *Golden Voyage I, II, III* (relaxing and joyful, stirring and at other times reflective, musical experience—fountains, bells, synthesizers, etc.) (White Swan Distributors)

Dan Gibson – *Solitudes* (a marvelous series of nature recordings. Note especially *Canoe Trip to Loon Lake* and *Tradewind Islands.* Note also the excellent *Solitudes Sampler*—just beautiful sounds of nature without synthesized music.) (Moss Music Group, Inc., 48 West Thirty-Eighth Street, New York, NY 10018)

Rautavaara – *Cantus Arcticus* (birds and haunting orchestral music)

John LaMontaine – *Birds of Paradise* (with natural sounds and orchestra; haunting, atmospheric piece of music) (available from the composer: Fredonia Discs/Press, 3947 Fredonia Drive, Hollywood, CA 90068; 213-851-3043)

The Natural Harp (ethereal harp and sounds of nature) (Northsound 22222)

Mozart Naturally (music of Mozart mixed with nature sounds) (Northsound 26222)

In the tranquility of evening, when only the swells move the surface of the sea, the eye is enraptured by the fabulous display of colors in the endless view over sea and land; colors fade toward midnight, the calmness becomes even more complete, until at last the night winds slowly begin to blow.

KURT ATTERBERG

CHAPTER 7

Angelic Music

There are regions so elusive in our life of feeling that only music can express such intangible and sublime visions of beauty.

LEOPOLD STOKOWSKI

. . . . the choir invisible, whose music is the gladness of the world.

FREDERICK DELIUS

Spiritual teachings inform us to "go to God first, and to others as God directs." We humans are attended by presences who are more highly evolved than we are. Many such helpers of God are open to us. The Kingdom of the Angels, the Devas and other nature beings, a Kingdom of life created before humankind blesses us continuously. If we do nothing else daily, we can remember our Guardian Angel or our Watcher with deep love and gratitude. Most of the blessings of our life are the result of our Guardian's attending love and care.

Angels, the radiant Hosts of God, are mentioned about three hundred times in the Bible and are also reverenced in other world religions and in many contemporary spiritual writings, such as Geoffrey Hodson's *The Brotherhood of Angels and Men*. Flower A. Newhouse, spiritual teacher and clairvoyant Christian mystic, has written with illumination and insight about the Kingdom of the Angels. Her books *Rediscovering the Angels* and *The Kingdom of the Shining Ones* are classics in their field and offer us much information into the ways of angels. Newhouse writes in *Kingdom of the Shining Ones*:

Among the countless orders of Angels, there are four great waves of Angelic life attuned primarily to earthly existence and to serving the lives which are active within the planet. There are many other great Angelic orders—all of them purposeful and glorious—but they do not concern us here. One of these four paths is that of the "Nature Wave." The second is called the "Life Motivation Wave." The third is associated with the releasement of Divine Wisdom's expression. The fourth is known as the "Wave of Love."

She explains how these great beings of light bless humankind with many different, empowering activities. Among these waves of angelic life are God's legions who bless nature and the elements, heightening their beauty, graceful forms, and colors.

Other angels help to direct God's healing light. These great ones focus renewing energies into hospitals, homes, places of work, churches, schools, and all areas that are receptive and needy. Other celestial messengers inspire humankind through the beauty and joy of the creative arts.

As we become more centered and attuned in light, we can hear the overtones of joy-filled harmonies and melodious sounds which the angels help to focus into our atmosphere. This music of the Watcher Angels and Guardian Angels (mentioned in all the world religions) remains near us throughout our lifetime, encouraging us to live finer lives, dedicated to truth and loving, unselfish service. Great Warrior Angels combat evil with power.

Angelic presences come through clearly in musical pieces such as Bruckner's Eighth Symphony. In Bruckner's words, the Adagio third movement is highly celestial, describing the "all-loving Father of mankind in His measureless wealth of mercy." Bruckner speaks of the Finale fourth movement of his Symphony no. 8 with these words: " . . . heroism in the service of the Divine, with trumpets as announcers of eternal life; the heralds of the idea of Divinity." Speaking generally of his music, Bruckner wrote: "And I heard, as it were, the voice of a great multitude, and as the voice of many waters, and as the voice of mighty thunderings."

Wagner's *Ride of the Valkyries* brings through the power of Warrior Angels; *Climb Every Mountain* from Rodgers and Hammerstein's *The Sound of Music* and Humperdinck's *Children's Prayer* (from *Hansel and Gretel*) activate the presence of one's Guardian Angel. The music of César Franck (*Panis angelicus; Psalm 150; Beatitudes*) was highly attuned to angelic presences. Franck himself well may have been from the angel line of unfoldment; Franck's students called him "the Seraph-father," and Franck's own writings seem to confirm this identification.

Beethoven describes the slow movement of his Piano Concerto no. 5 (*Emperor*) with the following words: " . . . a Guardian Angel watching over the pilgrim on his/her journey." Richard Strauss, in his inimitable tone poem *Death and Transfiguration*, suggests so beautifully the Angel of Transition, who helps us across into greater God-light at the time of our passing from earthly life. Sensing the depth of this music, the great conductor Leopold Stokowski spoke of this piece as "Death and Illumination."

Our consciousness is not limited to time. At any moment, in joy or in crisis, through inspiration or desperation, we can come into deeper attunement with light, which enables us to receive new inpourings in many forms from higher sources in God's creation. So it is with many of the great composers. In the midst of many good works, they seem to have had those moments when they were especially inspired. During these times, light poured through them, and angelic harmonies filled their being and atmosphere. Some composers, like Handel during his writing of *Messiah*, even saw the Angel Hosts and gave them full credit for whatever inspiration they were able to transmit into notes and melodies. As a result of feeling their empowerments, Handel did not charge for any performance of *Messiah*. He never even felt that he was the composer of *Messiah*.

Other musical compositions seem to have been especially inspired by angels. Wagner's Prelude to *Lohengrin*, Act 1, and the holy music from *Parsifal* create an unforgettable celestial atmosphere and the calls of angels (Walter – Sony MK 42050). Grieg's Piano Concerto, especially the magical second movement, contains angel calls. Likewise, Grieg's *Nocturne,* from the *Lyric Suite*, evokes an Angel of the Night, who blesses nature. Water Angels and the Nereids of the deep come through various "green" musical compositions of Debussy, such as *The Engulfed Cathedral*. Chopin's Nocturne in G, op. 37, no. 2, includes celestial sounds which are gossamer-like in their softness and transparency. Chopin wrote about his nocturnes as follows:

> Like butterflies upon the garden beds,
> Nets of bright sound. I follow them: in vain.
> I must not brush the least dust from their wings:
> They die of a touch; but I must capture them (in music)
> Or they will turn to a caressing flame,
> And lick my soul up with their flutterings.

Gounod, the French composer, offers us very powerful vibrations of angelic beings and heavenly choirs, especially in his *Easter Mass, Te Deum, Death and Life, Unfold Ye Portals of Creation*, and in the very powerful *Sanctus*, from the *Saint Cecilia Mass*.

Rachmaninov's *Vespers* and his *Liturgy of Saint John Chrysostom* contain celestial moments, and the hauntingly beautiful *Vocalise* closely suggests an angel call and quickens the presences of celestial beings (get the version sung by Anna Moffo, conducted by Leopold Stokowski – RCA Gold

Seal 7831-4-RG). Be sure to hear the cleansing choirs of adoration that come through the final minutes of Mahler's Symphony no. 2 *(Resurrection)*. Alan Hovhaness's music often awakens angelic awareness, especially his beautiful and meditative piece *Mysterious Mountain*. Alan Rosner's lovely *Responses, Hosanna and Fugue* contains some very beautiful, celestial moments, and William Alwyn's *Lyra Angelica* (Angel Songs – Chandos 9065) is a haunting experience and brings an inbreaking of angelic visitations. Vangelis's *Antarctica Echoes* (from the soundtrack, *Antarctica*, Polydor 815732-2) beautifully evokes the higher spheres of God-light and the celestial worlds of angels.

The new openness to the presence of angels in our midst seems to be bringing us closer to this kingdom and its many activities. Certain pieces of music seem especially to bless listeners who hear them and bring angelic vibrations into any atmosphere where they are played. Angelic music brings light. It is usually joyful, piercingly clear and bright. Often, such music echoes the singing of celestial choirs contained in bell-like and harplike sounds. Certain pieces of music also bring in strong healing energies (Mozart's Symphony no. 40 is good for clearance and purification) and are especially beneficial when played in hospitals, nursing homes, or in rooms with mentally disturbed patients. Dr. Bernie Siegel, the eminent physician, wrote me several years ago, asking me to recommend special pieces of soothing music that might help to quiet patients awaiting surgery, and it was a pleasure to work with him.

Other angelic music, such as Gluck's *Dance of the Blessed Spirits*, awakens the quality of joy.

The writer, Gwen Hulbert, offers these beautiful words about Angels of Music and Song:

> Our joy and our life is to Sing.
> As Angels of Song we form a choir, each note adding to the whole—to chant harmonies unimagined in your world.
> The tones come from our hearts, not from lungs and vocal cords.
> With the intonation of different qualities, such as valor, serenity, or joyousness, the harmonies change. Were you to see us, you would note the colors of our auras also changing in glowing harmony—music made visible!
> To worship and adore God in absolute purity of tone, in full attunement with each other, so that we may sing as One—that is our quest.

In all of the following pieces of music, angels' songs and presences are near. I invite you to find and listen to these selections. This music is especially striking and opens doorways into angelic atmospheres. Listen to these pieces repeatedly; let your consciousness open to heavenly echoes.

Grieg
  Nocturne (from *Lyric Suite*)
    This music brings into the atmosphere an Angel of the Night, who blesses nature and life forms.
  Piano Concerto
    This great nature concerto rises into angelic heights. Listen especially to the sublime slow movement (second movement), if possible, in versions with pianist Radu Lupu or Stephen Bishop-Kovacevich.

Gluck
  Dance of the Blessed Spirits
    This music emanates energies of joy and renewal.

Beethoven
  Piano Concerto no. 5 *(Emperor)*, second movement
    The quiet transparency of this music quickens the listener to angel presences. It is one of Beethoven's most beautiful and haunting achievements. He imitates an old pilgrim song, evoking the Guardian Presence watching over and leading the pilgrim. It is easy, listening to this music, for a listener to reflect on the words, "He gives His Angels charge over thee." (Try to find the magical rendition by Christoph Eschenbach and Seiji Ozawa on DGG, but others will do almost as well. It is important for the pianist to maintain the lighter, transparent atmosphere of this incredibly lovely and open music.)

Mozart
  Laudate Dominum, Psalm 116 (from *Vesperae Solennes de Confessore*)
  Ave Verum Corpus (I especially like the Te Kanawa/Colin Davis renditions on Philips 412873-2 PH)
  Piano Concerto no. 21 (slow movement)
    Both pieces raise the listener into celestial realms.

Brahms
  Piano Concerto no. 2, third movement
    The melodies in the cello and piano bring openings into the angelic realms.

Berlioz
  Hosanna (from *L'Enfance du Christ*)
  Sanctus (from *Requiem*)
    The choral singing here is strong but also light-filled and transparent, lifting the listener upward in consciousness into angelic openings and receptivity.

Humperdinck
  Children's Prayer (from *Hansel and Gretel*)
  This beautiful music, leading into high strings, always brings into
  the atmosphere the nearness of a person's Guardian Angel. Get the
  beautiful high strings Ormandy version, if possible, on Sony MLK
  45736 or the choral rendition on Resmiranda 8001 and another choral
  version, conducted by Stokowski on RCA 09026.

Vaughan Williams
  Fantasia on a Theme of Thomas Tallis
  The soaring strings in this one-of-a-kind masterpiece echo angelic
  harmonies (Barbirolli on EMI).
  Shepherds of the Delectable Mountains (from *Pilgrim's Progress*)
  The chorus of angels welcomes the Pilgrim into celestial regions,
  upon his transition from earth life.

Franck
  Panis angelicus (Pavarotti's version contains the celestial echoes of a
  boys' choir, and Stokowski's orchestral version with the Philadelphia
  Orchestra is also wonderful – Biddulph WHL 011. A beautiful choral
  version exists on Resmiranda 8001.)

Mahler
  Symphony no. 2 (Resurrection) (conducted by Stokowski on Intaglio
  749)
  The rising finale reaches into the celestial realms—chorus and
  orchestra reveal the heavens opened.
  Symphony no. 8 *(Symphony of a Thousand)*
  This great work, demanding one thousand players, is a cosmic vision,
  lifting the listener into great light.

Handel
  Hallelujah Chorus (from *Messiah*)
  Probably the greatest angel music ever composed. Handel saw
  angels descending and filling his room as he received their inspired
  thought forms while composing this part of *Messiah*. Note also the
  tremendous finale *(Amen)* which rises at the end, *if* the conductor
  understands the notes. I especially enjoy a large *Messiah* with full
  choir and orchestra, such as Sargent's version on EMI Classics for
  Pleasure (or Chesky) or Beecham's on RCA.

Bohm
  Calm as the Night (for organ)
  A quiet, meditative, yet very powerful piece of music, suggesting the
  eternal serenity of the heavens.

Chopin
  Nocturne in E-flat (op. 9. no. 2)

Piano Concerto no. 1 (slow movement) (get the Gilels/Ormandy version on Sony SBK 46336)

Andante Spianato (played by Arthur Rubinstein)

All these pieces open up the listener to angelic tones and harmonies.

Wagner

Ride of the Valkyries

Strong sounds of empowering Warrior Angels cleanse the atmosphere and call the listener to take courage (get Arthur Fiedler's version on RCA).

Prelude and *Good Friday Music* from *Parsifal* (Stokowski on Pearl 9448)

The music of the Holy Grail, lifting the listener into Hosts of attending, shining Presences.

Prelude (Act I) to *Lohengrin*

Wagner actually saw angels descending and rising in the golden radiance of the Grail music.

Evening Star (Tannhäuser) (Get Montovani's enchanting version on London.)

Pilgrims' Chorus (from *Tannhäuser*) (This is a fervent prayer offered in consecration.)

Bruckner

Symphony no. 8 (Adagio)

This is music of the night, suggesting forests and high mountain peaks. The symphony is Bruckner's painting of the Archangel Michael and his legions' combat with the dark forces. Bruckner's words about the Adagio (slow movement) of this symphony read as follows: "The quiet rule of the Deity—the all-loving Father of mankind."

Respighi

Church Windows (Archangel Michael)

Pines of Rome, third movement *(Pines of the Janiculum)*

This section of the work suggests the nature devas and angelic presences. The movement ends in a beautiful "suspension of time," with the nightingale's entrancing song.

Paul Horn

Inside the Taj Mahal (minus the chants)

The flute tones, soaring upward in the ambient, transparent acoustics of the marvelous Taj Mahal, link the listener with angelic harmonies.

Mendelssohn

How Lovely are the Messengers and *Sanctus* (from *Elijah*) (Erato ECD 75147)

The reverence and devotion of Mendelssohn's sacred music here can raise the listener into angelic contact.

J. S. Bach

Sanctus (from B Minor Mass)

Powerful, cosmic music; soaring celestial choirs join with angelic forces.

Anton Rubinstein

Angelic Dream (from *Kamenoi Ostrov*)

Magical music, moving one into angelic realms with beautiful, suggestive themes (available on CD called *Quiet Nights* and conducted by Henry Adolph on Vox Cameo Classics ACD 8763).

Schubert

Ave Maria

The rising, devotional quality of the music attracts angelic forces.

Bach-Gounod

Ave Maria

Also very beautiful, devotional music.

Gounod

Sanctus (from *Messe Solennelle*)

This is a very ceremonial kind of angelic music, which welcomes the angels into the atmosphere—very powerful. (I really like Jessye Norman's version on Philips, conducted by Sir Alexander Gibson.)

Albert Thomé

Adagio Religioso

Contains the theme of the Holy Spirit (available through the Christward Ministry, 20560 Questhaven Road, Escondido, CA 92029; 1-619-744-1500).

Rodgers and Hammerstein

Climb Every Mountain (from *The Sound of Music*) (RCA PCD1-2005)

According to the findings of Flower A. Newhouse, this music seems to contain the encouragements of one's Guardian Angel to do better and to achieve necessary overcomings in our lifetime. It brings in the tone and power of great courage.

Prologue (from *The Sound of Music*)

Calls of angelic and deva presences, echoing to each other from great Alpine peaks.

Pachelbel

Canon in D (get the Paillard version on RCA or Erato—the tempo is just right)

Braga

Angel's Serenade (Musical Heritage Society)

Casals

Song of the Birds (an exquisite miniature, filled with a hovering presence) (Harnoy on Pro Arte CDD418 or Victoria de los Angeles's ravishing vocal rendition of *Traditional Catalan Songs* on Collins 13182)

Marx-Gerda
  Guardian Angels (sung by Mario Lanza on RCA-BMG)

Elgar
  Pomp and Circumstance no. 1 (Land of Hope and Glory)

Eugene Friesen
  Cathedral Pines (a beautiful angel meditation for cello and pipe organ – Living Music LD-0007)

Celestial Bells (available from The Christward Ministry, 20560 Questhaven Road, Escondido, CA 92029; 1-619-744-1500)
  Many persons have described angelic presences and angel calls in terms of bell-like sounds. This beautiful recording brings through the transparent, celestial qualities of angel calls with their open, clear textures. The Questhaven Handbell Choir plays twenty-six angelic pieces of music, including *Jubilance* by Sherman, *Be Thou My Vision* by Butler, *Panis angelicus* by Franck, *Let There Be Peace on Earth* by Morse, and *O Holy Night* arranged by Morse.

Certain hymns, from various denominations and traditions, contain angel songs and words that praise these great Hosts with joy and devotion:

Hymns
  O Holy Night (by Adam)
  Ye Watchers and Ye Holy Ones (tune: *Lasst Uns Erfreuen*)
  Ye Holy Angels Bright (tune: *Darwall's 148th*)
  Angels from the Realms of Glory (tune: *Regent Square*, Henry T. Smart)
  Angels We Have Heard on High (tune: *Gloria*)
  (These hymns can be found in the Congregational Hymnal, United Church of Christ.)

You can never go wrong playing these pieces of great music. Angel music is always highly therapeutic, inspirational, and spiritually elevating. It brings noticeable empowerment and clears the aura.

> *Let the bright Seraphim in burning row,*
> *Their loud uplifted Angel-trumpets blow;*
> *Let the Cherubic Host, in tuneful choirs*
> *Touch their immortal harps with golden wires;*

Let their celestial concerts all unite,
Ever to sound His praise in endless morn of Light.

HANDEL, *SAMSON*

With prayer, let us expect the Angel's trumpet.

TERTULLIAN

About angelic intelligences and divine guidance—I owe my life
work to these spiritual guides whom I try to follow as a spiri-
tually blind man must be led through life.

ALAN HOVHANESS

So shall I join the choir invisible
Whose music is the gladness of the world.

ANONYMOUS

An Angel, not being composed of material substances, cannot
reflect the sun's rays in order to be visible. Therefore, we see
Angels either because the Angel assumes a material body mo-
mentarily or because our interior eye is opened, the inward eye
by which we see.

EMMANUEL SWEDENBORG

CHAPTER 8

Music and Global Spirituality

Raise the stone
and you shall find me;
Cleave the wood
and there am I.

LOGIA OF CHRIST

It is the whole my being, Lord Christ, that you would have me
give you, tree and fruit alike, the finished work as well as the
harnessed power, the opus together with the operation.

TEILHARD DE CHARDIN

A close look at the great composers' lives and music shows how often a higher inspiration sparked their efforts. Many of the composers who have acknowledged the Divine Presence, which has worked with them and through them, have been outside particular religious institutions or orthodox affiliations. Yet, as we examine their diaries and letters, we find that many frequently and openly named the Divine according to their own experience of direct communion and contact. In some instances composers called this Presence "God" or "Christ," though they often acknowledged that their inspirations were connected to cosmic sources of power larger than particular religions or movements, transcendent, yet extremely close and intimately present in their lives.

Regardless of any particular religion or philosophy held by these artists, whenever they were open and receptive, divine radiance came upon them, illumining their creativity like a golden fire. In these instances the composer became a connective channel, or recipient, who was able to transmit creatively closer communion between humankind and the Creator. As Corinne Heline put it, "The highest mission of music is to serve as a link between God and men (and women). It builds a bridge over which angelic hosts can come closer to mankind."

If we look at the personalities of great composers, we may find certain unrefined weaknesses or challenges yet unbalanced in their character and temperament. But even in the midst of such shortcomings, a deeper motivation and higher impulses often outshined these imperfections. It is wise to remember *not* to judge anyone, especially those whose inner motivation may be stronger than their outer failures. Even with all the composers' human limitations and irresponsible behavior, such as Beethoven's temper tantrums and brusqueness, Wagner's egomania, Delius's selfishness, etc., it seems that the divine light has always invaded their human efforts, often lifting and transforming ordinary works into timeless masterpieces that stimulate humankind's evolution. Beethoven seemed aware of his human frailty as well as realizing his divine gift when he said, "Divine One, Thou lookest into my inmost soul, Thou knowest that love of man and desire to do good live therein. . . . O God, give me strength to conquer myself; nothing must chain me to life."

Research into the lives of the great composers reveals many instances where their dedication to God was strong. Mozart wrote in his journals, "I prayed to God, and the symphony began." J. S. Bach affirmed, "The aim and final reason for all music should be nothing else but the glory of God and the refreshment of the spirit." Beethoven, coming closer to God through much personal suffering, stated in his diary his final acceptance of himself as a composer and a man: "I will humbly submit to all life's chances and changes, and put my sole trust in Thy immutable goodness, O God." The great Bohemian composer Antonín Dvořák always prefaced his scores with the words "Thanks be to God," and the devotional Austrian mystic and master composer Anton Bruckner dedicated his ninth symphony "To Beloved God." The motto on many of Vivaldi's scores was "Glory to God and the blessed Mary." Rachmaninov wrote these words at the end of his last major work, *Symphonic Dances*, "I thank thee, Lord."

Handel described his ecstatic experience while writing the *Messiah* as follows: "I did think I did see all Heaven before me—and the great God Himself. Whether I was in my body or out of my body as I wrote it, I know not. God knows." Haydn told of his joy in the Lord Christ: "God has given me a cheerful heart. . . . Whenever I think of the Dear Lord, I have to laugh. My heart jumps for joy in my breast." While composing *Parsifal*, Wagner set forth his spiritual credo: "I believe in God, Mozart, and Beethoven, and in their disciples and apostles; I believe in the Holy Spirit and the truth of art—one and indivisible: I believe that the art of music proceeds from God and dwells in the hearts of all enlightened men. . . . I rejoice in one thought and consideration, the results of which might yet bring a great healing to the world . . . that I should be able to make clear Christ."

Although accused of being an agnostic, Ralph Vaughan Williams made the following proclamation: "Music is not a science only, but a divine voice. . . . Divine Grace is dancing; dance ye therefore." Leoš Janáček, speaking about his *Slavonic Mass*, said, "I want to show people how to talk with God." Hector Berlioz, writing to a friend about *L'Enfance du Christ*, said, "It seems to me to contain a feeling of the infinite, of divine love."

César Franck, a Christ-oriented mystic composer, speaking to his friend and student d'Indy, said, "The joy of the world is transformed and flourishing by the Word of Christ." Speaking of his own faith, in his biography of Franck, d'Indy says, "The origin of music . . . is to be found incontestably in religion. The earliest song was a prayer. To praise God, to celebrate the beauty, the joy, and even the terrors of religion, was the sole object of all works of art for nearly 800 years." Arthur Abell in transcribing his conversation with his friend Brahms, wrote, "Who else of all the countless millions of men who have trod this earth could compare with Christ? He taught righteousness, honesty in our dealings with our fellow men and He knew there is a life beyond the grave and that we earn it by faith and by keeping the commandments. Christ came as a great example to us, not as an exception." Also Brahms, regarded by some as a crusty agnostic, made this statement of faith to Arthur Abell: "I feel vibrations that thrill all of me. These vibrations are of the Spirit illuminating the soul power within, and in this exalted state, I see clearly what is obscure in my ordinary moods. Then I feel capable of drawing inspiration from above, as Beethoven did. . . . I realize that I and my Father are one."

The composer Gustav Mahler was reared a Jew, but his longing for the Spirit was so strong that his deepest aspirations far exceeded any one faith or religion. We hear his devotion and heightened spiritual contact as they come through so strongly inspired in his own words, which he wrote for the choral finale of his Symphony no. 2 *(Resurrection):*

> O all pervading pain,
> You I have escaped.
> O all-conquering death,
> Now you are conquered.
> With wings that I have won for myself
> In fervent loving aspiration
> Will I soar
> To the light that no eye has ever seen.
> I shall die, that I may live.
> Arise, yes. You will arise
> My heart, in a moment.
> What you have borne will carry you to God.

From these and many other recorded statements in the journals and letters of the great composers, it is clear that when the Spirit has inspired the uplifted soul and the surrendered ego, and where talent has been cultivated sufficiently, great artistic expression can follow.

In music and in our lives, we are emerging out of chaos into a new order. The cult of ugliness, glorification of the ego, and selfish, narrow provincialism are slowly exhausting themselves; many persons are moving into new horizons of beauty, self-giving, and planetary cooperation. Today a new synthesis in the arts is emerging slowly, combining the best of the old with the new and unexpected. However, much of today's music seems transitional. Many styles of cerebrally oriented music are already undergoing change and are moving into a more melodic, neoromantic, feeling kind of music which opens the heart center. In the same way some New Age music is moving beyond mere faceless electronic sounds that promote "stresslessness" and musical escapism. Much New Age music is now moving more toward genuine attunement with nature and with the deeper Gaia principles of reverence for all lives on earth and a deeper spiritual attunement with the Creator.

It is clear that in the midst of increasing stresses and conflicts, many persons are seeking and helping to birth a spiritual renaissance. The recovery movement and other newly forming groups are expressing a new hunger for the Divine, often coming about through necessity, not just by choice. Some artists also share this development. George Rochberg, a contemporary American composer who spent many years in serialism and atonal experiments, recently stated his new artistic credo: "The business of art is to praise God." And John Nelson, formerly Music Director and Conductor of the Indianapolis Symphony Orchestra, described his love of God and the planetary Christ in an interview published in the *Christian Herald* in May, 1979:

Some of the blocks [in a person] arise because of your own inadequacies, and others because of circumstances, and often I get these two confused. If I don't do my work well and then something doesn't go right, it's my fault, my frustration. Other times I have done my work well and I have been stopped. Both have been present in my life.

I do believe as a Christian that if I do my work well and I follow what I know to be God's Will for me, then things are made rather clear, or—if they're not made clear—you know they're not clear for a reason, and you accept the situation.

Later in the interview, Nelson talked about the difference between straight talent and creative gifts that he believes are inspired by the Christ light:

There is special joy in finding a singer who brings not only a beautiful instrument, his voice, to a part, but the inner [Christlike] conviction. You can find soloists all over the place who will deliver the music beautifully and well, but there must be something deeper than that.

Irrespective of one's particular religious affiliation, every person is *potentially* spiritual in his or her deepest make-up. Whatever their inclination or tradition, as persons decide to draw upon this spiritual impulse and soul energy in praise and gratefulness, their lives open and the divine light enters their efforts. Many unexpected adventures then take such individuals along new roads of travel in the Spirit. Such lives begin to speed forward, through increased testings and the all-embracing Spirit, and many unseen helpers of God heighten each moment of the day.

Certain pieces of music have been deeply inspired by a love of God and the Christ. In most of these works Christ is perceived as the inspiration and empowering presence of love and light, not as a dogma or an ancient, exclusive, or punitive figure. Seen in this way, Christ in his great radiance works through all world religions and faith communities as the great world archetype for every person's larger completion in God. Christ, who has inspired countless beautiful works of art and many musical masterpieces, becomes for each of us the inspiring presence of love and the deeper impetus for our own larger life expression. Beyond mere theology, the living Christ is a presence of love in every receptive person's consciousness, a principle of all-inclusive, unconditional love, and an open door leading into the greater, infinite light of God. Much music that is spiritual in its deepest essence has been inspired by a love and an attunement to the presence of the Christ and the angels, whether named or unnamed. Such music inspires and transforms our consciousness; it can raise our spirits and change our attitudes and behaviors, even as we are experiencing it.

Following is a list of musical selections, composed in the light of inspiration and devotion to God and the various spiritual traditions of humankind:

Handel – *Messiah* (Beecham – RCA or Marriner – London)

Draeske – *Christus* (Bayer 100175-9) (a powerful, often majestic choral work describing the life of the Christ from nativity to resurrection and ascension)

Wagner – *Parsifal (Legend of the Holy Grail)* (Knappertsbusch – Philips)

J. S. Bach – *Jesu, Joy of Man's Desiring* (Vanguard)

  – *B Minor Mass* (DGG)

  – *St. John Passion* (EMI)

  – *St. Matthew Passion* (EMI)

Berlioz – *Requiem* (Philips or Walsingham 8000) (available through Allegro Imports)

  – *Te Deum* (DGG)

Paganini – *The Convent of Mont St. Bernard* (Plotino – Dynamic – Qualiton Imports)

Werner Josten – *Sacred Concerto* (Stokowski – CRI)

Otto Olsson – *Te Deum* (BIS)

  – *Requiem* (Propius: May Audio Marketing)

Andrew Lloyd Webber – *Requiem* (London)

George Harrison – *Liverpool Oratorio* (EMI)

Lou Harrison – *The Heart Sutra*

  – *Mass to Saint Anthony*

Arvo Pärt – *Te Deum* (ECM)

  – *Magnificat* (ECM)

  – *Berlin Mass* (ECM or Koch Schwann)

John Tavener – *We Shall See Him as He Is* (Chandos); *Akathist of Thanksgiving* (Sony)

Cherubini – *Coronation Mass* (EMI)

Paco Peña – *Missa Flamenca* (Nimbus)

Rossini – *Gloria Mass* (Vogel – Dynamic)

Mendelssohn – *There Shall a Star from Jacob* (from *Christus*) (Resmiranda)

  – *Elijah* (Philips or Erato)

Ronald Senator – *Holocaust Requiem* (Spiegelman – Delos 1032)

Jewish Liturgical Music (Harmonia Mundi 83)

Chanukah (MK 427133)

Jehova Mi Roca – (Jul Rivera, guitar) (beautiful, strong devotional music) (Beracha Music, Escondido, CA 92027; 1-619-741-3128)

Global Meditation (spiritual music from 40 countries) (Relaxation Company, 20 Lumber Road, Roslyn, NY 11576)

Paul Winter – *Missa Gaia* (Living Music) (global spirituality)

Celestial Songs of the Upanishad (Oriental Records, P.O. Box 387, Williston Park, NY 11596)

Indian Songs of Devotion (Lakshmi Shankar) (Auvidis)

Tibetan Buddhism (Tantras of Gyuto) (Nonesuch Explorer)

Martin Luther King: A Musical Testimony (lyrics – Maya Angelou)
   (Decca 425 212-2)
Cimarosa – *Requiem* (Philips)
Paul Ben-Haim – *Sweet Psalmist of Israel* (Sony)
Morton Gould – *Symphony of Spirituals* (Louisville)
   – *Spirituals for Orchestra* (Mercury or Everest)
Tchaikovsky – *Liturgy* (Chante du monde)
   – *Vespers* (Melodiya)
Puccini – *Gloria Mass* (Philips or Erato)
Kaplan – *Glorious* (the Psalms) (North American Liturgy Resources,
   11036 North Twenty-third Avenue, Phoenix, AZ 85029)
Bloch – *Sacred Service* (Sony or Chandos)
   – *Prayer* (Centaur)
Vivaldi – *Gloria* and other sacred choral music (London and Philips)
Hovhaness – *Magnificat* (Crystal)
Philip Green – *St. Patrick's Mass* (Wireless)
   – *The Man from Galilee* (Wireless, P.O. Box 64422, St. Paul, MN
   55164-0422)
Vaughan Williams – *The Sons of Light* (Lyrita)
   – *Pilgrim's Progress* (EMI)
   – *Fantasia on Christmas Carols* (London)
Virgil Fox (organ) – *The Christmas Album* (Bainbridge and The Virgil
   Fox Society, 88 Chestnut Street, Brooklyn, NY 11208)
   – *Great Protestant Hymns* (RCA)
Malotte – *The Lord's Prayer* (CBS)
Elgar – *The Light of Life* (EMI)
   – *The Apostles* (EMI or RCA)
   – *The Kingdom* (EMI or RCA)
Parry – *Jerusalem* (Hyperion)
   – *I Was Glad* (Hyperion)
Fauré – *Requiem* (Rutter – Collegium)
Mahler – *Symphony no. 2 (Resurrection)* (Stokowski – RCA or
   Klemperer – EMI or Kaplan – MCA)
Mozart – *Ave Verum Corpus* (Philips)
   – *Masses (miscellaneous)* (DGG and Philips)
   – *Coronation Mass* (Philips)
   – *Exultate, Jubilate* (Philips)
Franck – *Beatitudes* (Erato)
   – *Panis angelicus* (Biddulph or London)
Brahms – *A German Requiem* (Telarc or EMI)

Rachmaninov – *Vespers* (Melodiya or Telarc)
– *Liturgy of Saint John Chrysostom* (Claves)
Herbert Howells – *An English Mass* (Hyperion)
– *Hymnus Paradisi* (EMI)
– *Missa Sabrinensis* and *Stabat Mater* (Chandos)
Darius Milhaud – *Sacred Service for Saturday Morning* (Qualiton Imports)
Liszt – *Christus* (Supraphon)
F. J. Haydn – *The Creation* (BIS)
– *Masses* (London)
Bruckner – *Symphony no. 9* (EMI)
– *Te Deum* (DGG)
Gounod – *St. Cecilia Mass* (EMI)
– *Requiem in C* (Claves 9326)
Diane Bish (organ) – *Hymns and Classics* (has the best *Lord's Prayer* by Malotte) (available from Diane Bish, 400 E. Seventh Street, Box 11, Bloomington, IN 47405-3085, 1-800-933-4844)
– *Morning Has Broken: A Symphony of Hymns and A Symphony of Psalms* (VQR, P.O. Box 303, Needham, MA 02192)
Lee Holdridge – *Hymns Triumphant, I, II* (beautiful choral/orchestral settings) (Birdwing Records, 9255 Deering Avenue, Chatsworth, CA 91311)
Spirit of African Sanctus (compiled by David Fanshawe) (beautiful African sacred music) (Saydisc 389)
Morton Feldman – *Rothko Chapel* (Brett – New Albion NA039CD)
Karl Haas – *The Story of the Bells* (Seaway Productions, 26501 Emery Industrial Parkway, Cleveland, OH 44128)
Medicine Wheel (Native American spirituality) (Spring Hill Music, Box 800, Boulder, CO 80306)
Jerre Tanner – *Boy with Goldfish* (Hawaii) (Albany Records, P.O. Box 5011, Albany, NY 12205)
Ben Steinberg – *Shomeir Yisrael* (beautiful Hebrew sacred music) (Allegro Imports)
Passover Seder Festival (Richard Tucker) (Sony)
Jan Peerce – *Art of the Cantor* (Vanguard)
– *Hebrew Melodies* (Bass/Ellstein – RCA 09026-61687)
Noam Sheriff – *Prayers and Psalms of Jerusalem* (Allegro Imports)
Mordechai Seter – *Midnight Vigil* (Bertini – Capriccio)
Jackson Berkey – *The Mountains and the Sea* (SDG 92)
Gregg Smith – *Magnificat; Prayer for Peace* (Premier 120)
Choral Evensong (Cleobury – EMI 754412)

Havergal Brian – *Symphony no. 4 (Psalm of Victory)* (Marco Polo) (Records International)

Akira Ifukube – *Symphonic Ode to Gautama the Buddha* (Records International)

Leoš Janáček – *Glagolitic Mass* (Sony or Supraphon)

Uuno Klami – *Psalmus* (Finlandia)

George Lloyd – *A Symphonic Mass* (Albany Imports)

Andrzej Panufnik – *Sacred Symphony* (Elektra Nonesuch)

Frederick Swann (organ) – *Hymns* (Gothic 58519)

Favorite Hymns and Anthems (choir and organ) (Gothic 49044)

R. Whiting – *God Be With You Till We Meet Again* (RCA)

Fischer – *Mass for Freedom* (DGG)

Zamfir – *To You, O God* (Mercury)

Johnny Cash – *Gospel Road* (Columbia)

Mario Lanza – *I'll Walk With God* (RCA)

Svend Tarp – *Te Deum* (Nelson – Marco Polo 9005)

Palestrina – *Pope Marcellus Mass* (and other masses) (Gimell)

Monteverdi – *Vespers of the Blessed Virgin* (1610) (London)

Byrd – *Mass for Five Voices* (Gimell)

Schubert – *Ave Maria* (RCA)

Beethoven – *Christ on the Mount of Olives* (Sony)

Enjoy Jesus – Hour of Power, Rev. Robert Schuller (Crystal Cathedral, Garden Grove, CA)

Spirit Alive – Monks of the Weston Priory (Weston, VT)

Alfred Hill – *Symphony (Joys of Life)* (Marco Polo) (Records International)

Dances of Universal Peace (honoring all the world religions) (SIRS Publications, 65 Norwich Street, San Francisco, CA 94110)

Music of the Whirling Dervishes (Finnadar)

Mass from the Monastery of Senegal (Arion) (Allegro Imports)

Hildegard of Bingen – *Canticles of Ecstasy* (Sequentia – Harmonia Mundi 05472-77320)

Elvis Presley – *Gospel Songs* (RCA)

GREGORIAN CHANTS AND OTHER EARLY MUSIC

I also recommend to you the very beautiful and exalted music of Ambrosian and Gregorian chant. Often such music is sung by monks or nuns who regard the music as "the basis for everything else." Because of its original, spiritual motivation, you can often feel a reverence and a privacy in Gregorian chant that removes it from earthly complexity, stress, and turmoil. Recently, a group of monks who produced a top-selling album of chants decided that the increasing popularity of their music was too demanding and distracting. They decided not to make any more such recordings, preferring instead to resume their quiet, unglamorized activity of service to God in a monastic lifestyle.

Gregorian music is not sensational; it does not contain many sudden changes or shifts in tempo. It connects you with the lifting spiral of the Eternal. Thus, these chants are often a good way to defuse after a stressful day. Their celestial resonance, often interrupted periodically by peals of bells sounding the Angelus, can focus you and also lift you out of the mundane. Recordings now exist which combine chant with the sounds of nature, such as ocean waves, waterfalls, desert winds, or birdsong. (*Praise Mary, Star of the Sea*, sung by monks, and *Ave Maria* by the Benedictine Sisters, both accompanied by natural sounds, are available through White Swan Distributors, 1705 Fourteenth Street, Box 143, Boulder, CO 80302.) Gregorian chant is coming back into popularity, because more people are seeking peace and simplicity, a lifestyle that is less demanding and more spiritually attuned and meaningful. This music also contains a spaciousness which resonates deeply with an increasing desire today to reconnect with the cosmos and the Creator.

Gregorian music is restful; it clears out the cobwebs of our confusion. It is something you can "disappear into," another world of peace and humble power that is a gentle yet powerful antidote to the frustrated ambitions, conflicts, cruelties, and uncertainties of our times. Without listening to this music as an escapist, you can find much in it that is constructive and empowering. Its style is minimalistic, repeating notes that move forward slowly with only gradual changes, suggesting an unhurried unfoldment and a subtle metamorphosis.

The hypnotic effects of a piece such as Henryk Górecki's impassioned, haunting *Symphony of Sorrowful Songs* (Symphony no. 3), an international bestseller, are not entirely unlike the inviting continuity of Gregorian chant. I also find some of the music of today's minimalist composers to be intriguing. Many notes, repeated in the midst of slow and subtle changes, can at times produce a hypnotic, even relaxing effect. Composers who have been called minimalist include Terry Riley, Steve Reich, John Adams, Philip Glass, John Tavener, and Arvo Pärt. Two especially beautiful pieces in this category are Philip Glass's Violin Concerto and his compelling piece *Itaipu*. Other such compositions include John Tavener's *Protecting Veil* for cello and strings, and *Eternal Memory*, also for cello and strings. Arvo Pärt sums up the power of simplicity in music (and in life) with these words:

Here I am, alone with silence; I have discovered that it is enough when a single note is beautifully played. This one note, or a silent beat, or a moment of silence comforts me.

I remember an unforgettable moment while listening to some early choral chants in Cambridge, England, in 1972. Night was falling, and a peaceful atmosphere filled the evening like a benediction. The sun shone through the stained-glass windows of the luminous, ancient chapel of King's College. Suddenly, a group of young boys, red-robed choristers, entered singing and began to walk down the center aisle of the chapel, as though they were fulfilling some nameless, ancient ritual. For the Evensong, the young boys began to sing Gregorian chants and beautiful polyphonic anthems, which included settings of some Psalms. I remember the powerful, mysterious sense of Holy Presence; the music made me feel transparent and filled with light. It lifted me in consciousness, and a timeless peace surrounded me there in the chapel. Shortly afterwards, I tried to suggest something of what I had felt in these lines:

> This evening boys are singing
> anthems ancient as their chapel home;
> A canticle of gold and pure soprano –
> song, arising from a holiness so young,
> thrills and shivers the stained glass:
> eyes of eternity, watching
> the choristers sing praises
> while music clear is playing, praying through their faces,
> shaping sounds in Angel light forever streaming
> from the One.
>
> From the plexus of the solar fires,
> music calls its kingdoms' choirs;
> all the chanters of the sounding hours,
> hearing the eternal echoes,
> growing through their heart and bone;
> create the marrow of all singing –
> sparks of music, now suddenly translucent,
> firing their flaming harmony,
> revealing Divinity alone.

When you wish to experience peace and the timeless, embracing presence of God, listen to varied selections of Gregorian chant and other early polyphonic compositions. Many recordings now exist, especially as a result of the recent interest. I especially like the recordings of the Schola Hungarica, on Hungaroton (available from Qualiton Imports). Some chants are sung by men, others by women (often monks and nuns). Hildegard of Bingen, the eleventh-century mystic abbess, poetess, naturalist, and "Sybil of the Rhine," was the first person to allow monks and nuns to live as friends under the same roof and sing together. She was a remarkable composer, and her music is now becoming increasingly available on CD.

Some very beautiful recordings of Gregorian chant and other traditional church music include the following:

From Evening to Evening (Hungaroton HCD 31086)

Salve Festa Dies (women's voices only) (Naxos 8.550712)

Hildegard of Bingen – *Feather on the Breath of God: Hymns and Sequences* (Hyperion CDA 66039)
    – *Spiritual Songs* (Editio Classics 77020-2)

Tradition of Gregorian Chant (DGG Archiv 4-435032)

Christmas (Abbey of St. Peter – Solemnes S.821) (Paraclete Press Distributors)

Abbess: St. Brigid (Dennis and Paula Doyle – Incarnation Music IM 102)

Mystical Chants (Choir of Vienna Hofburgkapelle – Special Music SCD 5118)

Salve Regina (Benedictine Monks – Philips 420 879)

Gregorian Chorale (Excelsior 2-4232)

Ave Maria (Gregorian chant sung by Benedictine Nuns – New World Company NWCD 150) (available from White Swan)

Dom Paul Benoit – *Interior Chant: Men's voices plus organ interludes* (available from Qualiton Imports)

Chill to the Chant (men's voices alternating with women's voices) (RCA 09026-62666)

Monks of the Monasterio de Silos – *Holy Week* (EMI CDZ 67195)

Benedictine Nuns of St. Cecilia's Abbey (Herald HAVPCD 157-DDD)

Creston – *Gregorian Chant for String Orchestra* (Lief – Vanguard OVC 4076) (lovely twentieth-century string chant)

Respighi – *Gregorian Concerto for Violin and Orchestra* (Nishizaki/ Choo Hoey – Marco Polo 8.220152 or Cappelletti-Bamert – Koch-Schwann 3-1124-2H1)

Brother Sun, Sister Moon (John Rutter and the Cambridge Singers) (American Gramophone Records AGCD 588)

St. Peter's Abbey, Solesmes, Monastic Choir (Paraclete, Box 1568, Orleans, MA 02653) (various recordings – all magnificent attunements)

Anonymous 4 – *An English Ladymass* (Harmonia Mundi HMU 907080) (four women's voices)

Choir of the Benedictine Monastery of Santo Domingo de Silos (Lara – EMI CDZ 62735) (award winning recording)

The Rose and the Ostrich Feather, vols. 1, 2, 3, 4 (Eton Choir Book) (Collins 13142, etc.)

Great Orthodox Slavic Liturgy (Harmonia Mundi 190105)

The Queen's Minstrel (Therese Schroeder-Sheker) (beautiful solo female voice) (Windham Hill Records WD-1074)

Ave Gracia Plena (Music in Honor of Mary, Mother of Jesus) (Rutter – Collegium COLCD 116)

Praise of the Mother of God in the Russian Church (Christophorus CD 74505)

Russian Hymns in Honor of the Mother of God (Koch Schwann 31307)

Ecce Sacerdos Magnus (Behold the Great Priest) (haunting sacred music in honor of Saint Martin of Tours, beautifully played on pan flute and organ) (Sacem SYPC 90017) (available from Allegro Imports)

Tavener – *Music for Our Lady* (Darlington – Nimbus NI 5360)

Tallis – *Spem in Alium* (forty-part motet) (Wulstan – Classics for Pleasure 4638) (available from Allegro Imports)

Alonso Lobo – *Requiem* (Summerly – Naxos 8.550682)

Victoria – *Sacred Choral Music* (Hill – Hyperion CDA 66129)

Palestrina – *Pope Marcellus Mass* (Phillips and the Tallis Scholars – Gimell CDGIM 339)

Josquin des Prez – *Mass of the Blessed Virgin* (Feuillie – Cybelia CY 881)

Jean-Claude Mara – *Gregorian Themes for Pan Flute and Organ* (RTV Communications, P.O. Box 290007, Fort Lauderdale, FL 33329)

O my soul, for thee what remains now to do,
But to bend thy pride before such a mystery!
O my heart, fill now with a love deep and pure
That alone can guide us to a heavenly abode.

BERLIOZ, *L'ENFANCE DU CHRIST*
Words of the invisible angelic chorus

Lord Christ, you who are as gentle as the human heart, as
fiery as the forces of nature, as intimate as life itself, you in
whom I can melt away and with whom I must have mastery
and freedom: I love you as a world, as this world which has

captivated my heart. It is you, I now realize, that my brother-men, even those who do not believe, sense and seek throughout the magic immensities of the cosmos.

PIERRE TEILHARD DE CHARDIN

CHAPTER 9

Gallery of Great Composers: Composer Keynotes

We composers are projectors of the infinite into the finite.

GRIEG

Music is not illusion, but rather revelation. Its triumphant power resides in the fact that it reveals to us beauties we find nowhere else, and that the apprehension of them is not transitory, but a perpetual reconcilement to life.

TCHAIKOVSKY

A composer is often an inspired receptor of impressions from interpersonal relationships, nature, and the larger universe. Creative artists use varied rhythms, colors, and harmonies to describe their feelings. Inspired composers often anchor a particular keynote into the planetary consciousness. This keynote seems to arise from a mixture of inspiration, inner perception, individual temperament, creative response, and purposefulness. From the works of each great artist, listeners may receive particular vibrations of energy that can bring them upliftment, new focus, and even healing.

For example, for most listeners, Mozart's music is clear and open; it is always "new" and flows like fresh, rushing streams. Mozart's energetic sounds usually awaken joy and vitality. His music can also help to break up tensions, and it often releases blocked energy and penetrates depression. His works have spiritual merriment. Most of all, Mozart's music often reaches through our resistances to touch our higher self. In his marvelous book *Sacred and Profane Beauty*, Gerardus van der Leeuw says, "In Mozart's music there is something of divine levity—an unearthly gaiety, which is like the whispered laughter of stars, sublime in spite of its exuberance." Recent articles describe music of Mozart as a deterrent to violence. An experiment conducted on college students at the University of California-Irvine indicates that listening to ten minutes of Mozart's piano compositions "significantly improves performance in intelligence tests taken just after listening." The finding was reported in the British scientific journal *Nature* by researchers from the university.

In Japan, recently, the price of wheat noodles, which were made while classical music was playing in the background, rose by more than fifty percent. While the noodles were drying, Vivaldi's *Four Seasons* and birdsongs were played. According to the Asahi News Service, researchers in Japan claim that the music of Mozart makes the density of the yeast used for brewing sake about ten times higher than normal. The frequency of the vibration from the music of certain composers seems also to affect the growth of vegetables.

In a deeper sense, God's glory, flowing through music, offers each of us a transcendent experience, a way to keep alive the connection between our soul and our outer bodies. Our soul contains all the qualities of Infinity. Music can remind each attentive listener that we can feel in our souls the emanations of the heavens.

Beethoven's music brings focus and empowers the will; it can often deepen a person's determination, especially Symphony no. 5, the *Egmont Overture*, and the *Emperor Concerto*. Much of J. S. Bach's music is nurturing and offers clarity and reassurance of our place and purpose within the cosmic order, especially Bach's *Jesu, Joy of Man's Desiring, Sheep May Safely Graze, Arioso, Come Sweet Death, Air on a G String,* and *Thou Art with Me.* Mendelssohn's music is often "green," awakening in listeners a greater sense of peace and harmony; listen, for example, to his beautiful Violin Concerto in E. And so, each of the great composers seems to have brought forth a valuable keynote, which can be felt as their music is experienced. Get to know the essence of the great composers. Their music is immortal, far ahead of the mass consciousness, and connected to the higher worlds. A well-made CD-cassette player costs only $100–$200, and if you buy wisely, you can purchase a collection of twenty-five outstanding CDs for about $125. Thus, for under three hundred dollars, you will be on your way toward building an enjoyable collection of music. Each selection that nurtures you is like a valuable friend that can empower you and change your life for the better.

An aim of this book is to teach you to use pieces of music like energy prescriptions to help you reduce stress, lessen pain, and increase the release of endorphins and peptides that energize you naturally. Music, wisely chosen, provides far more than just entertainment. It can make you feel better about your life and more connected in the world. Musical selections are like tuning forks which can attune you to the larger cosmic harmony.

In my university music appreciation courses, although I am not a trained musician, I try to help people of different ages, backgrounds, and cultures learn to listen to and enjoy beautiful music. I love to introduce students to music of all types, music that often contains a variety of moods and colors. It is fascinating to watch how a particular song or concerto opens up hidden pockets of feeling and perception within them.

A recent story in a California newspaper told of a shopkeeper in a local mall who used Mozart's music to drive away "unruly teenagers" who were gathering outside the entrance to his store after school each day. At first, the young people reacted loudly (and profanely) to the "lousy elevator music" they were hearing. Most of them left. But, the young people still wanted to meet, and so within a few days they returned to the same location. Within a week, they began to resist Mozart's music less. Their manners (and language) improved. One young fellow even began holding the door for customers. Two weeks later, when the store owner gave up and offered to play the music the teenagers preferred, they accepted but also asked the owner to continue playing Mozart. Once in a while, the shopkeeper even served them doughnuts.

While some of your musical tastes might change through the years, other tendencies may become even stronger with time. Feeling your own deepest desires, temperament, and momentum, you will be led to find the composers and musical works that speak most directly to you. As your sensitivity increases, you will probably even want to hear several interpretations of favorite compositions, much like hearing different singers perform the same song.

Again, remember to keep a list of the musical selections that help you the most. Observe how they affect you and when they are most helpful for you. Like very close friends, such pieces of music will never fail you. They can absorb your negative moods better than most people can, and you can return to them repeatedly with trust and confidence. The effectiveness of music as a powerful healing agent in your life lies in its continuous becoming. Music never stands still; it is always new and forever alive, bringing into your consciousness fresh potencies of melody, rhythm, and harmonizing energies. Experience musical selections as large power stations or as beautiful healing fountains. Feel their liquid streams of sound pouring through you. Visualize your music bathing and cleansing you.

As I introduce the following great composers and their music, I mean for my descriptions to be suggestive, not literal. For each great creative artist, I have tried to share my personal impressions and the feelings and inner responses of others. You may hear entirely different qualities in a piece of music or even in a composer's total output. This is natural. However you might experience the music, my hope is that you will continue to risk hearing new pieces. Let my comments be springboards to help you find the music most inspiring to you—music that will be therapeutic and enjoyable.

Here are sketches of some of the world's most well-received composers and their famous masterpieces. I have included the element—Fire, Earth, Air, Water—which seems to be most dominant in the music. I have also listed the astrological sun sign of each composer. An appendix lists the birthdays of many of the composers mentioned in this chapter and elsewhere in the book. You may wish to coordinate your choice of musical selections with meditation and a celebration of a particular composer's birthday or anniversary. (See my book *Lifestreams*, Quest Books, Wheaton, IL 60189, 1988.)

ANTONIO VIVALDI
(Pisces—Water)

I like Vivaldi's beautiful melodies—somewhat like Mozart in mood: pleasing, effervescent, and joyful, as well as reflective. His music is Baroque —in other words, uncomplicated, clearly focused, bright and melodic, warm and genial. His music lightens the atmosphere. It does not intrude and is always like good company. At times you can hear imitations of nature songs and bird calls (notice these in the flute concerto *Il Gardellino*).

In my work with people and music, I have found that Vivaldi's bright and happy music is good for relieving depression and bringing emotional and mental clearance. In nursing homes, Vivaldi's music seems to cleanse the environment of negative moods, offering vitality and rhythmical clarity. Likewise, his concertos for flute, violin, or piccolo can aid digestion and are good company during meals. You can also write letters to a friend to the background of Vivaldi.

Main works: The Four Seasons; mandolin concertos; flute concertos; *Gloria; Credo;* piccolo concertos; sacred choral works. (Vivaldi composed more than five hundred concertos!)

GEORG PHILIPP TELEMANN
(Pisces—Water)

I find much in Telemann that is similar to the qualities of Vivaldi's music. Again, vitality and clear melodies are always present. A sense of freedom and easy flow pervades the music. Telemann's music is gentle, yet ordered and strong.

You can plan your day to the background of a Telemann concerto. His music is good for clearing your mind while driving to work in the morning. The melodies are cheerful and can help you relieve stress. Telemann's music gets you through traffic on the freeway. His slow movements, like Vivaldi's, are also intimate friends in the quiet hours of the night.

Main works: Music for the Banquet Table; Suite for Flute and Strings; *Water Music;* miscellaneous concertos.

GEORGE FRIDERIC HANDEL
(Aquarius-Pisces—Air-Water)

You can easily feel the majesty and nobility present in Handel's music. His finest music contains strong feelings and emotions, along with a directed activity and movement. It is often formal, traditional, and conventional. In true Baroque and early Classical style, Handel's music stays within boundaries, yet within the containment, the melodic line soars and uplifts the spirit. Handel's music can be thunderous, ceremonial, majestic, and at times ornate (listen to the oratorios *Solomon* or *Judas Maccabaeus*). In many of his compositions, Handel found inspiration from the Bible and world mythology. Often, power and genuine celestial joy supersede human merriment. Handel's music is inspired and raises human consciousness to view divine heights. His music can lift us beyond our outer personality. It helps us to do better. The outstanding modern composer Alan Hovhaness, also a Pisces composer, has said, "Handel is to me the greatest of all the composers."

I believe that the greatest music Handel ever composed is *Messiah*, especially the *Hallelujah Chorus*. One listener I know always sees "golden sunbursts" when she hears this music. The writer Stefan Zweig, in his book *Tides of Fortune*, describes Handel's unique experience as a receptor for this transforming music. According to Zweig, as the melodies and celestial sounds poured into Handel's room, the composer was so inspired and "on fire" that he could hardly keep his pen moving fast enough to represent what he was hearing. During these moments Handel reported seeing the Heavenly Host, who filled him with these Christ-empowered sounds. Handel's words about angelic visitations during his composition of *Messiah* read as follows:

I did think I did see all Heaven before me—and the great God himself. Where I was, in my body or out of my body as I wrote it, I know not. God knows!

Main works: Messiah; harp concertos; organ concertos; *Water Music; Ode to Saint Cecilia; Royal Fireworks Music; Israel in Egypt; Judas Maccabaeus; Solomon;* flute sonatas.

JOHANN SEBASTIAN BACH
(Pisces-Aries—Water-Fire)

For me Bach's music brings through the power and grandeur of God. His music is universal and cosmic, describing the immensity of the galaxies moving in their orbits. It is orderly and contained, yet vast. His textures are thickly orchestrated, yet even solo instruments sound clearly through the overall musical fabric. Bach's music is both masculine and feminine, powerful and nurturing (listen, for example, to the violin concertos). Reason and emotion are blended with total sureness of technique. Microcosms move within the macrocosm.

Bach composed all his music in a spirit of worship and with a deep desire "to glorify God." It is the unfailing statement of how light illumines darkness and how the larger divine order of the universe works through the limitations of earthly existence. At its best, Bach's music echoes the celestial choirs whose music is continuously filling the earth. The choruses from his cantatas are powerful and inspiring.

Bach's music brings a refreshment of the spirit and can change people's lives. I remember how the power and joy of the third *Brandenburg Concerto* helped a friend find courage to save his marriage. At a coffeehouse near our home, I often see customers responding happily as they hear the cheerful melodies of Bach's *Brandenburg Concerto no. 4*, which the proprietor frequently plays. Listen to Bach's music to clear and activate your mind. The great cellist Pablo Casals tried to play some piece of music by Bach every day of his life. The guitarist Andres Segovia loved Bach's music deeply. Bach's music can be performed successfully on most instruments.

Main works: Toccata and Fugue in D; B Minor Mass; *Saint Matthew Passion; Saint John Passion; Brandenburg Concertos; Magnificat; Christmas Oratorio;* suites for orchestra; *Jesu, Joy of Man's Desiring; Sheep May Safely Graze.* Listeners may enjoy beginning their Bach musical experience by listening either to the six *Brandenburg Concertos* or orchestral transcriptions (preferably conducted by Leopold Stokowski) of such beautiful Bach melodies as *Air on a G String, Arioso, Thou Art with Me, Come Sweet Death,* and *Sleepers Awake.* Do not miss the organist Virgil Fox playing his transcription of *Come Sweet Death* (Bainbridge CD). Note pianist Wilhelm Kempff's beautiful transcriptions of Bach's *Chorales* (DGG 439672).

CHRISTOPH WILLIBALD GLUCK
(Cancer—Water)

I like the simplicity and naturalness of Gluck's music. It is always in good taste and unifies feelings with ideas of form.

A piece of beautiful music that is always cleansing is the joyful *Dance of the Blessed Spirits*. This ten- to twelve-minute piece of music seems to clear the air and brings a purifying uplift to the listener. It is celestial music, which always activates one's sense of joy.

Main works: Concerto in G for Flute; *Don Juan; Orfeo ed Euridice.*

FRANZ JOSEPH HAYDN
(Aries—Fire)

Haydn's music is sharp and fresh; it sparkles with zestful tunes and rhythms. Haydn himself said that as he composed his music, he heard it crackle like notes flying from a spindle. His music is optimistic, joyful, clean, and always in good spirit. It offers a cleansing kind of energy— it effervesces, but in a way that is quite different from Mozart's. Haydn's music is buoyant and also well-mannered. It is said that in joy and gratitude, Haydn always dressed in his finest garments and wore his costliest wig when he sat down to compose, for he felt that when he was in the presence of music, he was also in the presence of the Creator.

Play Haydn's music to disperse depression or gloom (listen to the flute quartets). Haydn will help you to see and feel the brighter sides of your circumstances. His music is like bright diamonds of energy that will shimmer through rigid attitudes or negative emotions. His choral music is often worshipful and luminous with joy. Haydn's music empowers the listener.

Main works: The Seasons; The Creation; the symphonies; quartets; organ concertos; masses; Trumpet Concerto in E-flat (an exceptional recording of this piece features Hardenberger/Marriner on Philips 420203).

WOLFGANG AMADEUS MOZART
(Aquarius—Air)

He was remarkably fond of punch, of billiards, and had an excellent billiard table in his house. He was kind-hearted and always ready to oblige, but so particular when he played that if the slightest noise were made, he instantly left off. He once

*said to me, 'Melody is the essence of all music. Who knows the
most knows least.'*

Michael Kelly

*Mozart, so devoted to trifling amusements, appeared a being of
superior order as soon as he sat down to a pianoforte. His mind
then took wing, and his whole attention was directed to the sole
object for which nature designed him, the harmony of sounds.*

A. Schlichtegroll

As I have mentioned, I find Mozart's music different in quality and
essence from that of other composers. It is elusive, mysterious, will-o'-the-
wisp, and even at times angelic (Mozart's masterpiece is *The Magic Flute*,
which describes the process of initiation in music). Mozart's music often
may seem to come from an entirely different "place." It is always elegant
and charming, sometimes humorous.

For me, it is the airy, unrestricted quality of Mozart's music that is
so beautiful. Working within the musical form and period of his time,
he somehow transcended it and achieved a transparent joy. Most likely
you will find newness and freshness in Mozart's music. It is almost never
tiresome.

Mozart's creative use of the orchestra and its instruments yields a music
that is crystalline in its clarity (I doubt that you will ever tire of playing
his piano concertos); listen for the many different instrumental parts. Yet
Mozart's music is also powerful and radiant. A certain poignancy in some
works reveals a human being who suffered greatly but never indulged
himself for long in moodiness. To me a devotional quality pervades his
music, along with an airy lightness. Mozart's music belongs to a world far
removed from this earth. See Robert Harris's superb book, *What to Listen
for in Mozart* (Simon and Schuster, 1991).

Main works: Magic Flute (opera); piano concertos; masses; string quartets; string quintets; serenades; symphonies (especially nos. 25, 29, 35, 36,
39, 40, 41); violin concertos; overtures; violin and piano sonatas. Some of
the finest interpreters of Mozart's piano concertos include Kempff, Perahia,
Bishop-Kovacevich, Haebler, Shelley, Rudolf and Peter Serkin, Ashkenazy,
and Uchida.

LUDWIG VAN BEETHOVEN
(Sagittarius—Fire)

Beethoven's is the music of a titan. His life and works break open new
entries into human emotions and the human condition. Beethoven was the

first real musical psychologist who probed the individual and collective psyche. Because of Beethoven's own suffering (including deafness and frequent human rejection) he was able to identify with humankind's sufferings, and thus, help humanity to grow. This is music that throbs with joys and sorrows. Emanating large fountains of primal energy, Beethoven's music unleashes great waves of power and new archetypes into the atmosphere. (Begin by listening to the *Egmont Overture.*) Sometimes defiant, sometimes peaceful, his music is full of fighting spirit, courage, and strong willpower, sometimes granitelike in its determination and force. But Beethoven's music, like the man himself, can also be tender and lyrical, devotional and warm. Listen to the Symphony no. 6 *(Pastorale),* the "green symphony."

In my work with clients and students, I find that for most people, listening to one piece of Beethoven's music at a single sitting is ample. To listen to some of his symphonies (especially nos. 3, 5, 6, 7, and 9) is like experiencing a complete lifetime of feeling in four or five movements.

For many listeners, Beethoven's music deepens empathy and awakens compassion and the desire for universal brotherhood (listen especially to the deeply cosmic Symphony no. 9 or the Fantasia in C for Piano, Chorus and Orchestra). Because of the feelings contained in Beethoven's music, his works can stir groups and crowds and lift them to higher levels of human achievement, fulfillment, and divine realization. Beethoven's music is like a royal warrior—robed in orange and purple. It is interesting to remember that when Leonard Bernstein gave his concert to celebrate the fall of the Berlin Wall, the work he chose to perform was Beethoven's Symphony no. 9, a celebration of global brotherhood-sisterhood. This symphony emanates beautiful streams of blue. David Tame, in his excellent book on the composer *Beethoven and the Spiritual Path,* describes the difference between New Age music and Golden Age music:

> Beethoven's music is genuine Golden Age music, already with us! Whenever he composed, Beethoven's intent and purpose was always the New Age ideal as expressed in Christ's two great commandments (to love the Lord thy God with all thy heart, soul, strength and mind, and to love thy neighbor as thyself). . . . Beethoven's works exert an effect upon atoms, upon molecules, upon the individual's consciousness, and upon society at large similar to that of a magnet placed beneath a sheet of paper upon which iron filings have been scattered. Beethoven's compositions organize and harmonize, dissipating all unreality, and transforming entropy into alignment with the Divine.

Main works: the nine symphonies; *Creatures of Prometheus; Missa Solemnis;* the five piano concertos; *Fidelio;* Violin Concerto; the string quartets; the piano sonatas.

FRANZ SCHUBERT
(Aquarius—Air)

I especially like the private world of Schubert. His music reminds me of a wanderer in eternity, never really at home on earth, yet warm and good-hearted while passing through. Schubert's music is that of a loner among friends, living between love and pain, sensing a peace behind life's conflicts and transience (these feelings surface most clearly in Schubert's chamber music).

Three of the most inspiring pieces of Schubert's music for me are *Rosamunde, Ave Maria,* and the Symphony no. 8 *(Unfinished).* People that I have worked with usually respond very favorably to these selections, finding in them reassurance, calm power, and deep, inward awakenings. The *Ave Maria* is music of unconditional love, devotion, and surrender that transmutes sorrow. One of the greatest pieces that Schubert ever composed is the beautiful and magical String Quintet, op. 163. This composition, created through divine inspiration, was composed just before Schubert's passing in 1828. He never heard it performed. It reveals the joy and essential generosity of Schubert, and it speaks deeply of his own inner processes. I especially recommend the orchestral arrangement of this work by the gifted conductor Dalia Atlas (ITM Classics 950005 – available from One World Records, 85 Fulton Street, Unit 3, Boonton, NY 07005). Also, note the beautiful performance of Schubert's songs by Elly Ameling at Tanglewood (Omega 1001).

Main works: Ave Maria; the nine symphonies (the *Symphony no. 8 (Unfinished)* is especially powerful and urges us "to keep on keeping on"); the masses; the string quartets; the songs; the piano sonatas; *Rosamunde.*

FELIX MENDELSSOHN
(Aquarius—Air)

Whereas Beethoven stirs up, Mendelssohn soothes and brings serenity. His music contains an aristocratic refinement and an ennobling joy. I often sense beautiful landscapes, painted in shades of green and turquoise, as I experience Mendelssohn's music.

I find Mendelssohn's music to be good for calming manic persons and situations. The Symphony no. 4 *(Italian)* and the overtures *Calm Sea and Prosperous Voyage* and *The Hebrides* bring in healing energies that cleanse the atmosphere. Mendelssohn's music also revives the sick and lonely, and relieves tiredness. Don't forget that in the nineteenth century, it was

Mendelssohn who rediscovered Bach and played his music in public after that great composer had been forgotten.

Main works: A Midsummer Night's Dream; the symphonies; Violin Concerto; *Elijah; St. Paul; Calm Sea and Prosperous Voyage* and *Hebrides Overtures; On Wings of Song; Songs Without Words* (piano solo).

FRÉDÉRIC CHOPIN
(Pisces—Water)

Like Mendelssohn's music, Chopin's works are always refined. But instead of painting outer landscapes, Chopin's music portrays soulscapes of feeling. A deep emotional content fills his piano works. I also hear nobility, some nostalgia, and romance in Chopin's compositions. His music is like water, ever shifting in its contours, shadings, and colors. Sometimes a quiet stream, again a torrent, his music is forever fluid, carrying the listener through a shifting kaleidoscope of human emotions.

I feel that the essence of Chopin is contained in these words about him from his contemporaries:

A man of exquisite heart and mind.

DELACROIX

His soul was a star and dwelt apart.
. . . . .
He was a lover of an Impossible so shadowy and so near the stellar regions.

GEORGE SAND

What others say on their knees, he uttered in tone-language—all the mysteries of passion and grief which man can understand without words, because there are no words in which they can adequately be expressed.

FRANZ LISZT

I have found that Chopin's music strikes deeply into human loneliness. Several introverts with whom I have worked responded favorably to Chopin's waltzes. One woman, who formerly was catatonic, came to life upon hearing a Chopin waltz (Nocturne, op. 9, no. 2 and the Piano Concerto no. 1, slow movement). The slow movement of Piano Concerto no. 1

emanates waves of unconditional love and beauty. It is an angelic piece. (Listen to the wonderful Gilels/Ormandy version on Sony SBK 46336.)

Main works: Etudes; preludes; impromptus; waltzes; nocturnes; ballades; the two piano concertos; scherzos; polonaises; mazurkas; *Andante Spianato.*

ROBERT SCHUMANN
(Gemini–Air)

A childlike quality is present in much of Schumann's music. Also, a dreamlike quality provides a sense of fantasy and color. For example, the very pictorial *Manfred Overture,* based upon the description of a tragic hero, written by the poet Lord Byron, is beautifully melodic and emotionally filled music which sweeps the listener along. A similar outpouring of strong moods and inner "feelingscapes" fills the beautiful Symphony no. 2. At its best, Schumann's music balances the inspiration of the mind with deep responses of the heart. Schumann died insane, however. You will feel some of his inner turmoil in his music; struggle and sadness are present. Yet his melodies are often beautiful and uplifting.

Other works of Schumann that I have found to be particularly enjoyable are these: *Träumerei (Dreams),* Symphony no. 1 *(Spring), Childhood Scenes,* and the Piano Concerto. Listen to the beautiful musical description of the cathedral rising luminous over the Rhine River (in the Symphony no. 3, *Rhenish).*

Main works: The four symphonies; *Manfred; Scenes from Faust;* quartets; Piano Concerto; Cello Concerto; miscellaneous piano works, such as *Childhood Scenes.*

JOHANNES BRAHMS
(Taurus–Earth)

Brahms's music combines a private, tender, and loving heart with a feisty and rustic personality. In Brahms's music you can hear the professor and the peasant—when a student saw egg in Herr Brahms's beard, he said that he knew what Brahms had eaten for breakfast that morning, but Brahms responded that he hadn't eaten eggs for a week! Intellectual and sometimes oblivious to his outward appearance, yet inwardly profound and very deeply feeling—these are the qualities of the man, and they also fill his music. Listen to the power and psychological complexity of the melodies and the thickly orchestrated harmonies trying to emerge. You can hear the working out of inner conflicts and great soul strength as you listen to Brahms's music. There is a toughness of fiber, thick sounds of orchestral melody, which seem to me to emerge out of deep forests and underbrush of struggle. Always a path leads into light and clearance.

For example, listen to the wonderful finale of the Piano Concerto no. 1 or the finales from Symphonies nos. 1 and 2. A deep love is alive in Brahms's heart and music, much like the idealized love (probably never consummated because of Brahms's earlier, untransferrable love for his mother) that Brahms felt for Clara Schumann, wife of Robert Schumann and a composer in her own right. Thus, Brahms's devotional and intellectual natures combine continuously in his music to provide the listener with strength and tenderness. Brahms's compositions are also filled with robust humor and celebration (for example, *Academic Festival Overture*).

Brahms's music also reveals a deep attunement with nature (especially in the Symphony no. 2); a hint of nostalgia appears from time to time (listen to the slow movements of Symphonies nos. 2 and 3).

Music of Brahms that I particularly enjoy includes: Lullaby (good for soothing neurotic moods); Symphonies nos. 1, 2, 3, and 4; the two piano concertos; the gorgeous Violin Concerto; and the late piano pieces. I especially love his Piano Quintet, a marvelous chamber music masterpiece.

Main works: The four symphonies; Violin Concerto; *A German Requiem*; the two piano concertos; miscellaneous chamber music; songs.

RICHARD WAGNER
(Taurus-Gemini—Earth-Air)

The key to appreciating Wagner's works is to realize that they contain human and superhuman energies. Wagner, the man, could be egomaniacal, racist, dishonest, and a revolting human being; Wagner, the music deva and receptive channel for music, could be a rare genius. At times in his music, Wagner reveals an almost egomaniacal concern for self-power, yet mysteriously, the Higher Ones of God seem to have used him and inspired Wagner to compose some of the most spiritually powerful music that anyone could ever hope to hear (listen to the Prelude to *Lohengrin*, Act 1 and the Prelude and *Good Friday Spell* to *Parsifal*). Thus, Wagner remains a contradictory figure in music. Reports from his contemporaries tell us that Wagner the man was unattractive, without scruples, totally self-centered, feeling that the world owed him a living; but as a composer Wagner seems always to have remained totally loyal and dedicated to the Muse of music—

single-minded and open to inspiration coming to him from higher angelic Hosts and the powers in nature.

Wagner's music is very powerful, filled with surging, spiraling energies, massive crescendos, and bolts of thunder. Such powerful music of nature and the cosmos brings a listener into deeper spiritual contact, cosmic awareness, and feelings of divinity and invincibility within the soul. Listen, for example, to the surging power of *Die Meistersinger Overture*, a piece that Hitler played to empower himself; then listen to the *Liebestod* (from *Tristan and Isolde*), a rising, power-filled outpouring of love, both human and transcendental.

You can use some of Wagner's works to ennoble and inspire your life. As in the case of Hitler's response, Wagner's music can also make people become overbearing and power-hungry, even to the point of insanity and dementia. Hitler listened to Wagner and worked himself up to a frenzy before going out to address his troops. Wagner's music is capable of bringing out the very best and the very worst in the consciousness of the listener. Recently, in a Copenhagen zoo, a rare okapi, upon hearing Wagner's opera *Tannhäuser* being rehearsed nearby, went into shock, collapsed, and died. The music was too strong and stressful *(San Diego Tribune*, 11 August 1994).

The Wagnerian music that I have found to be most uplifting and inspiring includes these works: *Ride of the Valkyries*, mighty calls from great Warrior Angels; Prelude to *Lohengrin* (Act I), filled with serenity and exaltation, and angelic Hosts descending to earth through the theme of the Holy Grail; the Prelude and *Good Friday Spell* from *Parsifal* remain as examples among the most deeply spiritual music ever composed. After Wagner completed his *Parsifal*, he died quickly. With this masterpiece, he seemingly had completed his life purpose.

Main works: The Ring Cycle; Parsifal; Meistersinger; Lohengrin; Tannhäuser; Tristan und Isolde; Flying Dutchman (listen especially to inspiring orchestral selections from these works, such as the *Prize Song* from *Die Meistersinger* and *Pilgrims' Chorus* from *Tannhäuser*); *Siegfried Idyll* is a beautiful love song that Wagner composed for his wife.

MAX BRUCH
(Capricorn—Earth)

Here is beautiful music, filled with unforgettable melodies and deep feelings of longing and devotion. You will never tire of hearing the stirring, love-filled, triumphant, and spiritually uplifting beauty of Bruch's Violin

Concerto no. 1. I believe that of all the music my dear wife Rosemary and I have shared together through the years, this piece remains her favorite. And it is a favorite for many other persons.

Bruch's music is inclusive, warm, and powerful. Listen also to the lovely *Scottish Fantasy for Violin and Orchestra*. Lively rhythms and beautiful melodies mingle together continuously.

Main works: Adagio on a Celtic Theme for Cello and Orchestra; *Ave Maria*; Concerto for Clarinet, Viola, and Orchestra; *Kol Nidrei* for Cello and Orchestra (very beautiful); Romanza for Viola and Orchestra; Serenade for Strings; Swedish dances; three symphonies.

CÉSAR FRANCK
(Sagittarius—Fire)

Franck's music is contemplative, filled with feelings of intimate devotion to God. It is largely empty of personal ego and channels into the atmosphere the harmonies of devas and angelic choirs. Franck's music can help us to become more receptive to nature and angelic presences beyond ourselves. It frees us to larger possibilities in the spirit. It is also filled with the powerful simplicity of true love. Franck's music reveals the sound of a world transformed by the Divine Presence—warm, spacious, privately enthroned. As Vincent d'Indy, Franck's student, said, "Franck's music is music of the center of the soul." His goodness and his strength as a person shine even more through his music.

His music puts us at ease because it demands nothing from a listener. It pours forth its song, not always familiar, but strangely beautiful, other-worldly—like rarefied air. Franck's music, that of the contemplative mystic, once inspired me to write these lines:

> Listen to the sounds of great cathedrals
> steepling the heavens;
> hear the praising panoply of Angels
> filling earth.

Main works: Miscellaneous organ works; Symphony in D Minor; Piano Quintet in F; Symphonic Variations for Piano and Orchestra; the *Beatitudes* (oratorio) *Mass*; *Panis angelicus* (sung by Pavarotti or the orchestral transcription, composed and conducted by Stokowski); *Les Eolides*; *Redemption*; *Psyche*.

ANTONÍN DVOŘÁK
(Virgo–Earth)

Dvořák's music is an earth music that brings joy and warmth. It contains many beautiful melodies drawn from his native Bohemia, the songs of the Native Americans, and Negro spirituals. A strong kinship with nature fills Dvořák's music (listen to the *Silent Woods* and the Symphony no. 8), along with feelings of love for humanity and friends. Much of Dvořák's music surges with spiritual joy, affirmation, and the unaffected simplicity of the home, hearth, and the good earth.

Dvořák's music has helped me in two specific counseling situations. I once tutored a young student who was at the time quite tense, angry, and troubled. The Largo from the Ninth Symphony helped him to relax and to concentrate. In another instance I can remember how much happier a woman was after just listening quietly to *Humoresque* (played on the violin by Fritz Kreisler or Mischa Elman).

One of the first musical favorites my wife Rosemary and I shared together was the Cello Concerto, which both of us had especially loved before we ever met each other. Its melodies are beautiful, triumphant, and filled with the lyrical songs of the heart. I have a vivid memory of seeing and hearing Yo Yo Ma playing this beautiful work so sensitively with conductor Zubin Mehta and the New York Philharmonic Orchestra.

Main works: The nine symphonies, especially nos. 6, 7, 8, and 9 (from the *New World)*; Cello Concerto; *Humoresque;* Slavonic dances; Piano Concerto; *Silent Woods; Stabat Mater;* Serenade in E; the *Wood Dove; Czech Suite;* miscellaneous chamber music.

EDVARD GRIEG
(Gemini–Air)

When I listen to the music of Grieg, I can easily envision the nature beings—elves, gnomes, fairies, as well as the rushing cascades of great waterfalls and fjords of Scandinavia. Grieg's music is filled with enchanting, lyrical cameos of smaller nature presences, but he also composed the "big" pieces, such as *Olav Trygvason* and *Peer Gynt.* In Grieg's music a Nordic freshness and open-air quality purifies the environment wherever it is played. A joy and vitality also permeate his music. It is enlivening and life affirming.

Pay special attention to Grieg's *Nocturne* (from *Lyric Suite*) and the slow movement of the Piano Concerto. These selections seem especially to bring in healing radiations. A famous pianist once said that Grieg's Piano Concerto is the greatest piano concerto ever composed.

Though Grieg's music is powerful in places, it is usually more lyrical and does not sound as primal or as awesome as Sibelius's musical landscapes. One of Grieg's most dramatic works is his Piano Concerto. Like Mendelssohn and Chopin before him, Grieg composed intimate tone portraits and vignettes of beauty. I find Grieg's music to be very therapeutic, and it is well-received almost unanimously by persons I counsel or teach.

Main works: Piano Concerto; *Holberg Suite; Peer Gynt; Olav Trygvason; I Love Thee* (song); miscellaneous piano works; *Lyric Suite; Two Elegiac Melodies;* Norwegian dances; *Landsighting* (cantata).

PETER ILYICH TCHAIKOVSKY
(Taurus—Earth)

Tchaikovsky and his music are strongly attuned to the nature kingdom. His music evokes inward dreams and reveries. There is a wistfulness to his music, which often stirs memories of fairy tales and magical realms. Sometimes, Tchaikovsky's music suggests a longing for another world, as though the composer never felt really at home on earth. Along with this quality, his works also contains Slavic power, drama, occasional tints of melancholy, and the Russian penchant for exploring the dark side of life.

Tchaikovsky's strong attunement with nature comes through his music, especially Symphony no. 1 *(Winter Dreams), Sleeping Beauty, The Nutcracker,* and occasionally in *Swan Lake.* A strong militant quality also is audible, for example in the martial sections of *Marche slave,* Symphony no. 5, and Symphony no. 6 *(Pathetique).*

Tchaikovsky's works contain a wide range of emotional content. Find those selections which are inspiring to you; you can "go down into grief" as you play some of Tchaikovsky's most deeply felt pieces (listen to the heartrending final movement of the *Pathetique* Symphony no. 6, or the slow movement of the Symphony no. 5). Good energy raisers include Piano Concertos nos. 1, 2, the Violin Concerto, Serenade for Strings, *Manfred Symphony, Capriccio Italien,* and selections from *The Nutcracker.*

Main works: The three piano concertos; the six symphonies; *Manfred Symphony;* Violin Concerto; *Sleeping Beauty; Swan Lake; The Nutcracker;* Serenade for Strings; *Marche slave; Capriccio Italien; Variations on a Rococo Theme; Fatum; Francesca da Rimini; Souvenir from Florence; The Snow Queen; Eugene Onegin* (opera after the literary work of Pushkin); Liturgy; Vespers; Cherubic Hymns.

FREDERICK DELIUS
(Aquarius—Air)

Delius's music is filled with the atmosphere of nature. The listener may feel a certain impersonality. In this sense, the music is removed, nontactile, airy, yet very real, and takes a person inside nature's flowing rhythms, rather than leaving one to listen just as an onlooker. Delius's music is like an elusive breeze, bringing fragrance and passing by quickly. This winsomeness reminds us of the evanescent quality of life, the mysterious mingling of relationships on earth and the changing seasons of nature. Delius's music is universal music, belonging both everywhere and nowhere.

Delius's works require time and attention. Some of my friends have said to me at first, "Nothing's happening! What's Delius saying?" But, gradually, as people give themselves to the music, most of them can enter into Delius's very private world. Sir Thomas Beecham, the great conductor, seems to have had a special affinity for Delius's music. A special favorite among those who love Delius's music is *On Hearing the First Cuckoo in Spring*. I find that his works (especially *Appalachia* and *Florida Suite*) are excellent for activating creative imagination. I remember with pleasure finger-painting to the sounds and harmonies of *Brigg Fair* and *Over the Hills and Far Away*. The music produced a freeing effect on me.

Main works: Appalachia; Song of Summer; Florida Suite; Cello Concerto; *A Mass of Life; On Hearing the First Cuckoo in Spring; Over the Hills and Far Away; Brigg Fair;* Piano Concerto; *A Song of the High Hills;* Violin Concerto; *North Country Sketches.*

GUSTAV MAHLER
(Cancer—Water)

"Everywhere and eternally the distance shines bright and blue."

MAHLER, ABSCHIED

Mahler's music spans the whole range of human emotion and describes the aspiration of the soul through the realms of nature into the larger cosmos. Suffering and torment are sometimes present, but at its best (Symphonies nos. 2, 3, 4, 8, 9) Mahler's music rises to peaks of joy, fulfillment, radiant love, and divine connection. Many listeners feel the presence of celestial choirs in the glory-filled finale of the Symphony no. 2 *(Resurrection)*. Listen to the wonderful versions of this work, as conducted by Walter, Klemperer, Kaplan, or Stokowski on Music and Arts. Feel the surrender of the soul in the expansive Adagio of the Symphony no. 9, marvelously realized in the recordings by Bruno Walter and Herbert von Karajan. The Symphony no. 4 is a beautiful song to nature. Listen to the exquisite renditions conducted by Wit, Kletzki, Szell, or Bernstein (Sony).

Assertiveness and power mingle with deep devotion and surrender in Mahler's great symphonies and songs. A bittersweet quality pervades Mahler's world. Suffering brings liberation. Resignation is replaced by release and transcendence.

Mahler's works are composed for a very large symphony orchestra, so be prepared for real bombardments of cosmic sounds filling the atmosphere. His Eighth Symphony is composed for more than one thousand performers, and it brings through a cosmic potency which Mahler reports that he clearly felt and envisioned. But along with the power, deep love and devotion fill his music, and the Ninth Symphony, for example, moves into final peace and illumination.

Leonard Bernstein, more than any other conductor, seems to have understood Mahler's complex psychological world. His recordings of Mahler's music offer rewards beyond compare.

Main works: The ten symphonies; *Song of the Earth; Songs of a Wayfarer; Youth's Magic Horn.*

ANTON BRUCKNER
(Virgo—Earth)

Anton Bruckner dedicated all of his music to God Almighty. His music is cosmic and mystical. It is the great outpouring of a devotional Christ-centered mystic. The Japanese conductor Tadaaki Otaka has said, "Bruckner is special; he is closest to God." Layer by layer and stone by stone, each unfolding melody from Bruckner's symphonies can lift you up toward mountain peaks that reach into infinite kingdoms of holy light.

His music always unfolds gradually, and often Bruckner likes to repeat his great themes, each time slightly differently, weaving an ascending spiral, spreading and opening on high. In many of Bruckner's symphonies and choral works, there is a confrontation with evil, as clarion trumpets penetrate the darkness, filling it with power and light.

Many of his symphonies last more than an hour; they are like a pilgrim's quest that requires patience and a willingness to accompany the composer, a loyal guide and pathfinder, who leads the listener on a sacred journey. Bruckner's scherzos are like interludes, often spiced with a pastoral flavor, nature beings, and folklike sections. These episodes in nature contrast with more powerful, expansive sections. Bruckner's finales take us home, alternating peace and sudden power, movement and stillness, gradually lifting us higher and higher until finally we seem to be left suspended in the majestic presence of the Infinite surrounded with great legions of heavenly beings (I think here of the wonderful, cosmic paintings of angels filling the heavens, by Gustave Doré). Though sometimes dark and nocturnal, Bruckner's music always eventually emerges into light and triumph.

In his outstanding article "Anton Bruckner," Manfred Seyfert-Landgraf contrasts the outer childlike qualities and naiveté of Bruckner with his deep inner devotion to God and the profound spirituality of his music. Bruckner mentioned to friends that at times, while he was composing, he "suddenly saw the heavens open, and God's Presence, Saint Peter and the Archangel Michael came to him, surrounded by a huge angelic choir."

Seyfert-Landgraf and others experience the nine symphonies of Bruckner as an initiation process. The later symphonies, not only nurturing, dramatic, and mighty in their own right, become "a revelation of the divine spiritual world."

Erich Schwebsch wrote these revealing words about Bruckner and his music:

> Bruckner is the musician of the human soul that has overcome all nervous trends of our time; he has found a new and peaceful relationship with the cosmic background of all existence. . . . Bruckner has become a cosmic musician. . . . He brings into the world, in harmony with it, a peaceful creative power which recognizes that a person cannot rage against the cosmic forces in self-destructive ecstasy. . . . Bruckner finds in the laws of the spirit a new impulse for the rebuilding of our ruined earthly world.

Bruckner's radiant music stands today as a powerful and healing bed-rock—a vision of an all-inclusive, cosmic love already filling our world and helping to stabilize whoever may be feeling alienated amid the outer conflicts and inhumanities of our times.

> *Bruckner is one of those rare geniuses whose natural fate it was to make the supernatural real, to force the Divine into the straitjacket of our human world.*
>
> WILHELM FURTWÄNGLER

Listen to the sounds of harps in Bruckner's symphonies, especially in the Adagio of the Eighth Symphony. These sounds, like the glissandos of waterfalls in the night, represent angel calls and presences in our lives.

Main works: The nine symphonies; *Te Deum; Psalm 150;* motets; masses; String Quintet.

ACHILLE CLAUDE DEBUSSY
(Leo-Virgo—Fire-Earth)

I wish to express in music the slow and arduous birth of beings and things in nature, then their gradual unfolding, culminating in an outburst of joy upon rebirth into a new life.

DEBUSSY

Debussy's music is music of the water kingdom, filled with glimpses into aquamarine worlds of nature, containing such beings as sylphs, naiads, sirens, and undines from the deep. Much of Debussy's music emanates turquoise and green color streams. *The Sea (La Mer)* is especially good for breaking up emotional tensions.

A listener might easily feel the exotic and nostalgic qualities in Debussy's works (you can feel these qualities clearly emerging from Three Nocturnes for Orchestra). The orchestration is precise; each instrument is a unique voice which contributes to the very sensual orchestral tone colors. Along with these, there is at times a peculiar healing quality in the music which frees the mind and breaks down rigidity.

Those pieces which have proven to be most beneficial to patients I have worked with include *Clair de lune* (which stimulates emotion, nostalgia, and reverie), *The Sea* (which disperses mental tension and charges the listener), *Sacred and Profane Dances* for harp and orchestra, and *The Engulfed Cathedral* (which often awakens deep soul memories of distant kingdoms, as the music rises up, out of the ocean depths, then returns to complete submersion and stillness). *Images* energizes the listener with a color bath of lively rhythms.

Main works: The Sea; Nocturnes; *Images; Prelude to the Afternoon of a Faun; Sacred and Profane Dances;* Clarinet Rhapsody; *Clair de lune; Pelléas et Mélisande* (opera); String Quartet.

RALPH VAUGHAN WILLIAMS
(Libra—Air)

Vaughan Williams's music paints vivid nature scenes in the English tradition, reminiscent of pastoral poems by William Wordsworth, Walt Whitman, or Matthew Arnold (listen to the powerful opening chorus and orchestral proclamation of Symphony no. 1, *A Sea Symphony*). Vaughan Williams composes music with an individualized and spiritualized mind and a devotional heart. His music is sensitive to the human condition, while also describing the larger cosmic order in life. It is easy to feel the essential nobility waiting potentially in humankind as one is listening to Vaughan Williams's works. The orchestral sound is powerful and robust.

Vaughan Williams is also a "modern" composer who experienced the horrors of war and fought through differences toward a vision of reconciliation. In some works, especially Symphonies nos. 4, 6, and 9, tensions and dissonances are present. Yet, in other works there is calm attunement with nature (*Lark Ascending*, Symphonies nos. 3 and 5) and compelling drama (Symphony no. 7, *Antarctica*, composed for the cinema). *Lark Ascending*, based upon George Meredith's poem, is a great favorite among many clients and friends.

I believe that Vaughan Williams's masterpiece among his many outstanding works is *Fantasia on a Theme of Thomas Tallis*, for strings. This work enters deeply into the listener's consciousness, penetrating the soul and lifting one in a spiral of weaving melodies that rises and resonates like a great cathedral of sound.

Main works: Lark Ascending; Job (A Masque for Dancing); Symphonies no. 1 *(A Sea Symphony)*, 2 *(A Londoner's Symphony)*, 3 *(A Pastoral Symphony)*, 5; *Fantasia on a Theme of Thomas Tallis; Fantasia on Greensleeves; Norfolk Rhapsody; A Pilgrim's Progress* (a morality play based upon John Bunyan's *Pilgrim's Progress); Serenade to Music; In the Fen Country*; Piano Concerto.

SERGEI RACHMANINOV
(Aries–Fire)

Sergei Rachmaninov has been called the "last Romantic." His music is utterly Slavic, containing powerful feelings that express a moving synthesis of joy and sorrow, a longing for one's homeland, a profound spirituality, and beautiful, lasting melodies which fill one's heart with love and power. Rachmaninov himself was manic-depressive and fought most of his life to overcome extreme melancholy.

Rachmaninov wrote these words about himself and his music:

The music of a composer should express his country of birth (culture), his love relationships, his religion, the books which have influenced him, and the paintings he loves. It should be the total product of the composer's experiences.

I am a Russian composer; the country of my birth has influenced my temperament and my view of the world. My music is the product of my temperament, and so it is Russian music. Love, bitterness, sadness or religious feeling—all of these become part of my music, and so the music becomes beautiful, or bitter, sad or religious. I simply write down the music that I hear in myself and as naturally as possible.

The great musician Josef Hofmann said of Rachmaninov, "He was made of steel and gold; steel in his arms, gold in his heart. I can never think of this majestic being without tears in my eyes, for I not only admired him as a supreme artist, but I also loved him as a man."

Rachmaninov's Symphony no. 2, lasting about an hour, emerges in the first movement, as though from distant mists of heroic bogatyrs [great warriors] and bell-like domes emitting fragrances through history. The music later rises to a blazing crescendo, sinks back, surges again, and ends with a powerful thwack on the drum. After a peppy, very Slavic-sounding scherzo, the third movement (Adagio) moves the listener into a beautiful, expansive meditation, led by the clarinet. The movement gradually recedes into silence. The final movement propels the listener forward toward a triumphant, manic conclusion for full orchestra.

Be sure to experience the power and beauty of Rachmaninov's music, dramatically contained in the following works:

Main works: The three symphonies; *Monna Vanna* (opera, Act 1); the four piano concertos; *The Bells* (choral symphony); *Rhapsody on a Theme of Paganini* (the eighteenth variation is a beautiful love song that has been used in many movies, most recently in the John Barry soundtrack to *Somewhere in Time)*; twenty-three piano preludes; *The Isle of the Dead*; *Symphonic Dances* (notice how the work ends in a dramatic blaze of power and the sustained sound of the gong stroke, which ends the work and hurls the listener, like a meteor, out into limitless space. This cosmic, expansive effect is brilliantly achieved by Leonard Slatkin and the Saint Louis Symphony in their marvelous recording – Vox Box 3-CD3X 3002. Rachmaninov wrote these words at the end of *Symphonic Dances*, his last major work: "I thank thee, Lord.")

Rachmaninov's *Vespers* and the *Liturgy of Saint John Chrysostom* are two of the most strikingly beautiful sacred choral works ever composed. They are especially good for worship and inspire reverence and deep devotion.

FIRE COMPOSERS

In addition to the composers mentioned, these artists usually compose very powerful fire music, galvanic and highly energizing.

Modest Mussorgsky. His music extracts beauty from grossness and ugliness; it describes evil versus good, the macabre versus the serene.

Night on Bald Mountain (used in *Fantasia,* by Walt Disney, and followed mystically by Schubert's *Ave Maria); Boris Godunov; Pictures at an Exhibition* (note the great power of the closing section, *The Great Gate of Kiev).*

Béla Bartók. Bartók's music is often strange and impersonal; strange forces move in the the night (note Piano Concerto no. 3 and portions of Concerto for Orchestra). In some of Bartók's pieces the music reminds me of a metallic mind and a heart trying to open. It is not what I would call "warm" music, but it is often dramatic and certainly "interesting." Bartók's shadow side surfaces in his music, often chaotic and hard-driving; yet in his own personal life he was kind and quiet. I consider Bartók's music to be important as a historical stage of musical development, but I have not found it to be terribly therapeutic or renewing. The slow movement of the Piano Concerto no. 3 is perhaps Bartók's warmest, most heartfelt moment. The Concerto for Orchestra offers mystery and power. Note Bartók's delightful pieces for children (Bartók loved children), performed lyrically on the guitar by Stephan Nagy on Pilz 160 262, a lovely recording.

Concerto for Orchestra; Viola Concerto; Music for Strings, Percussion and Celesta; Piano Concerto no. 3.

Vincent d'Indy. He composes music of power, soaring melody, and wide open spaces; the music portrays some powerful forces of nature.

Symphony on a French Mountain Air (a beautiful, expansive nature piece that can really "blow through" a listener like fresh winds penetrating a person on Alpine mountain heights); *Istar; Mediterranean Diptych; Song of the Forest; Summer Morning on the Mountain; Souvenirs* (symphonic poem); Symphony no. 3; Prelude to *Fervaal.*

Franz von Suppé. This music is filled with drama and upliftment for the emotions and contains very strong energies and movement that can help to dispel moodiness and blocks in the temperament.

Poet and Peasant; Light Cavalry; Boccaccio Overtures.

Hector Berlioz. The keynote in Berlioz's music offers very strongly dramatic and intense, powerful energy. There is a certain manic, even wild quality to some of Berlioz's pieces, and it is filled with romantic fervor and wonderful melodies.

Te Deum; Requiem; Fantastic Symphony; Harold in Italy; Damnation of Faust; La Marseillaise; L'Enfance du Christ; Messe Solennelle.

Manuel de Falla. He uses strong, colorful melodies and rhythms that often disperse negativity and blockage in the mental-emotional areas. I consider *Nights in the Gardens of Spain* to be a genuine masterpiece of twentieth-century music. The music takes the listener inside the mysteries of the night, revealing beautiful, moonlit gardens and clear-flowing fountains. Ernesto Halffter, Falla's disciple, said of Falla and his sacred music, especially of his last work *Atlantida,* "An exemplar of Christian humility, a profoundly religious spirit, he abstained from writing any sacred music which might not possess the grandeur expressive of the mystic impulse."

The Three-Cornered Hat; La Vida Breve; Nights in the Gardens of Spain; El Amor Brujo; Harpsichord Concerto; *Atlantida; El Gran Teatro del Mundo*

Jean Sibelius. This great Finnish musical giant opens our ears to the music of the nature devas—strong, strangely removed, at times other than human, but at its best very beautiful, alluring, epic, and inspiring. Note the storm erupting in the *Karelia Overture* or in *The Tempest;* the thunder from the forests clearly audible in the crashing timpani of Symphonies nos. 1 and 4. Much of Sibelius's music was inspired by ancient Finnish mythology, especially the national epic *Kalevala* and tone poems for orchestra such as *The Bard, Luonnotar,* and *Pohjola's Daughter.* Listen to devas singing in *Autre Fois* or *Once Upon a Time.*

Finlandia; the seven symphonies; Violin Concerto; *Swan of Tuonela; En Saga; Oceanides; Tapiola; Tempest; The Dryad; The Bard; Karelia Overture and Suite; Origin of Fire; Night Ride and Sunrise.*

Alexander Glazunov. He composes strong nature music *(The Seasons, The Forest,* and *The Sea)* and lyrical yet powerful Russian melodies *(Stepan Razin;* the symphonies). Note also Glazunov's *From the Middle Ages* and *Characteristic Suite.*

EARTH COMPOSERS

Music by these earth composers is usually less explosive, often more calming and congenial. (Scriabin is an exception.)

Jules Massenet. He composed with deep feeling and emotion, expressing strong devotion and spiritual fervor which includes musical evocations of beautiful landscapes.

Meditation from Thais; Manon; Alsatian Scenes; The Juggler of Notre Dame; Sleep of the Blessed Virgin.

Sir Arthur Sullivan. Here is music of drama and deep feelings, and of worship. His orchestrations have flare, clarity, and strength.

Te Deum; Irish Symphony; miscellaneous overtures; Gilbert and Sullivan operas; Cello Concerto.

Alexander Scriabin. This is music that is at once strange, otherworldly and at times hauntingly beautiful in a way that is not "human." Cyril Scott, in his illuminating work *Music: Its Secret Influence Through the Ages,* says that Scriabin's works are often like "Deva-music . . . filled with ecstasy and . . . an intense loveliness, but not an earthly loveliness; his music reaches an unutterable grandeur . . . incomparable with anything we have seen or experienced on earth. It is grandeur of mighty Beings, flashing forth Their unimaginable colors and filling the vast expanses with Their song." Nevertheless, though beautiful, this music has not always proved uplifting or therapeutic, in my experience.

Poem of Ecstasy; Divine Poem; Poem of Fire; Piano Concerto; piano sonatas; symphonies.

Edward MacDowell. This American composer brings us music of nature that is at once American and also typical of the nineteenth-century European tradition; dramatic music, often with colorful themes.

The two piano concertos; *Celtic Sonata; Indian Suite; Woodland Sketches;* Suite no. 1 for Large Orchestra.

Ellen Taaffe Zwilich. This contemporary composer gives the listener a fascinating musical experience. Her works contain richly colored, beautiful sonorities and some lovely melodies. Her music is very modern, and her compositions are filled with energy. She also emphasizes instrumental detail; individual voices emerge clearly (as in her striking Flute Concerto).

Concerto Grosso; Celebration; Symbolon; Flute Concerto; Symphonies nos. 1, 2, and 3.

Keith Jarrett. Jarrett is a marvelous contemporary composer, who writes a variety of musical pieces that synthesize the genres of jazz, New Age, and classical. Recently, his beautiful composition *Elegy for Viola* has appeared on CD (ECM 1450), and Jarrett's lovely piano concerto *Celestial Hawk* is also worth seeking out. Note especially Jarrett's striking rendition of Shostakovich's twenty-four Preludes and Fugues for solo piano (ECM 2-78118-21469).

AIR COMPOSERS

Air composers' music is often more elusive and changeable, bringing frequent shifts in tempo, mood, and atmosphere.

Richard Strauss. Strauss's music is moving, but perhaps is not always as profoundly spiritual, like the best of Wagner's music. It contains strong rhythms, intense emotional outbursts, and stirring melodies which flash into the receptive temperament (for example, *Don Juan* and *Also Sprach Zarathustra*). Some of Strauss's music is very uplifting *(Alpine Symphony)* and even spiritual, such as *Death and Transfiguration*. The finale of *Death and Transfiguration* most closely describes the radiant light and angelic welcome of the soul making his/her transition from earthly life.

Don Quixote; Metamorphosen for Strings; Der Rosenkavalier; horn concertos; Processional Entry; Festival Prelude; Joseph's Legend; Violin Concerto; Dance Suite after Couperin.

Charles Ives. This music can be discordant but also very beautiful in its more serene moments.

Symphonies nos. 2, 3, 4; *The Pond; The Celestial Country.*

Leo Delibes. This is airy, dancelike music, very melodic, that breaks up emotional and mental congestion while also enlivening the body with its energies.

Coppélia; Sylvia; Lakmé.

Gustav Holst. His music combines melody and warmth with strangeness. Note the warmth and beauty of *Venus* from *The Planets*.

The Planets; Hymn of Jesus; St. Paul's Suite; Festival Te Deum; Egdon Heath; Somerset Rhapsody: Brook Green.

Philip Glass. Glass is a modernist who composes in the minimalist style. While some of his works might seem repetitive, at his best a laserlike propulsion and directed energy are present in the music. Lately, Glass has been composing in a more melodic, neoromantic style. Listen to the power of *Itaipu* and the lyricism in the *Low Symphony*.

Violin Concerto; *The Light; Itaipu; Akhnaten* (opera); *Satyagraha* (opera); *The Photographer; the Low Symphony;* organ works.

WATER COMPOSERS

Water music often appeals strongly to the emotions and the heart. It contains many nuances of feeling.

Ottorino Respighi. Respighi has composed strong melodic and dramatic works which fill the listener with multicolored showers of sound. I find Respighi's music enlivening, inspiring, and enriching.

Ancient Dances and Airs; Boticellian Triptych; The Birds; The Pines of Rome; The Fountains of Rome; The Festivals of Rome; Church Windows; Suite for Organ and Orchestra (get the beautiful, strong performance of the San Diego Chamber Orchestra, conducted by Donald Barra, Koch 3-7215).

Leoš Janáček. Janáček's music is Slavic and is filled with strong rhythms and effusive power. His melodies are very striking, as in the rising brass fanfares contained in *Sinfonietta. Taras Bulba* is a mighty symphonic poem about a great political-folk hero. The piece culminates in a full paean of triumph, written for organ and full orchestra. Janáček's *Glagolitic Mass* contains monumental grandeur and strength. It takes the listener down into the ancient roots and spiritual depths of the Slavic essence and culture. (Note Mackerras's version on Supraphon or Bernstein's on Sony.)

Maurice Ravel. This music often describes the beautiful and the ugly in watery nature, more than in humanity. Sharp rhythms and pinpointed structures combine to bring out force and feelings, sharp wit, and mystery.

Ravel's *Bolero* is a very popular but potentially harmful piece of music. The particular rhythms and discords and the finale in which the orchestra is completely torn apart, have a destructive effect on the listener's astral body, depleting and scattering one's vitality. The energies of such a piece can be very stressful. On the other hand, *The Fairy Garden* (from *Mother Goose*) is an enchanting piece of nature music.

Daphnis and Chloe; piano concertos; *Rapsodie Espagnole; Pavane for a Dead Princess; Ship on the Ocean; Mother Goose.*

Georges Bizet. This is music of refinement, filled with clear, beautiful melody that is usually therapeutic and vitalizing.

Symphony in C; *Children's Games; Roma; Patrie Overture; L'Arlesienne Suites; Carmen; Te Deum.*

Heitor Villa-Lobos. Here is a very exotic, at times profound, music that is reminiscent of the deep South American forests and jungles. Villa-Lobos's music is spontaneous, alive, free, at times seemingly eruptive and undisciplined, yet at its best, wonderfully colorful, daring, and appealing.

Origin of the Amazon River; Bachianas Brasileiras 1-9; Choros; Forest of the Amazon; Harp Concerto; Guitar Concerto; Genesis; Amazonas; piano concertos; Dawn in a Tropical Forest; Magdalena; Discovery of Brazil.

Nikolai Rimsky-Korsakov. Listen to the colorful, beautiful Russian melodies, clothed in exotic orchestral tones—a sparkling music which often uplifts.

Symphonies nos. 1, 2; Scheherazade; Golden Cockerel; Invisible City of Kitezh; Dubinushka; Christmas Eve; Russian Easter Overture (conducted by Stokowski on RCA Silver Seal 60487).

> *The real musical genius writes for no other purpose but to express his own Soul, and in so doing, finds life's greatest satisfaction and joy.*
>
> FREDERICK DELIUS

> *. . . the figure of some superhuman herald crossing the skies, a bringer of light. . . . The end comes with solemn glory. . . . The aftermath is like a sunset, melancholy, of a haunting beauty of the moment and of the loveliness embracing the world. . . . Serge Koussevitsky called this symphony Sibelius' "Parsifal."*
>
> OLIN DOWNES describing the Seventh Symphony of Sibelius

The Deeper Mysteries of Music

Think of our solar system, its colossal size. I have the impression that there are many solar systems, that ours is a very big one, but that there are others which are much larger. And that their distance from other solid bodies floating in the atmosphere, this distance is enormous. I have also the impression that not only is there endless space and the endless mass of the solar systems that are in that space, but there is endless time and endless mental power, that there are great masses of mind which are ours; this little earth that we live on is only a small part. We all live on this same planet. We breathe the same air and we are under the power of the light which the sun gives. No sunlight; no existence on this earth. We are all under the same conditions, and it is our privilege to make the best of those conditions—of the air we breathe, of the light we receive from the sun, THAT LIFE-GIVING LIGHT.

LEOPOLD STOKOWSKI

In the spheres a wonderful harmony of sound is being produced eternally, and from that Source have all things been created.

FLORENCE CRANE

To some it is evident that every sound gives forth a color equivalent. Likewise, the vibratory movements of musical notes and phrases combine to express meaningful patterns or shapings, called *archetypes*, which reside in a superphysical field of thought and feeling. Both the colors and forms of music can be observed clairvoyantly. In addition, some persons feel the colors of musical works, and scientific advances have expanded to give us new directions toward demonstrating the colors of music. The Russian composer Alexander Scriabin envisioned a time when a cosmic color organ would reveal simultaneously the colors and formations emanating from every piece of music as it was being played.

The study of the relationship of color animation and sound is called *synesthesia* by some researchers, although the term implies relationships among other senses. I am sure this science will be developed further in our lifetimes. Both Leopold Stokowski, the famed maestro of symphony orchestras, and Walt Disney were interested in the combination of color and sound, and together they produced the great movie classic *Fantasia*, which is an animated union of color, music, and movement—a dramatic representation of the energies released through sound and vibration.

Since I as yet do not see music colors and forms clairvoyantly, but only feel them, I am very much indebted to the Reverend Flower A. Newhouse, spiritual teacher and Christian mystic, who has shared her valuable insights with me and who has described with her clairvoyant perception the colors and musical forms of selections that have been found to be therapeutic for many listeners. I am also grateful for the observations shared by another clairvoyant teacher, Geoffrey Hodson, in his books *Music Forms, Kingdom of the Gods*, and *Clairvoyant Investigations:*

> Each note, when sounded or sung, produces . . . a typical form in su-
> perphysical matter. These forms are colored by the way the sound is
> produced, and the size of the form is decided by the length of time
> in which a note is sounded or sung. . . . The composer originates and
> establishes the form, partly by the play of his consciousness during the
> process of composition and partly by his own performance of the piece.

Music never stands still. Each note and phrase plays its part in building a continuously shifting array of shapes, colors, and consistencies which the total piece is vibrating into the atmosphere and the listener's consciousness. A clairvoyant can describe only the most outstanding color highlights and patterns which a musical work is building as it is being played. The composer—by his/her own thought forms and consciousness during the creation of a piece of music—and the performers who interpret the music together bring through the essence and harmonies of the music originally "heard." Likewise, a sensitive artist or listener, by moving inside the music he/she is experiencing, can at times contact mystically the mind and "atmosphere" of the composer. In this way we can understand what Leonard Bernstein meant, during his performance of a Mahler symphony, when he said, "But I *am* Gustav Mahler!"

The more reverently and expectantly you can experience a piece of music, the more its mysterious beauty and hidden essences will open to you, revealing far greater depth and power.

I want to share with you a list of some musical selections, as viewed clairvoyantly by F. A. Newhouse, for their colors and patterns of form. Consider these descriptions with open mind and heart, allowing the music, hereafter, to bathe you and fill you with its own distinctive color potencies and archetypal patterns.

Beethoven
> Symphony no. 1 (first movement): The music is bright orange and arouses the listener to action.
>
> Symphony no. 5: Here is royal purple, interwoven with saffron—his music comes forth like great waves that envelop an audience. The first four notes are an angel call.
>
> Symphony no. 6 (Pastorale): The emanation is gold and green.
>
> Symphony no. 9: This music contains deva chants and urges human-kind to aim higher, toward global unity and inclusive love. Beethoven's patterns are always large. Colors are blue and others outside our spectrum.

Elgar
> Pomp and Circumstance March no. 1: The highlight is flame and yellow hues; these colors for a time circulate like waves that fold into one another. Then, in the center of these waving colors appears an archetype somewhat resembling a beacon or torch. Gradually, this figure begins to unfurl what looks like a large white streaming flag. From this flag emanate other white flags, unfurling notes on either side of the central figure. This music is an ordination piece from the angelic kingdom, according to Reverend Newhouse. Such powerful anthems increase in power when they end going up. The final, rising notes emanate colors and energies that resemble a surging fountain.

Tchaikovsky
> Andante (from Swan Lake, Act 2, Dance of the Swans): There are beams of golden light; harp tones create bursts of light whose colors are outside our spectrum.
>
> Piano Concerto no. 1 (finale of first movement): The music contains a chant of praise and fulfillment; the blaze of light is yellow and orange.

J. S. Bach
> A Mighty Fortress: Yellow waves of power move out into the atmosphere, forming an anvillike figure.

Liszt
> Liebestraum: This music looks like smoke waves—a feminine figure moves in white at the center; there is purple and some rose, with aqua during the dancelike tunes.

Schubert

Ave Maria: Another clairvoyant-teacher, Corinne Heline, in her book *The Cosmic Harp*, describes the color of this music as primarily "rose-lavender—the synthesis of love and sorrow."

Symphony no. 8 (*Unfinished*): In the first movement the keynote is "Keep on striving." The main color is orchid, and the music is good for healing pain.

Debussy

Clair de lune: The main colors are saffron and pink, interspersed with a fountain-like figure spraying out its power; also, a pan-pipe shape is giving forth opalescent bubbles.

Herbert

Ah, Sweet Mystery of Life: A chalice in gold is emanating golden beams; hands held upwards move toward the chalice—rose streams flow.

Gounod

Sanctus (from *Saint Cecilia Mass):* Reverend Newhouse feels that Gounod may well be from the deva kingdom. This piece sends forth rose tones which blend into pink; other colors are orchid and white.

Goin' Home (Negro spiritual): There is an orange hill, with a male figure climbing; also, apricot hues.

Silent Night: This creates pink shades, like camellias; some petals are deep rose, others are more pink.

Sibelius

Finlandia: Here is a deva song blessing the earth with spiritual incitements. The music brings in mystic streams of orchid and white, rinsing through the earth and continuously emitting bright green beams. (No wonder that this stirring piece awoke the Finns to patriotic resistance against Russian invasion!)

Adam

O Holy Night: The music sounds an Archangel call; the crystal light of the higher world is mingling with green coming from the earth.

Mine Eyes Have Seen the Glory: The colors are green and white like plumes of fiery power; heavenly choirs are descending to bless. The plumes change into an archetype of the American flag. According to the Reverend Newhouse, this piece is the Planetary Logos's baptism of the earth.

Grieg

Nocturne (from *Lyric Suite*): There are silver, shimmering sea green waves of power; an angel of the night blesses nature's many forms of life.

Piano Concerto (second movement): There are waves of blue, splashed with a rose color that contains some burgundy tints; large thought forms appear like great cornucopias, with flowing, seedlike shapes of shining, varied colors. In the outer movements, which are more powerful, the color resembles a shimmering gold. The music of the whole concerto is a paean of praise.

I Love Thee (song): This noble and sublime deva music emanates thought forms of hearts and praying hands, against a rose and pink background; bursts of golden flashing colors come in from the higher worlds.

Rachmaninov

Piano Concerto no. 2 (finale): The triumphal theme reveals earth dwellers moving up upon a varicolored mountain toward resplendent light. In the second movement the color is a healing blue-green, permeated by electric flashes of light. The music emanates feelings of gratitude and recovery (from deep depression).

Chopin

Nocturne, op. 9, no. 2: Special notes create a turning bell-like music form of peach color that spins around in unison with the music; latter part has blue mist veiling bright forms which dance through veils into openness and continue to rotate all about the atmosphere.

Deep River (Negro spiritual): Deep blue currents move through the atmosphere horizontally; midway through the piece a gold-domed city appears, shining above the azure waves (the city represents one view of Paradise, on the inner planes).

Malotte

The Lord's Prayer: Blue tones; slowly an archetype of a white altar takes form; leaning against the altar are two large, praying hands; at the end of the piece only the praying hands remain—all blue and orchid have disappeared.

Humperdinck

Children's Prayer (from *Hansel and Gretel*): Great reservoirs of light, one giving rise to another in fountain-like bursts of creation; at last, one glorious stream of light emerges from the base of the fountain and lifts the prayers originating in humans up to God. The towering column of light keeps ascending, and as it does, the base of the fountain rises and widens, becoming more luminous and expansive.

Franck

Panis angelicus: This is a Christ blue-lavender piece; blue waves, with a lily-like archetype are facing downward in the beginning, fluidic, then later they turn upward. Three-quarters of the way through the piece, bell-shaped tones appear. Blue tones resolve, like sunset and become lighter blue.

Handel

Hallelujah Chorus (from *Messiah*): Golden sunbursts emanate from the music. Angelic Hosts gather with human beings.

Wagner

Parsifal (Grail Music): The music is white with some blue. The archetype indicates a feeling of sacrifice.

Scriabin

Piano Concerto (slow movement): An archetype indicating prayer lifts itself as the music plays. The music is a sustained prayer, which emanates rose and lavender.

Insights into the colors and forms of great music help me to feel more deeply the great beauty of shapes and colors that inspired music delivers powerfully into our atmosphere. I look forward to the day in the future when more persons will be able to "see" into great music and in this way will be able to share its healing energies with others. I am grateful to Reverend Newhouse for sharing her visions.

> *We should seek to perfect our understanding and appreciation of good music as we do our comprehension and assimilation of spiritual realities. Just as much inspiration is given by a great symphony as is imparted by a remarkable book.*
>
> FLOWER A. NEWHOUSE

> *In the future I have the vision of an extended keyboard, from which more power and an extended range can be brought in.*
>
> LEOPOLD STOKOWSKI

> *In a world that certainly seems to have gone completely insane, the arts are becoming ever more precious. When I look around me, or when I contemplate the daily barrage of depressing news, I cling to the notion that perhaps MUSIC and the other arts represent a rare refuge for us all, if we can but preserve their purity.*
>
> GUNTHER SCHULLER

Music for the Future

Would to God your horizon may broaden every day! The people who bind themselves to systems are those who are unable to encompass the whole truth and try to catch it by the tail; a system is like the tail of truth, but truth is like a lizard: it leaves its tail in your fingers and runs away, knowing full well that it will grow a new one in a twinkling.

IVAN TURGENEV
(in a letter to Leo Tolstoi)

In the education of the future, music for every person will be deemed as necessary as the reading and writing at present; for it will be clearly seen that it is a most powerful means for bringing life, health and strength.

PRENTICE MULFORD, THOUGHT FORCES

Originally, music was the testimony of the human soul. It was an integral part of the life of the community. Laws of harmony were followed, and only music, not "noise," was allowed into a society. As each person added his stone to the building of a great cathedral, so everyone's "tone" contributed to the evolving melody of the human world. But with the rise of individualism, many people began living for themselves alone, thus producing chaos in the world. Now, in the final years of the twentieth century, we move again toward synthesis. The truth is always evolving, always new. Just to survive, man, woman, and child must help each other. To move forward into the light of greater truth ahead, we must come together more constructively and lovingly. Great music can help us to move in this direction.

Today we are realizing once again the potential power of beautiful music to integrate the personality and temperament, to awaken each of us to our own soul, and to link us to supernal forces of light that surround us. It is becoming increasingly clear again that great music inspires us, relieves our tensions, and strengthens our lives. To be fed by beautiful music is a necessity.

The finest music is always uplifting and transforming; it also unlocks creativity. Once, while teaching a class in creative writing, I played a piece of Bartók's music and witnessed a man suddenly shout for joy because a certain musical phrase helped "bring through" the ending to a short story which he had tried to finish for seven years. I recall a woman artist who painted great angels moving in light as she listened to the full-volume chorus from Haydn's *Creation*.

Beautiful music is also dynamic and exciting; it heightens feelings, enhances life's scenes, and deepens relationships. It is thrilling to notice how many moviemakers are turning to the great classics for inspiration for their scenes and soundtracks. The English composer Ralph Vaughan Williams, a long time ago, realized the great potentials of film and multimedia when he said, "Film contains potentialities for the combination of *all* the arts such as Wagner never dreamed of." Vaughan Williams and other composers, such as Malcolm Arnold, John Addison, Nino Rota, Erich Korngold, Wojciech Kilar, and many more have written original soundtracks for movies. Other soundtracks, unfortunately, are not so original. Here is a substantial list of movies whose producers have borrowed from the great composers and their musical masterpieces:

The Great Race – J. S. Bach
Somewhere in Time – Rachmaninov
Fantasia – J. S. Bach; Dukas; Ponchielli; Beethoven; Schubert;
  Mussorgsky; Tchaikovsky
Song of Norway – Grieg
Barry Lyndon – Handel
Hot to Trot – Mouret
Alien – Hanson
2001: A Space Odyssey – Johann Strauss; Ligeti; Richard Strauss
Clockwork Orange – Beethoven; Mahler
Turning Point – Tchaikovsky; Wieniawski; Prokofiev
Death in Venice – Mahler
Elvira Madigan – Mozart
Interlude – Albinoni
Kramer vs. Kramer – Purcell; Vivaldi
A Little Romance – Vivaldi
Requiem for a Heavyweight (TV production) – Sibelius
Apocalypse Now – Wagner
Ordinary People – Pachelbel
The Witches of Eastwick – Mozart
My Geisha – Puccini

Moonstruck - Puccini
A Room with a View – Puccini
Diva – Catalani
Driving Miss Daisy – Dvořák
Brief Encounter – Rachmaninov
Who Framed Roger Rabbit? – Liszt
Raging Bull – Mascagni
Excalibur – Wagner; Orff
Four Seasons – Vivaldi
Elephant Man – Barber
So Fine – Wagner; Verdi
All the Marbles – Leoncavallo
Father of the Bride – Pachelbel
Havana – Elgar
Lorenzo's Oil - Donizetti
Pretty Woman – Verdi
Prince of Tides – Haydn
Wayne's World – Tchaikovsky
Indecent Proposal – Vivaldi
JFK – Mozart
Jennifer 8 – Puccini
Frankie and Johnny – Debussy
Godfather 3 – Mascagni
Regarding Henry – Mozart
Platoon – Barber
Raising Cain – Grieg
Howard's End – Beethoven
Silence of the Lambs – J. S. Bach
A League of Their Own – Boccherini
Hudsucker Proxy – Khachaturian

Several more contemporary composers are producing some of their finest creations for film soundtracks. Among my favorites are Lee Holdridge *(Other Side of the Mountain Part 2, Forever Young, Forever Free, Jonathan Livingston Seagull, Old Gringo)*; Maurice Jarre *(Ryan's Daughter, Shogun, Doctor Zhivago)*; Georges Delerue *(Promise at Dawn, King of Hearts, A Little Romance)*; John Barry *(Somewhere in Time, Born Free, The Dove)*; Basil Poledouris *(Blue Lagoon, Lonesome Dove, Lassie)*; and Bernard Herrmann *(Obsession, Citizen Kane, Jane Eyre, The Kentuckian, Cape Fear, Taxi Driver, Vertigo, and Psycho)*. The soundtracks for the movies just mentioned contain many beautiful, powerful, and lasting melodies, which can affect the listener's moods and also may emanate healing, revitalizing energies. My own personal favorite remains *The Sound of Music*, by Rodgers and Hammerstein. I also love the deep feelings expressed in John Barry's music *(Born Free, Somewhere in Time, Out of Africa, Indecent Proposal)*.

Today, we are just waking up to the incredible potency of great music and what it can mean to our lives. The possibilities of music as a healing force are enormous. I believe that in the coming years, great music sensitively and perceptively used will prove even more to be a major catalyst to better health and well-being—in homes, at places of work, in hospitals, schools, stores, shopping malls, penal institutions, with mothers at birthing, language study, in the creative arts, and in recovery groups, hypnotherapy, and massage therapy.

In these final decades of the twentieth century, we are beginning to rediscover how powerfully the currents of beautiful music can enter our bones, brains, and soul consciousness. Like a healing salve, inspired melodies, rhythms, timbres, and vibrations of sound can unlock cramps and blockage in our physical, emotional, and mental layers. Even beyond these areas, great music stirs us and awakens tingles in our souls, causing us to open our hearts to life's larger, eternal horizons.

I believe that eventually music will be more widely accepted as the greatest art form, for it truly contains unlimited powers of transformation for each person. Music is always moving and becoming, and it carries us beyond our present limitations and self-imposed boundaries. It is the healing lubricant for good which brings us into closer union with our work, our friendships, and our Creator. The finest music opens our hearts and minds, wielding a subtle magnetism capable of joining together groups and masses of humanity. True music inspires persons to live more unselfishly, in greater kindness to each other, and in fuller service to God.

I AM MUSIC

I am Music, most ancient of the arts. I am more than ancient; I am eternal. Even before life began upon this earth, I was here— in the winds and the waves. When the first trees and flowers and grasses appeared, I was among them. And when Man came, I at once became the most delicate, most subtle and most powerful medium for the expression of Mankind's emotions.

When persons were little better than beasts, I influenced them for their good. In all ages I have inspired humans with hope, kindled their love, given a voice to their joys, cheered them on to valorous deeds, and soothed them in times of despair. I have played a great part in the drama of life, whose end and purpose is the complete perfection of each person's nature. Through my influence, human nature has been uplifted, sweetened and refined. With the aid of men and women, I have become a Fine Art. I have a myriad of voices and instruments. I am in the hearts of all men and women and on their tongues, in all lands among all peoples; the ignorant and unlettered know me, not less than the rich and the learned. For I speak to all persons in a language that all understand. Even the deaf hear me, if they but listen to the voices of their own souls. I am the food of love. I have taught men and women gentleness and peace; and I have led them onward to heroic deeds. I comfort the lonely, and I harmonize the discord of crowds. I am a necessary luxury to all men. I am MUSIC.

ANONYMOUS

CHAPTER 12

Women Composers

The World Mother: there IS such a wondrous and glorious Being on our earth . . . and she is very near to human mothers during pregnancy and at the time of birth. . . . She ever seeks human agents and human helpers who will serve in her name and endeavor to live in her presence. While women especially represent her, she also needs men of honor . . . to guard with knightly loyalty all women and children. . . . A great Mahatma once wrote: "Not until woman bursts the bonds of her sexual slavery, to which she has ever been subjected, will the world obtain an inkling of what she really is and of her proper place in the economy of Nature."

GEOFFREY HODSON, from THE GODDESS RE-AWAKENING,
compiled by Shirley Nicholson

Man and woman always meet each other as *four*. The masculine and feminine energies of every man resonate with the feminine and masculine energies of every woman. In the ancient Chinese spirit of yang and yin, regardless of our particular gender, we meet ourselves and each other as mixtures and moving proportions of these basic universal life energies. In a woman the currents of yin often express themselves in being a nurturer, a wife and/or mother, a householder, a kind and gentle helper, a good listener, a giver, an affiliator, and a caregiver. Yang often expresses itself in a woman's capabilities, decision-making power, artistic self-expression, bodily fitness, management, business expertise, ability to negotiate, assertiveness, good judgment, good education, clear thinking, direct communication, and honest verbal expression. In the world today, many women are expressing more of their masculine capabilities and talents, without undermining or compromising their yin (or feminine) side.

For men, yang in its constructive forms includes leadership, command, reliability, being the warrior who finishes the task, good communicative-verbal abilities, producing useful results through work, mentoring others (especially younger men and women), making a contribution in the arena of the world, living with integrity, and developing job skills. Men can express their yin energies in some of the following ways: artistic creativity; close, caring friendships (with both sexes); exchange of feelings; compassion for others; forgiving rather than getting even; playing/working together toward win-win outcomes; and nurturing others.

Today, it is a thrilling possibility for man and woman to meet not just as equals, but as persons who come closer to each other as friends and who can learn how to love and understand each other more and more deeply as human beings, not just as genders. It is extremely pleasing to me in my work as a counselor and teacher any time I see myself and others progressing in self-awareness and in closer, more communicative relationships. Every person is different and responds differently. Working toward balance and harmony within oneself and in one's relationships is really like learning how to make beautiful music or, perhaps more exactly, learning to *be* music. Interestingly, Pythagoras's teachings about the musical octave find their correspondence in his discoveries of the tones of human behavior and response, as indicated in his teachings of number— the inner mathematics of our psyche and temperament. (See my books, *Living Your Destiny* and *Taking a Count of Your Life*, Samuel Weiser, York Beach, ME.)

Women's music is appearing in more concerts and recordings by women composers, conductors, and performing artists. The flourishing Women's Philharmonic in San Francisco, for example, is conducted by JoAnn Falletta. Additionally, more and more music by women is being performed by men and women. These recordings cut across various categories, including rock, pop, country, folk, jazz, classical, New Age, and world music. A really good survey of women composers may be found in Dr. Anne Gray's book *The Popular Guide to Classical Music* , Birch Lane Press. Note also *Ladyslipper Music by Women Catalogue*, P.O. Box 3124-R, Durham, NC 27715; 1-800-634-6044.

Although in previous chapters I have mentioned several women composer and performer recordings, I would like to focus particularly on some of those musical compositions by women that I have found especially enjoyable and rewarding.

Saint Hildegard of Bingen – *Hymns and Sequences* (Gothic Voices – Hyperion CDA 66039)
– *Ordo virtutem (The Play of Virtues)* (Sequentia – Tindemans and Thornton – Editio 2-77051)
– *Symphoniae (Spiritual Songs)* (Sequentia – Editio 77020)
– *Sacred Songs* (Augsburg Early Music Ensemble) (Christophorus CHR 74584)

– *Lauds of Saint Ursula & Her 11,000 Virgins* (Focus 911, Albany Distributors)

– *Feast of St. Hildegard; Ave generosa* (ARS Musici AM0942-2)

– *O clarissima mater* (from *Chill to the Chant*) (women's voices) (Sequentia – RCA 09026 62666)

– *Canticles of Ecstasy* (Harmonia Mundi 05472-77320)

Saint Hildegard, an eleventh-century German abbess, mystic, naturalist, healer, spiritual teacher, writer, and herbalist, as well as a celestially inspired composer, wrote very beautiful sacred choral music that is nurturing and elevating, even angelic.

Ave Maria – Gregorian chants with waterfall sounds (sung by the Benedictine Sisters of Mount Saint Scholastica of Atchison, Kansas) (Invincible 1102) (White Swan Distributors)

Ave Maria – Gregorian chant (sung by the Benedictine Nuns of Saint Cecilia's Abbey, Isle of Wight, England) (New World Company, Paradise Farm, England) (White Swan Distributors)

Anonymous 4 – *An English Ladymass* (Harmonia Mundi)

– *Love's Illusion* (Harmonia Mundi 907109)

Salva Festa Dies: In Dulci Jubilo (female voices) (Turco-Naxos 8.550712)

Sister Marie Keyrouz – *Hymns to the Virgin* (Harmonia Mundi – 901497)

Russian Hymns in Honor of the Mother of God (Russian choral) (Koch Schwann CD 313 0437 H1)

Praise of the Mother of God in the Russian Church (Linke – Christophorus CD 74505) (Qualiton Imports)

Ave Gracia Plena – Music in Honor of the Virgin Mary (Rutter – Collegium COLCD 116)

Lakshmi Shankar – *Bhajan: Janama Marana* (by the saint-poetess of the sixteenth century, Mirabai (Ravi Shankar Music Circle-RSMC D-102)

Abbess: Saint Brigid (Paula and Dennis Doyle, composers) (Incarnation Music, P.O. Box 1061, Glendale, CA 91209-1061) (A celebration of beautiful Irish hymns to Saint Brigid and Saint Patrick, very renewing and healing)

Fanny Mendelssohn-Hensel – *Piano Trio* (Largo 5103)

– *Concert Aria for Soprano and Orchestra* (Capriccio 10-449)

Fanny was the sister of Felix Mendelssohn. She was four years older than he and was a very talented pianist and composer. Brother and sister were very close. When Fanny died, Mendelssohn did not last long without her. Her Piano Trio is very colorful and beautiful. The Aria emanates vitality and passion—beautiful melodies.

Clara Schumann – *Piano Concerto* (Cheng/Falletta – Koch 3-7169 or Jochum/Silverstein – Pro Arte 395)

Thekla Badarzewska-Baranowska – *A Maiden's Prayer* (Budapest Strings – Laserlight 14-039 or solo piano – Naxos 8 550646)

Margaret Buechner – *The American Civil War* (Varineau – Nord-Disc 2028) Very beautiful, moving, melodic, and dramatic music, filled with variety and historical color.
    – *The Liberty Bell* (Nord-Disc 2034) (actual sound of Liberty bell)
    – *The Old Swedes Church* (Schmohe – Nord-Disc 2-2026-2)
    – *Elizabeth* (Schmohe – Nord-Disc 2-2026-2)
    – *Erlkönig* (symphonic poem) (Varineau – Nord-Disc 2024)
    – *The Flight of the American Eagle* (Nord-Disc 2030)

Augusta Holmes – *Orchestral Works (Irlande, Andromede, Pologne, The Night of Love* (Marco Polo 8.223449) Beautiful strong atmospheric music by a nineteenth-century woman.

Cecile Chaminade – *Concertino for Flute and Orchestra* (Wiesler Augin – BIS CD 529)

Anne-Marie Orbeck – *Symphony* (Dreier – Aurora ACD 4925) Highly pleasing and melodic music, at times quite dramatic.

Amy Beach – *Symphony no. 1 (Gaelic)* (Järvi – Chandos CHAN 8958) Absolutely sensational, beautiful music.
    – *Piano Concerto* (Boehm/Landau – Vox PVT 7196
Likewise marvelous and colorful music.
    – *Grand Mass in E-flat Major* (May – Newport Classic NCD 60008)
    – *Trio for Violin, Piano and Cello* (Vox Box CDX 5029)

Germaine Tailleferre – *Concertino for Harp and Orchestra* (Falletta – Koch 3 7169-2)

Suzanne McIntosh – *Healing Journeys* (cello – beautiful, peaceful, healing music) (P.O. Box 383, Lexington, KY 40585)

Henriette Bosmans – *Poéme for Cello and Orchestra* (Spanjaard NM 92040) (Records International)

Minuetta Kessler – Alberta Concerto for Piano and Orchestra (Vesterman/Block – MMC 2009) (Records International)

Lili Boulanger – *Psalm 24; Psalm 129; Old Buddhic Prayer; Pie Jesu* (Markevitch – EMI CDM 7-64281-2) The music describes a world all its own, at times sounding more inward and delicate, beautiful and celestial, at other times bursting with power and strength.

Ethyl Smyth – *Mass in D* (Brunelle – Virgin 7 91188-2) High-powered dramatic choral piece.
    – *The Wreckers* (Conifer 51250)
    – *Sonatas* (Troubadisc 01403)

Ida Gotkovsky – *Song of the Forest* (Nozy – Rene Gailly CD 87 058 – Qualiton Imports) Very beautiful and dramatic nature music.

Liliane Riboni – *Jeanne d'Arc* (Rauber – Bourg BGC 18 – Qualiton)

Franghiz Ali-Zadeh (Baku) – *Mugam Sayagi* (Muslim meditation) (Kronos Quartet – Nonesuch 79346)

Wendy Mae Chambers – *Symphony of the Universe* (Vuksic and Hyning – Newport Classic NPD 85552) (Allegro Imports) A very unusual and modern thriller, especially the movement called *Cosmos,* scored for cathedral pipe organ, four sets of chimes, crotales, two gongs, six tam-tams, and forty-nine handbells.

Rachel Portman – *The Joy Luck Club* (soundtrack) (Hollywood Records HR-61561-2) A beautiful, haunting soundtrack.

– *Road to Wellville* (Varese Sarabande 5512)

Lucrecia Kasilag – *Violin Concerto* (Philippine composer) (Lozada/Feliciano – Marco Polo 8.220419) Melodic, often exotic music.

Leonora Milà – *Tirant Lo Blanc* (ballet) (Wright – Regis Tro RTAC 005) (Qualiton) This music, based on the life of Tirant lo Blanc, a fifteenth-century knight, written by Joanot Martorell, contains many moods and varied colors. It is highly accessible music, containing melodic and kinetic scenes.

– *Piano Concerto no. 2* (Mila-Martinez – Regis Tro-002)

Nancy Van de Vate – *Besakih Temple* (Vienna Music Masters VMM 3006) A very mysterious, serene, and lovely piece of music honoring the largest shrine on the island of Bali; the peacefulness of the music mingles with feelings of imminent violence of the volcanic eruption.

Grazyna Bacewicz – *Concerto for Orchestra* (Rowicki – Olympia OCD 311)

– *Symphony* (Koch)

Marta Ptaszynska – *Marimba Concerto; Winter's Tale for Strings* (Muza PNCD 075)

Sofia Gubaidulina – *Offertorium* (Kremer/Dutoit – DGG-427336-2)

– *Meditation* (Klug/Berlin – Classics 0011132BC)

Peggy Glanville-Hicks – *Sinfonia da Pacifica* (Mills – Vox Australis VAST013-2)

– *Etruscan Concerto* (MusicMasters 01612-67089-2)

Diane Bish – *Symphony of Psalms; Symphony of Hymns; Morning Has Broken* (Bish/McMurrin, VQR, Box 302, Needham, MA 02192) Bish is a dramatic, spiritually uplifting composer and artist—a terrific organist and international television artist *(The Joy of Music).*

Galina Ustvolskaya – *Symphony no. 5 (Amen)* (Stephenson – Conifer 194)

Elinor Remick Warren – *The Legend of King Arthur* (Kawalla – Cambria
   CD-1043) Powerful and nurturing music.
   – *Good Morning, America!*
   – Suite for Orchestra
   – *The Crystal Lake*
   – *Along the Western Shore*
   – *Symphony in One Movement* (Kawalla – Cambria CD-1042)
Joan Tower – *Silver Ladders*
   – *Island Prelude*
   – *Sequoia*
   – *Music for Cello and Orchestra* (Slatkin – Nonesuch 79245-2) I believe
   that Joan Tower's music is powerful, melodic, and very colorful.
   – *Fanfare for the Uncommon Woman* (Slatkin – RCA 60778-2) In its
   way this short piece is a strong statement like Copland's *Fanfare for
   the Common Man.*
   – *Island Rhythms* (Louisville 006)
Katherine Gladney Wells – *Minor Reflection* (Slatkin – RCA 60778-2)
Suzanne Joly – *Petite Suite for Orchestre*
   – *Fantasie concertante*
   – *Triptyque*
   – *Ode à la Jeune Fille*
   – *Rupestre* (Chevreux – Cybelia CY 873) (Qualiton Imports)
Elena Kats-Chernin – *Stairs* (Iwaki – Vox Australis VAST006)
Shulamit Ran – *Symphony* (Barenboim – Chicago Symphony Collection)
Katherine Hoover – *Da Pacem* (Piano and String Quartet) (Koch 3-7147)
Libby Larsen – *Overture – Parachute Dancing* (Martin – Leonardo LE
   327, Box 1736, Cathedral Station, New York, NY 10025)
   – *Symphony: Water Music* (Marriner – Nonesuch 9 79147-2)
   This wonderful Minnesota composer creatively explores the realms
   of wind, water, and sky. Look for a recording of *The Atmosphere as
   a Fluid System,* premiered in 1992 by the Women's Philharmonic in
   San Francisco with Eugenia Zukerman as flute soloist.
Odaline de la Martinez – *Canciones* (Lorelt LNT 103)
Judith Weir – *Airs from Another Planet* (Lorelt LNT 103)
Pauline Oliveros – *Saint George and the Dragon* (Mode, Box 1026, New
   York, NY 10116)
   – *The Roots of the Moment* (hat Art 6009)
Ruth Crawford Seeger – *Two Movements for Chamber Orchestra*
   (Pittman – Delos DCD 1012)
Ellen Taaffe Zwilich – Symphony no. 1
   – Prologue and Variations

– *Celebration* (Nelson – New World Records NW336-2)
– *Flute Concerto* (Dwyer/Sedares – Koch 3-7142-2)
– *Symphony no. 2 (Cello)* (Smith – Louisville LCD002)
– *Symbolon; Trumpet Concerto* (Mehta – New World NW-372-2)
(powerful dynamics)
I love the powerful and colorful music of Zwilich. Her sonorities are full of energy and kaleidoscopic drama. Her music also moves steadily forward—highly enlivening, yet also containing sections of mystery, introspection, and reflection.
Adriana Holszky – *Space* (Davies-Koch 3-1417)
Kaija Saariaho – *Du cristal . . . à la fumee (From Crystal into Smoke)* (Salonen – Ondine ODE 804-2) This is a more modern orchestral piece, by a contemporary Finnish composer, describing in musical sounds the shaping and reshaping of varied biological and scientific models and patterns. Quiet passages that contain many shifting timbres mix with powerful, dramatic sections. In nature such combinations of sounds might remind the listener of the northern lights, water lilies, crystals, and spirals. A very intriguing piece, at times peaceful, at times disturbing.
Watch and Pray (spirituals and art songs by African-American women composers) Works by Margaret Bonds, Florence Price, Julia Perry, Undine Smith Moore, and Betty Jackson King, beautifully rendered with piano. (Koch International 3-7247-2H1)
Enya – *Enya*
– *Shepherd Moons*
– *Watermark* (Reprise – White Swan) Haunting and beautiful; often good for going down into grief and loss.
Lynette Johnson – *Twilight Airs*
– *Songs for Celtic Harp* (Sierra Classical, P.O. Box 5853, Pasadena, CA 91117) Very inspirational and also stress-relieving music. Her *Historical Suite* won a 1991 prize for original composition.
Georgia Kelly – *Seapeace* (harp)
– *Gardens of the Sun* (White Swan)
Jessita Reyes – *Native Flute Collection* (White Swan)
Paula Horne – *Heart Songs of Black Hills Woman* (White Swan)
Carole Koenig – *After Shadows* (hammered dulcimer) (Carole Koenig, c/o 42223 Village 42, Camarillo, CA 93012)
Marnie Jones – *Journeys* (harp, flute, Indian drum, crystal goblets, etc.) (Thrival Productions, 4608 Chowen Avenue South, Minneapolis, MN 55410)
Mary Anderson – *Voyage* (Celtic harp and natural sounds)

Nóirín Ní Riain (Irish singer of beautiful Irish songs and ballads and Irish sacred music) – *Soundings* (with orchestra)
  – *Caoineadh na Maighdine* (Irish religious traditional songs)
  – *Good People All* (with monks of Glenstal Abbey)
  – *Stór Amhrán* (Irish traditional songs)
  – *Vox de Nube* (ancient chant)
  (All of these beautiful, ancient songs are available from Sounds True Catalog, 735 Walnut Street, Dept. FC6, Boulder, CO 80302, 1-800-333-9185)
Thea Musgrave – *Chamber Concerto no. 2* (Pittman – Delos DCD 1012)
  – *Orfeo II for Flute and Strings* (Still/Braithwaite – Koch KIC 7140)
  – *Song of the Enchanter* (Comissiona – Ondine ODE 767 Koch)
Elizabeth Maconchy – *Quintet for Clarinet and Strings* (Hyperion CDA 66428)
Loreena McKennitt – *Parallel Dreams*
  – *The Visit*
  – *To Drive the Cold Winter Away*
  – *Elemental*
  – *Mask and Mirror* (Celtic vocal music available from White Swan Music, 1705 Fourteenth Street, Box 143, Boulder, CO 80302)
Victoria Jordanova – *Requiem for Bosnia* (CRI 673)
Joan LaBarbara – *73 Poems* (Lovely Music 3002)
Kim Robertson and Singh Kaur – *Crimson 1–7* (beautiful singing in the Hindu-New Age tradition, accompanied by transparent harp tones) (available from White Swan)
Kim Robertson and Bettine Clemen – *Love Song to a Planet*
Kim Robertson – *Tender Shepherd*
  – *Moonrise*
  – *Water Spirit*
  – *Celtic Christmas*
  – *Gratitude* (beautiful harp music, some folk, some New Age—very nurturing and lovely) (White Swan)
  I find Robertson's tones so beautiful and clear. She plays exquisitely on her harp(s). Recordings are especially clear.
Cynthia Lynn Douglas – *An Open Heart* (harp and other instruments) (very clear and beautiful music) (White Swan)
Kay Gardner – *Garden of Ecstasy*
  – *Ouroboros: Seasons of Life* (Oratorio) (Ladyslipper CD LR 115)
  – *Fishers Daughter*
  – *Sounding . . . Inner Landscape* (meditations with guided imagery) (White Swan)

– *Rain Forest* (Martin-Leonarda LE327 – Leonarda Productions, P.O. Box 1736, Cathedral Station, New York, NY 10025)

Silvia Nakkach – *Seeker* (meditative world music) (White Swan)

Sue Richards – *Morning Aire* (Celtic harp) (White Swan)

Joemy Wilson – *Celtic Dreams*
  – *Gifts I, II*
  – *Carolan's Cup*
  – *Carolan's Cottage*

(All these CDs are clear, magical, and lovely. The chief instrument is the hammered dulcimer, played to perfection by Joemy Wilson.)

Princess Grace of Monaco (with Richard Pasco) – *Birds, Beasts and Flowers* (a beautiful collection of lovely music and poetry centered around the theme of nature) (Nimbus NI 5354)

In these critical years, when the feminine must come forward in the consciousness of both men and women, it is good to remember the healing power and the long undervalued achievements of women throughout the ages. In the words of ancient wisdom:

> To enumerate the achievements of Womanhood, is to write the history of the world. To enumerate the ecstasies of illumination, is to enumerate the visions of Womanhood. To study cooperation is to perceive the hand of Womanhood.

In our culture and in our spirituality today, all people will benefit as they empower the feminine, especially in the qualities of kindness, respect, reverence, forgiveness, enthusiasm, loyalty, and devotion. Opposing the tired, empty, desperate gasps of rage, greed, heartless aggression, retaliation, cruelty, and violence is the peaceful, loving compassion of the heart in action. Nicholas Roerich, Russian artist, philosopher, and mystic, and a great champion of woman and the eternal feminine, wrote these words in *The Realm of Light* which can help us to redeem ourselves, our society, and our world as we approach the close of the twentieth century.

> *The Mother of the World! . . . A mother's heart, a woman's heart is a great treasure. It kindles us, lights up the family. Who taught you to pray? Who will understand and forgive? The mother. The Woman. Who will inspire to a great task? The Beloved One, the Friend—the Woman. Woman, the inspirer of beauty, knows all the power, all the synthetic might of Beauty. This is the great Cosmic Law, the law of Majesty, the law of greatness and equilibrium. Striving toward Beauty will be as the key to knowledge. Better than others, the woman*

knows the element of fire, that element with which is bound the nearest future. . . . What is needed now is the unity of women which will weave the sparkling threads from the hearth through all Hierarchies into the Infinite; remember women, remember mothers, wives and sisters, remember that you are united by the beauty of spirit. It is you who are to weave and unfurl the banner of peace. You can preserve children from disintegration and show them the meaning of heroism and self-sacrifice. You shall say the sacred word; culture! Far up lies the celestial path. . . . Make everything as well as possible. Make everything beautiful!

REALM OF LIGHT, NICHOLAS ROERICH

In these transformational times, many men are learning how to feel and nurture with the heart in joy and laughter, as they resolve their anger, pain, and deep grief. At the same time, many women have already become the vessels of love for the Spirit, as they now contact the power of the mind and realize and express their strength, unique purpose, and creative destiny.

My world is my music. . . . I picture the orchestra sitting and waiting for me to put music on their stands. [I] start [with the flow of ideas, which I notate by hand]. . . . [Composers] start with an idea and work their way out. That's why a piece of music isn't whole until it's performed.

ELLEN TAAFFE ZWILICH

Appendix to the Text

The following lists of musical compositions add to the suggestions contained in the individual chapters of this book. For further reference, please consult a *Schwann Opus Catalogue*. Two other sources are especially helpful as guides to finding your music: the *Stevenson Guide to Musical Recordings* and the *CD Guide to Classical Music*, by Douglas C. Brown (order from CD Guide, Box 7388, Ann Arbor, MI 48107-7388).

1. CHIEFLY CLASSICAL MASTERPIECES

Addinsell, John – *Warsaw Concerto* (Dichter/Marriner – Philips)
  Stirring piece; romantic; inspired by the tragedies and losses of war; good for emotional release; strong interaction between piano and orchestra; lasting melodies.
Albéniz, Isaac – *Suite Española* (Fruhbeck de Burgos – London)
  Pictorial music of Spain; lovely melodies; awakens feelings and imagination; energizing rhythms.
Anderson, Leroy – *Sleigh Ride; Bugler's Holiday; Typewriter; Syncopated Clock* (Fennell – Mercury or Anderson – MCA)
  Activates body, emotions, and mind; clear rhythms and melodies.
Alfvén, Hugo – *A Legend of the Skerries and Symphony no. 4 (From the Seaward Skerries)* (Järvi – BIS)
  Mysterious and powerful landscapes; feelings of remote, yet enchanting nature.
Arensky, Anton – *Symphonies nos. 1, 2* (Svetlanov – Vox 8187)
  Beautiful Russian melodies.
Atterberg, Kurt – *Symphony no. 3 (West Coast Pictures)* (Ehrling – Caprice 21364)
  Depicts rugged, stormy seascapes of Scandinavia (Sweden).
Bacarisse, Salvador – *Concerto for Guitar & Orchestra* (Yepes/Alonso – DGG)
  Slow middle movement ideal for contemplation and guided imagery; musically embodies the deep feelings, memories, and landscape of Spain.

Bach, Johann Sebastian – *Toccata and Fugue in D* (Stokowski – EMI, RCA, or London)
A cosmic experience; great expanse; powerful and majestic; good for release of emotions; cleanses and lifts the spirits and reveals infinities of space.
　– *Brandenburg Concertos* (Casals – Sony or Suk – Vanguard or Marriner – Philips)
Extremely exhilarating; delightful colors and tones; helps the listener to focus, and directs activity; good for mental refreshment and clarity.
　– *Come Sweet Death* (Stokowski – EMI or RCA; Virgil Fox on organ – Bainbridge)
Caressing, embracing, and beautiful, this is music that deepens understanding and awakens unconditional love; extremely therapeutic; deepens relaxation and meditation.
　– *Violin Concertos* (Szeryng/ Marriner – Philips or Grumiaux/Davis – Philips)
Good for mental focus and poise.
　– *Piano (or Keyboard) Concertos* (Schiff – London)
Music of warmth and dignity; inspirational and centering.
　– *Transcriptions for Orchestra* (Stokowski – Pearl GEMM CDS 9098) (including ten of Stokowski's orchestrations not previously available)
　– *Jesu, Joy of Man's Desiring* and *Sheep May Safely Graze* (Flagstad/Boult – London is vocal/instrumental; or Stokowski/Vanguard or Marriner – Angel is orchestral only)
Music of spiritual devotion; opens heart center and awakens aspiration.
　– *A Bach Program* (Stokowski – RCA or Ormandy – Odyssey or Pikler – Chandos or Bamert – Chandos)
Marvelous samplers of Bach's music, transcribed for full orchestra; these pieces awaken a variety of emotions and inner responses; this is music of universal joy and compassion, filled with the sense of God's grandeur.
　– *Goldberg Variations* (harpsichord) (Landowska – RCA)
Elegant and refreshing; bubbling and effervescent.
Bantock, Sir Granville – *Hebridean Symphony; Celtic Symphony; Pagan Symphony* (Handley – Hyperion or Boult – Intaglio)
Prompts creativity and imagination; lovely melodies and varieties of mood. Brings in the sense of ancient, bardic times.
Barber, Samuel – *Adagio for Strings* (Munch – RCA or Bernstein – DGG or I Musici – Philips)
Contacts deep emotions; good for releasing grief; swells to a mighty crescendo and recedes into silence.

– *Second Essay for Orchestra; Music for a Scene from Shelley*
(Golschmann – Vanguard 4016 or Zinman – Argo 436288)
Dramatic music, excellent for creative arts and visualization work; also
useful for emotional release and catharsis.
– *Violin Concerto* (Hu Kun/Boughton – Nimbus or Oliveira/Slatkin
– Angel)
Beautiful melodies; evokes landscapes of reverie and imagination.
Beethoven, Ludwig van – *Symphony no. 5* (Furtwängler – DGG and
EMI or Kleiber – DGG or Karajan – DGG)
In places deeply powerful and stirring, in others reflective; awakens
courage to overcome.
– *Symphony no. 6 (Pastorale)* (Reiner – RCA or Walter – Sony or
Furtwängler – EMI or Klemperer – EMI)
First two movements especially good for emotional cleansing and
upliftment; joyful memories move into storm movement, ideal for
emotional stirring, followed by *Hymn of Thanksgiving*, a summation
of release in gratitude.
– *Symphony no. 9 (Choral)* (Furtwängler – Music and Arts or Kubelik
– Orfeo or Stokowski – London Weekend or Bernstein – DGG, a live
recording to celebrate the fall of the Berlin Wall)
Music that paints the creation out of the void and culminates in the
magnificent *Hymn to Brotherhood;* a work that inspires universal love
and understanding among nations; third movement meditative and
serene.
– *Piano Concerto no. 4* (Moravec/Turnovsky – VAI 1021)
– *Piano Concerto no. 5 (Emperor)* (Arrau/Davis – Philips or Eschen-
bach/Ozawa – DGG or Kempff/Leitner – DGG or Horowitz/Reiner –
RCA)
Inspires courage and joy; energizing and uplifting piece; middle move-
ment is serene and angelic. A complete piece of music therapeutically,
stimulating physical, emotional, mental, and intuitive faculties.
– *Violin Concerto* (Heifetz/Munch – RCA or Mutter/Karajan – DGG
or Chung/Tennstedt – EMI)
Another therapeutic piece; soulful melodies, strong in energy.
– *Choral Fantasy for Piano and Chorus and Orchestra* (Kissin/
Abbado – DGG)
Stirring and empowering; finale expresses joy and high velocity.
– *String Quartets nos. 14, 16* (Bernstein – DGG-435779)
Exalted; orchestral harmonies majestic and centering; good for deep
reflection.

Benoit – *Rubens Cantata* (De Vocht – Eufoda 1158) (available from Records International, P.O. Box 1140, Goleta, CA 93116 – 1140)
Beautiful, strong music of praise.

Berlioz, Hector – *Harold in Italy* (Suk/Fischer-Dieskau – Supraphon)
Music of wide emotional range; at times peaceful and melodic, but with manic moments; rich in melodic content; emotionally stirring.
– *Symphonie Fantastique* (Freccia – Chesky or Martinon – EMI or Bernstein – Sony or EMI or Muti – EMI)
Pictorial music; describes inner workings of man in love and his ecstasy and agony for his beloved; third movement *Scenes in the Country* is especially lovely. *March to the Scaffold* depicts the hero being led to the guillotine for his own execution.
– *Te Deum* (Tagliavini/Davis – Philips or Bardot/Gouinguene – Thesis)
Powerful, sacred choral music containing many emotionally and spiritually uplifting moments.

Bizet, Georges – *Symphony in C* (Martinon – DGG or Beecham – EMI or Bernstein – Sony)
Elegant and rhythmically enlivening; good for both energizing and reverie.
– *Carmen and L'Arlesienne* (Selections) (Beecham – EMI or Munch – London Weekend or Stokowski – Sony)
Enlivening and uplifting with strong rhythms and impressive melodies.

Blackwood, Easley – *Symphonies nos. 1, 5* (Munch and DePreist – Cedille CDR 90000 016)
Athletic and contemporary, yet lyrical music.

Bloch, Ernest – *Schelomo* (Piatigorsky/Munch – RCA or Rostropovich/ Bernstein)
Brooding, emotional Hebraic piece; in sections prophetic and powerful; good for reflection and deep feeling response.
– *America: An Epic Rhapsody* (Stokowski – Vanguard or Schwarz – Delos)
Beautiful melodies; moods range from brooding to heroic.
– *Baal Shem; Abodah, God's Worship* (Mordkovitch/ Gerhardt – RCA or Guttman/Serebrier – ASV)
Reflective, devotional music in the Hebraic tradition.
– *Sacred Service* (Bernstein – Sony or Simon – Chandos)
Joyous and mighty evocation of worship and praise.
– *Mystical Poem (Violin Sonata No. 2)* (Galperine/Aguessy – Adda)
Very beautiful, spiritually penetrating music.

Boccherini, Luigi – *Guitar Quintets* (P. Romero, Marriner – Philips or Tokos–Naxos)

Beautiful, pleasant melodies; good for centering; music awakens joyfulness.

Bois-Vallée – *Adagio Religioso* (Bonneau – Philips 6511-001)
Devotional, quiet, and reassuring; music that brings peace.

Bolcolm, William – *Fantasia Concertante* (Davies – Argo 433-077)
Lively, fun-filled, and dramatic music.

Borodin, Alexander – *Symphony no. 2* (Temirkanov – RCA or Smetacek – Supraphon)
Singularly Russian, exploring feelings of power, mystery, movement, and triumph.

– *Nocturne for String Orchestra* (Stokowski – EMI or Ormandy – Sony)
Peaceful, exotic, good for relieving stress; awakens reverie and calmness.

Bossi, Marco Enrico – *Concerto for Organ and Orchestra* (Sacchetti/ Frontalini – Bongiovanni GB 5512-2)
Very melodic and powerful piece, filled with splendor and good energy.

Brahms, Johannes – *Symphony no. 1* (Furtwängler – DGG or Walter – Odyssey or Païta – Lodia)
Solid and earthy, yet tender and warm; final movement moves toward climax, crescendo, and release into triumph; good for emotional/mental cleansing.

– *Symphony no. 2* (Monteux – London or Philips; Furtwängler – EMI or C. Kleiber – Testament)
Brahms's nature symphony; lyrical and at times very dramatic.

– *Piano Concerto no. 1* (Bishop-Kovacevich/Sawallisch – EMI or Gilels/Jochum – DGG or Rubinstein/Reiner – RCA)
Extremely stirring music; finale especially conducive to emotional clearance and uplift.

– *Piano Concerto no. 2* (Gilels/Reiner – RCA or Bishop-Kovacevich/ Davis – IMP or Horowitz/Toscanini – RCA)
One of the greatest piano concertos ever composed; at times deeply reflective while at others eruptive and volcanic; quiet third movement with cello melodies emerging so beautifully; this movement especially good for devotion.

– *Lullaby* (Ormandy – Sony)
Especially warm piece of music; simple and healing.

– *A German Requiem* (Klemperer – Angel or Kempe – EMI or Shaw – Telarc)
Brahms's spiritual testament; powerful, tender, and melodic; repays repeated listening.

Britten, Benjamin – *Four Sea Interludes,* from *Peter Grimes* (Giulini – EMI or Slatkin – RCA or Pesek – Virgin or Bedford – Collins)
Tone pictures of the sea; in some places stirring, in others pensive and brooding; activates both visceral and emotional release.

Bruch, Max – *Violin Concerto; Scottish Fantasy* (Lin/Slatkin – CBS or Chung/Kempe – London or Hefetz/Sargent – RCA) (Accardo – Philips 432-282)
Melodic and inspiring, emotionally uplifting.

– *Ave Maria* (Berger – EBS-6060)

Bruckner, Anton – *Symphony no. 3* (Szell – Sony or Böhm – London or Sinopoli – DGG)
A mysterious and dramatic musical journey; slow movement especially beautiful and nurturing.

– *Symphony no. 4, Romantic* (Jochum – DGG or Böhm – London or Walter – Sony or Karajan – DGG or EMI; Sawallisch – EMI); *Symphony no. 7* (Chailly – London) – *Symphony no. 8* (Van Beinum – Philips or Jochum – EMI or DGG or Horenstein – Music and Arts or VOX or Furtwängler – DGG) – *Symphony no. 9* (Giulini – DGG or Horenstein – Music and Arts or Furtwängler – DGG)
Music of devotion and expansive consciousness; the Eighth Symphony is linked esoterically to the Archangel Michael and describes the conquest of evil by forces of Light.

Bruneau, Alfred – *Orchestral Highlights* (Lockhart – Marco Polo 8.223498)
Beautiful dramatic music.

Butterworth, George – *A Shropshire Lad; The Banks of Green Willow; Two English Idylls* (Boughton – Nimbus)
Atmospheric music that paints pastoral scenes; mostly quieting to the emotions, with some melancholy.

Byrd, William – *Mass in Four Parts; Mass in Five Parts* (Phillips and Tallis Scholars – Gimell)
Celestial, devotional music; brings feelings of great majesty and connects listener with upward, cathedrallike spirals of energy.

Canning, Thomas – *Fantasy on a Hymn of Justin Morgan* (Stokowski – Everest 9004)
Peaceful and devotional, with an early American feeling; inspiring and worshipful.

Canteloube, Joseph – *Songs of the Auvergne* (Davrath/de la Roche – Vanguard or De los Angeles/Jacquillat – Angel or Te Kanawa/Tate – London)
A wide range of music, including lively songs, love songs with mellow flavor, and pastoral scenes of French countryside; lyrical and

energizing; awakens feelings. (See also the beautiful song *Bailero* performed by cello and orchestra in the version by Julian Lloyd Webber and conducted by Charles Gerhardt on RCA 60695-2-RG.)

Caplet, Andre – *Le Miroir de Jesus* (Bender – Region SPT 94010) (Qualiton Imports)
Exquisite.

Castelnuovo-Tedesco, Mario – *Guitar Concertos (3)* (Yamashita(s) /Slatkin – RCA)
Beautiful, sunny, melodic music; brings cheerfulness.
– *Guitar Concerto in D* (Williams/Ormandy – Sony)
Strong Spanish flavor; highly melodic and rhythmically pleasing; energizing.

Catalani, Alfredo – *Loreley: Dance of the Water Nymphs* (Toscanini – RCA)
Marvelously pictorial and scintillating; evokes imagination and movement.

Chabrier, Emmanuel – *Orchestral Works: España, Festival Polonaise, Pastoral Suite, etc.* (Ansermet – London)
Light music that airs out the system; good for light moments; parts are energizing.

Chaminade, Cecile – *Concertino for Flute and Orchestra* (Galway/Dutoit – RCA)
Pleasing music for flute; emotionally stimulating.

Charpentier, Marc-Antoine – *Midnight Mass* (Willcocks – Angel)
Reverent and inspiring.

Chausson, Ernest – *Symphony in B-flat; Festival Evening* (Plasson – Angel or Munch – RCA or Ansermet – London)
Dramatic and reflective; music contains nostalgic feelings and some sense of struggle to move beyond sadness and longing.

Chávez, Carlos – *Sinfonia India* (Bernstein – Sony or Mata – VOX)
Exotic, stimulating, celebrational, evoking landscapes of ancient Mexico and Indian cultures.

Chopin, Frédéric – *Andante Spianato and Grande Polonaise* (Brendel – Vanguard or Zimerman/Giulini – DGG)
Spiritually elevating; brings out deep feeling and aspiration.
– *Piano Concerto no. 1* (Gilels/Ormandy CBS or Simon/Beissel – Vox)
Positive energy flow with profoundly meditative slow movement that awakens the heart center and love.
– *Waltzes* (Lipatti – EMI or Simon – VOX)
Provide wonderful energies for renewal and vitality; melodies and rhythms activate physical body and emotional nature.

Clementi, Muzio – *Sonatas for Piano* (Horowitz – RCA and Sony)
Good for mental focus and stability; enlivening and centering; increase
vitality.

Cooke, Arnold – *Concerto for Clarinet and String Orchestra*
(T. King/Francis – Hyperion)
Some lovely pastoral flavors here; mellowness allows for centering and
good feeling.

Copland, Aaron – *Appalachian Spring* (Copland – RCA); *Billy
the Kid* (Bernstein – Sony or Ormandy – RCA); *Old American
Songs* (Warfield/Copland – Columbia); *Lincoln Portrait* (Sand-
burg/Kostelanetz – Sony or Jones/Schwarz – Delos or Heston/
Abravanel – Vanguard); *Quiet City* (Bernstein – DGG or Copland –
Sony or Abravanel – Vanguard); *Tender Land* (Copland – RCA or
Sedares – Koch 3-7092-2); *Our Town* (Abravanel – Vanguard); *The
Red Pony* (Sedares – Koch or Copland CBS)
Uniquely expansive and lyrical American music; many beautiful
melodies; dramatic, reflective, and devotional times as well; powerful
energy raisers; also good for imagination and for building feelings of
reflection and triumph.

Corelli, Arcangello – *Concerti Grossi* (I Musici – Philips or Marriner –
London)
Stabilizing music with lovely melodies and pleasing flavor; for mental
poise and order. Brings the Baroque sense of order and mental-
emotional focus.

Cras, Jean – *The Loves of Children* (Stoll – Cybelia)
Pure, naive, and mysterious beauty.

Davey, Shaun – *Relief of Derry Symphony* (Tara CD 3024) (Koch)
A beautiful, stirring, modern yet melodic work; celebrational music
that incorporates bagpipe into full orchestra.

Dawson, William Levi – *Negro Folk Symphony* (Järvi – Chandos 9226)
Contains some deeply spiritual and magnificent music by a sadly
neglected American composer. May there be more!

Debussy, Claude – *Engulfed Cathedral* (Stokowski – London or Simon
– Cala)
Arouses deep, archetypal memories of another age, perhaps the lost
continent of Atlantis; oceanic music that pulls the listener in; stimulates
creative visualization and imagination.

– *Clair de lune* (Ormandy – Columbia or Sony; or Stokowski – EMI)
Nostalgic; calls up feelings of reverie.

– *The Sea (La Mer)* (Munch – RCA or Boulez – Sony or Bernstein –
Sony or Ansermet – London Weekend)

Marvelously pictorial, suggestive scenes; right for emotional release; brings power and mystery; breaks up emotional tension.

– *Nocturnes* (Boulez – Sony or Abbado – DGG or Haitink – Philips or Stokowski – EMI)

Mysterious and evocative pieces; *Festivals* is a particularly energetic piece that activates the body and deep feelings.

– *Prelude to the Afternoon of a Faun* (Monteux – London or Karajan – DGG or Bernstein – Sony)

Expansive and reflective, at times rising to heights of reverie and winsomeness; good for relieving heaviness and lethargy.

– *Sacred and Profane Dances for Harp and Orchestra* (Badings/Haitink – Philips)

Again, the sounds of another world, mysterious and alluring; the harp penetrates the listener's consciousness with its exotic, hypnotic melodies.

Delibes, Léo – *Coppélia; Sylvia* (Mari – Angel)

Beautifully melodic, enlivening music; good for movement and energy release; lively rhythms relieve depression.

Delius, Frederick – *On Hearing the First Cuckoo in Spring* (Beecham – Angel)

Very calming and ethereal nature music.

– *Appalachia* (Barbirolli – EMI or Hickox – London)

Beautiful, haunting melodies that evoke distant memories.

– *Florida Suite* (Beecham – Angel or Boughton – Nimbus)

Musical pictures of the beauty of the nineteenth-century Florida coast, depicting night on the river and the echoes of Negro spirituals mixing with the intoxicating fragrances of orange groves; wonderful for reverie and reflection.

– *Summer Night on the River; Song before Sunrise; La Calinda; In a Summer Garden* (Barbirolli – Angel)

More beautiful, atmospheric music; good for creative imagination.

Dello Joio, Norman – *Triumph of Saint Joan Symphony* (Sedares – Koch Schwann)

Dramatic themes, containing powerful energies of Joan of Arc, a warrior Angel of Light.

De Luca, Edmond – *The Conquerors of the Ages* (Linz – Alshire ALCD 41)

Dvořák, Antonín – *Amid Nature; Carnival* (Kubelik – DGG); *Czech Suite* (Dorati – London)

Slavic delights, depicting festive flavors and a strong feeling for nature; good energy raisers.

– *Cello Concerto* (Fournier/Szell or Rose/Ormandy or Gendron/
Haitink or Rostropovich/Karajan – DGG or Piatagorsky/Munch –
RCA or Du Pre/Barenboim – EMI)
Melodious, noble, and inspiring; finale especially moving, composed in
loving memory of a close relation of Dvořák.
– *Symphony no. 8* (Walter – Columbia or Munch – RCA or Barbirolli
– EMI)
A nature painting in melody; uplifts the spirits; energizing and lyrical.
– *Symphony no. 9, From the New World* (Walter – Columbia or
Kertész – London or Toscanini – RCA or Bernstein – Sony)
A description of the magical, beautiful sights of early America, a new
world; combines Native American Indian-like tunes with Slavonic
flavors and stirring melodies; uplifts the spirits; note especially the
famous and deeply moving Largo (second movement), which brings
deep peace, reflection, and release.
– *Slavonic Dances* (Szell – Sony or Kubelik – DGG)
Moving rhythms and lovely colors enliven the listener.
Dyson, Sir George – *Symphony* (Hickox – Chandos 9200)
A friendly, warm work, filled with many colors and variety.
Elgar, Sir Edward – *Enigma Variations* (Monteux – London Weekend
or Boult – Angel)
Varied musical portraits of the composer's friends; some of the music
bubbles and is powerful; other sections are more pensive and quiet,
such as *Nimrod*, the beautiful and moving ninth variation.
– *Sea Pictures* (Baker/Barbirolli – Angel)
Songs of power and devotion with sea (orchestra) accompanying;
nostalgic in places and inspiring.
– *Starlight Express* (Handley – EMI)
Music of variety; some sections energetic and songful, others more
quiet; good for creative imagination.
Enesco, Georges – *Roumanian Rhapsodies* (Dorati – Mercury)
Stirring music, sparkling in melody and rhythmic vitality; good for
movement and physical stimulation.
van Eyck, Jacob – *Der Fluyten Lust-Hof* (Kosofsky – Titanic)
Transparent music for solo recorder; excellent for clearance and relief
of stress; also to be played while eating.
Falla, Manuel de – *Nights in the Gardens of Spain* (Rubinstein/Jorda
– RCA or Haskil/Markevitch – Philips or de Larrocha/Fruhbeck de
Burgos – London)
Scenes of nocturnal mystery; haunting melodies; marvelous for
painting memories and imagination.

Fanshawe, David – *African Sanctus and Salaams* (Philips)
Unique piece of music, brings in great energy and exotic, spontaneous singing in praise; also filled with nature sounds; stimulates the whole person; good for body movement, dance, and singing.

Fauré, Gabriel – *Requiem* (Willcocks – EMI or Rutter – Collegium)
Reverent; excellent for deepening devotion. *In Paradise* is especially beautiful and celestial.

Fétis, François-Joseph – *Symphonic Fantasy for Organ and Orchestra* (Priestman – Koch Schwann)
Beautiful and melodic music that contains many empowering, energizing moments.

Finzi, Gerald – *Intimations of Immortality* (Handley – Lyrita or Hickox – EMI)
Poetic musical journey; deepens aspiration. (See Wordsworth's poem by the same title.)
– *Cello Concerto* (Ma/Handley – Lyrita or Wallfisch/Handley – Chandos)
Lyrical and moving, in the English pastoral tradition.

Le Flem, Paul – *Symphony in A (Celtic)* (Schnitzler – Timpani)
Original and beautiful treatments of Bretón melodies and the bardic legends and wild forests.

Foster, Stephen – *Songs* (Smith/Gregg Singers – Vox or Hampson – EMI)
– *Commemoration Symphony to Stephen Foster* (beautiful choral-orchestral arrangements of many of Foster's songs by the composer Robert Russell Bennett) (Legacy)
Arousing friendliness and warmth; good for awakening feelings.

Franck, César – *The Beatitudes* (Rilling – Hanssler Classic)
Music of praise, love, and devotion, based upon the teachings of the Christ.
– *Symphony in D Minor* (Monteux – RCA or Dutoit – London or Hampton, solo organ – Musical Heritage)
Music of deep aspiration and spiritual beauty; good for solitary listening experience; rises to the heights.
– *Panis angelicus* (Pavarotti – London)
Angelic, exquisitely devotional; uplifting. Title means "The Bread of Angels." Music brings in angelic vibrations.
– *Psyche* (Strauss – Connoisseur Society)
Music of mystery and expansive beauty; good for increasing imagination and poetic sensitivity.

Fučík, Julius – *Marches* (Neumann – Supraphon)
Stirring and enlivening; stimulates physical body.

Gabrieli, Giovanni – *Music for Brass and Organ* (Biggs/Burgin – Columbia MS-6117 or Biggs/Gregg Smith Singers – Sony) – *A Venetian Coronation* (McCreesh – Virgin)
Stirring and stimulating to body and emotions. Beautiful brass, organ, and choirs that sing antiphonally.

Gade, Niels – *Symphonies nos. 5, 6* (Järvi – BIS 356)
Highly romantic and melodic.

Gershwin, George – *Concerto in F; Rhapsody in Blue* (Previn/Angel or Entremont/Ormandy – Sony)
Jazzy in spots, sometimes containing lovely melodies that inspire the emotions.

Ginastera, Alberto – *Panambi; Ollantay; Estancia* (Borejko – Largo 5122) (Qualiton)
Exotic, rhythmical, and powerful; listen especially to the beautiful, five-minute finale of *Panambi,* called *The Dawn.*

Giuliani, Mauro – *Concertos for Guitar and Strings* (P. Romero/ Marriner – Philips)
Very uplifting, beautiful melodies and harmonious sounds; good for any time. Music enlivens imagination and brings focus.

Glass, Philip – *Violin Concerto* (Kremer/Dohnányi – DGG 135369)

Glière, Reinhold – *Soprano Concerto* (Hulse/Hickox – Chandos 9094)
Unique and haunting music.

Gluck, Christoph – *Dance of the Blessed Spirits* (Stokowski – EMI)
Gorgeous and uplifting; music of joy and peace that clears the atmosphere.

Gould, Morton – *Declaration Suite and Fall River Legend* (Mitchell – RCA 09026-61651)
Strong, lyrical, and appealing.

Gounod, Charles – *St. Cecilia Mass,* especially *Sanctus* (Prétre – EMI or Norman/Gibson – Philips [for *Sanctus* only])
Music of devotional fervor and aspiration; very powerful in sections; good for release.
– *Unfold Ye Portals of Creation* (Condie/Ormandy – Sony)
Powerful; good for release and spiritual aspiration.

Grechaninov, Alexander – *Symphonies nos. 1, 2* (Edlinger/Wildner – Marco Polo 8.223163)
Beautiful, romantic Slavic pieces, filled with lasting melodies. A real winner!

Grieg, Edvard – *Piano Concerto in A* (Lupu/Previn – London or Curzon/Fjeldstad – London or Zimerman/Karajan – DGG or Andsnes/Kitaenko – Virgin)

Perhaps the greatest piano concerto ever composed in the sense of its balance and total beauty; powerful outer movements with nature-filled and enchanting slow movement in the middle; a total experience.

– *Holberg Suite* (Karajan – DGG)
Varied moods; mostly lyrical and awakening impressions of nature.

– *Peer Gynt* (Hollweg/Beecham – Angel)
Tonal palette with many colors and melodies recalling Scandinavian landscape and folk songs; also nature beings.

Griffes, Charles Tomlinson – *Three Poems of Fiona MacLeod; Golden Peacock; Pleasure Dome of Kubla Khan* (Ozawa – New World or Schwarz – Delos)
Impressionistic and poetic pieces; mysterious and exotic.

Grofé, Ferde – *Grand Canyon Suite* (Cash/Kostelanetz – Sony or Ormandy – Sony or Bernstein – Sony or Kunzel – Telarc)
Pictorial and evocative music; good for imagination; stimulates physical body. Note: watch out for very powerful, actual thunderstorm incorporated into the Telarc recording.

Guilmant, Alexandre – *Organ Concerto* (Preston/Braithwaite – ABC Australia – 8.770008) (Albany Imports)

Guy, Barry – *After the Rain* (Hickox – NMC 0135)
Throbbing and deep instrumental threnody.

Handel, George Frideric – *Harp Concerto, opus 4, no. 6* (Zabaleta/Kuentz – DGG Musikfest)
Elegant, centering, and appealing during meals.

– *Israel in Egypt* (Mackerras – DGG)
Lovely choral sections that inspire spiritually.

– *Messiah* (Hogwood – Oiseau Lyre or Sargent – EMI Classics for Pleasure or Beecham – RCA)
Music of deep adoration and praise to the Christ; Handel believed this music was "given to him" and he never charged for a single performance; attunes the listener spiritually to the Christ and the angels.

– *Water Music* (Van Beinum – Philips or Harnoncourt – Telefunken)
Sparkling melodies and rhythms; good for cleansing and artistic creativity.

– *Let the Bright Seraphim*, from *Samson* (Te Kanawa/Willcocks – BBC-REP 413 or Philips)
Joyful song of praise; very energizing.

Haydn, Franz Joseph – *Piano Concertos* (Alpenheim/Dorati – Vox); *Trumpet Concerto* (Hardenberger/Marriner); *The Creation* (Marriner – Philips 6769047); the *Masses* (Guest – London or Bernstein – Sony);

Symphonies (Dorati – London or Jochum – DGG or Bernstein – Sony or Beecham – EMI or Szell – Sony or Davis – Philips); *Symphonies nos. 82-87, 93-99* (Bernstein – Sony 47550, 47553, 47557 – Note: Bernstein's classic perfomances—so joyful)
Music that breathes and gives off sparks of vitality; excellent "up" music; good also for mental centering and clarity.

Heenan, Ashley – *A Maori Suite* (Heenan – Kiwi SLC-72)
Exotic piece of music from New Zealand, arousing love, devotion, action, and aspiration.

Herbert, Victor – *Ah! Sweet Mystery of Life* (Sills/Kostelanetz – Angel)
"For 'tis love, and love alone, the world is seeking/And 'tis love, and love alone that can repay!/'Tis the answer, 'tis the end and all of living./For it is love alone that rules for aye!" Sweet uplifting songs.

Hill, Alfred – *Symphony, The Joy of Life* (Marco Polo) (Records International)
Music that lifts the listener into expanded feelings of devotion and power.

Hindemith, Paul – *Mathis der Maler, Symphony* (Bernstein – DGG or Sony)
Awakens reverence and imagination and brings through power.

Holst, Gustav – *Jupiter,* from *The Planets* (Boult – EMI or Mackerras – Virgin or Dutoit – London)
Jupiter is very refreshing; the other movements are varied in mood.

Honegger, Arthur – *Summer Pastorale* (Bernstein – Sony)
A quiet, lyrical piece portraying a time and scene in nature.

Hovhaness, Alan – *Mysterious Mountain* (Reiner – RCA 5733-2 or Schwarz – Delos or RCA (BMG) 09026-61957)
A beautiful meditative experience; takes listener into private worlds of melody and offers a tonal landscape that is good for deep meditation.
– *Magnificat* (Whitney – Poseidon 1018, not yet on CD)
Inspires joy and rapture in the Divine Presence; synthesis of East and West in style and descriptive content.
– *Prayer of Saint Gregory* (Clark – Koch KIC 7221)
– *Talin* (Sobol/Flagello – Kenwest CD 508 – 21 Napier Place, London W14)
Piece for clarinet and strings that is introspective in most places; quieting to the emotions. Also exists as a Viola Concerto.
– *Avak the Healer* (Nixon, Stevens/Gold – Crystal CD 806)
An especially lovely and mystical composition by Hovhaness.
– *And God Created Great Whales* (David Amos – Crystal CD 810, a

wonderful recording, or Kostelanetz – Columbia M-30390, not yet on
CD, or Schwarz – Delos, also a beautiful CD)
Combines actual whale songs with a shimmering orchestral back-
ground; great for imagination and guided imagery.
Hummel, Johann Nepomuk – *Mandolin Concerto* (Hladky – Turnabout
TV 340035, not yet on CD)
Soothing and good for centering.
d'Indy, Vincent – *Symphony on a French Mountain Air* (Casadesus/
Ormandy – Sony Portrait or Thibaudet/Dutoit – London or Thiollier/de
Almeida – Naxos 8550754)
Suggestive of Alpine scenes, at times releasing great power and at
others offering a ruminative mood; inspires creativity and relieves
lethargy and depression.
   – *Medde; Karadec; Souvenirs* (Nopre – Marco Polo 8.223654)
Ireland, John – *The Holy Boy* (Dilkes – EMI)
Reverent and quieting.
Janáček, Leoš – *Sinfonietta* (Ančerl – Supraphon or Mackerras – London
or Neumann – Supraphon)
Brassy, celebrational music; activates body and emotions.
   – *Slavonic (or Glagolitic) Mass* (Kubelik – DGG or Bernstein – Sony
or Ančerl – Supraphon)
Music of praise; stirring and majestic; good for releasing anger. The
composer's description of it is as follows:

Always the scent of the woods—that was the incense. I felt a cathedral
grow out of the giant expanse of the woods and the sky stretching far
into the misty distance.

    A flock of white sheep were ringing the bells. Now I hear the voice of
each archpriest in tenor solo, a maiden angel in the soprano and in the
choir our people.

    The tall firs, their tips lit up by the stars, are the candles and during
the ceremony I see the vision of Saint Wenceslas, and I hear the language
of the missionaries, Cyril and Methodius.

Jongen, Joseph – *Symphonie Concertante for Organ and Orchestra*
(Fox/Prétre – EMI or Murray/De Waart – Telarc)
A real showpiece for drama of organ and orchestra; highly stirring in
places, meditative and reflective in others; stimulates the whole person;
spiritually elevating. Finale is a nonstop blaze of triumph.
Joplin, Scott – *Piano Music* (Rifkin – Nonesuch)
Moving rhythms; activates body.

Josten, Werner – *Sacred Concerto I-II* (Stokowski – CRI)

Kabalevsky, Dmitry Borisovich – *The Comedians* (Barra – Koch Schwann)
Buoyant, energizing, and pleasing.
– *Requiem* (Kabalevsky – Olympia)

Kaplan, Abraham – *K'Dusha Symphony* (Congregation B'Nai Amoona, 324 S. Mason Road, Saint Louis, MD 63141) (cassette)
A compelling symphonic-choral work sanctifying God's name on earth as it is sanctified in heaven by the angels.

Ketélbey, Albert – *In a Monastery Garden; Bells Across the Meadow* (Lanchbery – Angel)
Simple, appealing music with pleasing melodies; awakens nostalgia.

Khachaturian, Aram – *Sabre Dance,* from *Gayaneh* (Khachaturian – EMI)
Exciting and high-voltage, enlivening the physical body; good for fast movement and dancing.
– *Symphony no. 3* (for organ and orchestra) (Stokowski – RCA or Tjeknavorian – ASV or Gluschenko – Chandos 9321)
Very strong and compelling music, even overwhelming, but magnificent.

Kodály, Zoltán – *Háry János Suite* (Szell – Sony)
Exotic sounds of the cimbalom combine with orchestral colors; stimulating to imagination.

Koechlin, Charles – *The Persian Hours* (Segerstam – Marco Polo); *The Jungle Book* (Segerstam – Marco Polo)
Both of these CDs contain many mysterious, exotic, and dramatically powerful moments of melodic music.

Korngold, Erich – *Symphony* (Downes – Chandos or Kempe – Varèse Sarabande)
A marvelous array of melody and power.
– *Violin Concerto* (Perlman/Previn – Angel or Heifetz/Wallenstein RCA)
Highly melodic and romantic; good for feelings.
– *Garden Scene* (Sakanov – London 440 081-2)
Richly warm and melodic serenade of love; music of intimacy.

Kreisler, Fritz – *Violin Music* (Elman – Vanguard or Perlman – EMI or Kreisler – EMI)
Charming melodies exuding a warmth and friendliness; good for intimacy and developing kindliness and friendship.

Lalo, Edouard – *Symphonie Espagnole* (Kyung Wha Chung/Dutoit – London)

Music of drama and lyrical warmth; good emotional/mental stimulus.

Larsson, Lars-Erik – *Pastoral Suite* (Wedin – BIS or Westerberg – Swedish Society 1020); *Symphonies* (BIS)
Nature-oriented melodies paint tonal pictures of Scandinavian rural life; kindles the imagination.

Lekeu, Guillaume – *Violin Sonata* (Philips)
Excellent for emotional/mental relaxation.
– *Adagio for String Orchestra* (DePriest – Radio Canada International)
Very calming.

Liadov, Anatol – *Enchanted Lake* (Svetlanov – Melodiya)
Mysterious and enchanting selection; promotes tranquility.

Lilburn, Douglas – *Symphonies nos. 1, 2; Aotearoa Overture* (Heenan – Kiwi or Hopkins – Continuum)
Magnificent music, majestic, lofty, and powerfully dramatic; describes nature in its pristine beauty, and eruptive force and grandeur; a celebration of New Zealand's mountains and forests, especially Mount Cook and Milford Sound, located on South Island. The overture is celebrational, elicits courage, strength, and imagination/visualization.

Liszt, Franz – *Battle of the Huns* (Ansermet – London or Kunzel – Telarc)
Dramatic, powerful cymbals and organ; good for release.
– *Bells of Strassburg* (Ferencsik – Hungaroton)
Dramatic and reverent music describing the overcoming of evil with the power of Light; the chorus of the heavens mixes with cathedral bells; good for encouragement.
– *Christus* (Forrai – Hungaroton or Dorati – Hungaroton)
Perhaps Liszt's greatest work; a mighty epic in music of the life of the Christ from beginning to crucifixion and resurrection.
– *Hungarian Rhapsodies* (Dorati – Mercury)
Beautifully colored and melodic dance music; wonderful for enlivening body and emotions; good for relieving lethargy. Note the beautiful, exotic sounds of the cimbalom.
– *Les Préludes* (Fricsay – DGG or Bernstein – CBS)
Dramatic tone poem, at times highly energetic with great climaxes; beautiful melodies; romantic sections.

Lyatoshinsky, Boris – *Slavic Concerto* (Rzhanov/Gnedash – Russian Disc 11059)
Powerful and melodic.

MacDowell, Edward – *To a Wild Rose* (Clark – Koch 3-7282)
Very pleasing; a natural for romance and reverie.
– *Suite no. 1* (Hanson – Mercury 4343372)

  – *Suite no. 2, Indian* (Hanson – Mercury)
Pictorial and dramatic; stimulates.
Mahler, Gustav – *Symphony no. 1, Titan* (Walter – Sony or Horenstein
  – Unicorn-Kanchana or Kubelik – DGG or Muti – EMI)
Marvelously poetic and dramatic; good for emotional release.
  – *Symphony no. 2, Resurrection* (Baker/Bernstein – Sony or Kaplan
  – MCA or Mehta – London or Stokowski – Intaglio)
Epic work; a tremendous statement of a spiritual seeker, culminating
in drama of celestial choirs; bells, organ, and orchestra; a worship
experience; good for spiritual inspiration and empowerment.
  – *Symphony no. 3* (Bernstein – Sony)
Noble and inspirational work describing the journey of the composer
and his interaction with nature; note the last movement, which is
especially suited for deep meditation; the finale brings feelings of
transcendent power.
  – *Symphony no. 9* (Walter – Sony or Horenstein – Music and Arts)
Total life statement; peaceful but intensely dynamic final movement.
Malipiero, Gian – *Symphonies* (Almeida – Marco Polo)
Colorful and dramatic music.
Martin, Frank – *Violin Concerto* (Olding/Iwaki – ABC 8.77004) (Albany
  Imports)
  – *Symphony; Passacaglia* (Bamert – Chandos 9312)
Martini, Giovanni – *Plaisir d'Amour* (Sills/Kostelanetz – Sony)
Beautiful song that awakens love.
Martinu, Bohuslav – *Symphony no. 6, Fantaisies symphoniques* (Munch
  – RCA or Ančerl – Supraphon)
A most dramatic symphony with many short, delightful moments of
melody; depicts eventual resolution and surrender; good for pictorial
imagination.
Mascagni, Pietro – *Messa di Gloria* (Colusso – Musicaimmage MR
  10001) (Qualiton Imports)
Massenet, Jules – *Sleep of the Blessed Virgin* (Frémaux – EMI or
  Beecham – EMI)
Peaceful and relaxing.
  – *Meditation,* from *Thais* (Karajan – EMI or DGG)
Linear; good for meditation and beautiful for listening.
McKuen, Rod – *Concerto for Balloon* (Stanford – Stanyan CD
  STZ103-2)
A twentieth-century masterpiece; alternating dramatic segments
with those that are meditative and floating; the finale which blends

synthesizer and organ is gorgeous; wonderful for imagination and deep reflection; joy-inspiring.

Mendelssohn, Felix – *Violin Concerto* (Fodor/Maag – RCA Silver Seal 09026 or Stern/Ormandy – Sony)
Warm and mellow; calming and reassuring; very nurturing and renewing.

– *Elijah* (Corboz – Erato or Hickox – Chandos)
Inspiring, spiritual work, especially in its choral selections.

– *Symphony no. 3, Scottish* (Munch – RCA or Maag – London Weekend)
Beautiful and radiant work, inspired by the Scottish countryside and Mendelssohn's visit to the Chapel at Holyrood Palace in Edinburgh.

– *Symphony no. 4, Italian* and *Symphony no. 5, Reformation* (Munch – RCA or Sinopoli – DGG)
Refreshing, light, and clearing. Symphony no. 5 is an especially beautiful statement of faith, containing the *Dresden Amen* motif.

Minkus-Lanchbery – *La Boyadere* (Bonynge – London 2-436-917-2)
Exotic and lovely music.

Milhaud, Darius – *Sacred Service for Sabbath Morning* (Senart – Adda Arcam 590143)

Moeran, E.J. – *Symphony* (Dilkes – EMI or Handley – Chandos)
Impassioned, wild, and beautiful, containing some strong nature scenes.

Monteverdi, Claudio – *Vespers of the Blessed Virgin, 1610* (Schneidt – DGG or Corboz – Erato or Gardiner – London)
Excellent for awakening reverence and producing spiritual openings (in the spirit of the Renaissance); meditative and healing.

Mozart, Wolfgang Amadeus – *Concertos for Flute* (Tast/Haenchen – Laserlight 15873)
All beautiful and refreshing.

– *Horn Concertos* (Tuckwell/Marriner – Angel)
Energizing, joyful, clearing.

– *Ave Verum Corpus* (Kiri Te Kanawa/Davis – Philips)
Beautiful and reverent; brings peace and celestial sounds.

– *The Magic Flute* (Böhm – DGG)
Based upon Masonic teachings; deeply esoteric and very inspiring description of the spiritual quest.

– *Cassations* (Nerat – Naxos 8.550609)
Exquisite music.

– *A Little Night Music, Serenade in G* (Walter – CBS or Marriner – EMI)
Gorgeous, charming; refreshing to the spirit.

– *Piano Concertos* (Rubinstein or Brendel or Perahia or Lupu or Ashkenazy – pianists performing on various labels)
All beautiful, some very pensive and inspiring sections mixed with music that is clear and effervescent.
– *Symphonies nos. 39, 40, 41* (Walter, Szell, Beecham, Davis, Bernstein – conductors performing these works on various labels)
Mozart's last three symphonies are special classics; they bring cleansing and clearance. No. 40 seems to be especially good for driving away negativity in the atmosphere.
– *Posthorn Serenade* (Szell – Sony)
Moving; sharp and cleansing.

Mundy – *The Voice of the Heavenly Father* (*Vox Patris Caelestis*) (Phillips – Gimell)
Inspiring and clear; a beautiful, radiant, polyphonic choral work.

Mussorgsky, Modest – *Night on Bald Mountain* (Stokowski – London or Ormandy – Sony or Reiner – RCA)
Pictorial and intriguing; explores the macabre versus transformation and ends peacefully, with bells followed by strings receding into silence.
– *Great Gate of Kiev*, from *Pictures at an Exhibition* (Diazmunoz – OM or Leibowitz – Chesky or Toscanini – RCA or Giulini – Sony) (Diazmunoz adds a magnificent pipe organ to score)
Inspires triumph and release into power; great theme, much drama. (Note: video *Pictures at an Exhibition* – Leonard Slatkin, conductor – St. Louis Symphony Orchestra, 718 N. Grand Boulevard, St. Louis, MO 63103.)

Novák, Vitezslav – *The Eternal Longing; In the Tatras; Slovak Suite* (Sejna – Supraphon 11 0682-2)
Uplifting and inspirational pieces, filled with the imagery of nature.

Olsson, Otto – *Requiem* (Ohlsson – Proprius PRCD 9086)

Orff, Carl – *Carmina Burana* (Blegen/Thomas – Sony or Popp/Fruhbeck de Burgos – Angel Studio)
Music with compelling drama and color; repetitions and montages of sounds with strong rhythms; good for release/clearance.

Pachelbel, Johann – *Canon in D* (Paillard – Erato)
Noble, gentling music; excellent for quieting nerves and for spiritual devotion; like a lullaby from the womb.

Palestrina, Giovanni Pierluigi – *Pope Marcellus Mass* (Willcocks – EMI or Phillips – Gimell)

Serene, celestial, beautiful; good for intense meditation; music that rises like perfume and circulates high among the Gothic arches of a great cathedral.

Paray, Paul – *Mass for 500th Anniversary of Joan of Arc* (Paray – Mercury 432 719)
Highly dramatic and charged with devotional energy.

Parry, Sir Hubert – *Symphonies* (5) (Bamert – Chandos); *I Was Glad; Jerusalem* (Hickox – Chandos); *Ode to the Nativity* (Willcocks – Lyrita)
Stately, exquisite music, with beautiful melodies; the Christmas ode is a marvelous, radiant work, ending with the angelic song of a radiant soprano.

Piston, Walter – *The Incredible Flutist* (Hanson – Mercury or Schwarz – Delos)
Colorful and dramatic; brings cheer and good energy.

Ponchielli, Amilcare – *Dance of the Hours,* from *La Gioconda* (Ormandy – Sony)
Stimulating; fast rhythms; quickens pulse.

Poulenc, Francis – *Concerto for Organ, Timpani and Strings* (Zamkochian/Munch – RCA or Duruflé/Prétre – EMI or Malcolm/Brown – London)
Powerful and dramatic; brings strong energy and potential for release of anger; cathartic.

Prokofiev, Sergey – *Alexander Nevsky* (Schippers – Sony or Bychkov – Philips or Järvi – Chandos)
Heroic Slavic music; mixes strong lyricism with some sorrow and stirring battle scenes; galvanizing for the energy.

– *Symphony no. 5* (Järvi – Chandos or Ansermet – IMP or Karajan – DGG)
One of the great Russian symphonic works; combines powerful melodies with strong rhythms: a powerhouse.

– *Symphony no. 7* (Martinon – Vox or Malko – EMI or Ruud – Simax or Previn – EMI)
Some beautiful melodies here, and some sadness and nostalgic moments; I like the beauty of the themes and the stirring finale.

Puccini, Giacomo – *Without Words* (Kostelanetz – CBS)
Romantic and dramatic.

Purcell, Henry – *Anthems* (Preston – DGG or Deller – Vanguard)
Majestic, devotional music; good for building faith and spiritual dedication.

Quilter, Rogers – *Where the Rainbow Ends; Country Pieces* (Leaper – Marco Polo 8.223444)

Rachmaninov, Sergei – *Piano Concerto no. 2* (Richter/Wislocki – DGG or Rubinstein/Reiner – RCA or Cliburn/Reiner – RCA or Wild/Horenstein – Chandos)
Dramatic music, building toward joyful overcoming theme in the finale which helped Rachmaninov's own depression to lift.
– *Piano Concerto no. 3* (Horowitz/Reiner – RCA or Gilels/Cluytens – Testament) (Allegro Imports)
Highly charged, manic joy.
– *Symphony no. 2* (Svetlanov – Mobile Fidelity or Previn – EMI or Bychkov – Philips)
Spacious Russian canvas of drama, color, and melody; the Adagio is particularly therapeutic and expansive, as a clarinet playing longingly over the orchestra.
– *Rhapsody on a Theme of Paganini* (Wild/Horenstein – Chandos or Chesky or Rubinstein/Reiner – RCA)
Many moments of power and rhythmic vitality; eighteenth variation is especially warm and appealing; awakens love (used in soundtrack to movie *Somewhere in Time,* by John Barry).
– *Transcriptions for Orchestra* (Kogosowski/Järvi – Chandos 9261)
Marvelous discovery of new orchestrations of Rachmaninov's *Trio Elegiaque, Variations on a Theme of Corelli,* and *Vocalise.* Beautiful, Slavic works.
– *Suites for Piano and Orchestra* (Mester – Citadel 88101)

Rautavaara, Einojuhani – *Cantus Arcticus* (Pommer – Ondine)
A brooding, meditative piece, combining haunting bird calls with orchestra sounding from the distant wilds of nature; good for imagination and creativity.

Ravel, Maurice – *Piano Concerto for Left Hand* (Browning/Leinsdorf – EMI or Gavrilov/Rattle – EMI or Béroff/Abbado – DGG)
Perky and very strong in places; a total experience emotionally, exploring many feelings.

Reinecke, Carl – *Piano Concertos* (Robbins/Van Remoortel – Genesis)
Powerful and joyful works that bring upliftment and openness.

Respighi, Ottorino – *Pines of Rome; Fountains of Rome; Roman Festivals* (Muti – EMI or Toscanini – RCA or Mata – Delos)
Some glorious color and varieties of sound here; the nightingale movement is especially evocative and soothing (third movement of *Pines*).
– *Ancient Dances and Airs* (Dorati – Mercury or Marriner – EMI)

Thoroughly enjoyable music filled with charm and changes of pace; a therapeutic quality comes through its grace and vitality.

– *Sinfonia dramatica* (Nazareth – Marco Polo)

Rheinberger, Joseph – *Organ Concertos* (Biggs/Peress – Columbia or Murray/Ling – Telarc)

Dramatic and powerful; good energizing music.

– *Suite for Organ, Violin and Strings* (Hoenchen – Capriccio CD 10-337)

– *The Star of Bethlehem* (Heger – Carus)

A very beautiful, devotional piece of Christmas music.

Rimsky-Korsakov, Nikolai – *Scheherazade* (Beecham – Angel or Temirkanov – RCA or Stokowski – RCA or London)

Has fairy-tale quality; soars with melody and also with powerful drama; good for visualization and creativity.

Rodrigo, Joaquin – *Concierto de Aranjuez* (P. Romero/Marriner – Philips)

– *Fantasy for a Courtier* (Segovia/MCA or Williams/Groves – Sony)

Lilting Spanish rhythms and tunes; middle movement of *Aranjuez* particularly lovely and expansive emotionally. Moods are romantic, interior, and vibrant. Rodrigo, blind from age three, wrote about the *Aranjuez Concerto* as follows: "The concerto should sound like the unseen breeze that ruffles the treetops—as strong as a butterfly, as dainty as a veronica."

Ropartz, Joseph-Guy – *Requiem; Psalm 129; Short Mass* (Piquemal – Adda 581266) (Qualiton Imports)

Beautiful sacred music.

Rossini, Gioacchino – *William Tell Overture; The Silken Ladder* (Reiner – RCA or Toscanini – RCA or Bernstein – Sony)

Alive, quickening; good for releasing tensions and anger.

Roylance, Dave and Robert Galvin – *Battle of the Atlantic Suite for Soprano, Orchestra and Chorus* (Garret/Connor – Conifer 74321-15008-2)

– *The Tall Ships Suite; Ocean Fantasia; The Grand Parade of Sail* (Hicks/Connor – Conifer 74321-18309-2)

Very dramatic and strong sections mix with lyrical moments; memorable tunes and lasting impressions.

Rubinstein, Anton – *Reve angelique (Angelic Dream)* (Adolph – Vox Cameo Classics ACD 8763)

Beautiful and mysterious angel music.

– *Two Cello Concertos* (Thomas/Ahronovitch – Koch Schwann CD 311)

Lovely, lyrical Slavic works.
– *Piano Concertos nos. 1, 2* (Banowetz/Walter – Marco Polo 8.223456)
Very dramatic, high-energy, romantic works.
– *Symphony no. 2 (Ocean)* (Gunzenhauser – Marco Polo 8.220449)
Music of the "seven seas" containing high energy and power.
Saint-Saëns, Camille – *Symphony no. 3, Organ* (Zamkochian, Munch –
RCA or Rawsthorne/Bátiz – ASV or Raver/Bernstein – Sony)
Electrifying piece, at times very quiet and reflective, but culminating
in grand finale, reminiscent of a cathedral rising stone by stone to the
heavens. The music builds archetypes.
Schmidt, Franz – *Intermezzo,* from *Notre Dame* (Karajan – DGG or
EMI)
Rising splendor; grand, expansive music of awe and joyous praise.
Schubert, Franz Peter – *Rosamunde,* selections (Böhm – DGG or Szell
– Sony)
Serene, joyous, reassuring.
– *The Last Quintet (op. 163)* (arranged *beautifully* for string orchestra
by the wonderful Israeli composer and conductor Dalia Atlas – ITM
950005) (One World Records Distributors)
– Symphonies (various labels)
All bright and lyrical; *Unfinished* (Symphony no. 8) in places very
haunting and mysterious; good for centering.
Schumann, Robert – *Piano Concerto in A* (Argerich/Rostropovich –
DGG or Zimerman/Karajan – DGG); *Symphonies nos. 1, 2 , 3, 4* (Muti
– EMI or Kubelik – DGG); *Träumerei (Dreams)* (Ormandy – Sony)
Mostly dramatic and very inspiring; beautifully lyrical.
Shchedrin, Rodion – *Anna Karenina* (ballet music) (Simonov – Russian
Disc 10030)
Shostakovich, Dimitri – *Song of the Forests* (Fedoseyev – Melodiya or
Yurlov – Russian Disc)
A most stirring and passionate song to nature in the great Russian
spirit.
Sibelius, Jean – *Finlandia* (Toscanini – RCA or Bernstein – Sony);
Karelia Suite (Ormandy – RCA or Saraste – RCA); *Symphonies nos.
1, 2, 4, 6, 7* (Maazel – London or Collins – Beulah or Bernstein – Sony
or Ashkenazy – London)
From the great nature deva and master painter of nature music,
compelling and surging melodies; one needs concentrated reflection
and immersion in order to appreciate and feel deeply into the pieces.
Sierra, Roberto – *Tropicalia; Idilio* (Mocal – Koss KC-1021)

Sinding, Christian – *Symphony no. 2* (Ingebretsen – Norsk Kulturrad NKF)
Wonderful, melodic Scandinavian music; expansive.

Smetana, Bedřich – *My Country (Má Vlast)* (Kubelik – DGG or Supraphon; or Talich – Supraphon)
Epic music of ancient Bohemia; rich variety of emotions; wide range of musical experience; powerful mantras of heroic memories.

Smolsky, Dmitri – *Dulcimer Concerto no. 1* (Raisky – Olympia 551)

Sowande, Fela – *African Suite* (Bernardi – CBC 5135)
Appealing and melodic, especially the lullaby.

Sousa, John Philip – *Marches* (Hunsberger – Philips or Fennell – Mercury)
Good energizers for body, encourage movement.

Stanford, Sir Charles Villiers – *Symphonies nos. 1-7* (Handley – Chandos 9279-82)
– *Irish Rhapsodies* (Handley – Chandos)

Still, William Grant – *Symphony no. 2 (Song of a New Race)* (Järvi – Chandos 9226)
A beautiful, noble, and powerful musical experience, often awakening deep aspiration.

Strauss, Johann II – *Die Fledermaus Overture; Waltzes* (Dorati – London or Boskovsky – London, Vanguard or EMI; or Bernstein – Sony)
Pleasing melodies, bringing uplift and joy; good for movement and dancing.

Strauss, Richard – *Aus Italien (From Italy)* (Kempe – EMI); *Also Sprach Zarathustra* (Reiner – RCA or Bychkov – Philips); *Dance Suite after Couperin* (Kempe – EMI or Wakasugi – Denon); *Don Juan* (Böhm – DGG); *Death and Transfiguration* (Previn – Telarc or EMI)
Highly varied music; some really dramatic (i.e., *Sunrise* from *Also Sprach Zarathustra)* and the ethereal beauty of the *Death and Transfiguration* finale which brings in angelic presences as they welcome the departing soul making his/her transition from earthly life.

Stravinsky, Igor – *Firebird* (Stokowski – London or Haitink – Philips or Boulez – Sony)
The Schwarz version on Delos also contains an enchanting story for children narrated with the music. Exotic, stimulating, powerful release music.

Sullivan, Sir Arthur – *Irish Symphony* (Groves – EMI) (coupled with the *Cello Concerto*)

Beautiful and exhilarating; one of the movements was used in a *Masterpiece Theater* story.

Sumac, Yma – *Chants of the Incas* (Capitol)
Exotic and haunting Peruvian songs, spanning multiple octaves.

Suppé, Franz von – *Poet and Peasant Overture; Light Cavalry Overture* (Bernstein – Sony)
Very stimulating; good to relieve lethargy or the doldrums.

Sviridov, Georgy – *Snow-Storm* (Fedoseyev – Olympia 520)

Takemitsu, Toru – *Viola Concerto; Eclipse; November Steps* (Ozawa – Philips 432176)

Tallis, Thomas – *Spem in alium, 40-part Motet* (Willcocks – Argo or Phillips – Gimell or Wulstan – EMI Classics for Pleasure) (Allegro Imports)
Celestial; uplifting, devotional music; builds into soaring and powerful finale.

Taneyev, Sergei – *Concert Suite for Cello and Orchestra* (Tang – Koch 3-1135-2)
– *Symphony no. 4* (Järvi – Chandos 8953)

Tchaikovsky, Peter – *Capriccio Italien* (Bernstein – Sony)
– *Piano Concertos nos. 1, 2* (Graffman/Szell – Columbia or Rodriguez/Tabakov – Elan or Horowitz/ Toscanini – RCA or Dichter/Leinsdorf – RCA)
– *Symphony no. 1, Winter Dreams* (Thomas – DGG or Markevich – Philips) *Symphony no. 4* (Markevich – Philips or Bernstein – Sony)
– *Symphony no. 5* (Monteux – RCA or Stokowski – London Weekend or Barbirolli – EMI or Bernstein – Sony)
– *1812 Overture* (Sharples – London or Temirkanov – RCA or Davis – Philips or Stokowski – London)
– *Romeo and Juliet* (Ozawa – DGG or Abbado – DGG)
– *Swan Lake* (Rowicki – DGG or Ormandy – Sony or Bernstein – Sony)
Combinations of martial rhythms, colorful melodies, and great emotional swings: some of the music very manic, other parts calm and reflective, nostalgic and filled with deep feelings and the Slavic spirit.

Telemann, Georg Philipp – Miscellaneous concertos on different labels. Lively and stimulating, bringing a Baroque sense of order, refreshment, and vitality.

Theodorakis, Mikis – *Canto Olympico* (Karitinos – Lyra INT 3107-2)
Strong and triumphant; energetic music
– *Symphony no. 3* (Knothe – Minos MCD 15009) (available from Greek Video Records and Tapes, 394 McGuinness Boulevard, Brooklyn, NY 11222, 1-718-383-9455)

Very powerful, celebrational sections, which take the listener back to the surging spirit of ancient Greece and its Golden Age. The music evokes the soul and essence of "Greek."

Thompson, Randall – *Suite for Oboe, Clarinet and Viola* (Christ – Crystal)
Calming and strengthening.

– *Symphony no. 2* (Bernstein – Sony or Schenck – Koch Schwann)
A beautiful, strong, and melodic piece of Americana.

Thomson, Virgil – *The River* (Stokowski – Vanguard 8013)
Americana at its finest: beautiful scenic music, great for imagination. Note the atmospheric sounds of the banjo.

Torroba, Frederico Moreno – *Iberian Concerto, Guitar and Orchestra* (Romeros/Marriner – Philips)

– *Concierto de Castilla* (Tröster/Przybylski – Thorofon CTH 2171)

– *Sonatina for Guitar and Orchestra* (Linhares/Wildner – Naxos 8.550483)

– *Interludio I, II* (Boucher/Dessaints – Analekta AN 2-9502) (Records International)
Refreshing, clear, and enlivening. Beautiful melodies.

Truscott, Harold – *Elegy* (Brain – Marco Polo 8.223674)

Turina, Joaquin – *Spring in Seville* (Udaeta – Claves 50-9310)

Vaughan Williams, Ralph – *Fantasia on a Theme of Thomas Tallis* (Stokowski – BBC live) (Allegro Imports)

– *Job* (Boult – Angel or Intaglio)

– *Lark Ascending* (Bean/Boult or Garcia/Menuhin – Arabesque)

– selections from his nine symphonies, especially nos. 1, 2, 3, 5 (Previn – RCA, various discs)

– *Oxford Elegy* (Willcocks – EMI or May/Darlington – Nimbus)
Music of nobility with English pastoral/dramatic/folk song ingredients; restores sense of order and rightness; splendid listening, often highly charged.

Verdi, Giuseppe – Choruses (miscellaneous labels)
Energizing. often triumphant.

Vivaldi, Antonio – *Four Seasons* (Galway – RCA – with flute or Stokowski – London Weekend or Brown/Marriner – Philips)

– *Guitar Concerto in D* (Yepes – London CS 6201)

– *Flute Concertos* (Rampal – Columbia)

– *Sacred Music* (Negri – Philips, various discs)

– *Gloria* (Willcocks – London)

– *Organ Concertos* (Isoir, Kuentz – DGG)

Very therapeutic music; alive and light; good for joyfulness and clearing; releases staleness. Research shows that Vivaldi's music is ideal for babies in the mother's womb.

Wagner, Richard – *Die Meistersinger Overture and Prelude; Parsifal, Prelude and Good Friday Music; Lohengrin, Prelude to Act 1; Flying Dutchman Overture* (for all selections: look for Furtwängler's, Walter's, and Klemperer's renditions for depth; Ormandy's and Stokowski's versions for color and grandeur; and Bernstein's for drama)
Powerful, demanding music; high voltage works which are uplifting and expansive; *Parsifal* is good for spiritual deepening and devotion. A beautiful meditative continuum comes from listening to the following musical sequence: Prelude to *Lohengrin* (Act l) and the descent of the Holy Grail, plus Prelude and *Good Friday Music* from *Parsifal.*

Weber, Carl Maria von – *Overtures* (Bernstein – Sony or Toscanini – RCA or Kubelik – DGG)
Very stirring and activating music; good for releasing tensions and anger.

Willan, Healey – *Symphony no. 2* (Mayer – CBC SMCD 5123)
A warm, romantic, strong, and lovely work for full orchestra; note especially the beautiful love-filled Adagio (second movement).

Yardumian, Richard – *Song of the Soul and Heart* (Brusilow – HNH-4043)
Gorgeous! (currently out of print; look for it!)

2. MISCELLANEOUS SELECTIONS

Adoro – *Domingo* (CBS)
Some beautiful love songs for tenor and orchestra.

Ancient Shepherd Pipes (Hillel – Folkways-FW-8724)
Haunting and lovely.

Anderson, Hans Christian (Danny Kaye, Jenkins – MCA 148)
Friendly music and good story for children and adults.

Anderson, Marian – *Spirituals* (RCA 7911 or Pearl 9318)
Very therapeutic; beautiful singing; deep, devotional experience.

Bayless, John – *Bach Meets the Beatles* (improvisations on Beatles melodies) (Pro Arte 211)

Bearns and Dexter – *Golden Voyage I, III, IV* (White Swan Distributors)
Music that cleanses the aura; purifying and elevating/relaxing; synthesizers, nature sounds, etc. What a shame that both composers died so young!

Beauty of Maori Song (Kiwi SLC-122)
Soulful songs and chants from New Zealand, often with mantralike qualities; some songs very activating, others meditative.

Behold the Great Priest (Ecce Sacerdos Magnus) In Honor of St. Martin of Tours (music composed for flute of Pan, organ, and orchestra by Jean-Claude Mara and Georges Bernes) (SYPC 90017) (Allegro Imports)
Haunting and lovely sacred piece.

Best Years of Our Lives (Friedhofer) (Preamble 1779)
Exhilarating with absolutely lovely melodies. One of the truly wonderful soundtracks.

Birds, Beasts and Flowers (Princess Grace of Monaco and Richard Pasco) (Nimbus NI 5354)
An elegant program of poetry, prose, and music.

Bok, Gordon – *Peter Kagan and the Wind; Bay of Fundy; Sea Djiril's Hymn* (Folk Legacy FSI 44; FSI 54; FSI 48)
Soothing voice; music that calms.

Born Free (John Barry soundtrack) (MGM-4368-ST)
Beautiful and stirring; African rhythms provide means for greater mental focus; no CD yet; just on record and worth looking for.

Brother Sun, Sister Moon (Riz Ortolani soundtrack) (Paramount CO 64-93393)
Exquisite soundtrack music; two beautiful songs (in Italian), the rest instrumental, suggesting the life of Saint Francis of Assisi.

Caravans (Mike Batt soundtrack) (CBS 467030-2)
Exotic film score containing Mideastern rhythms and melodies; exceptionally energizing and at times nostalgic.

Carolan's Receipt (Derek Bell, Irish harp – Shanachie)
Lively and cheerful sounds.

Chants of Yogananda (Haridas, piano – Living Joy, 14618 Tyler Foote Road, Nevada City, CA 95959)
Reverent, joyful music of praise and devotion.

Chariots of Fire (Vangelis soundtrack) (Polydor)
Very powerful music; fine for indecision and lethargy treatment.

Nat King Cole – *Stardust; When the World Was Young* (K-tel-PTP-2508-A or Capitol)
Extremely relaxing, nostalgic; good for relieving tensions.

Collins, Judy – *Colors of the Day* (Elektra TC-55030)
Melodic love songs and ballads; pleasing instrumental accompaniment; mellow; stirs imagination.

The Cowboy Poetry Gathering (Rhino 71573; Rhino Records, 10635 Santa Monica Boulevard, Los Angeles, CA 90025)
Unique blend of poetry and music.

Danny Boy (White/Gerhardt – RCA ARL1-3442)
Irish ballads, some enlivening, others exploring melancholy and nostalgia.

Dark Eyes (Dmitri Hvorostovsky and Ossipov Russian Folk Orchestra) (Kalinin – Philips 434 080)
Unforgettably beautiful and often dramatic Russian folk songs in the true Slavic idiom.

de Hartmann – *Journey to Inaccessible Places* (P. O. Box 5961, Grand Central Station, New York, NY 10163)
Mysterious music, often hypnotic in its rhythms and suggestive of inner landscapes.

– *Sacred Hymns* (Keith Jarrett, piano – ECM 1174)

– *Seekers of the Truth; Reading of a Sacred Book; Words for a Hymn to the Sun* (Cecil Lytle – Celestial Harmonies Distributors)

Denver, John, and Placido Domingo – *Perhaps Love* (CBS); *Seasons of the Heart* (Denver only) (RCA AFL1-4256)
Some really lovely music here; melodic, inspiring, and with uplifting words; good for relieving depression and self-pity.

Diamond, Neil – *Jonathan Livingston Seagull* (CBS)
Haunting music that both inspires and captivates; in some places very soft, in others strong.

Dr. Zhivago (Maurice Jarre soundtrack) (MGM – Sony)
Contains famous *Lara's Theme* and much inspiring music.

Domingo, Placido – *Zarzuela Romances* (Moreno-Buendia – EMI 7-49148)

E.T. (John Williams soundtrack) (MCA-6109)
Music that alternates between mystery and forcefulness; good for inspiration in the more dynamic places.

Echoes of a Waterfall (Drake – Hyperion)
Romantic harp music of the nineteenth century; transparent; provides openings; energizing and relaxing.

Environments – Psychologically Ultimate Seashore and *Optimum Aviary* (Syntonic Research SD-66001)
Soothing sounds; good for deep meditation.

Evening Bells (Gedda – Seraphim S-60225)
Glorious Russian sounds of balalaika and folk songs.

Fiddler on the Roof (soundtrack) (RCA LSO-1093)
Some festive music; basically energizing.

Fiedler, Arthur – *Those Were the Days* (RCA LSC-3261)
Nostalgic spirit of yesteryear; good spirit; inspiring.

Flagstad, Kirsten – *Great Sacred Songs* (London OS-25038)
Inspiring, devotional hymns and anthems, especially Parry's *Jerusalem*.

Flicka (Fredrica von Stade – CBS MK 44609)
Lovely popular songs.

Flowers from the Silence (David and Amanda Hughes – Vedic Research
Institute, 415 South Bernardo, Sunnyvale, CA 94068)
Quiet music; Oriental flavor, at times a bit austere, yet compelling and
meditative; nature sounds and various contemporary sounds.

For a Child's Heart (Synergetic Media, SMC-7801)
Beautiful songs for children; joyous and very devotional.

Fox, Virgil – *Heavy Organ at Carnegie Hall* (RCA ARD1-0081)
Powerful organ music of Bach, energizing and enlivening.

Galway, James – *Song of the Seashore* (RCA ARL1-3534); *The Long
White Cloud and Waiata Poi* (RCA-AFL1-4063)
Flute music of the Orient and New Zealand—poetic, nostalgic, tender.

Garfunkel – *Angel Clare* (Columbia KC-31474)
I especially like the rendition of *Barbara Allen* which is very caressing
and warm.

Gibson, Dan – *Solitudes* (Dan Gibson Productions, Box 1200, Station Z,
Toronto, Ontario M5N 2Z7, Canada)
Extremely therapeutic musical sounds of nature, including gentle
streams, gurgling brooks, heavy and light surf, sounds of the prairie,
redwood forests, etc. This "nature music" is also good for reverie and
relaxing to the body. Try to avoid the synthesizer CDs.

Gillespie, Dizzy – *A Night in Tunisia* (Turtle Island Quartet – Järvi –
Chandos 9331)

Glorious (Abraham Kaplan – North American Liturgy Resources,
Phoenix, AZ 85029) (cassette)
Celebrational psalms, beautifully arranged for chorus and instruments.

The Good, the Bad and the Ugly (Ennio Morricone soundtrack) (Liberty
LO-05172)
Haunting and evocative music suggesting feelings of the West, the
desert, and the echoes off canyon walls; good for emotional release.

Hoffmann - *Music for the Glass Harmonica* (Philips 9500397 or Vox)
Exotic sounds that suggest both antiquity and timelessness.

Horn, Paul – *Inside the Taj Mahal* (White Swan Distributors)
Marvelously meditative music; some for solo flute has the floating
ambience that takes the listener upward in consciousness. (Leave out
the chanting tracks.)

Hymns Triumphant I, II (Holdridge, arranger – Birdwing BWD 2023; 2058)
Beautiful and devotional arrangements; many great hymns; powerful choral singing; good for upliftment and reverence.
Iasos – *Angels of Comfort* (Inter-Dimensional Music, Box 594, Sausalito, CA 94965)
Floating music for synthesizer; lifting music that goes nowhere but is here now; makes no demands upon the listener; suggests peacefulness.
Inkuyo – *Land of the Incas* (White Swan Distributors)
Haunting Andean music.
Jackson, Mahalia – *Hymns* (Folkways FTS-31102)
Music of praise; reveals a large, loving heart; deeply devotional.
Javanese Court Gamelan (Nonesuch H-72074)
Exotic sounds of gongs and Balinese music that is both praise-filled and worshipful; stimulates the body and emotions.
Kennedy, Calum – *Scottish Songs* (Golden Hour GH593)
Music filled with energy and warmth; promotes warmth and friendliness.
Kleinsinger – *Tubby the Tuba* (Jenkins – MCA-148)
Story and music combine to bring joy and good humor; uplifting.
Lanza – *I'll Walk with God; Lanza Collection* (RCA 3-09026-60889)
A voice filled with ardor and devotion; music that inspires and uplifts.
Lecuona, Ernesto – *Maria la O* (Guerrero – Montilla CDFM 731)
Beautiful zarzuela from Cuban composers.
Lee, Riley – *Oriental Sunrise* (Celestial Spaces – Plumeria, Box 54, Kailua, HI 96734)
Music for koto; meditative, relaxing, expansive; good for hyperactivity release.
Liberace – *The Best of Liberace* (Decca 73-7209)
Music of exuberance, flair, and good spirit.
Lutunn Noz – *Celtic Music for Guitar* (Musical Heritage Society 5577)
Marvelously uplifting music, good for release of tightness; also good for relieving boredom.
Malotte – *The Lord's Prayer* (Mormon Tabernacle Choir – CBS 21988; phone: 1-800-771-4053)
Music that ennobles and uplifts; good for deepening devotion and dedication to God.
Mantovani – Miscellaneous albums, particularly *Evening Star* (London 921) (note especially the Montovani arrangements of hymns on London Weekend 433-875-2)
Pleasant, reassuring music; quite linear in places, thus building stability.

McDonald, Susann – *World of the Harp* (Delos DMS 3005)
Magnificent for clearance; the harp sounds and the melodies played here help one to ventilate immediately. (Note especially Albert Zabel's *The Source.*)

Missa Criolla (Philips); *Missa Luba* (Philips)
Modern settings of the Mass, bringing out exotic flavors and energizing rhythms.

Montoya, Carlos – *Malagueña* (RCA AFL-12380)
Compelling guitar music, alternating between reflective and introspective, and strong, earthy rhythms; good for clearing out the system.

Morgan, Melissa – *Music to Soothe and Relax* (solo harp) (Box 4024, San Diego, CA 92104)
Music of varying moods, sometimes more forceful, other times more spatial and nondirected; in general, it defuses pressures and tensions.

Murooka – *Lullaby from the Womb* (Capitol ST-11421)
Music to help the birthing process; Dr. Murooka suggests good music for pregnancy and also includes the sound of a mother's heartbeat along with the music.

Music for Zen Meditation (Tony Scott) (White Swan Distributors)
Mysteriously unfolding, like flower petals.

Music of the Lone Ranger (James King – Intersound, Box 1724, Rosewell, GA 30077)
Here it is, all those mysterious, atmospheric "in between" pieces of music that so beautifully caught the spirit of the scenes and dramas of the Lone Ranger's and Tonto's episodes.

Musical Sea of Tranquility (Chris Valentino, harp) (Jonella Record Company, Box 522, Englewood, NJ 07631)
An absolutely wonderful, relaxing disk, featuring harp playing classical melodies and ocean waves flowing in the background.

National Anthems of the World, especially *Star-Spangled Banner* (Everest 3329)
Powerful melodies and stirring rhythms; good for overcoming lethargy and boredom.

New Troubadours – Winds of Birth (Lorian Association, Box 1095, Elgin, IL 60120)
Songs of the new Aquarian planetary age of brotherhood, cooperation and joyfulness in the Spirit; cuts across barriers of rigidity and blockage.

Norman, Jessye – *Sacred Songs* (Gibson – Philips)
Powerful, devotional music; I especially like the consciousness-raising rendition of *Sanctus* by Gounod.

Nun's Story (Franz Waxman soundtrack) (Stanyan)
Dramatic and reflective music.

O Sanctissima: Music for Prayer (flute and harp) (PHD Productions, Huntington Beach, CA)
Ideal for reflection, quiet, and prayer; soothing.

Oklahoma! (soundtrack) (Columbia OS-2610)
Marvelous, perky tunes and energizing music.

Old Gringo (Lee Holdridge soundtrack) (Crescendo GNPD 8017)
Marvelous, melodic and dramatic piece, filled with Hispanic rhythms, guitar melodies, and pathos.

Coyote Oldman – *Tear of the Moon* (Incan pan pipes and Native American flute) (available through Four Winds Trading Company)
Haunting, meditative, and deeply evocative music.

Paco de Lucia – *Master of the Spanish Guitar* (Philips 6695001)
Music of power and songfulness; explores many different emotions; good for reverie and clearance.

Parkening, Christopher – *Bach* (Angel 47191)
All the great Bach favorites, played on a clear-sounding guitar; this music is healing and quieting, getting inside the listener and bringing cleansing.

Partita Teresiana (DiVietri, guitar solo – Teresian Records, Box 2525, San Rafael, CA 94912)
Music recorded in a monastery; has reverent, devotional beauty to it; melodies soar and offer an uplifting quality of spirit.

Pavarotti, Luciano – *O Sole Mio, Neapolitan Songs* (London) *Mattinata; Passione; Mama*
Powerful and passionate songs of love, friendship, and reflection; brings out heart chakra energy.

Peerce, Jan – *Bluebird of Happiness* (RCA-VIC-1553)
Moving solos of melodic and emotional depth; Peerce's voice has power and tonal richness; arouses deep feelings.

Philip, Hans-Erik – *Fiskerne* (soundtrack) (Danica CD 8127)
Hauntingly beautiful, melodic music for viola and orchestra.

Psalms of David (Willcocks – EMI-TC-CSD-3656 or Virgin or Priory)
Deeply mantralike in their repeated cadences, these melodies of devotion get inside the listener in a cleansing way.

Rampal, Jean-Pierre – Miscellaneous albums (Sony)
You cannot go wrong buying Rampal's tasteful, elegant expressions of music. The flute sounds help to unwind the emotions, and they clear out the system. Note especially *Songs for Children* (CBS MK-39669).

Rey, Cemal Resit – *Turkish Rhapsody; Scenes from Turkey* (Simsek – Hungaroton 31483) (Qualiton Imports)

Rey is one of the five great Turkish composers, joining Ahmet Adnan Saygun, Ferit Tuzun, Ulvi Cemal Erkin, and Necil Kazim Akses. Rey's music is strong, often exotic and energizing.

Robertson, Kim – *Tender Shepherd; Angels in Disguise; Gratitude; Moonrise; Love Song to a Planet; Water Spirit; Wild Iris; Windshadows I, II* (Gourd Music, Box 585, Felton CA 95018) (White Swan Distributors)

Kim Robertson plays the harp as beautifully and as clearly as any harpist that I have heard. All her albums for me are refreshing, cleansing, and healing.

Rodgers, Richard – *Victory at Sea* (Gerhardt – Quintessence PMC 7032 and RCA)

Strong, powerfully compelling music; breaks up blockage.

Rota, Nino – *Symphony on a Love Song* (Bernart – Nuova Era7063)

Romantic, fluid, and elegant orchestral work.

Saygun, Ahmet – *Viola Concerto* (Gunes/Aykal – Koch Schwann 311002 H1)

A beautiful, exotic, and powerful poem in music by an outstanding Turkish composer; melodic, intriguing, and mysterious.

Somewhere in Time (John Barry, composer) (soundtrack) (MCA)

Ultimately satisfying; deeply romantic, expansive, warm music; includes Rachmaninov's eighteenth variation from *Rhapsody on a Theme of Paganini;* music that awakens deep soul memories and loving emotions; provides a continuum mood of remembrance.

Son of the Morning Star (Craig Safan soundtrack) (Intrada MAF7037D)

Wonderful soundtrack, somewhat of a mixture, moving between deeply elegiac, lyrical moods and powerful, epic moments; has a Native American quality to it also.

Sound of Music (Rodgers and Hammerstein soundtrack) (RCA LSOD-2005)

One of the greatest pieces of music ever composed; the *Prologue, Climb Every Mountain,* and *Edelweiss* are especially therapeutic and should be played in sequence if possible; brings in the joy of the angels and the strong currents of encouragement.

Spirit Alive (Monks of the Weston Priory, Weston, VT 05161)

Contemporary songs of joy and the Christian spirit; these songs are simple statements of wellsprings of devotion, excellent for sing-along, either by oneself or in groups of friends.

Star Wars (soundtrack) (Warner Brothers 2BSK-3257)
  Bold, energetic score replete with suspense and involvement; excellent
  for tiredness or mild depression.
Stenhammar, Wilhelm – *Chitra* (for Tagore play) (Järvi – BIS CD-476)
Stivell, Alan – *Renaissance of the Celtic Harp* (Polydor 2424-069)
  Deeply soulful experiences in this music of ocean waves and haunting
  melodies played on the Celtic harp. Good for reverie and introspection.
  (See also first part of Alan Stivell's *Harps for the New Age*.)
Superman (John Williams, composer) (soundtrack) (Warner Brothers)
  Strong, enlivening music; filled with drama and excitement; good for
  combating lethargy and "the blahs."
Talbot, John Michael – *Come to the Quiet* (Birdwing BWR-2019)
  Contemporary monklike songs of devotion; a strong feeling of solitude
  and contemplation accompanies the music; good for spiritual aspiration.
Ten Commandments (soundtrack) (Paramount 1006)
  Epic music, strong and demanding; some memorable melodies and
  strong rhythms.
Theodorakis, Mikis – *Music for Bouzouki and Orchestra* (Galata
  GAL-503)
  Very stimulating Greek rhythms; arouses desire to dance; good for
  lifting one out of introversion.
– *Zorba the Greek* (ballet) (Records International)
  Beautiful and uplifting music in the true Greek spirit.
Tibetan Bells – I, II (White Swan Distributors)
  Music for strong focus and mental centering; deep resonances and
  cosmic expanse of gonglike sounds.
Traditional Catalan Songs (Victoria de los Angeles and Geoffrey Parsons
  – Collins 13182)
  Utterly beautiful, winsome cameos, including *Song of the Birds*, a
  favorite of Pablo Casals.
Tremolo (Teña/Ramos – Musical Heritage 972)
  Music of Spain, intoxicating with its rhythms and melodies, highlighted
  by Teña's castanets.
Vanity Fair (Neel – Citadel Records CT-6013)
  The pleasing little melody *Vanity Fair*, by Anthony Collins, is
  especially charming in its direct appeal.
A Venetian Coronation 1595 – Gabrieli(s) (McCreesh – Virgin VC
  91110-2)
  Glorious antiphonal choirs – music of ancient Venice.

When You Wish Upon A Star (CBS-37200 and Daniel Kobialka – Li-Sem 115)
Walt Disney songs; marvelously uplifting, especially in meditative flowing version by Kobialka.

Whistle While You Work (Mormon Tabernacle Choir – CBS M-35868)
A marvelous pick-up for early morning; tones the day ahead with joy and focus.

Windwalker (soundtrack) (Jenson – Cerebrus Records, CST-0202)
Marvelous music of the West, combining melodies and instrumental sounds that bring to mind Paul Horn's *Inside the Taj Mahal* and other exotic flute melodies; good for reflection and some stirring up.

Winter, Paul – *Callings; Canyon; Whales Alive; Missa Gaia; Wolf Eyes; Earthbeat* (Living Music Records, Box 68, Litchfield, CT 06759) (White Swan Distributors)
Music that combines instruments and nature calls of animals and ocean; I do not personally like the "jazzy" saxophone sections, but this is mostly ennobling music that deepens one's appreciation of and affiliation with nature.

Wright, Danny – *Curtain Call* (lovely solo piano) (Moulin D'Or – NIW 932)

Yas-Kaz – *Darkness in Dreams* (especially *Jungle Book*) (Celestial Harmonies 11092)
Jungle Book, with its intriguing animal calls and tropical flavors, provides a pleasing, open-air meditational experience. Especially children enjoy it.

Yellow River Concerto (by Xian Xianghai) (Ormandy – RCA-ARL-1-0415 or Nuova Era or Hong Kong)
Beautiful Oriental melodies.

You Light Up My Life (Debby Boone – Warner Brothers BS-3118)
Sparkling and uplifting love song; very romantic and inspiring; expresses intimacy and caring.

Zamfir, Music for Flute of Pan (various albums on miscellaneous labels, especially Mercury and Philips)
Exotic sound of the Pan flute makes this music excellent for defusing from busyness; also good for creative imagination. Note: see especially these Zamfir recordings: *Rocking Chair, Classics by Candlelight,* and *Lonely Shepherd.*

Zimmer, Hans – *Millennium (Tribal Wisdom)* (Narada)
Used as soundtrack to the excellent book and television series honoring the different cultures and tribes of humankind.

3. CHRISTMAS MUSIC

Anonymous 4 – *On Yoolis Night* (Medieval carols and motets) (Harmonia Mundi)

Arnold, Malcolm – *Commonwealth Christmas Overture* (Arnold – Reference Recordings)

Bach Choir Family Carols (Willcocks – London)

Bach, J. S. – *The Christmas Oratorio* (Jochum – Philips or Gardiner – DGG)

– *Christmas Music* (Pommer – Laserlight 15 274)

Baez, Joan – *Noël* (Vanguard VRS-9230)

Ball, Patrick – *The Christmas Rose* (Celtic harp) (Fortuna 17077-2)

Barabas, Tom – *Magic in December* (Barabas Productions, 2530 Bancroft Street, San Diego, CA 92104) (beautiful solo piano Christmas music) (TB101CD)

Battle, Kathleen – *A Christmas Celebration* (Slatkin – EMI CDC-7-47587-2)

Bax – *Christmas Eve* (Thomson – Chandos 8480)

Belafonte, Harry – *To Wish You a Merry Christmas* (BMG 2626-2-R)

Belanger – *Noels for Strings* (Turovsky – Chandos 9098)

Berlioz, Hector – *L'Enfance du Christ* (oratorio) (Munch – RCA Gold Seal 09026)

Boyd, Liona – *A Guitar for Christmas* (CBS MK 37248)

– *Christmas Dreams* (A & M Records – Canada Cd 9513)

Bridge, Frank – *The Christmas Rose* (Williams – Pearl SHE CD 9582)

Britten, Benjamin – *A Ceremony of Carols* (harp, orchestra, and choir) (Flämig – Laserlight 15 273 or Willcocks on EMI)

Bruch, Max – *Salute to Christmas* (Gronostay – Koch Schwann 313 013 H1)

Brunelle, Philip – *Serenade for a Christmas Night* (Brunelle – Virgin VC 7 91088-2)

Burchfield, Jonathan – *A Classic Christmas* (Music Valley Pub., 107 Music City Circle, Nashville, TN 37214)

Candlelight Carols (Jones – London 430 456-2) (Christmas at Trinity Church, Boston)

Carol Concert (Heltay – IMP PCD 1026)

Carols for Today (Canterbury Cathedral) (Wicks – Conifer)

Carols from Kings (Willcocks – EMI Classics for Pleasure CFP-4586)

Christmas Carols from King's College (Ledger – EMI CDC 7-47500-2)

Casals, Pablo – *El Pesebre, The Manger* (Casals – Columbia/Sony)

Cathedral of Saint John the Divine (Christmas Eve) (Pizarro – Westenburg -Vanguard VBD 71212)

Celebration: Christmas Fanfares and Carols (Thomas – Nimbus NI5310)

Celestial Bells (Handbell Favorites) (Christward Ministry, 20560 Questhaven Road, Escondido, CA 92029)

Chadwick, George – *Noël*, from *Symphonic Sketches* (Hanson – Mercury 434 337-2)

Chantons Noël (Let's Sing of Christmas) (Corboz – Erato 2292-45641-2)

Charpentier – *Pastorale for the Birth of Jesus Christ* (Harmonia Mundi HMC 901082)

Christmas Bells (Westminster Concert Bell Choir – Gothic G-49055)

Christmas Carols of European Nations (Venhoda – Supraphon 11 0299-2)

Christmas Carols from Saint Johns (Guest – Chandos 8485)

Christmas Carols (Londonderry Boys Choir) (Ross CD 6644-4)

Christmas at Kings (Willcocks – London Weekend 430 146-2)

Christmas at St. Thomas Cathedral (New York) (Hancock – Stradivari SCD 8006)

Christmas Carols (Westminster Cathedral Choir – Point 2660102)

Christmas Eve at Notre Dame de Paris (Cochereau – FY-FYCD006)

Christmas in the Alps (Laserlight 15 279)

Christmas in Europe (Quaresima – Laserlight 15 149)

Christmas in Russia (Russian choral) (Koch – Schwann 313 044 G1)

Christmas Masterpieces (Flummerfelt – Gothic G 47931)

Christmas Music from Kings (Willcocks – EMI)

Christmas Organ and Chimes (Ross 6645-2)

Christmas Songs from Europe (Ameling – Peters, cassette only)

Christmas Spirituals (Odetta – Vanguard 79079)

Christmas Traditions (London Symphony – Special Music Company SCD-4558)

Christmas Treasures (includes *Guardian Angels* by Marx-Gerda and Humperdinck's *Evening Prayer* conducted by Leopold Stokowski) (RCA 09026-61867-2)

Christmas under Capricorn (carols arranged for orchestra by nineteen Australian composers) (Abbott – Tall Poppies TPO16) (Albany Distributors)

Christmas with the New York Harp Ensemble (von Wurtzler – Music Masters)

Constantinescu – *The Nativity* (Basarab – Olympia OCD 402)

Dickens, Charles – *A Christmas Carol (Scrooge)* (Audioworks CD, 1230 Avenue of the Americas, New York, NY 10020 or Gielgud – BMG-7678-35904-2)

Dragon – *Lullaby of Christmas* (Peck – Decca DL-78009)

Enchanted Christmas – Harp and Chamber Ensemble (Mendieta – Sugo SR9311)

An English Christmas (Beat – MCA MCAD 5900)

Favorite Carols At Christmas (Jackson and Robinson – Chandos 6588)

A Festival of Christmas (Walters – Musical Heritage Society, 1710 Highway 35, Ocean, NJ 07712, MHS 522676W)

A Festival of Christmas Carols (Davis – Philips 416 249-2)

Fiedler, Arthur – *White Christmas* (Fiedler – DGG 419 414-2)

Fox, Virgil – *The Christmas Album* (Bainbridge BCD 2505)

Gade, Niels – *The Holy Night* (Rasmussen – Kontrapunkt 32149) (Allegro Imports)

Galway, James – *Christmas Carol* (Galway – RCA-RCD 1-5888)

The Glorious Sound of Christmas (Ormandy – Columbia)

Gould, Morton – *A Musical Christmas Tree* (Gould – RCA 7931)

Greg Smith Singers: Holiday Greetings (Smith – Essex Entertainment, Inc., 560 Sylvan Avenue, Englewood Cliffs, NJ 07632)

Gregorian Chant (Christmas Mass) (Monks of Benedictine Abbey – Musikfest 427 014-2)

Christmas Chant (Benedictine Nuns of St. Cecilia's Abbey – New World Company, Paradise Farm) (White Swan Distributors)

Hampson, Thomas – *Christmas* (Wolff – Teldec T2 73135)

Handel, George Frideric – *Messiah* (Willcocks – EMI Import CDB 7 67114-2 or Sargent, two different performances—Classics for Pleasure CFPD 4718 and Chesky CD 106, or Beecham – RCA 09026-61266-2)

Harp of Christmastide (King – Ambitus 97 812 CD)

Hely-Hutchinson – *Carol Symphony* (Rose – EMI CDM 7 64131-2)

The Holly and the Ivy (carols for chorus and orchestra) (Currie – ASV CDWHL 2073)

Holst, Gustav – *Ceremony of Carols* (Willcocks – EMI import)

Ives – *A Christmas Carol* (Western Wind – Musical Heritage or Vox; or John Williams – Philips)

Jackson, Mahalia – *Silent Night* (Williams – Columbia CK 38304)

Jessye Norman at Notre Dame (Philips D 100861)
  – *Christmastide* (Philips 420180)

The Joy of Christmas (Crystal Cathedral: Rev. Robert Schuller – RFJ-8101)

Just Wright for Christmas (Danny Wright – piano, plus violin, oboe, and English horn) (Moulin D'Or, 1148 West, Pioneer Parkway, Suite E, Arlington,TX 76013)

Te Kanawa, Kiri – *Christmas* (London 414632-2)

Kelly, Georgia – *Winter Classics* (harp, cello, violin, guitar) (Global Pacific R2 79337)

Kiev Christmas Liturgy (Amvrosy – Erato 2292-45961-2)

Knabel, Rudi – *German Christmas in the Alps* (Pilz 75900)

Kunzel, Erich – *Christmas with the Pops* (Kunzel – Telarc CD 80226)

La Montaine, John – *The Nine Lessons of Christmas* (Fredonia Discs, 3947 Fredonia Drive, Hollywood, CA 90068)

Lanza, Mario – *Christmas* (RCA 6427-2 RG)

Liberace – *'Twas the Night Before Christmas* (includes *The Rosary*) (Special Music 4629)

Magic Christmas (Dinu Radu, pan flute) (Laserlight 15 148)

Majesty of Christmas (Raver – Columbia CK 40944)

Mantovani – *Great Songs of Christmas* (Bainbridge BCD6238)
 – *Christmas Favorites* (Mantovani – London 820 540)

Marjorie, Jean – *Slumber Song* (Carmel Records MJ2002CD)

Medieval Carols (Summerly – Naxos 8.550751)

Merry Christmas (Walter – Naxos 8.550188)

Mormon Tabernacle Choir: Noel (Ottley – Bonneville Communications)
 – *Silent Night* (Ottley – Columbia MK 37206)
 – *Christmas* (Ottley – Laserlight 12 198)

Music Box of Christmas Carols (Weight – Vanguard VBD 10015)

A Natural Christmas (a mingling of beautiful carols with the sounds of nature, such as wolves, loons, a sleigh drawn by horses, and other wilderness sounds; lovely) (NorthSound, 1-800-336-5666)

Noel (Dirksen and Major – VQR, P.O. Box 302, Needham, MA 02192)

Noel, Noel (Joel Cohen – Erato ECD 75569)

An Old Fashioned Christmas (McCrorie – Abbey CDMVP 829)

An Old World Christmas (Musikfest 413 657-2)

On Christmas Day (American Boychoir – Rykodisc 30129)

On Christmas Night (Willcocks – London 425 499-2)

Once in Royal David's City (Willcocks – EMI Classics for Pleasure)

Ormandy, Eugene and Philadelphia Orchestra (Ormandy – Columbia MK 6369); *Joy to the World* (RCA 6430-2-RG)

Ortiz, Alfredo – *Christmas Harps* (Box 911, Corona, CA 91718)

Pahlen, Kurt – *Navidad Criolla* (Milan 7313835604-2)

Parry, Hubert – *Ode on the Nativity* (Willcocks – Lyrita-SRCS-125)

Paulus, Stephen – *So Hallowed Is the Time* (Brunelle – Pro Arte)

Pavarotti, Luciano – *O Holy Night* (London 414044)

Les Petits Chanteurs: Noel (Houdy – Auvidis A 6123)

Pierné, Gabriel – *The Children at Bethlehem* (de Rozel – Erato 2292-45008-2)

Popp, Lucia – *Czech Pastorely* (Praga PR 250 019)

Price, Leontyne – *Christmas Songs* (Price – Karajan London Jubilee 421 103-2)

Rejoice and Sing (Stultz – Afka SK-510)

Respighi, Ottorino – *Adoration of the Magi, from Botticellian Triptych* (Tortelier – Chandos)

– *Laud to the Nativity of the Lord* (Korn – RCA 7787)

Rheinberger, Josef – *The Star of Bethlehem* (Heger – Carus 83.111 CD)

Rimsky-Korsakov, Nikolas – *Christmas Eve (Holy Night)* (Tjeknavorian – ASV DCA 772)

Robertson, Kim – *Celtic Christmas I, II* (Invincible, P.O. Box 13054, Phoenix, AZ 85002)

Romanian Byzantine Hymns and Christmas Carols (Carstoi – Electrecord ELCD 101)

A Rose of Such Virtue (Musica Antigua of Albuquerque – Dorian Discovery DIS-80104)

Rosenberg – *Holy Night* (Erickson – SR Records RELP-5007)

Rutter, John – *Christmas with the Cambridge Singers* (Rutter – Collegium COLCD 111)

– *Christmas Day in the Morning* (Rutter – Collegium 121)

– *Carols from Clare* (Rutter – EMI CDM 7 69950-2)

– *The Holly and the Ivy* (Rutter – London 425500-2)

– *Christmas Night* (Rutter – Collegium COLCD 106)

– *Dancing Day* (Bartle – Marquis Classics, Canada, ERAD 135)

Ryba – *Czech Christmas Mass* (Smetáček – Supraphon-Fidelio 1809)

– *Pastorals* (Chvala – Supraphon 11 0330-2)

Saint-Saëns, Camille – *Christmas Oratorio* (Flämig – Laserlight)

St. Paul's Christmas Concert (Rózsa: Christmas Sequence) (Scott – RPOCD 7021)

Schmitt, Georges – *Joy to the World* (pan pipes) (Saydisc 357)

Schroeder-Sheker, Therese – *In Dulci Jubilo* (Celestial Harmonies)

Schwarzkopf, Elisabeth – *The Christmas Album* (Mackerras – EMI CDM 7 63574-2)

Scotto, Renata – *Christmas at Saint Patrick's Cathedral* (Anselmi – VAI Audio Vaia 1013)

Seeger, Ruth Crawford – *American Folksongs for Christmas* (Seeger Family – Rounder CD 0268/9)

Shaw, Robert – *Many Moods of Christmas* (Shaw – Telarc 80087)

Sing We Merrily (Choral Christmas) (Delos DE3125)

Sing We Noel (Pearson – Delos DE 3128)

Sing We Now of Christmas (Swann/Crystal Cathedral Choir – Gothic G 49036)

Star of Wonder (Hooper – Reference Recordings RR21CD)

Sukay – *Navidad Andina (Andean Christmas)* (Sukay Records, 3315 Sacramento Street, San Francisco, CA 94118)

Sutherland, Dame Joan – *The Joy of Christmas* (Bonynge – London 421 095-2)

Tallis Scholars – *Christmas Carols and Motets* (Phillips – Gimell CDGIM 010)

Tesh, John – *Winter Song* (grand piano, guitar, and orchestra) (GTS 3-4572-2)

– *A Romantic Christmas* (GTS 3-4569-2)

Vaughan Williams, Ralph – *Hodie* (Willcocks – Angel or Hickox – EMI D 13514)

Vienna Choir Boys: Christmas (RCA 7930-2-RG)

Wagner, Roger – *To Catch a Christmas Star* (Wagner – Delos CD 3072)

Willcocks, David – *O Come All Ye Faithful* (London 417 898-2)

Williams, John – *Joy to the World* (Sony SK 48232)

Worcester Cathedral Choir: Joy to the World (Hunt – Helios CDH 88031)

Zamfir: Christmas (panflute and orchestra) (Brott – Philips 314 510 309-2)

4. AN EASTER PROGRAM

J. S. Bach – *Come Sweet Death*, organ solo

– *Jesu, Joy of Man's Desiring* (Flagstad)

> *Jesu, joy of man's desiring,*
> *Holy wisdom, love most bright:*
> *Drawn by Thee, our souls aspiring*
> *Soar to uncreated Light.*
> *Word of God, our flesh that fashioned,*
> *With the fire of Light impassioned,*
> *Striving still to truth unknown,*
> *Soaring, dying round Thy throne;*
> *Through the way where hope is guiding,*
> *Hark what peaceful music rings,*

Where the flock in Thee confiding
Drink of joy in deathless springs.
Theirs is beauty's fairest pleasure,
Theirs is wisdom's holiest treasure.
Thou dost ever lead Thine own
In the love of joys unknown.

TEXT BY ROBERT BRIDGES

Ludwig van Beethoven – *Hallelujah*, from Christ on the Mount of Olives

Hallelujah, Hallelujah, Hallelujah, Hallelujah,
Unto God's Almighty Son!
Praise the Lord, ye bright angelic choirs, in holy songs of joy.
Praise the Lord in holy, holy songs of joy.
Man, proclaim His grace and glory.
Hallelujah, Hallelujah, Hallelujah, Hallelujah,
Unto God's Almighty Son.
Praise the Lord, praise the Lord,
In Holy songs of joy.

Gabriel Fauré – *In Prayer*

If the voice of a child can reach you
Listen, O my Father, to the prayer of Jesus Christ kneeling
before you;
If you have chosen me to teach your laws on earth,
I shall know how to serve you, King of Kings, O Light.
Place on my lips the solitary truth,
That he who doubts reveres you with humility.
Do not abandon me,
Give me the sweetness needed to cure the ills;
Relieve the pain and misery;
Reveal yourself to me, in whom I place my faith and hope.

Charles Gounod – *Sanctus*, from *St. Cecilia Mass*
– *Unfold Ye Portals*, from *Redemption*

Unfold! Unfold! Unfold! Ye portals everlasting!
With welcome to receive Him ascending on High.
Behold the King of Glory!
He mounts up through the sky
Back to heavenly mansions hasting,
Unfold – Unfold, for lo, the King comes nigh.

But who is He, the King of Glory?
He who Death overcame, the Lord in battle mighty.
But who is He, the King of Glory?
Of hosts He is the Lord, of angels and of powers;
The King of Glory is the King of the Saints.

George Frideric Handel – *Hallelujah Chorus*, from *Messiah*
Franz Liszt – *Resurrexit, He Is Risen*, from *Christus*
Gustav Mahler – Finale from Symphony no. 2, *Resurrection*

With wings that I have won
in fervent, loving aspiration,
will I soar to the Light
that no eye has ever seen.
I shall die that I may live.

Richard Wagner – Prelude to Act 1 of *Lohengrin*, music of the Holy
  Grail and the descent of angels from on High
Hugo Wolf – *Night is Almost Ended*

Night is almost ended,
Already I feel morning breezes blowing.
The Lord who says: "Let there be Light."
Then all the darkness must vanish.
From the vault of Heaven, throughout the whole world
The rejoicing angels fly:
The sun's rays light up the universe.
Lord, let us fight, let us win.

Other Recommended Listening at Easter
(Found on Various Labels)

J. S. Bach – *St. Matthew Passion; St. John Passion; Easter Oratorio*
Anton Bruckner – Adagio from Symphony no. 7; Adagio from Symphony no. 8
Paul Creston – Symphony no. 3, third movement; *Resurrection*
Sir Edward Elgar – *The Apostles; The Kingdom*
Joseph Foerster – *Symphony no. 4, Easter* (Smetaček – Supraphon 11-1822-2011)
César Franck – *Beatitudes; Redemption; Panis angelicus*
Franz Josef Haydn – *The Seven Last Words of Christ*
Alan Hovhaness – *Magnificat*
Pietro Mascagni – *Easter Hymn* (from *Cavalleria Rusticana*)
Giovanni Pergolesi – *Stabat Mater*
Randall Thompson – *Alleluia*
Antonio Vivaldi – *Kyrie; Gloria*
Richard Wagner – Prelude and *Good Friday Music,* from *Parsifal*

5. MUSIC OF NATURE AND THE SEASONS

Miscellaneous

Alturas – *From the Heights* (South American nature scenes) – *Enchanted Land* (Terra Nova Records, P.O. Box 455, Sunland, CA 91041-0455)
Alwyn, William – *Pastoral Fantasia* (Hickox – Chandos-9065)
The Ancient Shepherd Pipes, Israeli (Folkways FW 8724)
Alfvén – *A Legend of the Skerries* and *Symphony no. 4, From the Seaward Skerries* (BIS CD-505)
Babbling Brook (Distributions Madacy, P.O. Box 1445, St. Laurent, Quebec, Canada H4L 4Z1) (Bach and brook: very healing)
Bamboo Waterfall (waterfalls, chimes, streams, ocean waves, wind, etc.) (Nature Recordings, P.O. Box 2749, Friday Harbor, WA 98250)
Beethoven, Ludwig van – *Symphony no. 6 (Pastorale)* (Böhm – DGG 2-413721 or Walter – Sony MYK 36720)
A Bell Ringing in an Empty Sky (Japanese) (Nonesuch-H72025)
Bliss, Sir Arthur – *Pastoral* (Hickox – Chandos 8886)
Bridge, Frank – *The Sea* (Handley – Chandos 8473)
Classical Loon (NorthWord Press, Inc., P.O. Box 1360, Minocqua, WI 54548)

Cry of the Loon (Special Music Company, 87 Essex Street, Hackensack, NJ 07601)

Loons on Mirror Lake and *Summer Waterfall* (Nature Recordings CDN 08)

Debussy, Claude – *Reverie* (Ormandy – CBS MFK 45543)
– *Nocturnes* (Simon – Cala CACD 1002)
– *The Engulfed Cathedral* (Simon – Cala 1001)

Dvořák, Antonín – *Symphony no. 8* (Barbirolli – EMI CDM 64193)

Elgar, Sir Edward – *Sea Pictures* (Baker/Barbirolli – EMI)

Evenson, Dean – *Desert Moon Song* (Soundings of the Planet – SP-7144 CD)
– *Peaceful Pond* (SP-7122-CD)

Friesen, Eugene – *Cathedral Pines,* from *New Friend* (Living Music LD-0007)

Gardens of the World (with Audrey Hepburn) (Conifer 74321-17841-2)

Gibson, Dan – *Solitudes* (Solitudes, P.O. Box 309, Mount Albert, Ontario, Canada L0G 1M0)

Glazunov, Alexander – *The Forest and The Sea* (Svetlanov – Melodiya SUCD 10-00156)

Gluck, Christoph – *Dance of the Blessed Spirits* (Seraphim S-60278)

Grieg, Edvard – *Piano Concerto* (Lupu/Previn – London 417728-2)

Grainger, Percy – *Hill Song 1, 2; Beautiful Fresh Flower* (Simon – Koch Schwann 3-7003-2)

Hadley, Patrick – *The Trees So High* (Bamert – Chandos 9181)

Harty, Sir Hamilton – *Children of Lir and Ode to a Nightingale* (Thomson – Chandos 417450-2)

Horn of Plenty: Conducted by David Amos (beautiful orchestral arrangements of Israeli melodies by Sarah Shoham) (David Amos, 5150 Norris Road, San Diego, CA 92115)

d'Indy, Vincent – *Symphony on a French Mountain Air* (Dutoit – London 430-278-2)

Jones, Michael – *After the Rain* (Narada ND 61020)

La Montaine, John – *Wilderness Journal* (Thoreau) (Fredonia)
– *The Birds of Paradise* (Fredonia, 3947 Fredonia Drive, Hollywood, CA 90068)

Mahler, Gustav – Symphonies nos. 4, 6, and 7 (miscellaneous labels)

Maxwell Davies, Peter – *Orkney Wedding with Sunrise* (Maxwell Davies – Unicorn-Kanchana 9070 or J. Williams – Philips 420946-2)

Meulemans, Arthur – *The Pine Tree Symphony* (Rahbari – Marco Polo 8.223418)

Moncayo, José – *Storm Land* (Alvarez – Crescendo 1697)

Naegele, David – *Temple in the Forest* (Valley of the Sun, Box 38, Malibu, CA 90265)

Noskowski, Zygmunt – *Morskie Oko Lake in the Tatras* and *The Steppe* (Olympia OCD 389)

Novák, Vitezslav – *Pan* (Bilek – Marco Polo 8.223325)
– *Slovak Suite* (Vajnar – Supraphon CO-1743 or Talich – Supraphon 11 1905-2)

Nystroem, Gösta – *Arctic Ocean* (Eros – Caprice 21332)

Panufnik, Andrzej – *Sinfonia Rustica* (Panufnik – Unicorn-Kanchana UKCD2016)

Peach Blossom Time (Chinese) (The Cowherds – Candide CE 31037)

Ponchielli, Amilcare – *Scena Campestre* (Frontalini – Bongiovanni GB 2115-2)

Respighi, Ottorino – *Pines of Rome; Fountains of Rome* (London 21024)

Serenity (Tranquil Moods-TR-2-7904: L.D.M.I., P.O. Box 1445, St. Laurent, Quebec, Canada H4L 4Z1)

Song of the Seashore (Japanese) (Galway, flute – RCA ARL1-3534) (beautiful Japanese folk songs of nature for flute, koto, orchestra)

Sounds of the Forest (Distributions Madacy, P.O. Box 1445, St. Laurent, Quebec, Canada H4L 4Z1)

Sowande, Fela – *African Suite* (Ace of Diamonds SDD 2214)

Stewart, Andrew – *Nature Meditations* (piano, chimes, flute, cello, and sounds of nature) (Relaxation Company – CD595)

Strictly for the Birds (Menuhin and Grappelli – EMI-CFP 4549)

Sullivan, Paul – *Sketches of Maine* (note *Troubled Night* with loons and thunder) (River Music WS101-2)

Takemitsu, Toru – *Far Calls, Coming Far* (Iwaki – ABC Classics 426 998-2)

Tingstad and Rumbel – *In the Garden* (Narada)

Tropical Rain Forest and Poetry (Beautiful blend of nature sounds and poetry readings) (Madacy 1305 – Quebec, Canada)

Vaughan Williams, Ralph – *Symphony no. 3 (Pastoral)* (Harper/Previn – RCA 60583-2)

Winter, Paul – *Whales Alive* (Payne – Living Music LD0013)

Zemlinsky, Alexander – *The Mermaids* (Chailly – London 417450)

The Four Seasons

Carlos – *Sonic Seasonings* (Columbia PG-31234)

Four Seasons (Milhaud: *Spring Concertino;* Rodrigo: *Summer Concerto;* Chaminade: *Autumn;* Serebrier: *Winter Concerto*) (ASV 855-Koch)

Glazunov – *The Seasons* (London 6509)

Palmgren – *Pictures from Finland* (Finlandia 544252)

Panufnik, Andrzej – *The Cosmic Tree (Arbor Cosmica)* (Elektra Nonesuch 9 79228-2)

Tchaikovsky – *The Seasons* (Columbia/Melodiya MG-35184)

Verdi – *The Four Seasons* (Angel SZ-37801)

Vivaldi – *The Four Seasons* (RCA LRL 1-2284; Philips 6500017)

Yoshimatsu, Takashi – *Unicorn Circuit* (Camerata 32CM-175)

Spring

Bax – *Spring Fire* (Chandos CHAN 8464)

Beethoven – *Spring Sonata, Sonata no. 5 in F for Violin and Piano* (DGG 2531300)

Bridge – *Enter Spring* (Pearl 9601)

Britten – *Spring Symphony* (Angel S-37562)

Debussy – *Printemps* (RCA Gold Seal 6719-2)

Delius – *On Hearing the First Cuckoo in Spring* (Seraphim S-60185)

Eto, Kimio – *Bright Morning* (koto) (World Pacific records, rare)

Farnon – *A Promise of Spring* (Reference Recordings RR-47)

Foerster – *Springtime and Desire* (Supraphon CD-72887)

Foulds – *April-England* (Lyrita)

Glazunov – *Spring* (Chandos 8611)

Grieg – *The Last Spring* (BIS 125)

Hadley – *The Hills* (EMI-Odeon SAN 393); *The Trees So High* (Chandos 9181)

Iasos – *Essence of Spring* (including brook and bird songs) (Interdimensional Music, Sausalito, CA)

Lajtha – *Symphony no. 4 (Springtime)* (Hungaroton 31452)

Magical Strings – *Spring Tide* (Flying Fish FF90282)

Mendelssohn – *Spring Song* (DGG 415118-2)

Miyagi – *The Sea of the Spring* (koto and flute) (Crystal CD 316)

Mortelmans – *Spring-Idyll* (Belgian) (Discover DICD 920100)

Nielsen – *Springtime in Funen* (Chandos 8853)

Rachmaninov – *The Spring* (Chant du Monde LDC 288069)

Respighi – *Spring,* from *Botticellian Triptych* (Argo ZRG 904)

Schumann – *Symphony no. 1, Spring* (Angel RL-32063)

Sibelius – *Spring Song* (BIS CD 384)

 – *A Spring in the Park* (from *Pelléas et Mélisande*) (ASV-CD DCA 649)

Sinding – *Rustle of Spring* (Arabesque 26578, piano or Naxos 8.550090, -orchestral)

Songbirds of Spring (World Disc Productions, 915 Spring Street, Friday Harbor, WA 98250)

Stravinsky – *Rite of Spring* (Sony 47629)

Strauss, Johann – *Voices of Spring* (London 433682)

Van Wyck – *Primavera (Spring)* (Claremont GSE 1509)

Zamfir – *Rhapsodie du Printemps* (Foster – Philips 412 221-2)

Summer

Atterberg – *Symphony no. 3 (West Coast Pictures)* (Caprice 21364)

Alfven – *Summer Rain* (from *Symphony no. 5*) (BIS)

Beethoven – *Symphony no. 6, Pastorale* (CBS-MYK 36720)

Brahms – *Symphony no. 2* (Philips Festivo 6570108)

Bridge – *Summer* (Chandos 8373)

Bush – *Summer Serenade* (Chandos 8864)

David – *The Desert* (Capriccio 10379)

Delius – *Florida Suite; A Song of Summer; Summer Night on the River; In a Summer Garden* (Teldec 4509 90845-2)

d'Indy – *Symphony on a French Mountain Air* (RCA 6805)

Dvořák – *Silent Woods* (BIS 245)

Hanson – *Summer Seascapes* (not yet recorded)

Honegger – *Summer Pastorale* (DGG-435438)

Hovhaness – *Mysterious Mountain* (RCA 5733)

Humperdinck – *Moorish Rhapsody* (*Desert Ride* and *Sunset*) (Marco Polo 8.223369)

Kallstenius – *A Summer Night Serenade* (Musica Sveciae MSCD 620)

Kodály – *Summer Evening* (Kontrapunkt 32153)

Lambert – *Summer's Last Will and Testament* (Hyperion 66565)

MacDowell, Edward – *Summer Idyll* (from *Suite for Large Orchestra*) (Mercury)

Melartin, Erkki – *Symphony no. 4 (Summer Symphony)* (Ondine 822)

Micha, Raymond – *Little Summer Air* (Musique en Wallonie 8801)

Moore – *Last Rose of Summer* (Galway – RCA 604214-2)

Peterson-Berger – *Summer Night* (from *Symphony no. 3*) (Musica Sveciae MSCD 630)

Prokofiev – *A Summer Day* (Ondine ODE-769-2 or Koch Schwann 3-7042-2)

Raff, Joachim – *Symphony no. 9 (In Summer)* (Auberson – ex libris - 6090)

Rimsky-Korsakov – *May Night* (Chandos 3-8327-29)

Schoeck – *Summer Night* (Claves 50-8502) (Qualiton)

Sibelius – *Symphony no. 6* (EMI CDD-63896)

Soft Summer Serenade (from *Peaceful Pond*) (Soundings of the Planet SP 7122)

Song of the Seashore (Galway – RCA CD 3534)

Suk – *A Summer Tale* (Supraphon CD 33CO-1030)

Vaughan Williams – *Symphony no. 3, Pastoral* (RCA 60583)

Zamfir – *Summer Rhapsody* (Philips 412221-2)

Autumn

Alwyn – *Autumn Legend* (Chandos 9065)

Gould – *Fall River Legend* (RCA 09026-61651)

Grieg – *Nocturne*, from *Lyric Suite* (Seraphim S-60032)

Hamilton – *Ripe Breath of Autumn* (Ribbonwood RCD 1004)

Ives – *The Pond* (CRI 163)

Kosma – *Autumn Leaves* (Reader's Digest RB7-115-4)

MacDowell – *Autumn Leaves* (Philips 9500095)

Panufnik – *Autumn Music* (Unicorn UKCD 2016)

Porter – *New England Episodes* (Bay Cities 1004)

Prokofiev – *Autumn* (Chandos 8806)

Respighi – *Autumnal Concerto* (Chandos 9232)

Ridout, Godfrey – *Fall Fair* (CBC SMCD5069)

Strauss, R. – *From Italy (Aus Italien)* (Naxos 8.550342)

Thomson, V. – *Autumn* (EMI CDM 64306)

Vaughan Williams – *In the Fen Country* (ASV 779); *Lark Ascending* (Angel 64022)

Zamfir, Gheorghe – *Colors of Autumn* (Philips 412 2211-2)

Winter

Barber – *Must the Winter Come So Soon* (from *Vanessa*) (RCA)

Barlow – *The Winter's Past* (Koch 37187-2)

Bax – *Winter Legends* (Chandos 8484)
 – *November Woods* (Chandos 8307)

Darnell, Dik – *Winter Solstice* (Native American) (Etherean Music, 9200 West Cross Drive #510, Littleton, CO 80123)

Grieg – *Piano Concerto* (Philips 412923)

Kelly, Georgia – *Winter Classics* (harp) (Global Pacific RZ-79337)

Larsson – *The Winter's Tale* (BIS CD-165)

Raff – *Symphony no. 11 (Spring)* (Tudor 787)

Rutter – *When Icicles Hang* (Collegium COLCD 117)

Sibelius – *Symphony no. 4* (London 430749); *The Tempest* (Chandos 8943)

Strauss, R. – *An Alpine Symphony* (Telarc 80211)

Sviridov – *Snow Storm* (Melodiya SUCD 10-00214)

Takemitsu – *November Steps* (Philips 432176-2)

Tchaikovsky – *Symphony no. 1, Winter Dreams* (DGG 25300078)

Vaughan Williams – *Symphony no. 7, Antarctica* (Angel 64020)

6. ADDITIONAL CHILDREN'S MUSIC

Prenatal and Infancy

"In the germ, when the first trace of life begins to stir, music is the nurse of the Soul; it murmurs in the ear, and the child sleeps; the tones are companions of his dreams—they are the world in which he lives."

BETTINI

Bach, J. S. – *Two Flute Concertos* (James Galway – RCA 65172)

Barry, John – *Somewhere in Time* (soundtrack) (MCA 5154)

Brahms – *Lullaby* (RCA 09026-60876)

Debussy – *Clair de lune* (Ormandy – RCA Silver Seal 09026-61211)

Dexter, Ron – *Golden Voyage I, III* (White Swan Distributors)

Humperdinck – *Children's Prayer* (from *Classical Jukebox*) (Ormandy – Columbia MLK 45736)

Koto Flute (Ransom Wilson, flute, and koto orchestra) (Angel 4XS-37325)

Mozart – *Piano Concerto no. 21*, slow movement (CBS 34562)

Pachelbel – *Canon in D* (RCA 65468)

Roth – *You Are the Ocean* (Heavenly Music, Box 1063, Larkspur, CA 94939)

Vivaldi – Miscellaneous concertos (especially flute and mandolin/guitar concertos)

The Story of Celeste (Cricket Records CR-16)

World of the Harp (Susann McDonald – Delos DCD 3005)

Ages 3-5

Play melodious music with clear rhythms but nothing heavy or raucous. Encourage your children to make and play their own instruments; teach them rhythms and open them to the mysteries of sounds.

Bizet – *Symphony no. 1 and Children's Games* (DGG-3335238)

Copland – *Lincoln Portrait* (Vanguard 4037); *Old American Songs* (Columbia MS-6497) The greatest version of *Lincoln Portrait* with Carl Sandburg and Andre Kostelanetz, on Sony, is not currently available. Keep looking for it.

Delibes – *Coppélia* (Columbia MT-31845)

Emperor and the Nightingale (Glenn Close) (Windham Hill CD 0706)

Golden Slumbers, Lullabies (Caedmon TC-1399)

Harsanyi – *The Story of the Little Tailor* (Angel S-36357)

Haydn – *Symphony no. 45; Toy Symphony; Trumpet Concerto* (miscellaneous)

Mendelssohn – *Overture and Selections from A Midsummer Night's Dream* (London STS-15084)

Music for Recorder (Kosofsky – Titanic 7)

Prokofiev – *Peter and the Wolf* (Angel 4XS-36644)

Rimsky-Korsakov – *Scheherazade* (Columbia MS-7509)

Snow White and the Seven Dwarfs (Disneyland Records)

Sousa – *Marches* (London 139)

Strauss, Johann, Jr. – *Blue Danube Waltz and other Strauss Waltzes* (Columbia D3S-789)

Villa-Lobos – *Little Train of the Caipira* (Everest 3041)

Weber – *Overtures* (DGG-3300294)

When You Wish Upon a Star (CBS-37200)

Ages 6-12

Introduce your children to music of many lands and to the beauty of the orchestra.

Mr. Bach Comes to Call (Classical Kids, 134 Howland Avenue, Toronto, Ontario, Canada M5R 3B5)

The Black Stallion (soundtrack) (Liberty L00-01040)

Blake, Howard – *The Snowman* (CBS 39216)

Boyd, Liona – *Paddle-to-the-Sea* (Oak Street Music, 301-140 Bannatyne Avenue, Winnipeg, Canada R3B 3C5)

Britten – *Young Person's Guide to the Orchestra*, coupled with *Saint-Saëns Carnival of the Animals* (Columbia MT-31808)

Diamond, Neil – *Jonathan Livingston Seagull* (Diamond – Columbia KS-32550)

Dohnányi – *Variations on a Nursery Song* (Chesky CD-13)

Hardy, Hagwood – *Anne of Green Gables* (Channel Productions, P.O. Box 454, Twin Falls, ID 83303)

Hepburn, Audrey – *Enchanted Tales* (Dove Audio, 301 N. Canon Drive, Beverly Hills, CA 90210) (Allegro Imports)

James, Terry – *Jonathan Livingston Seagull* (Richard Harris – ABC-DSD-50160)

Makarova, Natalia and Stravinsky – *The Firebird* (fairy tale and music) (Delos DE 6005)

Mozart – *Symphony no. 41, Jupiter* (DGG3335114)

Mozart's Magic Fantasy (a lovely, engaging children's story of *The Magic Flute*) (A & M Records of Canada, 939 Warden Avenue, Scarborough, Ontario, M1L 4C5, Canada)

The Nonesuch Explorer Series of Music from All Over the World (Nonesuch Records)

Seraphim Guide to the Instruments of the Orchestra (Seraphim S-60234)

Tchaikovsky Comes to America (Children's Group, 561 Bloor Street West, Suite 300, Toronto, Ontario, M5S I46 Canada)

Tchaikovsky – *1812 Overture* (London 417087 or DGG 429984) – *The Snow Queen* (narration in English with piano music by Tchaikovsky) (Delos DE 6004)

Three Cheers for Pooh (Musical Heritage Society MHS 4617)

Vivaldi's Ring of Mystery (Children's Group, 561 Bloor Street West, Suite 300, Toronto, Ontario M5S I46 Canada)

Zamfir – Music for flute of Pan (various albums on miscellaneous labels, especially Mercury and Philips)

Miscellaneous

Ann Rachlin – *Fun with Music* (vols. 1-20) (EMI, England)
Beautiful stories, such as *Romeo and Juliet* and *Sleeping Beauty*, accompanied by classical music in the background, perfectly woven into the story line.

Rabbit Ears Stories:
1. *East of the Sun, West of the Moon*
2. *The Boy Who Drew Cats*
3. *The Monkey People*
4. *Rumpelstiltskin*
5. *The Fool and the Flying Ship*
6. *Peachboy*
7. *Koi and the Kola Nuts*
8. *The Tiger and the Brahmin*
9. *Anansi*

10. Finn McCoul
(Source: Rhino Records, 2225 Colorado Ave., Santa Monica, CA 90404)

Betty Ballantine – *The Secret Oceans* (Bantam 483B) (2 cassettes)

J. M. Barrie – *Peter Pan* (Random House cassettes – ISBN 0-679-42949-2)

James Herriot Collection of Stories (Cassettes – Listen for Pleasure, 25 Mallard Road, Don Mills, Ontario, Canada M3B 1S4)

Jean Giono – *The Man Who Planted Trees* (Robert J. Lurtsema, narrator) (Earth Music Productions, Paul Winter, P.O. Box 68, Lichfield, CT 06759)

E. B. White – *Charlotte's Web* (Bantam Audio Cassette – ISBN 0-553-47048-5)

C. S. Lewis – *The Chronicles of Narnia* (four cassettes – ISBN 1-55994-501)

Ludwig Bemelmans – *Madeline Stories* (Carol Channing, reader) (ISBN 1-55994-654-7)

George Kleinsinger – *Tubby the Tuba* (Channing/Kunzel – Caedmon CPN 1623)

Music Lists

SLAVIC SACRED CHORAL MUSIC

1000 Years of Russian Monastery Music (Koch Schwann CD 3131 079H1)

Bortnyansky, D. – *Concertos for Choir* (Polyansky – Melodiya SUCD 10-00266, SUCD 10-00030-032)

Bulgarian and Russian Orthodox Chants, Boris Christoff (Konstantinov – Balkanton 050046)

Byzantine Music of the Sixth – Fifteenth Century (Yanchenko – Melodiya SUCD 10-00276)

Chaliapin Sings: The Russian Creed, by Archangelsky (Pearl GEMM CD 9314)

Chants of the Slavonic Liturgy (Benedictine Monks of Chevetogne – Harmonia Mundi HMA 190507)

Chesnokov, P. – *Vesper Mass* (Georgievsky – Melodiya SUCD 10-00598)

Christmas in Russia (Koch Schwann DC 313 004G1)

Collection of Sacred Russian Choral Music (Glinka Choir – MCA AED-68004)

Diletsky, N. – *Choral Works* (Ikonnik – Melodiya SUCD 10-00271)

Gedda, Nicolai – *Russian Liturgical Chant* (Evetz – Philips 434 174-2) – *Russian Songs and Romances* (Nekrasov and Popov – Melodiya MCD 244)

God in Russia (Koch Schwann CD 313 003H1)

Gretchaninov – *Holy Radiant Light* (from *An American Tribute*: Mormon Tabernacle Choir, CBS MK 42133); *Vespers Liturgy* (Klochkov – Gega 158)

Holy Radiant Light; The Sacred Song of Russia (Patterson – GDCD 007) (Paraclete Press, Orleans, MA 02653)

Hristov, Dobri – *Liturgy* (Klochkov – Gega GD-126)

Ippolitov-Ivanov, Mikhail – *Liturgy; Vespers* (Abalyan – Sony 64091)

Kastalski, A. – *Liturgy* (Zaboronok – Harmonia Mundi LDC 288013)

Kiev Christmas Liturgy; Moscow Liturgic Choir (Erato 2292-45961-2)

Komitas (Sogomon Sogomonyan) – *Mass* (Liturgy) (Keshishyan – Melodiya SUCD 10-00275); *Divine Liturgy* (Keshishyan – New Albion NA033 CD)

Light of Christ Illumineth All Men (Matveyev – Melodiya SUCD 10-00279)

Liturgical Music of Russia (Diakoff – Cascavelle VEL 1023)

Midnight in Moscow – (*Evening Bells, I Pray to the Power of Love* – Bortnyansky, *O Lord, Save Thy People*) The Don Cossack Choir (Serge Jaroff – Musicfest 413 257-2)

Millennium of Russian Baptism; Hymns of Holy Easter (Olympia OCD 261)

Monks of Zagorsk from Paris (Pierre Verany PV.789031)

New York Russian Chorus (Lieberman – Priceless D12450)

Nikolsky – *Liturgy* (Kurilo – MCA AED-10432)

Poznan Choir (Zaborowski – MCA-AED-10353)

Praise of the Mother of God in the Russian Church (Linke – Christophorus CD-74505)

Rachmaninov – *Liturgy of St. John of Chrysostom* (Minin – Melodiya SUCD 10-00012)

– *Vespers* (Sveshnikov – Melodiya SUCD 10-00601)

Russian Hymns in Honor of the Mother of God (Koch Schwann CD 313 047H1)

Russian Liturgical Music – Tompkins Vocal Ensemble of Budapest (Radioton HCD31408)

Russian Mass (Koch Schwann CD 3-1212-2)

Russian Orthodox Chants (UNESCO D8301)

Russian Orthodox Music (Great Voices of Bulgaria) (Mihaylov – Auvidis Ethnic B6786)

Russian Polyphonic Choral Music (Minin – Melodiya MA 3028)

Russian Sacred Choral Masterpieces (Spassky – Monitor MCD 61468)

Russian Sacred Music (Polyansky – Melodiya SUCD 1000258)

Russian Sacred Music – *The Lord is My Light* (Multisonic 31 0051-2)

Sacred Easter Service; Cantus (Arshavskaya – LAD MK 417125)

Sacred Hymns of Old Russia (Verhoeff – Koch Schwann CD 313 033H1)

Sacred Music from the Ukraine (Koch Schwann CD 313 034H1)

St. Ivan Rilsky (Atanassov – Balkanton 050056)

Serbian Grand Liturgy (Jade – JACD 021 12 19.06)

Shchedrin, R. – *The Sealed Angel* (Minin – Melodiya SUCD 10-00004)

Shvedov, K. – *Liturgy of St. John of Chrysostom* (Kornev – Melodiya SUCD 11-00318)

Tchaikovsky – *Ten Hymns* (Oukov – Melodiya/Chant du Monde LDC 278 728)
– *Choral Works (Invocation to Sleep)* (Polyansky – Melodiya SUCD 10-00015)
– *Vespers* (Tchernoushenko – Chant du Monde LDC 278 749)
Vedel, A. – *Choral Concertos nos. 1-7* (Ikonnik – Melodiya SUCD 10-00268)
– *Choral Concertos nos. 8-15* (Ikonnik – Melodiya SUCD 10- 00269)

MUSIC OF ANGELS AND DEVAS

Adams-Weatherly – *The Holy City* (Pickwick – Voices from the Holy Land)
Aeoliah – *Angel Love* (White Swan Music, 1705 Fourteenth Street, Box 143, Boulder, CO 80302)
– *Angel Love for Children* (White Swan)
Alwyn – *Lyra Angelica* (Hickox – Chandos, or Alwyn – Lyrita)
Archangelsky – *Russian Creed* (Chaliapin – Pearl)
Bach, J. S. – *Come Sweet Death* (organist, Virgil Fox – Bainbridge)
– *Sanctus,* from *B-Minor Mass* (Gardiner – Archiv, or Adolph – Pilz)
– *Toccata and Fugue* (Stokowski – London or Angel)
Bach-Gounod – *Ave Maria* (various labels)
Beethoven – *Piano Concerto no. 5, Emperor,* second movement (Arrau – Philips, or Perhia – Sony)
– *The Heavens are Telling* (Resmiranda Music, or Mormon Tabernacle Choir – Columbia or Sony)
Berglund, Erik – *Angel Beauty* (White Swan Music 1705 Fourteenth Street, Box 143, Boulder, CO 80302)
– *Angelic Harp Music* (White Swan)
– *Harp of the Healing Waters* (White Swan Music)
Berlioz – *Hosanna,* from *L'Enfance du Christ* (Munch – RCA 2-09026-61234)
– *Sanctus,* from *Requiem* (Davis – Philips)
Boisvallee – *Adagio Religioso* (Philips)
Bortnyansky – *Sacred Concertos* (Polyansky – Melodiya)
Braga – *Angel's Serenade* (RCA)
Brahms – *Piano Concerto no. 2,* third movement (Gilels, Jochum – DGG)
Bruckner – *Adagio,* from *Symphony no. 8* (Horenstein – Vox, Haitink – Philips)
Casals – *El Pesebre (The Manger)* (Casals – Sony or Columbia)

– *Sacred Choral Music* (Segarra – Koch Schwann)

– *Song of the Birds* (Casals – Sony or Harnoy – Pro Arte or [sung] de los Angeles – Collins)

Chopin – *Nocturne in E-flat, opus 9, no. 2* (Ormandy – Sony) (orchestral version)

– *Piano Concerto no. 1*, slow movement (Gilels/Ormandy – Sony)

Deep River (traditional) (Alex Jones: Pickwick – Voices from the Holy Land)

De Vocht – *Mass in Honor of the Angels* (Benoit – Rene Gailly International CD)

Elgar – *Pomp and Circumstance March no. 1* (Davis – Philips) (Land of Hope and Glory)

Enya – *Angels* (Reprise)

Fauré – *In Prayer* (Battle – DGG)

– *Sanctus and In Paradisum*, from *Requiem* (Rutter – Collegium)

Franck – *Panis angelicus* (Resmiranda Music or Pavarotti – London or Stokowski – Biddulph)

– *Psalm 150* (Resmiranda, or Mormon Tabernacle Choir – Sony)

Gluck – *Dance of the Blessed Spirits* (Monteux – London)

Gounod – *Choral Mass* (Erato – Corboz)

– *Sanctus*, from *St. Cecilia Mass* (Norman – Philips, or Prétre – Angel EMI)

– *Te Deum* (Munk – Danica)

Grieg – *Nocturne*, from *Lyric Suite* (Ormandy – Sony)

– *Piano Concerto*, second movement (Lupu/Previn – London)

Handel – *Hallelujah Chorus*, from *Messiah* (Sargent – EMI or Beecham – RCA)

– *Largo*, from *Xerxes* (instrumental; Marriner – Angel), or *Holy Art Thou* (choral version; Resmiranda Music, 179 West State Street, Windsor, VT 05089) (Fiedler – RCA)

– *Let the Bright Seraphim*, from *Samson* (Beecham – Angel Seraphim)

– Miscellaneous choruses (Ormandy and Mormon Tabernacle Choir – Sony)

– *Thanks Be to Thee* (Resmiranda Music)

Haydn, F. J. – *The Creation* (Atzmón – BIS)

Herbert – *Ah, Sweet Mystery of Life* (Sills / Kostelanetz – Angel)

Hovhaness – *Fra Angelico* (Hovhaness – Crystal)

– *Mysterious Mountain* (Reiner – RCA)

– *The Holy City* (Lipkin – CRI)

Humperdinck – *Children's Prayer*, from *Hansel and Gretel* (choral version, Ormandy – Columbia) (Stokowski – RCA 09026, 61887-2)

Hymns – *O Holy Night; Ye Watchers and Ye Holy Ones; Ye Holy Angels Bright; Angels from the Realms of Glory; Angels We Have Heard on High; All Creatures of Our God and King; Holy, Holy, Holy; Come Down O Love Divine* (various labels)

Ja Pan Payong – *The Sleeping Angel* (Nimbus 5319) (Fong Naam)

Lieuwen, P. – *Angelfire* (Freeman – Pro Arte) (New Mexico Angel Ritual)

Liszt – *Prayer to the Guardian Angel* (organ, Bousseau – Adda CD 581089; piano, Block – OM80504 CD)

Mahler – Finale from *Symphony no. 2, Resurrection* (Bernstein – Columbia – Sony, or Rattle – EMI Angel)

Malotte – *The Lord's Prayer* (Mormon Tabernacle Choir – Sony)

Mendelssohn – *He Watching Over Israel,* from *Elijah* (Corboz – Erato)

Mozart – *Ave Verum Corpus* (Davis – Philips)
– *Laudate Dominum, Psalm 116,* from *Solemn Vespers* (Kiri Te Kanawa – Philips)

Oldfield, Terry – *Star of Heaven* (NWC 184 – White Swan)
– *Angel* (NWC 192 – White Swan)

Olsson – *Te Deum* (Ek – BIS)
– *Requiem* (Propius/May Audio Marketing)

Palestrina – *Pope Marcellus Mass* (Tallis Scholars – Gimell)

Rachmaninov – *Liturgy of St. John Chrysostom* (Minin – Melodiya)
– *Vespers* (Shaw – Telarc or Sveshnikov – Melodiya)
– *Vocalise* (Moffo/Stokowski – RCA 7831-2RG)

Respighi – *The Archangel Michael,* from *Church Windows* (Simon – Chandos or Cobos – Telarc)

Robertson, Kim – *Angels in Disguise* (White Swan Music))

Rodgers and Hammerstein – *Prologue* and *Climb Every Mountain,* from *The Sound of Music* (Andrews – RCA)

Rosner – *Responses,* from *Responses, Hosanna and Fugue* (Amos – Harmonia Mundi)

Roylance, Dave and Bob Galvin – *Distant Shores* from *Battle of the Atlantic Suite* (Garrett/Connor – Conifer 74321-15008)

Rubinstein – *Angelic Dream,* from *Kamennoi Ostrov* (F. Slatkin – Angel or Adolph – Vox Cameo Classics – AED 8763); *Quiet Nights*

Schubert – *Ave Maria* (Ormandy – Sony or Stokowski); *Fantasia,* (soundtrack – Disneyland)

Shchedrin – *The Angel* (choral song, Melodiya)
– *The Sealed Angel* (Melodiya)

Sibelius – *Finlandia* (Choral Version, Ormandy – Sony) (Barbirolli – EMI) (nature devas' chants of praise)
– *Swan of Tuonela* (Ormandy – EMI or Barbirolli – EMI)

Strauss, R. – *At Parting,* from *Four Last Songs* (Norman and Masur – Philips)
– Finale, from *A Hero's Life* (Karajan – EMI; Previn – Angel)
– *Transfiguration,* from *Death and Transfiguration* (Previn – Telarc)
Vangelis – *Antarctica Echoes,* from *Antarctica* soundtrack (Polydor)
Vaughan Williams – *Fantasia on a Theme of Thomas Tallis* (Boult – EMI, or Boughton – Nimbus)
– *The Delectable Mountains,* from *A Bunyan Sequence* (Best – Hyperion)
Vivaldi and F. J. Haydn and M. Haydn – Masses (various labels)
Wagner – *Brunnhilde's Immolation,* from *Die Götterdämmerung* and *Die Walküre* (Flagstad – EMI or RCA); *The Angel,* from *Wesendonk Songs* (Flagstad/Sargent – EMI)
– *Evening Star,* from *Tannhäuser* (Mantovani – London)
– *Liebestod,* from *Tristan und Isolde* (Flagstad – AS) (divine love)
– *Pilgrim's Chorus,* from *Tannhäuser* (Resmiranda Music)
– *Prelude to Lohengrin, Act I* (Kempe – EMI Laser) (Angels' descent and Holy Grail theme and archetype)
– *Prelude to Parsifal and Good Friday Music* (Kempe – EMI Laser)
– *Prize Song,* from *Die Meistersinger* (EMI) (theme of angelic choirs)
– *Ride of the Valkyries* (Fiedler – RCA, or Stokowski – London)

THE MUSIC OF NATURE, THE ELEMENTS, AND THE SEASONS

Adler – *Wilderness Suite* (music honoring the National Parks) (Ketcham – RCA)
Alfvén – *From the Seaward Skerries* (tone poem of the sea) (Järvi – BIS CD 505)
Alwyn – *Autumn Legend; Angel Songs* (Hickox – Chandos, Lyrica Angelica or Alwyn – Lyrita)
Ancient Shepherd Pipes (Israeli nature music) (Folkways FW 8724)
Atterberg – *Symphony no. 3, West Coast Pictures* (music of the ocean and Nordic lands – Sweden) (Ehrling – Caprice CAP21364)
Barber – *Music for a Scene from Shelley; Essays nos. 1, 2, and 3 for Orchestra* (Schenck – Stradivari SCD 8012 or Golschmann – Vanguard)
Bax – *Spring Fire; Tintagel; Mediterranean; Winter Legends* (Thomson – Chandos)
Beethoven – *Symphony no. 6, Pastorale* (Walter – Sony or Böhm – DGG)
Bliss – *And the Flocks Lie Strewn* (pastoral and choral) (Hickox – Chandos)
Bridge – *The Sea* (Handley – Chandos)

Britten – *Four Sea Interludes* from *Peter Grimes* (Previn – EMI)

Bruckner – *Symphony no. 4* (Böhm – London); *Symphony no. 8* (Horenstein – Intaglio)

Butterworth – *Banks of Green Willow; Two English Idylls* (Boughton – Nimbus)

Classical Loon I, II (NorthWord Press, P.O. Box 1360, Minocqua, WI 54548)

Coyote Oldman – *Tear of the Moon* (Native American music) (Coyote Oldman Music)

Cry of the Loon (Special Music Company; Madacy, Quebec, Canada)

d'Indy – *Symphony on a French Mountain Air* (Dutoit – London)

Darnell, Dik – *Following the Circle; Winter Solstice* (Native American environmental) (Etherean)

David – *The Desert* (Guida – Capriccio)

Debussy – *Prelude to the Afternoon of a Faun; Engulfed Cathedral, The Sea, Three Nocturnes* (Simon – Cala; Ansermet – London)

de Falla – *Nights in the Gardens of Spain* (Rubenstein-Jorda – RCA)

Delerue – *A Summer Story* (Virgin)

Delius – *On Hearing the First Cuckoo in Spring; Sea Drift; Appalachia* (Boughton – Nimbus)

Douglas Spotted Eagle – *Sacred Feelings* (Thunderstorm) (Soar)

Elcano, Philip – *Rain Dance* (Desert Productions)

Elgar – *Sea Pictures* (Baker/Barbirolli – EMI)

Evenson, Dean – *Ocean Dreams; Peaceful Pond; Desert Dawn Song; Evensong* (Soundings of the Planet)

Fanshawe – *African Sanctus* (Philips)

Farnon – *Lake of the Woods* (Reference Recordings)

Finzi – *Intimations of Immortality; A Severn Rhapsody* (Hickox – EMI; Boult – Lyrita)

Galway – *Song of the Seashore* (beautiful Japanese nature folk songs) (RCA)

Gentle Surf; Sounds of the Forest; Waterfall Suite (Distributions – Madacy)

Ginastera – *Pampeana no. 3* (Argentinian pampas) (Whitney – Philips or Mata – Dorian)

Glazunov – *Forest; The Sea* (Svetlanov – Melodiya or Järvi – Chandos)

Glière – *Concerto for Coloratura Soprano* (Sutherland – London)

Gluck – *Dance of the Blessed Spirits* (Monteux – London)

Grieg – *Piano Concerto* (Lupu/Previn – London or Andsnes/Kitaenko – Virgin)

Hanson – *Symphony no. 2, Romantic* (Hanson – Mercury or Slatkin – EMI)

Harty – *Ode to a Nightingale* (Thomson – Chandos)

Honegger – *Summer Pastorale* (Bernstein – Sony)

Hovhaness – *Mysterious Mountain* (Reiner – RCA); *Symphony no. 46, To the Green Mountains* (Jordania – Koch);
– *And God Created Great Whales* (Amos – Crystal)

Klami – *Sea Pictures* (Segerstam – Finlandia)

Koechlin – *Jungle Book* (Segerstam – Marco Polo)

Koh, Bunya – *Confucian Temple Rites* (nature and spirituality) (Sunrise 8503)

Le Flem, Paul – *Symphony no. 1* (Schnitzler – Radio France/Records International, Box 1140, Goleta, CA 93116-1140)

Listen to the Loons (Solitudes – Dan Gibson Productions)

Locke, Kevin – *Dream Catcher* (Earth Beat)
– *The Flash of the Mirror* (Meyer Sound Studios, P.O. Box 1738, Bismarck, ND 58502)

Mahler – *Symphony no. 3* (Bernstein – Sony)

Mendelssohn – *Calm Sea and Prosperous Voyage Overture* (Chmura – DGG)

Meulemans – *Pine Tree Symphony* (Rahbari – Marco Polo)

Moeran – *Symphony in G Minor* (beautiful wild ocean scenes) (Dilkes – EMI or Handley – Chandos)

Montaigne – *Wilderness Journal* (Thoreau) (Dorati – Fredonia)

Novák – *In the Tatras; Slovak Suite* (Smetaček – Supraphon)
– *Pan* (Bilek – Marco Polo)

Oldfield, Terry – *Reverence* (New World Company, England)

Ravel – *Fairy Garden,* from *Mother Goose; Daphnis and Chloe* (Martinon – EMI or Munch – RCA)

Reger – *The Virgin's Slumber Song* (Fox and Natale – Bainbridge)

Respighi – *Pines of Rome; Fountains of Rome* (Muti – EMI or Toscanini – RCA)

Rodrigo – *Music for a Garden* (concerto) (Bátiz – EMI)

Rosenschoon – *Timbili* (African classical) (Mbande/Tiemeyer – Claremont)

Sainton – *Moby Dick* (film score) (RCA)
– *The Island* (Bamert – Chandos)

Schoeck – *Summer Night* (Goritsky – Claves)

Schumann – *Symphony no. 1, Spring* (Munch – RCA)

Sibelius – *Finlandia* (deva initiation call); *The Tempest; The Bard; Autre Fois (Once Upon a Time); Symphony no. 4* (Järvi – BIS)

Silverbird, J. Reuben – *The World in our Eyes* (Native American vision of creation with nature sounds) (Celestial Harmonies)

Songbird Symphony (NorthWord Press, Inc., P.O. Box 1360, Minocqua, WI 54548)

Songbirds of Spring (pastoral countryside with church bells) (National Audubon Society CDN 07)

Tanner, Jerre – *Boy with Goldfish* (Hawaian) (Holdridge – Albany)

Tchaikovsky – *Symphony no. 1, Winter Dreams* (Jansons – Chandos)

Valentino, Chris – *The Musical Sea of Tranquility* (Jonell Record Company)

Vaughan Williams – *A Sea Symphony* (Haitink – EMI)

– *In the Fen Country; Lark Ascending; Northern Ballads* (Boult – EMI)

– *Symphony no. 3, A Pastoral Symphony* (Previn – RCA)

Villa-Lobos – *Amazon; Genesis; Erosion: Origin of the Amazon River* (Duarte – Marco Polo)

– *Discovery of Brazil* (Duarte – Marco Polo)

Wagner – *Forest Murmurs; Ride of the Valkyries; Evening Star* (Stokowski – London; Mantovani – London)

Winter, Paul – *Missa Gaia; Whales Alive* (Living Music)

Wolf Talk (NorthWord Press, Inc., P.O. Box 1360, Minocqua, WI 54548)

Zemlinsky – *The Mermaids* (Chailly – London)

MUSIC FOR STRESS REDUCTION, RELAXATION, AND FOCUS

New Age Selections

Aeoliah – *Majesty; Love in the Wind*

William Aura – *Lovely Day*

Patrick Ball – *Celtic Harp; From a Distant Time; Secret Isles*

Tom Barabas – *Magic in December; You're the End of the Rainbow*

Bruce Becvar – *Take It to Heart*

Spencer Brewer – *Emerald*

Jim Chappell – *Dusk*

Patrick DiVietri – *Partita Teresiana; Invocation* (beautiful guitar)

Evenson – *High Joy; Peaceful Pond; Whistling Woodhearts; Tropic of Paradise; Ocean Dreams; Desert Moon Song*

George Parker Franchell – *Rannveig and Chrysalis* (Jonaubri Productions, 436 Washington Avenue, Oneida, NY 13421)

Max Highstein – *The Healer's Touch*

Alex Jones – *Kali's Dream; Pranava*

Daniel Kobialka – *Path of Joy; Sunspace; Journeys in Time; Goin' Home*
Carolyn Margrete – *Emerald Season*
Steven Pasero – *Winter Heartsong for Guitar; Nutcracker Suite* (guitar)
Kim Robertson – *Moonrise; Water Spirit; Wind Shadows I, II; Celtic Christmas*
Mike Rowland – *The Fairy Ring; Solace; Silver Wings*
Liz Storey – *Solid Colors*

Classical Selections and Miscellaneous

Carol Adee – *Bach to Nature* (Well-Tempered Productions – from Allegro Imports)
J. S. Bach – *Jesu, Joy of Man's Desiring; Sheep May Safely Graze*
Beethoven – Symphony no. 6 *(Pastorale)*
Corelli – *Concerti Grossi*
Dvořák – *Silent Woods; Cello Concerto*
Grieg – *Holberg Suite; Morning* (from *Peer Gynt)*
Handel – *Largo* (from *Xerxes); Water Music*
Mendelssohn – *Songs without Words*
Mozart – Flute and piano concertos
Pachelbel – *Canon in D*
Rodrigo – *Aranjuez Concerto; Music for a Garden*
Vaughan Williams – *Lark Ascending; Flos Campi*
Vivaldi – *The Four Seasons;* miscellaneous concertos

Composers' Birthdates

January 1	Robert De Cormier	(1922)
January 2	Sir Michael Tippett	(1905)
	Gardner Read	(1913)
January 3	Boris Liatoshinsky	(1895)
	Victor Borge	(1909)
January 4	Josef Suk	(1874)
	Giovanni Pergolesi	(1710)
January 5	Frederick Converse	(1871)
January 6	Max Bruch	(1838)
	Alexander Scriabin	(1872)
January 7	Ulysses Kay	(1917)
	Sigismond Thalberg	(1812)
	Francis Poulenc	(1899)
	William Hurlstone	(1876)
January 8	Jean Gilles	(1669)
	Jaromir Weinberger	(1896)
	Andrej Ocenas	(1911)
	Robert Starer	(1924)
January 9	John Knowles Paine	(1839)
	Luis Gianneo	(1897)
January 10	Jean Martinon	(1910)
	Akiro Miyoshi	(1933)
January 11	Christian Sinding	(1856)
	Reinhold Glière	(1875)
	Maurice Duruflé	(1902)
January 12	Ermanno Wolf-Ferrari	(1876)
January 13	Vasily Kallinikov	(1866)
	Richard Addinsell	(1904)
	Ami Maayani	(1936)
January 14	Gasparo Spontini	(1774)
	Albert Schweitzer	(1875)
January 15	Elie Siegmeister	(1909)

January 16	Ernesto Halffter	(1905)
January 17	François Gossec	(1734)
	Henk Badings	(1907)
January 18	Emmanuel Chabrier	(1841)
January 19	Boris Blacher	(1903)
January 20	Johann Schein	(1586)
	Guillaume Lekeu	(1870)
	Walter Piston	(1894)
January 21	Alexander Tcherepnin	(1899)
	Ernest Chausson	(1855)
January 22	Charles Tournemire	(1870)
	Henri Dutilleux	(1916)
January 23	Muzio Clementi	(1752)
	Rutland Boughton	(1878)
January 24	Jean Daetwyler	(1907)
	Norman Dello Joio	(1913)
	Gottfried von Einem	(1918)
	Leon Kirchner	(1919)
January 25	Witold Lutoslawski	(1913)
January 26	Stéphane Grappelli	(1908)
January 27	Wolfgang Amadeus Mozart	(1756)
	Juan Arriaga	(1806)
	Edouard Lalo	(1823)
	Jerome Kern	(1885)
January 28	Vittorio Rieti	(1898)
January 29	Georg Wagenseil	(1715)
	Daniel Auber	(1782)
	Frederick Delius	(1862)
	Havergal Brian	(1876)
January 30	Johann Quantz	(1697)
	Charles Loeffler	(1861)
	Charles Haubiel	(1892)
January 31	Franz Schubert	(1797)
	Philip Glass	(1937)
February 1	Victor Herbert	(1859)
	Camargo Guarnieri	(1907)
February 2	Giovanni Pierluigi da Palestrina	(1525)
	Fritz Kreisler	(1875)
	Candelario Huizar	(1888)
February 3	Felix Mendelssohn	(1809)
	Luigi Dallapiccola	(1904)

February 4	Bernard Rogers	(1893)
February 5	Ole Bull	(1810)
	Kara Karayev	(1918)
February 6		
February 7	William Boyce	(1710)
	Wilhelm Stenhammar	(1871)
	Eubie Blake	(1883)
	Quincy Porter	(1897)
	Edmond de Luca	(1909)
February 8	André Grétry	(1741)
	Matthijs Vermeulen	(1888)
February 9	Alban Berg	(1895)
February 10	Jerry Goldsmith	(1929)
February 11		
February 12	Jan Dussek	(1760)
	Roy Harris	(1898)
February 13	Fernando Sor	(1778)
February 14	Alexander Dargomyzhsky	(1813)
February 15	Michael Praetorius	(1571)
	Georges Auric	(1899)
February 16	John Corigliano, Jr.	(1938)
February 17	Arcangelo Corelli	(1653)
	Henri Vieuxtemps	(1820)
	Sir Edward German	(1862)
	Leevi Madetoja	(1887)
	Paul Fetler	(1920)
	Lee Hoiby	(1926)
	Ron Goodwin	(1925)
February 18	John Parry II	(1776)
	Giovanni Vitali	(1632)
February 19	Luigi Boccherini	(1743)
	Arthur Shepherd	(1880)
	Grace Williams	(1906)
	Luis Gesensway	(1906)
February 20	Toshiro Mayazumi	(1929)
February 21	Leo Delibes	(1836)
	Charles Marie Widor	(1844)
February 22	Frédéric Chopin	(1810)
	Niels Gade	(1817)
	Ingvar Lidholm	(1921)
February 23	George Frideric Handel	(1865)

February 24	Arrigo Boito	(1842)
	Samuel Wesley	(1766)
February 25	George Harrison	(1943)
February 26	Anton Reicha	(1770)
	Frank Bridge	(1879)
	Rudolf Moralt	(1902)
February 27	Sir Hubert Parry	(1848)
	Wilhelm Peterson-Berger	(1867)
February 28	John Alden Carpenter	(1876)
	Elias Parish-Alvars	(1808)
February 29	Gioacchino Rossini	(1792)
March 1	Glenn Miller	(1904)
March 2	Bedřich Smetana	(1824)
	Carl Ruggles	(1876)
	Ruy Coelho	(1892)
	Kurt Weill	(1900)
	Marc Blitzstein	(1905)
	Robert Simpson	(1921)
	Allfred Bruneau	(1857)
March 3	Henry Wood	(1869)
	Frederico Moreno Torroba	(1891)
	Lee Holdridge	(1944)
March 4	Antonio Vivaldi	(1678)
	Carlos Surinach	(1915)
March 5	Arthur Foote	(1853)
	Heitor Villa-Lobos	(1887)
	Patrick Hadley	(1899)
	Anthony Hedges	(1931)
March 6	Josef Bayer	(1852)
March 7	Maurice Ravel	(1875)
	Juan Jose Castro	(1895)
	Tomaso Vitali	(1663)
March 8	C. P. E. Bach	(1714)
	Ruggiero Leoncavallo	(1858)
	Paul Juon	(1872)
	Nikos Skalkottas	(1904)
	Alan Hovhaness	(1911)
March 9	Matthias Monn	(1717)
	Samuel Barber	(1910)
March 10	Pablo de Sarasate	(1844)
	Dudley Buck	(1839)

	Arthur Honneger	(1892)
March 11	Anthony Heinrich	(1781)
	Henry Cowell	(1897)
	Xavier Montsalvatge	(1912)
March 12	Thomas Arne	(1710)
March 13	Hugo Wolf	(1860)
	Enrico Toselli	(1883)
March 14	Georg Philipp Telemann	(1681)
	Johann Strauss I	(1804)
March 15	Colin McPhee	(1901)
March 16	Nikolai Lopatnikoff	(1903)
March 17	Josef Rheinberger	(1839)
	John LaMontaine	(1920)
	Paul Horn	(1930)
March 18	Nikolai Rimsky-Korsakov	(1844)
	Gian Malipiero	(1882)
	Ctirad Kohoutek	(1929)
March 19	Max Reger	(1873)
	Elizabeth Maconchy	(1907)
	Dinu Lipatti	(1917)
	Normand Lockwood	(1906)
March 20		
March 21	Johann Sebastian Bach	(1685)
March 22	Hamish McCunn	(1868)
March 23	Dane Rudhyar	(1895)
	Ludwig Minkus	(1826)
	Franz Schreker	(1878)
	Geoffrey Bush	(1920)
March 24		
March 25	Béla Bartók	(1881)
March 26	Pierre Boulez	(1925)
March 27	Vincent d'Indy	(1851)
	Ferde Grofé	(1892)
	Ruperto Chapi	(1851)
March 28	Jacob Avshalamov	(1919)
	Murray Adaskin	(1906)
March 29	Sir William Walton	(1902)
	Richard Rodney Bennett	(1936)
	Vangelis	(1943)
March 30	Guillaume de Machaut	(1300)
	Sergey Vassilenko	(1872)

March 31	Franz Josef Haydn	(1732)
April 1	Sergei Rachmaninov	(1873)
	Ferruccio Busoni	(1866)
	William Bergsma	(1921)
April 2	Franz Lachner	(1803)
	Anis Fuleihan	(1900)
April 3	Mario Castelnuovo-Tedesco	(1895)
April 4		
April 5	Louis Spohr	(1784)
	Albert Roussel	(1869)
	Richard Yardumian	(1917)
	Herbert von Karajan	(1908)
April 6	Carlos Salzedo	(1885)
	Vano Muradeli	(1908)
	Andrew Imbrie	(1921)
	André Previn	(1929)
April 7	Michio Miyagi	(1894)
	Ravi Shankar	(1920)
	Ikuma Dan	(1924)
April 8	Giuseppe Tartini	(1692)
	Sir Adrian Boult	(1889)
April 9	Aulis Sallinen	(1935)
April 10	Eugene D'Albert	(1864)
	Claude Bolling	(1930)
April 11	William Byrd	(1543)
	Jean Mouret	(1682)
	Alberto Ginastera	(1916)
April 12	Josef Lanner	(1801)
April 13	Félicien David	(1810)
	Sir William Sterndale Bennett	(1816)
April 14	Morton Subotnick	(1933)
April 15	Domenico Gabrieli	(1651)
April 16	Seth Bingham	(1882)
	Federico Mompou	(1893)
	Leo Weiner	(1885)
April 17	Harald Saeverud	(1897)
	Artur Schnabel	(1882)
April 18	Franz von Suppé	(1819)
	Leopold Stokowski	(1882)
	Miklós Rózsa	(1907)
April 19	David Fanshawe	(1942)

April 20	Nikolai Miaskovsky	(1881)
April 21	Randall Thompson	(1899)
	Bruno Maderna	(1920)
	Easley Blackwood	(1933)
	John McCabe	(1939)
April 22	Giuseppe Torelli	(1658)
	Michael Colgrass	(1932)
April 23	Arthur Farwell	(1872)
	Dame Ethyl Smyth	(1858)
	Albert Coates	(1882)
	Sergei Prokofiev	(1891)
April 24	Giovanni Martini	(1706)
April 25	Enrico Bossi	(1861)
	Sparre Olsen	(1903)
	Luis Herrera de la Fuente	(1916)
April 26	Erland von Koch	(1910)
April 27	Friedrich von Flotow	(1813)
April 28	Hermann Suter	(1870)
April 29	Sir Thomas Beecham	(1879)
	Wallingford Riegger	(1885)
	Duke Ellington	(1899)
	Rod McKuen	(1933)
	Harold Shapero	(1920)
	Peter Sculthorpe	(1929)
April 30	Franz Lehár	(1870)
	Ellen Taaffe Zwilich	(1939)
May 1	Hugo Alfvén	(1872)
	Leo Sowerby	(1895)
May 2	Alessandro Scarlatti	(1660)
	Hans Christian Lumbye	(1810)
	Alan Rawsthorne	(1905)
	Maurice Thiriet	(1906)
	Jan Hanus	(1915)
	Derek Healey	(1936)
May 3	Pete Seeger	(1919)
May 4	Mariana Martinez	(1744)
	Emil von Reznicek	(1860)
	Mátyás Seiber	(1905)
	Marisa Robles	(1937)
May 5	Hans Pfitzner	(1839)
	Abraham Kaplan	(1931)

May 6	Rabindranath Tagore	(1861)
	Godfrey Ridout	(1942)
May 7	Johannes Brahms	(1833)
	Peter Ilyich Tchaikovsky	(1840)
May 8	Giovanni Paisiello	(1740)
	Louis Moreau Gottschalk	(1829)
	David van Vactor	(1906)
	Keith Jarrett	(1945)
May 9	Dietrich Buxtehude	(1637)
	Adolph von Henselt	(1814)
	August De Boeck	(1865)
May 10	Milton Babbitt	(1916)
May 11	Anatol Liadov	(1855)
	Irving Berlin	(1888)
	William Grant Still	(1895)
	Josip Slavenski	(1896)
May 12	Jules Massenet	(1842)
	Gabriel Fauré	(1845)
	Sir Lennox Berkeley	(1903)
May 13	Sir Arthur Sullivan	(1842)
	Ottokar Nováček	(1866)
	Joseph Achron	(1886)
May 14	Claudio Monteverdi	(1567)
	Lou Harrison	(1917)
	Joly Braga-Santos	(1924)
May 15	Lars-Erik Larsson	(1908)
	Arthur Berger	(1912)
	John Lanchbery	(1923)
	Andrei Eshpai	(1935)
May 16	Woody Herman	(1913)
May 17	Erik Satie	(1866)
	Nicolai Berezowsky	(1900)
	Werner Egk	(1901)
	John Vincent	(1902)
	Peter Mennin	(1923)
May 18	Karl Goldmark	(1830)
	Henri Sauguet	(1901)
	Roger Matton	(1929)
May 19	Arthur Meulmans	(1884)
	Albert Hay Malotte	(1895)
May 20	Jerzy Fitelberg	(1903)

May 21	"Fats" Waller	(1904)
May 22	Richard Wagner	(1813)
	Gordon Binkerd	(1916)
May 23	Edmund Rubbra	(1901)
	Jean Francaix	(1912)
	Pio Barrios	(1885)
May 24	Paul Paray	(1886)
	Martin Kalmanoff	(1920)
May 25	Miles Davis	(1926)
May 26	Ernst Bacon	(1898)
	William Bolcom	(1938)
May 27	Jacques Halévy	(1799)
	Joachim Raff	(1822)
	Claude Champagne	(1891)
	Thea Musgrave	(1928)
	Ramsey Lewis	(1935)
May 28	Giovanni Sgambati	(1841)
	Sir George Dyson	(1833)
	Gyorgy Ligeti	(1923)
May 29	Isaac Albéniz	(1860)
	Erich Korngold	(1897)
	Fela Sowande	(1905)
	Yannis Xenakis	(1922)
May 30	Ignaz Moscheles	(1794)
	Pauline Oliveros	(1932)
	Benny Goodman	(1909)
May 31	Akira Ifukube	(1914)
June 1	Ignaz Pleyel	(1757)
	Ferdinando Paër	(1771)
	Mikhail Glinka	(1804)
June 2	Sir Edward Elgar	(1857)
	Robin Orr	(1909)
	Louis Vierne	(1937)
	Marvin Hamlisch	(1944)
June 3	Curtis Mayfield	(1942)
June 4	Elizabeth Whitehouse	(1955)
June 5	Adolf Wiklund	(1879)
	Marcel Tournier	(1879)
	Daniel Pinkham	(1923)
June 6	Sir John Stainer	(1840)
	Aram Khachaturian	(1903)

	Vincent Persichetti	(1915)
June 7	George Szell	(1897)
June 8	Robert Schumann	(1810)
June 9	Otto Nicolai	(1810)
	Gaetano Braga	(1829)
	Carl Nielsen	(1865)
	Albéric Magnard	(1865)
	Cole Porter	(1893)
	Ingolf Dahl	(1912)
June 10	Tikhon Khrennikov	(1913)
June 11	Carlos de Seixas	(1704)
	Richard Strauss	(1864)
June 12	Carlisle Floyd	(1926)
	Werner Josten	(1885)
	Alexander Tansman	(1897)
	Maurice Ohana	(1914)
June 13	Anton Wranitsky	(1761)
	Carlos Chávez	(1899)
June 14	Tomaso Albinoni	(1671)
June 15	Franz Danzi	(1763)
	Edvard Grieg	(1843)
	Guy Ropartz	(1864)
	Paul Gilson	(1865)
	Robert Russell Bennett	(1894)
	Otto Luening	(1900)
	Paul Patterson	(1947)
June 16	David Popper	(1843)
June 17	Charles Gounod	(1818)
	Igor Stravinsky	(1882)
	Einar Englund	(1916)
	Don Gillis	(1912)
June 18	Eduard Tubin	(1905)
June 19	Alfredo Catalani	(1854)
June 20	Jacques Offenbach	(1819)
June 21	Hilding Rosenberg	(1892)
	Alois Hába	(1893)
June 22	Walter Leigh	(1905)
June 23	Carl Reinecke	(1824)
June 24	Harry Partch	(1901)
	Pierre Fournier	(1906)
	Jose Siqueira	(1907)

	Terry Riley	(1935)
June 25	Gustave Charpentier	(1860)
	William Russo	(1928)
June 26		
June 27		
June 28	Joseph Joachim	(1831)
	Richard Rodgers	(1902)
	George Lloyd	(1913)
June 29	Bernard Herrmann	(1911)
	Chou Wen-Chung	(1923)
	Ezra Laderman	(1924)
	Jose Moncayo	(1912)
June 30	Georg Benda	(1722)
	Laszlo Lajtha	(1892)
July 1	Hans Werner Henze	(1926)
July 2	Christoph Gluck	(1714)
July 3	Leoš Janáček	(1854)
	Gene Gutché	(1907)
July 4	Louis Claude Daquin	(1694)
	Stephen Foster	(1826)
	Flor Peeters	(1903)
	Alec Templeton	(1910)
July 5	Josef Holbrooke	(1878)
	Paul Ben-Haim	(1897)
	George Rochberg	(1818)
	Gordon Jacob	(1895)
July 6	Alberto Nepomuceno	(1864)
	Vladimir Ashkenazy	(1937)
July 7	Gustav Mahler	(1860)
	Gian Carlo Menotti	(1911)
July 8	Percy Grainger	(1882)
	George Antheil	(1900)
July 9	Ottorino Respighi	(1879)
	David Diamond	(1915)
	Paul Chihara	(1938)
July 10	Henri Wieniawski	(1835)
	Carl Orff	(1895)
	Yasuchi Akutagawa	(1925)
July 11	Carlos Gomes	(1836)
July 12	George Butterworth	(1885)
	Oscar Hammerstein	(1895)

	Amadeo Roldan	(1900)
July 13	Per Norgaard	(1932)
July 14	Gerald Finzi	(1901)
July 15	Harrison Birtwistle	(1934)
July 16	Goffreddo Petrassi	(1904)
July 17	Isaac Watts	(1674)
July 18	Bernard Wagenaar	(1894)
	R. Murray Schafer	(1933)
July 19	Klaus Egge	(1906)
	Boyd Neel	(1905)
July 20	Déodat de Sévérac	(1872)
July 21	Jean Rivier	(1896)
July 22	Cecil Effinger	(1914)
July 23	Franz Berwald	(1796)
	W. G. Whittaker	(1873)
	Leon Fleisher	(1928)
July 24	Adolph Adam	(1803)
	Ernest Bloch	(1880)
July 25	Alfredo Casella	(1883)
July 26	John Field	(1782)
	Serge Koussevitsky	(1874)
July 27	Enrique Granados	(1867)
	Ernst von Dohnányi	(1877)
	Otar Taktakishvili	(1924)
July 28	Rued Langgaard	(1893)
	Larry Pruden	(1925)
July 29	Sigmund Romberg	(1887)
	Rudi Stephan	(1887)
	Mikis Theodorakis	(1925)
July 30	Paul Anka	(1941)
July 31	C. W. Orr	(1893)
August 1	Benedetto Marcello	(1686)
	Jerome Moross	(1913)
August 2	Sir Arthur Bliss	(1891)
	Karl Hartmann	(1905)
August 3	Louis Gruenberg	(1884)
	Richard Adler	(1921)
August 4	William Schuman	(1910)
August 5	Ambroise Thomas	(1811)
	Oskar Merikanto	(1868)
	Oscar Espla	(1886)

	Stjepan Sulek	(1914)
August 6	Nikolai Budashkin	(1910)
August 7	Sir Granville Bantock	(1868)
	Ernesto Lecuona	(1896)
	Saburo Moroi	(1903)
	Karel Husa	(1921)
August 8	Cécile Chaminade	(1857)
	André Jolivet	(1905)
	Roger Nixon	(1921)
August 9	Albert Ketélbey	(1875)
August 10	Alexander Glazunov	(1865)
	Douglas Moore	(1893)
August 11	Anton Arensky	(1861)
	Alun Hoddinott	(1929)
August 12	Sergei Slonimsky	(1932)
August 13	John Ireland	(1879)
	George Shearing	(1919)
August 14	Samuel Sebastian Wesley	(1810)
	Kaikhosru Sorabji	(1892)
August 15	Marion Bauer	(1887)
	Samuel Coleridge-Taylor	(1875)
	Jacques Ibert	(1890)
	Lukas Foss	(1922)
August 16	Gabriel Pierné	(1863)
August 17	Peter Benoit	(1834)
August 18	Antonio Salieri	(1750)
	Sir Ernest MacMillan	(1893)
	Herman Berlinski	(1910)
August 19	Georges Enesco	(1881)
August 20	Jacopo Peri	(1561)
August 21	Lili Boulanger	(1893)
	Roman W. Zajaczek	(1927)
August 22	Claude Debussy	(1862)
	Karlheinz Stockhausen	(1928)
August 23	Moritz Moszkowski	(1854)
	Ernst Krenek	(1900)
	Constant Lambert	(1905)
	Harold Truscott	(1914)
August 24	Theodore Dubois	(1837)
August 25	Alexei Haieff	(1914)
	Leonard Bernstein	(1918)

August 26	Zakharia Paliashvili	(1871)
	Humphrey Searle	(1915)
August 27	Umberto Giordano	(1867)
	Eric Coates	(1866)
	Sri Chimnoy	(1931)
August 28	Karl Böhm	(1894)
August 29		
August 30		
August 31	Amilcare Ponchielli	(1834)
September 1	Johann Pachelbel	(1653)
	Engelbert Humperdinck	(1854)
	Othmar Schoeck	(1886)
September 2	Saverio Mercadante	(1795)
	Dai-Keong Lee	(1915)
	Gideon Waldrop	(1919)
September 3	Pietro Locatelli	(1695)
	Anthony Collins	(1893)
	Otto Ketting	(1935)
September 4	Anton Bruckner	(1824)
	Darius Milhaud	(1892)
September 5	Giacomo Meyerbeer	(1791)
	Amy Beach	(1867)
	John Cage	(1912)
	Gail Kubik	(1914)
	Peter Racine Fricker	(1920)
September 6	Wayne Barlow	(1912)
	William Kraft	(1923)
	Yevgeny Svetlanov	(1928)
September 7	Leonard Rosenman	(1924)
September 8	Nicolas de Grigny	(1672)
	Antonín Dvořák	(1841)
	Willem Pijper	(1894)
September 9	Girolamo Frescobaldi	(1583)
	Edward Burlingame Hill	(1872)
September 10	Boris Tchaikovsky	(1925)
September 11	Johann Peter	(1746)
	Frederick Kuhlau	(1786)
	Ashley Heenan	(1925)
	Arvo Pärt	(1935)
September 12	Salvador Bacarisse	(1898)
	Ernst Pepping	(1901)

September 13	Clara Schumann	(1819)
	Arnold Schoenberg	(1874)
	Ray Green	(1909)
	Robert Ward	(1917)
	Maurice Jarre	(1924)
September 14	Maria Luigi Cherubini	(1760)
	Michael Haydn	(1737)
September 15	Horatio Parker	(1863)
	Bruno Walter	(1876)
	Frank Martin	(1890)
	Henry Brant	(1913)
September 16	Orlandus Lassus	(1530)
	Nadia Boulanger	(1887)
September 17	Vincenzo Tommasini	(1878)
	Charles Tomlinson Griffes	(1884)
	Hendrik Andriessen	(1892)
September 18	Arthur Benjamin	(1893)
	Pablo Sorozabal	(1897)
	Joseph Tal	(1910)
September 19		
September 20	Ildebrando Pizzetti	(1880)
	Uuno Klami	(1900)
September 21	Gustav Holst	(1874)
	Thomas de Hartmann	(1885)
	Moses Pergament	(1893)
	Lodewijk de Vocht	(1887)
September 22	Mikolajus Ciurlionis	(1875)
September 23	William Dawson	(1899)
	Norman Cazden	(1914)
September 24	Andrzej Panufnik	(1914)
	Vaclav Nelhybel	(1919)
September 25	Jean Philippe Rameau	(1683)
	Leon Boëllmann	(1862)
	Roberto Gerhard	(1896)
	Dmitri Shostakovich	(1906)
September 26	Henry Gilbert	(1868)
	George Gershwin	(1898)
	Hisatada Otaka	(1911)
September 27	Cyril Scott	(1879)
September 28	Florent Schmitt	(1870)
	Vivian Fine	(1913)

September 29	Orlando Gibbons	(1583)
September 30	Johan Svendsen	(1840)
	Sir Charles Villiers Stanford	(1852)
October 1	Paul Dukas	(1865)
	Vladimir Horowitz	(1904)
October 2	Kenneth Leighton	(1929)
October 3	Steve Reich	(1936)
October 4	Heinrich Schütz	(1585)
October 5	Cyril Rootham	(1875)
	Silvestre Revueltas	(1899)
October 6	Karol Szymanowski	(1882)
October 7	William Billings	(1746)
October 8	Louis Vierne	(1870)
	Toru Takemitsu	(1930)
October 9	Camille Saint-Saëns	(1835)
	Roger Goeb	(1914)
	Einojuhani Rautavaara	(1928)
October 10	Giuseppe Verdi	(1813)
	Paul Creston	(1906)
October 11		
October 12	Ralph Vaughan Williams	(1872)
	Healey Willan	(1880)
	J. Leigh Isolfsson	(1893)
October 13	Gösta Nystroem	(1890)
October 14	Ciprian Porumbescu	(1853)
	Alexander Zemlinsky	(1871)
October 15	Dag Wirén	(1905)
October 16	Charles Lloyd	(1849)
	Jan Zelenka	(1679)
October 17	Héraclius Djabadary	(1891)
	Herbert Howells	(1892)
October 18	Shin'ichi Suzuki	(1898)
October 19	Vittorio Giannini	(1903)
	Karl-Birger Blomdahl	(1916)
October 20	Charles Ives	(1874)
October 21	Marie-Joseph Canteloube	(1879)
	Malcolm Arnold	(1921)
	Dizzy Gillespie	(1917)
October 22	Franz Liszt	(1811)
October 23	Ned Rorem	(1923)
	Manos Hadjidakis	(1925)

	Miriam Gideon	(1906)
October 24	Luciano Berio	(1925)
	George Crumb	(1929)
October 25	Johann Strauss, Jr.	(1825)
	Georges Bizet	(1838)
	Alexander Gretchaninov	(1864)
	Jean Rogister	(1879)
	Don Banks	(1923)
October 26	Domenico Scarlatti	(1685)
	Johan Roman	(1694)
October 27	Niccolò Paganini	(1782)
	Dominick Argento	(1927)
October 28	Howard Hanson	(1896)
October 29		
October 30	Elizabeth Coolidge	(1864)
October 31	Louise Talma	(1906)
November 1	William Mathias	(1934)
	Victoria de los Angeles	(1923)
	Roger Quilter	(1877)
November 2	Karl Ditters von Dittersdorf	(1739)
	Douglas Lilburn	(1915)
November 3	Samuel Scheidt	(1587)
	Vicenzo Bellini	(1801)
	James Kalnins	(1904)
	Vladimir Ussachevsky	(1911)
November 4	Arnold Cooke	(1906)
November 5	Johann Christian Bach	(1735)
	Eugene Zádor	(1894)
November 6	Ignacy Jan Paderewski	(1860)
	John Philip Sousa	(1854)
November 7	William Alwyn	(1905)
November 8	Sir Arnold Bax	(1883)
November 9	Burrill Phillips	(1907)
November 10	Martin Luther	(1483)
	François Couperin	(1668)
	Henri Rabaud	(1873)
November 11	Alexander Borodin	(1833)
	Aaron Avshalomov	(1894)
	Ernest Ansermet	(1883)
November 12	Carlo Pedrotti	(1817)
November 13	George Chadwick	(1854)

	Joonas Kokkonen	(1921)
November 14	Leopold Mozart	(1719)
	Johann Hummel	(1778)
	Aaron Copland	(1900)
November 15	Frederico de Freitas Branco	(1902)
November 16	Paul Hindemith	(1895)
	Alfred Hill	(1870)
November 17	David Amram	(1930)
	Joseph Kaminski	(1903)
November 18	Jean Baptiste Loeillet	(1680)
	Carl Maria von Weber	(1786)
	Eugene Ormandy	(1899)
	Louis Mennini	(1920)
November 19	Daniel Lesur	(1908)
	Mikhail Ippolitov-Ivanov	(1859)
November 20	Daniel Gregory Mason	(1873)
November 21	Henry Purcell	(1695)
	Francisco Tárrega	(1852)
	Sigfrid Karg-Elert	(1877)
	Malcolm Williamson	(1931)
November 22	Jacob Obrecht	(1450)
	Joaquin Rodrigo	(1901)
	Benjamin Britten	(1913)
	Gunther Schuller	(1925)
	Fikret Amirov	(1922)
November 23	Thomas Tallis	(1505)
	Manuel de Falla	(1876)
	André Caplet	(1878)
November 24	Scott Joplin	(1868)
November 25	Sergei Taneyev	(1856)
	Bernard Stavenhagen	(1862)
	Virgil Thomson	(1896)
November 26		
November 27	Charles Koechlin	(1867)
November 28	Jean Baptiste Lully	(1632)
	Anton Rubinstein	(1829)
	Alexander Kastalsky	(1856)
	Randy Newman	(1943)
November 29	Gaetano Donizetti	(1797)
November 30	Carl Loewe	(1796)
	Charles Henri Alkan	(1813)

	Sergey Liapunov	(1859)
	Ture Rangström	(1884)
December 1		
December 2		
December 3	Anton von Webern	(1883)
	Halsey Stevens	(1908)
	Nino Rota	(1911)
	Irving Fine	(1914)
December 4	Sir Hamilton Harty	(1879)
	Andre Campra	(1660)
December 5	Vitezslav Novák	(1870)
	Francesco Geminiani	(1687)
December 6	Henryk Górecki	(1933)
December 7	Hermann Goetz	(1840)
	Pietro Mascagni	(1863)
	Rudolf Friml	(1879)
	Ernst Toch	(1887)
	David Jones	(1912)
December 8	Jean Sibelius	(1865)
	Manuel Ponce	(1882)
	Bohuslav Martinu	(1890)
December 9	Leopold Kozeluch	(1752)
	Joaquin Turina	(1882)
December 10	César Franck	(1822)
	Olivier Messiaen	(1908)
	Morton Gould	(1913)
December 11	Hector Berlioz	(1903)
	Mieczyslaw Karlowicz	(1876)
	Elliott Carter	(1908)
December 12	Kurt Atterberg	(1887)
December 13	Phillips Brooks	(1835)
December 14	Joseph Jongen	(1873)
	Manolis Kalomiris	(1883)
	Ron Nelson	(1929)
December 15	Jean d' Ockeghem	(1425)
December 16	Ludwig van Beethoven	(1770)
	François Adrien Boïeldieu	(1775)
	Zoltán Kodály	(1882)
	Georgy Sviridov	(1915)
	Rodion Shchedrin	(1932)
December 17	Domenico Cimarosa	(1749)

	Fernando Lopes-Graca	(1906)
	Augusta Holmes	(1847)
December 18	Edward MacDowell	(1861)
December 19	Otto Olsson	(1879)
December 20	Josquin Des Pres	(1450)
	Vagn Holmboe	(1909)
	Henry Hadley	(1871)
	John Harbison	(1938)
December 21	Zdenek Fibich	(1850)
	Leroy Robertson	(1896)
December 22	Giacomo Puccini	(1858)
	Franz Schmidt	(1874)
	Deems Taylor	(1885)
	Robert Kurka	(1921)
	Edgard Varèse	(1883)
	Alan Bush	(1900)
December 23	Ross Lee Finney	(1906)
	Hans Henkemans	(1913)
December 24	Charles Cadman	(1881)
December 25	Joseph Saint-Georges	(1739)
December 26	Victor Hely-Hutchinson	(1901)
December 27	Oscar Levant	(1906)
December 28	Roger Sessions	(1896)
December 29	Tomás Bretón	(1850)
	Pablo Casals	(1876)
	Peggy Glanville-Hicks	(1912)
December 30	Josef Foerster	(1859)
	Dmitri Kabalevsky	(1904)
	Sir David Willcocks	(1919)
	Andre Messager	(1853)
December 31	Ernest Moeran	(1894)
	John Denver	(1943)

Bibliography

FOR FURTHER STUDY AND READING

Abell, Arthur. *Talks with the Great Composers*. Verlag, Germany: G. E. Schroeder, 1964.

Abrams, Jeremiah, ed. *Reclaiming the Inner Child*. Los Angeles: Jeremy Tarcher, 1990.

Ackerman, Diane. *The Natural History of the Senses*. New York: Random House, 1990.

Alberti, Luciano. *Music of the Western World*. New York: Crown Publishing, 1968.

Andrews, Donald Hatch. *The Symphony of Life*. Lee's Summit, Mo.: Unity Books, 1966.

Assagioli, Roberto. *Psychosynthesis*. New York: Viking Compass, 1965.

Baker, Richard. *The Magic of Music*. New York: Universe Books, 1975.

Bancroft, Anne. *Weavers of Wisdom: Women Mystics of the Twentieth Century*. New York: Penguin Books, 1989.

Bayles, Martha. *Hole in Our Soul*. New York: Macmillan, 1994.

Benjamin, Edward B. *The Restful in Music*. Boston: Crescendo Publishing, 1964.

Birosik, Patti Jean. *The New Age Music Guide*. New York: Collier Books, 1989.

Bonny, Helen. *Music and Your Mind*. New York: Harper & Row, 1973.

Braider, Jackson N. *For God and Country: Forty Hymns of Joy and Celebration*. Providence, R. I.: Newport Classic, 1992. (CD included)

Brown, Douglas C. *CD Guide to Classical Music*. Ann Arbor, Mich: CD Guide, 1992 and 1993.

Burke, John. *Musical Landscapes*. Exeter, Devon, England: Webb and Bower Publishers, 1983.

Carlson, Richard and Benjamin Shield. *Healers on Healing*. Los Angeles: Jeremy Tarcher, 1989.

Cayce, Edgar. *Music As the Bridge*. Virginia Beach: A.R.E. Press, 1972.

Combs, Allan and Mark Holland. *Synchronicity*. New York: Paragon House, 1990.

Commins, Dorothy. *All About the Symphony Orchestra.* New York: Random House, 1961.

Cousins, Norman. *The Anatomy of an Illness.* New York: W. W. Norton, 1979.

Cross, Milton and David Ewen. *Encyclopedia of Great Composers and Their Music.* Garden City, N. Y.: Doubleday, 1962.

Cunningham, Lawrence. *Mother of God.* San Francisco: Harper and Row, 1982.

Diamond, John. *BK, Behavioral Kinesiology.* New York: Harper and Row, 1979. (Published in paperback with title *Your Body Doesn't Lie.* New York: Warner Books, 1980.)

———. *The Life Energy in Music.* Valley Cottage, N.Y.: Archaens Press, 1981.

Eadie, Betty. *Embraced by the Light.* Placerville, Calif.: Gold Leaf Press, 1992.

Einstein, Alfred. *Greatness in Music.* New York: Oxford University Press, 1941.

Gal, Hans, ed. *The Musician's World.* New York: Arco, 1966.

Galway, James. *Music in Time.* New York: Harry N. Abrams, 1983.

Gammond, Peter. *The Meaning and Magic of Music.* New York: Golden Press, 1970.

Gilder, Eric, and June Port. *Dictionary of Composers and Their Music.* New York: Ballantine, 1978.

Graham, Lanier F. *The Rainbow Book.* Berkeley: Shambhala, 1975.

Gray, Anne. *The Popular Guide to Classical Music.* New York: Birch Lane Press, 1993.

Gutheil, Emil. *Music and Your Emotions.* New York: Liveright, 1952.

Haas, Karl. *Inside Music.* New York: Anchor Books, 1984.

Hadden, J. Cuthbert. *Composers in Love and Marriage.* London: John Long, 1913.

Hall, Manly P. *Music Through the Ages* (a talk). Los Angeles: The Philosophical Research Society, 1972.

Hart, Mickey, and Frederic Lieberman. *Planet Drum.* San Francisco: Harper Collins, 1991.

Headington, Christopher. *The Orchestra and Its Instruments.* Cleveland: World Publishing, 1965.

Heline, Corinne. *Beethoven's Nine Symphonies.* Santa Barbara: J. F. Rowny Press, 1965.

———. *Music: The Keynote of Human Evolution.* Santa Barbara: J. F. Rowny Press, 1965.

———. *The Cosmic Harp.* La Canada, Calif.: New Age Press, 1969.

————. *The Esoteric Music of Richard Wagner.* La Canada, Calif.: New Age Press, 1974.

————. *Color and Music in the New Age.* Los Angeles: New Age Press, 1977.

————. *Healing and Regeneration Through Music.* Los Angeles: New Age Press, 1978.

————. *Healing and Regeneration Through Color.* Los Angeles: New Age Press, 1979.

Saint Hildegard of Bingen. *Symphonia.* Translated by Barbara Newman. Ithaca, N.Y.: Cornell University Press, 1988.

Hodson, Geoffrey. *Music Forms.* Wheaton, Ill.: Theosophical Press, 1976.

————. *The Brotherhood of Angels and of Men.* Wheaton, Ill.: Theosophical Press, 1973.

————. *Clairvoyant Investigations.* Wheaton, Ill.: Theosophical Press, 1984.

Holmes, John L. *Conductors on Record.* London: Gollancz, 1982.

Houston, Jean. *Godseed: The Journey of Christ.* Wheaton, Illinois: Quest Books, 1992.

Hurd, Michael. *The Orchestra.* New York: Quarto Publishing, 1980.

Ismael, Cristina. *The Healing Environment.* Millbrae, Calif.: Celestial Arts, 1976.

Johnson, James. *Freedom from Depression.* New York: Logos International, 1982.

Johnston, William. *Silent Music.* New York: Harper & Row, 1974.

Kelly, Thomas R. *A Testament of Devotion.* New York: Harper and Row, 1941.

Kennedy, Joan. *The Joy of Classical Music.* New York: Doubleday, 1992.

Keyes, Laurel. *Toning.* Santa Monica: DeVorss, 1973.

Khan, Sufi Inayat. *The Mysticism of Sound.* Netherlands: Servire BV, 1979.

Lebrecht, Norman. *The Maestro Myth.* New York: Citadel, 1991.

Leonard, Richard Anthony. *The Stream of Music.* Garden City: Dolphin-Doubleday, 1962.

Levith, Murray J. *Musical Masterpieces in Poetry.* Neptune, N.J.: Paganiniana Publications, 1984.

————. *Musical Masterpieces in Prose.* Neptune, N.J.: Paganiniana Publications, 1981.

Lewis, Richard, ed. *In Praise of Music.* New York: Orion Press, 1963.

Libbey, Ted. *Building a Classical CD Collection.* New York: Workman Publishing, 1994.

Lingerman, Hal A. *Living Your Destiny*. York Beach, Maine: Samuel Weiser, 1992.

———. *Life Streams*. Wheaton, Ill.: Quest Books, 1988.

Menuhin, Yehudi, and Curtis Davis. *The Music of Man*. Sydney, Australia: Methuen, 1979.

Merritt, Stephanie. *Music, Mind and Imagery*. New York: Plume, 1990.

Moody, Raymond. *Life after Life*. New York: Bantam Books, 1977.

———. *The Light Beyond*. New York: Bantam Books, 1988.

Morgenstern, Sam, ed. *Composers on Music*. New York: Pantheon, 1956.

Morse, Melvin. *Closer to the Light*. New York: Ivy Books, 1990.

Munch, Charles. *I Am a Conductor*. New York: Oxford University Press, 1955.

Murchie, Guy. *The Seven Mysteries of Life*. Boston: Houghton Mifflin, 1978.

Nette, Paul. *Book of Musical Documents*. New York: Philosophical Library, 1948.

Newhouse, Flower A. *Speak the Word*. Vista, Calif.: The Christward Ministry, 1942.

———. *Insights Into Reality*. Edited by Stephen Isaac and Phyllis Isaac. Escondido, Calif.: The Christward Ministry, 1975.

———. *The Kingdom of the Shining Ones*. Escondido, Calif.: The Christward Ministry, 1955, 1975.

———. *The Journey Upward*. Escondido, Calif.: The Christward Ministry, 1978.

———. *Rediscovering the Angels*. Escondido, Calif.: The Christward Ministry, 1976.

Ortmans, Kay. *Reminders from Well-Springs*. Ben Lomond, Calif.: Well-Springs Foundation, 1969.

Podolsky, Edward. *The Doctor Prescribes Music*. New York: Frederick A. Stokes, 1939.

Previn, André, ed. *Orchestra*. London: MacDonald & Jane's, 1979.

Rael, Joseph. *Being and Vibration*. Tulsa, Okla.: Council Oak Books, 1993.

Ralph, W. Arthur. *The Messiah—A Spiritual Interpretation*. Great Britain: Arthur Stockwell, Ltd., 1980.

Retallack, Dorothy. *The Sound of Music and Plants*. Santa Monica: DeVorss, 1973.

Rosicrucian Fellowship. *The Musical Scale*. Oceanside, Calif.: 1949.

Roustit, Albert. *Prophecy in Music*. Albert Roustit, 1972.

Rutledge, Lyman V. *Earth Music*. Boston: Branden Press, 1970.

Salter, Lionel. *The Illustrated Encyclopedia of Classical Music*. London: Salamander Books, 1978.

Schaefer, John. *The Virgin Guide to New Music.* London: Virgin, 1990.

Schafer, R. Murray. *The Tuning of the World.* New York: Alfred Knopf, 1977.

Scott, Cyril. *Music—Its Secret Influence Throughout the Ages.* New York: Samuel Weiser, 1969.

Shearer, Tony. *The Praying Flute.* Santa Fe, N.M.: Bear & Company, 1991.

Slonimsky, Nicolas. *The Road to Music.* New York: Dodd, Mead & Company, 1947.

Stebbing, Lionel. *Music, Its Occult Basis and Healing Value.* E. Grinstead, Sussex, England: New Knowledge Books, 1961.

Stevenson, Victor, ed. *The Music Makers.* Middlesex, England: Harry Abrams, 1979.

Storr, Anthony. *Solitude.* New York: Ballantine Books, 1988.

Sullivan, J.W.M. *Beethoven, His Spiritual Development.* New York: Vintage, 1955.

Tame, David. *Beethoven and the Spiritual Path.* Wheaton, Ill.: Quest, 1994.

Teilhard de Chardin, Pierre. *Hymn of the Universe.* New York: Harper and Row, 1965.

———. *Prayer of the Universe.* New York: Harper & Row, 1965.

———. *The Heart of Matter.* New York: Harvest Pub., 1978.

Thompson, Oscar. *How to Understand Music and Enjoy It.* New York: Premier-Fawcett, 1958.

Tompkins, Peter. *The Secret Life of Plants.* New York: Avon, 1973.

Treitler, Leo. *Music and the Historical Imagination.* Cambridge, Mass.: Harvard University Press, 1989.

Van de Leeuw, Gerardus. *Sacred and Profane Beauty in Art.* New York: Abingdon Press, 1965.

Verny, Thomas, and John Kelly. *The Secret Life of the Unborn Child.* New York: Delta, 1988.

Verny, Thomas, and Pamela Weintraub. *Nurturing the Unborn Child.* New York: Delacorte Press, 1991.

Wall, Steve. *Wisdom's Daughters.* New York: Harper Collins, 1993.

Walter, Bruno. *Of Music and Music-Making.* New York: W.W. Norton, 1957.

Warner, Marina. *Alone of All Her Sex.* New York: Vintage Books, 1983.

QUEST BOOKS
are published by
The Theosophical Society in America,
Wheaton, Illinois 60189-0270,
a branch of a world organization
dedicated to the promotion of the unity of
humanity and the encouragement of the study of
religion, philosophy, and science, to the end that
we may better understand ourselves and our place in
the universe. The Society stands for complete
freedom of individual search and belief.
For further information about its activities,
write, call 1-800-669-1571, or consult its Web page:
http: / / www.theosophical.org

The Theosophical Publishing House
is aided by the generous support of
THE KERN FOUNDATION,
a trust established by Herbert A. Kern
and dedicated to Theosophical education.

38204000014963

MANOOS
PUBLIC LIBRARY